Inside Microsoft® Office SharePoint® Server 2007

Patrick Tisseghem

PUBLISHED BY
Microsoft Press
A Division of Microsoft Corporation
One Microsoft Way
Redmond, Washington 98052-6399

Library of Congress Control Number: 2007924644

Printed and bound in the United States of America.

1 2 3 4 5 6 7 8 9 QWT 2 1 0 9 8 7

Distributed in Canada by H.B. Fenn and Company Ltd.

A CIP catalogue record for this book is available from the British Library.

Microsoft Press books are available through booksellers and distributors worldwide. For further information about international editions, contact your local Microsoft Corporation office or contact Microsoft Press International directly at fax (425) 936-7329. Visit our Web site at www.microsoft.com/mspress. Send comments to mspinput@microsoft.com.

Acquisitions Editor: Ben Ryan
Project Editor: Kathleen Atkins
Developmental Editor: Devon Musgrave
Editorial and Production Services: Custom Editorial Productions, Inc.

Body Part No. X13-68386

Contents at a Glance

Table of Contents

Acknowledgments

It was in April 2002 that Chris Volckerick of Microsoft Belgium motivated me to attend the SharePoint 2003 Products and Technologies airlift in Redmond. Attending that event was a major turning point in my professional life, since from that moment on, SharePoint has become my main focus. I want to thank him for this.

Over the years, many people helped me to become more successful and guided me to become a better SharePoint trainer and evangelist. I want to thank people like Mike Fitzmaurice, Mike Ammerlaan, Mauricio Ordonez, Rob Barker, Doug Mahugh, Christin Boyd, Randall Isenhour, and many others in Redmond for the support they have given me over the past years and the many opportunities for creating and delivering training material and white papers on the subject. Many thanks also to Ted Pattison for the close relationship we have developed and the excellent work we have done creating and delivering the Ascend and TouchDown material during the past two years. I could not have accomplished this without him. Special thanks also to the team within Microsoft Press who made all of this possible.

About eight years ago, Wim Uyttersprot and I started a company called U2U, which has become very successful over the years. Having Wim as a partner is one of my blessings of the last ten years, and I want to thank him especially for all the support and hard work. Also a big thank you to the trainers and consultants at U2U who support me and inspire me in my work.

Last but not least, of course, a big thank you to my family: my wife, Linda, and my two wonderful daughters, Laura and Anahi. Being on the road most of the time and, when home, working on projects in the evenings and on the weekends, I acknowledge that I am not your ordinary husband and father. But I am fortunate to have a strong wife taking care of the family while I am gone. I could not have reached this level without her. I see my daughters evolving into mature and independent women, all thanks to her.

Thanks to everybody I did not mention here. I have met hundreds of students the past two years in many countries around the world. I hope they have good memories of the trainings and I wish them all the luck. Have a good reading!

Introduction

Introducing Microsoft Office SharePoint Server 2007 in your organization is an excellent decision when there is a need to deliver a platform for collaboration, enterprise content management, integration of business processes and data, exposure of business intelligence data, and much more. There are a great amount of solutions and features immediately available out of the box, but in many real-world scenarios, you'll have to configure, tune, customize, and extend all of these pieces so that SharePoint addresses all of the needs of your business. This is exactly what this book covers. This book explains the many different options from a developer perspective to accomplish all of this.

This book is based on my experience over the past two years working closely with product teams to create and compile training material for Independent Software Vendors (ISVs) and deliver numerous workshops, seminars, and talks.

Target Audience

This book primarily targets developers who have experience with ASP.NET 2.0 and know their way around both Windows SharePoint Services 3.0 and Microsoft Office SharePoint Server 2007. As the title indicates, only topics that are related to Microsoft Office SharePoint Server 2007 are covered. Another book, *Inside Microsoft® Windows® SharePoint® Services 3.0* by Ted Pattison and Daniel Larson (Microsoft Press), covers development topics for the Windows SharePoint Services 3.0 platform. I recommend that you read that book first because many development techniques are explained there in detail, such as building Web Parts, creating event handlers, the major classes in the object model that provide access to content stored in SharePoint, and much more.

How This Book Is Organized

My primary occupation is to train people how to be successful developers for Microsoft SharePoint Products and Technologies. Therefore, my writing style and the organization of the material covered are very straightforward and practical, and I use a lot of walkthroughs to get you started. Descriptions of the chapters follow.

Chapter 1: Introducing Microsoft Office SharePoint Server 2007

Chapter 1 is an overview of some of the fundamentals to know before continuing. Many terms and concepts are explained, and an overview discusses the development options you have within Windows SharePoint Services 3.0. The chapter concludes with a walkthrough covering the out-of-the-box workflow support delivered by Microsoft Office SharePoint Server 2007 on top of the Windows SharePoint Services 3.0 integration of the Windows Workflow Foundation.

Chapter 2: Collaboration Portals and People Management

This chapter is divided into two parts. First, you'll learn what a collaboration portal is and how it differs from an individual site. Several topics are covered such as the provisioning process, the site hierarchy and the page model, the publishing cycle, and customization and branding of the portals. Chapter 6, "Customizing and Branding Publishing Portals," goes a step further and discusses more customization and extensibility options. The second part is all about user profiles, audiences, personal sites, and social networking support.

Chapter 3: Customizing and Extending the Microsoft Office SharePoint 2007 Search

Chapter 3 is the most elaborate chapter and covers the new search administration object model, the customization of the Search Center, the various options to programmatically execute a search query, and the steps for building a custom security trimmer that filters the results for a user before they get displayed in the search results page.

Chapter 4: Working with the Business Data Catalog

In this chapter, you'll learn how to create application definitions using the declarative approach as well as the programmatic approach via the object model exposed by the Business Data Catalog. Another section also covers the techniques for programmatically accessing the content delivered via the Business Data Catalog in custom Web Parts.

Chapter 5: InfoPath Forms Services

This short chapter covers the different steps to take to deploy and deliver electronic forms in the browser.

Chapter 6: Customizing and Branding Publishing Portals

This chapter builds on Chapter 2, "Collaboration Portals and People Management." You'll learn how to customize the provisioning process, how to configure publishing portals for forms-based authentication (using the out-of-the-box authentication providers and custom providers), the customization of the publishing console, and the advanced techniques for creating custom master pages, page layouts, and field controls. However, this chapter also covers how to set up variations and the options for allowing users to publish pages to the portal using their familiar Microsoft Office Word 2007 environment.

Chapter 7: Integrating with Excel Services

Chapter 7 begins by providing information for administering and configuring Excel Services. Later in the chapter, you'll learn how to publish a spreadsheet, take snapshots, communicate with a spreadsheet via the Web service, and go through the steps for creating user-defined functions to extend the functionality to server-side Microsoft Office Excel workbooks.

Chapter 8: Policies and the Records Repository

The final chapter discusses development options for creating your own information management policies and the Records Center and its configuration. The chapter concludes with the steps for building a custom document router.

System Requirements

You'll need the following hardware and software to build and run the code samples for this book:

- Microsoft Windows Server 2003 with Service Pack 2
- Microsoft Office SharePoint Server 2007 Enterprise Version
- Microsoft Visual Studio 2005 Standard Edition or Microsoft Visual Studio 2005 Professional Edition
- Microsoft Visual Studio 2005 Extensions for Windows SharePoint Services 3.0
- Microsoft SQL Server 2005 Express (included with Visual Studio 2005) or Microsoft SQL Server 2005
- Microsoft Office Professional 2007
- 600 MHz Pentium or compatible processor (1 GHz Pentium recommended)
- 1 GB RAM (2 GB or more recommended)
- Video monitor (800 × 600 or higher resolution) with at least 256 colors (1024 × 768 high color 16-bit recommended)
- CD-ROM or DVD-ROM drive
- Microsoft mouse or compatible pointing device

Configuring Your Development Environment

When developing with SharePoint, you have the option to develop locally or remotely. When developing locally, you either have Windows Server 2003 installed with Microsoft Office SharePoint Server 2007 up and running or you make use of Microsoft Virtual PC 2005/2007 with an image running a SharePoint installation. With the remote option, you configure your development environment with all of the necessary .NET assemblies (basically copy the DLLs to your local machine and deploy them in the global assembly cache), build projects locally, deploy them to a SharePoint server, and then test and debug this way. Note that developing locally is preferred in order to be productive and avoid potential problems with deploying code, testing, and debugging.

Code Samples

The language used in the book is C#, and sample code is available only in C#. All of the examples are wrapped up in single Visual Studio 2005 projects and can be downloaded from the book's companion content page at the following address:

http://www.microsoft.com/mspress/companion/9780735623682/

Microsoft Press provides support for books and companion content at the following Web site:

http://www.microsoft.com/learning/support/books/

Questions and Comments

If you have comments or ideas regarding the book or the companion content, or if you have questions that are not answered by visiting the preceding Web sites, please send them to Microsoft Press via e-mail to

mspinput@microsoft.com

Or via postal mail to

Microsoft Press
Attn: Editor, *Inside Microsoft® Office SharePoint® Server 2007*
One Microsoft Way
Redmond, WA 98052-6399

Please note that Microsoft software product support is not offered through the preceding addresses.

Chapter 1
Introducing Microsoft Office SharePoint Server 2007

- Learn about Microsoft Office SharePoint Server 2007 services and solutions.
- Learn about the Shared Services Provider delivering Microsoft Office SharePoint Server 2007 services to all the sites associated with it.
- Explore what sort of Web Parts, Features, and site definitions are available in addition to Windows SharePoint Services 3.0 after installing Microsoft Office SharePoint Server 2007.
- Experience one of the Microsoft Office SharePoint Server 2007 custom workflows.

Microsoft Office SharePoint Server 2007 Services and Solutions

Microsoft Office SharePoint Server 2007 without Windows SharePoint Services 3.0 is like *a horse without feet*. It is important to understand, before continuing to read this book, that a very intimate connection exists between Microsoft Office SharePoint Server 2007 (often abbreviated as MOSS 2007) and Windows SharePoint Services v3 (WSS 3.0). The latter is playing the role of the solutions platform; the former delivers additional solutions and services on top of this. In this chapter, I'll cover some of the important pieces of the solutions platform along with a general overview of the services and solutions delivered with Microsoft Office SharePoint Server 2007.

Windows SharePoint Services 3.0: A Solutions Platform

The Windows SharePoint Services 3.0 solutions platform is covered in detail in *Inside Microsoft® Windows® SharePoint® Services 3.0* (Microsoft Press), authored by Ted Pattison and Daniel Larson, and it is recommended that you first read that book before reading this one. Let me highlight, however, a number of important topics from their book that you should keep in mind for the rest of my book.

Windows SharePoint Services 3.0 is best described as a site-provisioning engine, enabling organizations to quickly set up a Web-based infrastructure for collaborating, storing, and managing content and documents. The installed infrastructure offers all of the needed ingredients to make this happen, allowing you to scale from a small team with a limited number of users and content toward supporting large organizations with thousands of users and millions of documents.

1

A number of enhancements have been made to the way information and documents are stored. These enhancements are important to keep in mind because solutions delivered by Microsoft Office SharePoint Server 2007 rely heavily on them. I'll briefly discuss two of them.

The first enhancement is versioning. Windows SharePoint Services 3.0 can now differentiate between minor (or draft) versions and major (or published) versions of a document. Associated with these states, you can have security, workflows, policies, or other behavior.

A second enhancement to keep in mind, since I'll refer to it often, is the concept of content types. Content types are objects you create and activate typically at the level of the site collection containing the definition of one specific type of content you want to make available to the SharePoint users via the list and document library containers. Content types are packaged definitions of what you intend to store in SharePoint sites. An example is a legal report, but do know that it is not restricted only to documents—as you'll see in Chapter 6, "Customizing and Branding Publishing Portals." A content type definition can include plenty of things such as columns, workflows, information management policies, document templates, and more. Taking the example of the legal report again, you can have three columns, an expiration policy enforcing that the document cannot be deleted before five years, and a custom Microsoft Office Word 2007 template associated. The creation of a content type can be done in the browser, delivered via a Feature or programmatically via the object model. (If you are unfamiliar with the Feature concept, see later for an explanation of what a Feature is all about.) Once the content type is defined, you can go to any of the lists and document libraries and configure the container to allow the user to create a new item or document based on this content type. Figure 1-1 shows a document library where the user is able to create a marketing report or legal report. Each type of report is defined as a content type, and specific metadata and behavior is associated with each of them.

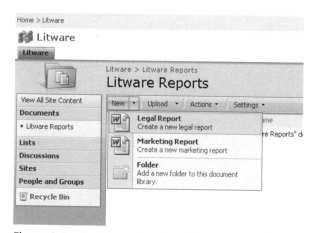

Figure 1-1   Creating and storing different types of reports in one document library

One of the strong points of Windows SharePoint Services, both version 3.0 and the previous version, is the integration with what some people like to call the "comfort zones" of the information workers—with that we mean the Microsoft Office client products such as Microsoft Outlook, Microsoft Word, and Microsoft Excel. Information workers are not required to leave their familiar environment to work with the content and documents stored in SharePoint containers or collaborate with other colleagues on these documents. The integration level with the new version of Windows SharePoint Services 3.0 is of course at its most when your information workers use Microsoft Office 2007 as their client. However, clients running previous versions of Microsoft Office (starting from Microsoft Office XP) do provide some level of integration with SharePoint.

The ease of use, excellent out-of-the-box experience, rich integration, and many self-service capabilities offered with Windows SharePoint Services 3.0 are, however, just the hood over a very powerful engine, platform, and template architecture. The engine and platform of the latest version are deeply integrated with ASP.NET 2.0—built on top of it—and designed according to the best practices and guidelines put forward by the ASP.NET product team. The template architecture is very sophisticated and delivers great power out-of-the-box but, more important, it was designed to be extensible. This means that in addition to the artifacts provided by Windows SharePoint Services, you have all you need to create your own templates, either full-blown site templates or building blocks—called Features.

Features are a major enhancement to the template architecture of Windows SharePoint Services 3.0. With Features, you can easily install and activate new functionality to the existing sites within your server farm. Think of it: You have a customer with 500 team sites, and the customer is asking for a new document library to support legal reports. This document library must be made available to the 500 team sites and requires custom metadata associated with it. Your approach in Windows SharePoint Services 3.0 can be to encapsulate the definition of that document library as a Feature containing all of the metadata in the schema expressed in the Collaborative Markup Language (CAML).

> **Note**   What is *CAML*? CAML is an XML-based language that plays a very important role within the whole SharePoint story, today and in the past. CAML is used for the definition of the schemas of sites, lists, document libraries, views, fields, and much more. Another role of CAML is that of a query language for retrieving and updating the items in lists and libraries.

After testing the Feature on your development machine, you can package it up as a SharePoint solution, basically a compressed cabinet file with the extension .wsp, and send it to the farm's administrator. He or she can then install and deploy the solution. The deployment involves several steps. All of the required files are copied to their dedicated places (the Global Assembly Cache, the Layouts folder, the Features folder, or other folders in the 12 hive). Next, the solution will take care of the installation of the Feature and administrators can take care of the activation of the Feature for site collections and sites within the SharePoint server farm.

Features are thus used to make *things* available in your server farm. These *things* can be new templates for lists and document libraries, custom workflows you've created using Microsoft Visual Studio.NET, new content types, fields, and even enhancements or modifications to the user interface of SharePoint, often called *light-up* Features. An example is a new option you make available to administrators in the Site Actions menu as shown in Figure 1-2.

Figure 1-2   An extra action in the Site Actions menu made available with a light-up Feature

Extending the template architecture is one thing, but there are many other options for extending your sites. The previous version of Windows SharePoint Services introduced the concept of Web Parts, building blocks of a page with the option to configure and personalize them and have the instances serialized as such in the content database. Windows SharePoint Services 3.0 continues to support Web Parts of course, but the Web Part infrastructure has changed. SharePoint 3.0 now uses the ASP.NET 2.0 Web Part infrastructure with a small layer on top to make it backward-compatible for the Web Parts targeting the previous version of Windows SharePoint Services. Building and deploying custom Web Parts adds more functionality to what you're receiving out-of-the-box with Windows SharePoint Services. An example of a custom Web Part is depicted in Figure 1-3 illustrating how you can deliver a master-detail view for employees and some of the particulars retrieved from a *Microsoft SQL Server* database.

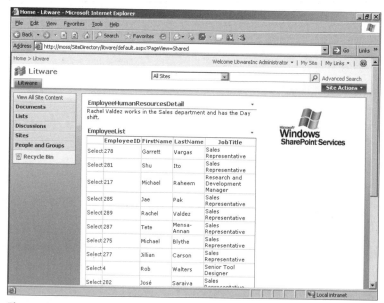

Figure 1-3   Master-detail view for employees delivered in a Windows SharePoint Services 3.0 page using custom Web Parts

Another extensibility option is the building of event handlers. *Event handlers* are classes within a .NET assembly that can execute code reacting on certain events that are triggered at various levels within the SharePoint environment. In Windows SharePoint Services 3.0, the scope is expanded to include—in addition to document libraries (the only scope in the previous version)—lists, content types, and even sites. Moreover, you now have synchronous *before* events in addition to the asynchronous *after* events. An example of a synchronous *before* event can be custom code that intercepts the deletion of an item in a list and cancels the action SharePoint wants to perform in the database because of a business rule you coded that forbids the deletion.

A last topic I want to touch briefly here is workflow. Windows SharePoint Services 3.0 can host the Windows Workflow Foundation (WF) engine. The engine is able to execute the workflows you've associated with the lists or document libraries (or content types). As you will notice, Windows SharePoint Services 3.0 by itself will not provide you with a lot of candidate workflows out-of-the-box. Only the three-state workflow is available. When activated, it allows you to associate a small workflow to track items in a list. However, you have the option to use Microsoft Office SharePoint Designer 2007 or Microsoft Visual Studio to create and deploy additional custom workflows. The core message here is that the platform, Windows SharePoint Services 3.0, has all of the infrastructure needed to perform workflow. Later in the chapter, you can read more about the custom workflows that Microsoft Office SharePoint Server 2007 is delivering out-of-the-box, and the first walkthrough of the book is going to illustrate it.

Microsoft Office SharePoint Server 2007 Services

After a successful installation of Microsoft Office SharePoint Server 2007, one of the additions on top of the Windows SharePoint Services 3.0 platform is a set of new services. The number of services actually depends on what license you are using. I don't want to dive into a discussion of the licensing model here in this book, but in short, and not going into details regarding the alternatives and possible combinations, Microsoft Office SharePoint Sever 2007 is licensed in two modes: standard vs. enterprise. Figure 1-4 displays all of the available services.

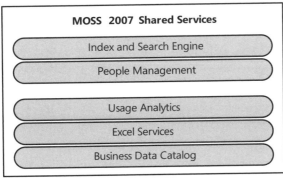

Figure 1-4   The different services delivered with MOSS 2007

Let me briefly discuss the various services available with a standard license of Microsoft Office SharePoint Server 2007. Each of these services will be discussed from a developer's perspective in later chapters.

- The first and most important one is Enterprise Search Services. These services consist of the index engine and search services that allow you to start crawling many possible content sources, build up an index file, and let your users execute their search queries against it.

- A second set of services is related to People Management. Users in a Windows SharePoint Services 3.0 environment are identified by an account name, display name, and e-mail. The Microsoft Office SharePoint Server 2007 adds more meat to this and can associate a user profile enriching the information related to these individuals. User profile information can be used in SharePoint sites to create a more dynamic and adaptive user experience. Users can become members of one or more audiences if they match up with the membership conditions defined. These audiences can be used to target information and personalize the experience of the user through the filtered visualization of parts of SharePoint pages and the content on them. User profile information also plays an important role in the personal sites that can be created per user, exposing parts of the user profile information to other users visiting the public part of these personal sites.

- Windows SharePoint Services 3.0, the platform, allows for auditing and logging of the actions users perform within a SharePoint site. The Microsoft Office SharePoint Server 2007 adds advanced usage analytics on top of the one provided by Windows SharePoint Services 3.0, providing a more granular auditing and logging not only of the work done in the collaboration workspaces but also of the work done with the different services. A good example is the auditing and logging that can be activated for the search queries performed by users.

If you decide to make the move to the enterprise license for Microsoft Office SharePoint Server 2007, two more services are available on top of all the previously listed services:

- The Business Data Catalog (BDC) is a middle layer that acts as a bridge between your SharePoint environment and basically any type of external data source (for example, an *SAP*, *Microsoft CRM*, traditional *SQL Server*, or *Oracle* database). Once the bridge is constructed, SharePoint users can interact with the data in a number of ways, as we will see later in Chapter 4, "Working with the Business Data Catalog," and the data can also be crawled by the indexing engine so that search results can contain data physically stored in external systems.

- Microsoft Excel 2007 spreadsheets can be published to your SharePoint environment. A new service, Excel 2007 Services, can render a thin client representation of a spreadsheet as well as any snapshot you may want to take from a spreadsheet. These snapshots can be isolated in their proper Web Part—the Excel Web Access Web Part. Also, Excel 2007 Services makes it possible for any environment that knows how to talk Web Services to interact in a programmatic and remote way with a Microsoft Excel spreadsheet published in a trusted SharePoint document library.

> **More Info**   Office Forms Server 2007 is another service component that helps you deliver Microsoft InfoPath 2007 forms to basically anybody in the world via a browser-based rendering of the forms. But, as you've probably noticed, I purposefully did not put it on the same level as the Business Data Catalog and the Excel Services, because the Office Forms Server 2007 is also packaged as a stand-alone product that can be installed on a Windows SharePoint Services 3.0 only installation. This is an interesting setup to choose if you just want to expand the collaboration and document management workspaces with Microsoft InfoPath 2007 forms in the browser—no need for the installation of a Microsoft Office SharePoint Server 2007. So, it is not really a Microsoft Office SharePoint Server 2007 service, but if you decide to go for the enterprise CAL, it is part of the package.

Microsoft Office SharePoint Server 2007 Solutions

You have to regard Microsoft Office SharePoint Server 2007 solutions as additional site definitions, Features, Web Parts, and different .NET assemblies adding extra functionality to your server farm. Figure 1-5 presents an overview of the major solution domains by the Microsoft Office SharePoint Server 2007.

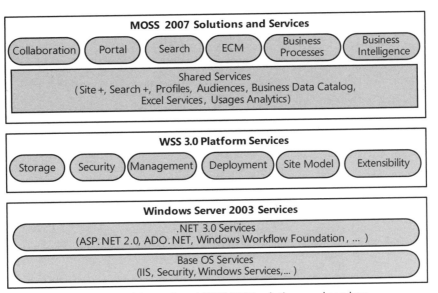

Figure 1-5   Overview of the various MOSS 2007 solutions and services

In the following paragraphs, I'll briefly describe the most important solutions you'll benefit from after the installation, assuming you opt for the enterprise license of Microsoft Office SharePoint Server 2007. For the sake of clarity, these solutions are organized into a number of categories. As with the services, each of these solutions will be discussed from a developer's perspective in subsequent chapters.

Collaboration Solutions

As discussed in the beginning of the chapter, Windows SharePoint Services 3.0 delivers the platform for collaboration, but by installing Microsoft Office SharePoint Server 2007, you'll receive a lot of additional features that enable you to build more powerful collaboration workspaces for your SharePoint users. Many of these features assist collaboration at the enterprise or divisional level rather than at the team level.

Slide Library   The *Slide library* is a new type of document library that enables the storage and management of individual slides extracted from a Microsoft PowerPoint presentation. The slides can be organized, versioned, and used for the creation of new complete Microsoft PowerPoint presentations.

Data Connection Library   The *Data Connection Library* allows for a centralized, securable, and manageable storage of data connection files (both .odc and .udcx based). Microsoft Office clients can use these data connection files to connect to data sources instead of embedding the data connection details or storing local data connection files. Utilizing data connections from trusted data connection libraries with Microsoft Office SharePoint Server 2007 is considered a best practice and, in some cases, is even required—such as when enforced by administrators working with Excel 2007 Services.

Collaboration Portal   A *collaboration portal* is a collection of site definitions and new features that enable you to provision portals (sometimes also referred to as corporate intranet sites) within your server farm. Figure 1-6 displays the out-of-the-box experience when provisioning a collaboration portal.

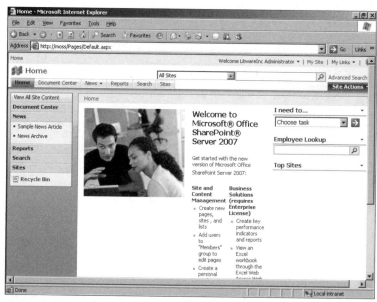

Figure 1-6   A collaboration portal brought to you by MOSS 2007

Portals come with a lot of subsites, many of them related to the other categories of solutions discussed a little bit later. One, however, is related to collaboration. The Document Center is a place in the portal where SharePoint users can collaborate and store information and documents in managed lists and document libraries as shown in Figure 1-7. Managed lists and document libraries are containers that are already configured with workflow, versioning, and other types of features that are important for working with information and documents at the enterprise or division level. Additionally, on the home page of the Document Center, you'll find two Web Parts that can aggregate the relevant documents and assigned tasks for the logged-on user—for example, created by workflows.

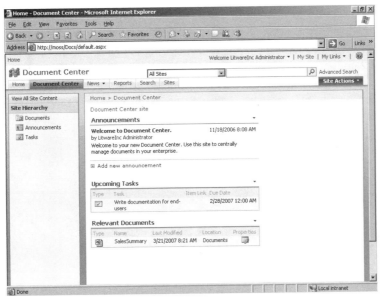

Figure 1-7   The Document Center with managed lists and document libraries. The home page displays the relevant documents and assigned tasks.

Search Center   Collaborative work often requires easy access to information and the people within your enterprise who possess that information. To find the information you need, there must be a solid search service scoped at the level of the enterprise. This is exactly what is delivered as a service with Microsoft Office SharePoint Server 2007. A new type of site called the *Search Center* is the place in your portal where you can expose a rich search experience for your users. It replaces the search box at the top of the pages with a site exposing a rich tab-based user interface fully customizable to meet the needs of everybody looking for a great search experience. Many new Web Parts are used within the different search pages, each of them customizable via properties in the tool pane.

Enterprise Content Management Solutions

Enterprise Content Management (ECM) will be covered in full detail in a number of chapters in this book. ECM is all about document management, Web content management, and records management. Microsoft Office SharePoint Server 2007 introduces many new types of solutions for SharePoint.

Publishing Features   *Publishing Features* encompasses a wide variety of features that enable controlled publishing of content and documents within collaboration portals or publishing portals. Many people also refer to it as Web Content Management (WCM) features, and these are new for SharePoint developers as a result of the integration of Microsoft Content Management Server (CMS) 2002 in the standard version of Microsoft Office SharePoint Server 2007. The basic idea here is that people from the IT department set up an infrastructure, based on the Windows SharePoint Services 3.0 platform, consisting of page layouts (a.k.a. templates in CMS 2002) with field controls (a.k.a. place holders in CMS 2002), workflows supporting the publishing cycle, and ASP.NET 2.0 artifacts such as master pages and navigation controls. Next, certain users acting in the role of content author or approver are then responsible for creating and managing the content published through the collaboration and/or publishing portals. Figure 1-8 summarizes all of this.

Figure 1-8   The different players and roles defined within a Web Content Management system

Workflow   Workflow by itself is not really a new solution delivered with Microsoft Office SharePoint Server 2007. As discussed in the beginning of this chapter, *Workflow* is actually

Windows SharePoint Services 3.0 that delivers the necessary plumbing integrating the Windows Workflow Foundation (WF) so that we can associate workflows with lists and document libraries. These workflows are then serviced by the different runtime components and services part of the Windows Workflow Foundation. So, what's different when installing Microsoft Office SharePoint Server 2007? Actually, there is no real change to the plumbing, but you will be able to use a number of new custom workflows. At the end of this chapter, you'll be able to experience one in a small walkthrough.

Document Converters   *Document Converters* are a new built-in framework for supporting a conversion of one type of document to another. Microsoft Office SharePoint Server 2007 makes a number of converters immediately available after installation. Examples include Info-Path to PNG, InfoPath to TIFF, and Word 2007 documents to Web pages. However, since all of this is delivered as a framework, developers are able to create additional converters to support other types of conversion scenarios. An example can be converting Microsoft Word documents to the new XML Paper Specification (XPS) format.

Information Management Policies   *Information Management Policies* ensure that content in SharePoint sites is created, stored, and managed the way the company wants it—and some policies may even be required, such as with federal legislation. Examples of policies include retention policies, labeling of documents, and the auditing and tracking of the operations performed on the content, such as viewing, opening, and editing documents. Again, the experience is a combination of a number of policies delivered out-of-the-box and a framework designed for creating your own custom policies.

Records Center   A *Records Center* is a new type of site and by design a safe place for records, not limited to documents. The Records Center site is equipped with all the gear to enforce policies and mechanisms to automatically route incoming records to specific containers based on pre-defined routers, also referred to as file plans. Moving documents from the collaboration spaces to the records repository is possible via an SMTP or a SOAP-based interface, and you'll be able to do this from within all of the sites and applications within and even outside of your server farm.

Business Process Management Solutions

Many organizations are looking for better ways to integrate their business processes and make it easier for the information workers to contribute to them. Microsoft Office SharePoint Server 2007 delivers a number of solutions that will help you achieve this.

Office Forms Server   The *Office Forms Server* is a new ASP.NET-based engine that makes it possible to deliver electronic forms based on Microsoft InfoPath 2007 templates in the browser, as shown in Figure 1-9. The reach of users with your InfoPath forms can be expanded enormously with the Office Forms Server.

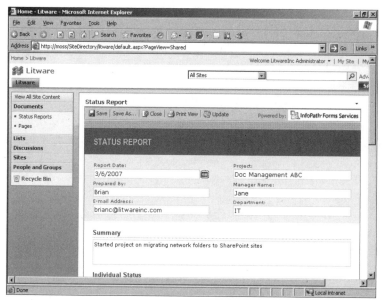

Figure 1-9   Microsoft InfoPath 2007 forms delivered in the browser

Single Sign-On   *Single sign-on* (SSO) enables application developers to silently allow users to log on to external databases or line-of-business (LOB) systems. Mappings between accounts at the level of these applications are stored in a secure credential store. SSO delivered with Microsoft Office SharePoint Server 2007 is pluggable, which means that you now are allowed to use non-SQL Server-based credentials to store the mapped credentials.

Business Data Web Parts   *Business Data Web Parts* is a set of rich and powerful Web Parts connecting to the business data delivered via the applications defined within the Business Data Catalog (BDC) repository. The various Business Data Web Parts are able to deliver a very rich out-of-the-box user experience, as shown in Figure 1-10, and there are many options for customization.

Business Intelligence (BI) Solutions

Microsoft Office SharePoint Server 2007 delivers a number of interesting features that can collectively support very rich types of business intelligence solutions that you may want to deliver on top of the SharePoint platform.

Report Center   The *Report Center* is a new type of site designed to assemble in one place all of the required infrastructure for storing and managing reports. There is also support for creating and provisioning dashboard pages.

Report Library   The *Report Library* is one of the core pieces in the Report Center, and, although it behaves pretty much like a normal document library, it is customized to store reports in many forms. These reports can be Excel spreadsheets and/or SQL Server Reporting Services reports. Reports have specific storage and versioning needs, and the Report Library delivers all of that.

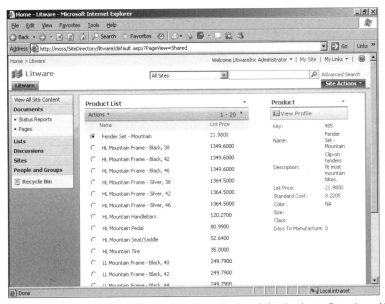

Figure 1-10   The Business Data List Web Part and the Business Data Item Web Part showing users a master-detail view on the product information stored in an external data source or LOB-system

Excel Web Access Web Part   The *Excel Web Access Web Part* is a connectable Web Part ready to render a complete Excel spreadsheet or individual objects contained within the spreadsheet—so-called snapshots, such as a chart or a pivot table. The rendering is done in a high-fidelity HTML presentation that is by default read-only, but as we will discuss later in the book, there is the option to provide the user with a parameter tool pane where he or she can specify new data values for the worksheets.

Filter Web Parts   A *Filter Web Part* is a Web Part that can slice or filter the data delivered typically within dashboard pages. A Filter Web Part can retrieve the filter value directly from the user or, as an example, can grab it behind the scenes from the profile of the current user. Filter Web Parts are by definition connectable and can map their filter values to parameters exposed by the reports or the Web Parts delivering the reports in the dashboards.

Dashboards   *Dashboards* are Web Part pages that are designed to host Filter Web Parts and Web Parts containing reports or snapshots of these reports. Together they deliver one integrated business intelligence experience to the visitors of your SharePoint site. Figure 1-11 shows an example of a dashboard in the Report Center.

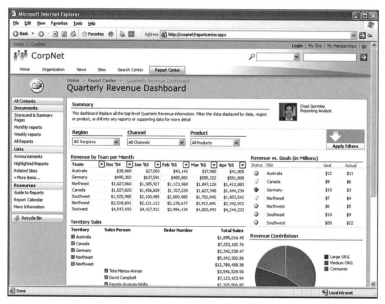

Figure 1-11   A dashboard delivering tailored data to sales persons

Shared Services Providers

We have summed up the different services available after an installation of Microsoft Office SharePoint Server 2007. All of them can be utilized and consumed by any type of SharePoint site within your server farm—team sites, wikis, blogs, and collaboration and publishing portals. We therefore appropriately refer to these services as *shared services*.

If you have been wandering around in SharePoint country for the last four years, you probably have experience with SharePoint Portal Server 2003 (SPS), and you might recognize the term *shared services*. SharePoint Portal Server 2003 basically introduced the first generation of shared services. During the installation of the product, a number of services are installed, supporting the enterprise-level features for collaboration and management of content and people within your organization. Many companies requiring multiple portals within the same server farm often dedicate one of their portals as the master portal, making it so that this master portal then shares all of its services to any other portal installed and connected to the same server farm. An example of such a scenario can be a multinational company with divisions in the United States and in Europe setting up a server farm with one global world-wide portal and a couple of country-level portals. The services—indexing, search, user profiles, audiences, and personal sites—associated with the master portal are shareable, and the installation of the country-level portals in the server farm does not include the installation of any local services anymore. These portals connect to the shared services of the master portal instead of installing their own unique services.

Although a good start, the way administrators must roll out a server farm with SharePoint Portal Server 2003 and many portals is often very challenging. Also, for both administrators and developers, it is very hard to deliver consistent and unified solutions to support information workers at all levels within the server farm. A major problem with the first generation of shared services is the restricted use of the services to only the portal sites and not directly outside of these environments. Collaboration sites at the level of the teams, team sites, and workspaces delivered with Windows SharePoint Servers 2003 have no out-of-the-box mechanism to leverage the services shared at the level of the portals.

In the past, you had within your SharePoint server farm two levels: portals and sites or workspaces. The portals were the places delivering extra services that were not available at the level of the sites and workspaces. A user had to navigate to the company's portal to execute a search query leveraging the index engine and only when working in the portal was he or she able to target pages with audiences. Sites and workspaces at the collaboration level (that is to say, Windows SharePoint Services v2) did not allow users to benefit from these services unless developers created extensions accessing these services in a custom way. Now, most of the time within an organization, you had more than one portal installation. Instead of installing every portal with its own services, administrators typically flagged one of the portals as being the master portal sharing the services to all of the other portals in the server farm. This way, visitors to SharePoint portals were using the same search and index engine, user profiles, audiences, and personal sites whatever portal they were navigating to. That was the first generation of shared services.

Microsoft Office SharePoint Server 2007 introduces the second generation of shared services. After a successful installation, one default, Shared Services Provider, is installed and configured. A Shared Services Provider, the new superpower in the SharePoint server farm, is an independent component within your Microsoft Office SharePoint Server 2007 environment with the role of providing services to anyone who is interested. A server farm has at least one Shared Services Provider. Multiple ones can be created and configured in case this scenario is required for your company. Whenever an IIS Web application (a.k.a. a virtual server) is extended and prepared for hosting SharePoint sites, it is associated with the default Shared Services Provider active in the server farm. The association with the Shared Services Provider ensures that all of the site collections hosted on the IIS Web application are able to consume and access the shared services.

To conclude, with Microsoft Office SharePoint Server 2007, shared services are not restricted to only the portals. Portals are now degraded to the level of normal citizens in SharePoint country. They are no longer superpowers with special privileges. As a result of the decoupling of the shared services from the portals and the move to put them under the governance of a Shared Services Provider, the services can now be used everywhere in the server farm. It is possible to open a team site and target a Web Part on a page to a specific audience. Another example is the support for search. When connected to a Shared Services Provider, the search with team sites can be promoted to the powerful Enterprise search leveraging the index file generated by the crawler and the rich search services. In addition, all of the new types of shared services such as the Excel 2007 Services or the Business Data Catalog are available everywhere in the server farm. This is very important to keep in mind for the rest of the book. I'll discuss the services in more detail and use one type of site, such as a collaboration portal or a publishing portal. However, know that the topics and techniques discussed can be applied to other types of sites as well.

Let's review the components that are installed when creating a Shared Service Provider in your server farm:

- A number of *SQL Server* databases store all of the data needed by the shared services. There is the *Shared Services Provider* database that stores the different pieces making up the configuration data for the various shared services, the usage information that is collected while people are working within the sites, the user profiles and the compiled audiences, and much more. Another database is related to the index and search engine that stores the metadata collected during crawling of the different content sources.

- A number of Windows Services are added to the list of services already up-and-running after a Windows SharePoint Services 3.0 installation. Examples are services supporting the conversion of documents on the SharePoint server and the search service.

- New site definitions and Features are copied to the \12\Template folder that is the basis for the diverse new MOSS solutions that you saw in Figure 1-5. Compared to the 5 site definitions that come with Windows SharePoint Services 3.0, you'll get 25 site definitions installed. And with Microsoft Office SharePoint Server 2007, you'll have 141 Features to play with (compared to the 35 when working with a pure Windows SharePoint Services 3.0 installation). Figure 1-12 is just a small representation of the number of additional Features installed.

- There is also a Microsoft Office Servers folder in the Program Files that stores specific .NET assemblies and other files (such as the list of noise words and thesaurus files).

- Finally, a new IIS Web application called the *Shared Services Provider Administration Application* gives access to all of the configuration and management tasks for the shared services.

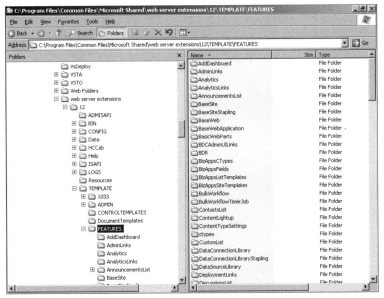

Figure 1-12   New site definitions and Features made available after a Microsoft Office SharePoint Server 2007 installation

In the next chapters, I will talk about many of the administrative tasks that are necessary at the level of the Shared Services Provider. To begin, Windows SharePoint Services 3.0 introduces a two-tier administration architecture consisting of two levels:

The first level is the administration of the server farm and IIS Web Application using the SharePoint 3.0 Central Administration, shown in Figure 1-13. This Web application gives you an Operations site and a Web Application site. The former is dedicated to administration at the level of the farm and the latter to administration for the various IIS Web Applications that are available on the machine.

A second layer of administration is at the site collection and site itself. In every site collection, there is the option to work with the site collection administration pages. The links are available at the level of the root site via the Site Actions menu and then the Site Settings menu item. Every individual site in a site collection has its own set of administration pages, again accessible via the same menu options.

Microsoft Office SharePoint Server 2007 introduces a third level of administration: at the level of the Shared Services Provider. The list of all Shared Service Providers active in your server farm can be reviewed via the SharePoint 3.0 Central Administration. Under every instance, lists of all of the IIS Web Applications associated with it are displayed.

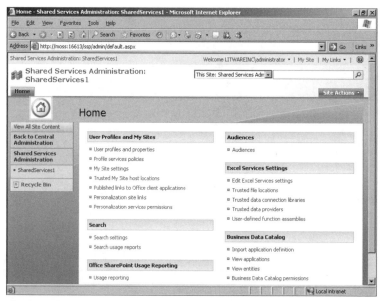

Figure 1-13   Administration at the level of the server farm and the IIS Web Application using the SharePoint 3.0 Central Administration

In most cases, you'll get to see only one Shared Services Provider, by default named *SharedServices1*. Administrators have the option to create additional Shared Services Providers, configure existing ones, restore Shared Services Providers, and change the bindings between IIS Web Applications and Shared Services Providers. All of this configuration and administration is neatly written down by Bill English in *Microsoft Office SharePoint Server 2007 Administrator's Companion* (Microsoft Press). I refer you to that book for further details since it is not a really a development topic.

The administration site associated with each of these Shared Service Providers is what is important in the context of this book. There are two options for navigating to it: the context menu of the item in the list of Shared Services Providers or the Quick Launch at the left of the screen. The result for both is exactly the same, as shown in Figure 1-13. In a lot of the chapters in the book, I'll come back to this Web application to discuss the various options available for configuring and managing the shared services.

Microsoft Office SharePoint Server 2007 Workflows

In the beginning of this chapter, I discussed the important building blocks that make Windows SharePoint Services 3.0 a true solutions platform. One of these components is the support for workflows that can be associated with lists, document libraries, or content types.

A number of new custom workflows, in addition to the three-state workflow that is part of a Windows SharePoint Services 3.0 installation, are available after installation of Microsoft

Office SharePoint Server 2007. They can be directly applied to one of the document libraries or lists in the SharePoint sites. To review the available workflows, create a new document library or list or use an existing one and open the Document Library Settings page using the Settings menu option on the toolbar. Next, under Permissions and Management, find the Workflow Settings page. If there are already workflows associated with the list or document library, you'll get an overview and the option to manage the workflows or add more. In case there are no workflows associated, you are instantly redirected to the Add a Workflow page. There are a number of workflows displayed here.

The Approval Workflow

This workflow is probably the principal one of the set of workflows available with Microsoft Office SharePoint Server 2007. The *Approval Workflow* supports the association of a serial approval or a parallel approval workflow with your document libraries. Draft documents, for example, can be routed through a number of approval steps before they are published as a major version in the document library, making these documents available to every visitor of your site. A small walkthrough will illustrate this in a moment.

The Collect Feedback Workflow

In many collaboration scenarios, there is the need to gather feedback from co-workers when authoring a document. The *Collect Feedback Workflow* can be used to route the document through a chain of people who are requested to give that feedback. All of the feedback is collected via the workflow, and the original author of the document can then process that feedback in the document.

The Collect Signatures Workflow

The *Collect Signatures Workflow* is a type of workflow that can be started only from the Microsoft Office 2007 clients and aims at collecting digital signatures from a number of people.

The Disposition Approval Workflow

The *Disposition Approval Workflow* is one that can be associated with the document library to manage the retention and expiration of a document. It organizes a structured flow to enable users to decide whether to retain or delete a document.

Deployment of Workflows

All of the discussed workflows are deployed as .NET assemblies in the global assembly cache, and most of them are making use of Microsoft InfoPath 2007 forms to interact with the users involved in the workflow. An example is a form that is shown when you associate the workflow with the list or document library. Another example is the form displayed when a task has been assigned to approve or reject the document. Because the interaction is done with

Microsoft InfoPath forms, the same forms are displayed both in the browser and the Microsoft Office 2007 clients when users go through the workflow.

Workflows are made available in the server farm as Features and scoped at the level of the site collection. Site collection administrators can see the list of activated Features by navigating to the Site Collection Features page, and they can deactivate the ones that are not needed, if desired.

Walkthrough: Working with the Approval Workflow

Let's see a workflow in action. In the daily life of an information worker, workflow is omni-present. Often, decisions involve one or more steps, sometimes involving interaction with other people. In this small walkthrough, for the purpose of refreshing or familiarizing yourself with the super-important concept of content types, you'll associate the approval workflow with a content type and define the parallel approval route. You'll start the workflow in the browser but also experience how the Microsoft Office 2007 clients integrate with workflows associated with the SharePoint document library.

Of course, a SharePoint site is the first thing needed. This can be any type of site since work-flow is available in all cases. For the walkthrough, we'll use a small team site created as a subsite in a portal.

The content type is created in a gallery called the *Content Types Gallery,* accessible via the Site Settings page. There are plenty of content types already defined in this gallery, and in the toolbar you'll find the Create link to define your own. Let's name the new content type *Customer Visit Report*–a report that everybody in the company has to create that summarizes a visit made to a customer. Content types are created in a hierarchy, and you'll create this one based on the Document content type out of the Document Content Types group. As a result, your content type already inherits a lot of metadata defined at the level of the Document content type. As a last step, put your new content type in your own group called *Litware Content Types.* Figure 1-14 shows all of the information needed for the new content type.

After clicking the OK button, you'll end up in the Site Content Type page where you can fur-ther detail what the content type is all about. There is custom metadata that needs to be associated with a customer visit report: the name of the customer, a date recording the visit, and a small description of the reason of the visit. This metadata must be defined as extra columns for the content type. The first one is a brand new column you create by clicking on the Add From New Site Column link. Name the column *Customer,* and for the sake of sim-plicity just type **Single line of text**. Note that the column will be created as a site column in the Site Columns Gallery. This means that you will be able to reuse that column in other content types or directly associate the column with the lists or document libraries you create in the site collection. You have the option to specify again your own group, for example, Report Columns.

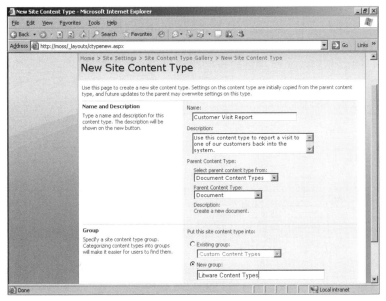

Figure 1-14   Creating a new content type

Repeat the steps, but this time for a column called *Date of Visit,* and define this one as type *Date and time.* Set the default value for *Today's Date.* The last custom field or column is one that already exists as a site column, so click on the Add From Existing Site Columns link. In the list showing the available columns from which to choose, select the *Report Description* field, transfer it to the second list, and click OK. You now have three extra columns defined for your content type.

There is also the requirement that the report is to be based on a specific Microsoft Word 2007 template. So, proceed and create a new document in Microsoft Word 2007 and use some of the artifacts that come with the rich user interface to design a good-looking template for your report. When finished, save the document on your file system. Go back to the browser and associate the template with the content type by choosing Advanced Settings and using the Upload option.

Let's concentrate now on the workflow. When creating a report, two people have to approve it: Mike and Tracy. Of course, you can utilize other users who are defined in your environment, invited to the SharePoint site, and have member rights (at a minimum) to perform the tasks. Mike and Tracy can work in parallel, but both have to approve the report. If one of them rejects the report, the workflow will be aborted.

On the Site Content Type page, choose Workflow Settings and click on the Add A Workflow link to start the process of defining the settings for the new workflow as displayed in Figure 1-15. Select Approval from the list of possible workflow candidates and assign it the name *Customer Visit Approval Workflow.* Keep the defaults for the Task and History List.

Workflows in SharePoint use these two lists to create tasks, get them assigned to the appropriate people, and log all of the steps performed in the workflow.

There is the option of having the workflow started automatically when a report is created or modified.

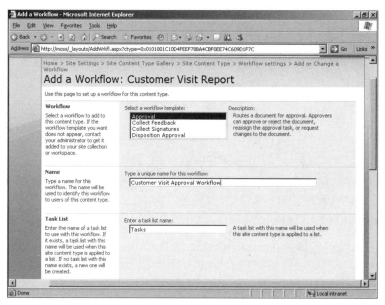

Figure 1-15   Associating an Approval Workflow to the content type

The next page is part of the custom workflow itself. This is actually a Microsoft InfoPath 2007 form embedded in the ASP.NET page. I'll discuss the details involved later in the book. For now, select the option to work in parallel mode assigning tasks to all participants simultaneously. Add *mikef* and *tracyt* in the textbox for the approvers and resolve the names. The only other option for this workflow is to select the check box for cancelling it in case one of the approvers rejects the document. Click OK to finish the job, which also ends the work for the definition of the content type.

It is now time to focus on the container—the document library—where users will store reports. Start by creating a new document library called *Reports* in your team site, and then open the Document Library Settings page using the Settings menu. Allow multiple content types from the Advanced Settings page and add the newly created content type to the list of content types associated with this document library. Right now, you have only one content type, the Document content type. Select the Litware Content Types group to see the content type that it contains, and add it to the list of content types associated with the document library, as shown in Figure 1-16.

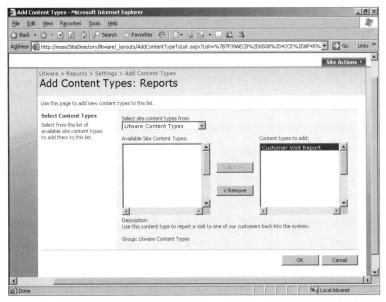

Figure 1-16   Adding the Customer Visit Report content type to the list of content types associated with a document library

Clicking on the Document content type enables you to remove it from the list so that you only have the Customer Visit Report content type available for the users.

Now play the role of a user creating a new report and navigate to the document library. Click the New button in the toolbar to start the creation of a new Customer Visit Report. As shown in Figure 1-17, the Microsoft Word 2007 clients nicely show the custom metadata defined at the level of the content type, and the document is created based on the template you've associated with it.

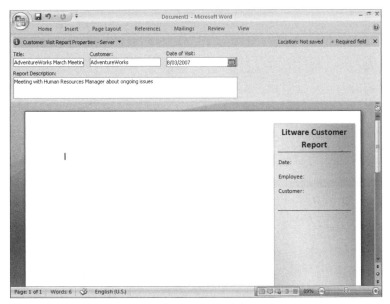

Figure 1-17   Creating a new Customer Visit Report

Save the document to the document library and notice that there is one extra field associated with the new item in the library: *Customer Visit Approval Workflow*. It has the value *In Progress*, indicating that a new workflow has been started. The value is actually a hyperlink that you can click on to go to a page for an overview of the status of the workflow. Figure 1-18 shows the two tasks created for Mike and Tracy and the information about the different steps already completed by the workflow.

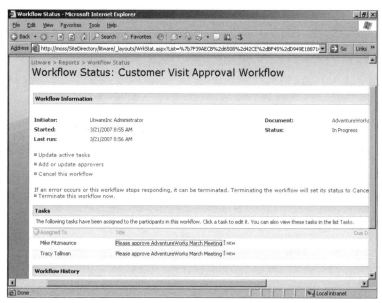

Figure 1-18   The workflow status page

Mike and Tracy have some work to do now that tasks have been assigned to them. To complete these tasks, log on with Mike (or any of the other accounts you're using) and learn how he can finish the task entirely in the browser. Completing the workflow tasks in the browser is a requirement if you do not have an Office 2007 client on your desktop.

So, Mike navigates to the same document library, opens the document in Microsoft Office Word, and reviews the content. When he is happy with it, he returns to the browser and navigates to the workflow status page. Here, he clicks on the task assigned to him and has the option of either approving or rejecting the document, as shown in Figure 1-19.

Mike is a nice guy and approves the document, completing his task in the workflow. The status page shows the change in the workflow, and now it is up to Tracy to finish her task. Note that since you've created a parallel approval workflow, Tracy can complete her task before Mike does. Assume that Tracy has Microsoft Office Word 2007 installed on her machine. This means that she can actually complete her task directly in the Word environment. She checks out the document and edits it. Notice in Figure 1-20 how the Microsoft Office 2007 clients can display a panel with an Edit Task button in case there is a workflow running for this document and there is a task assigned to the current user.

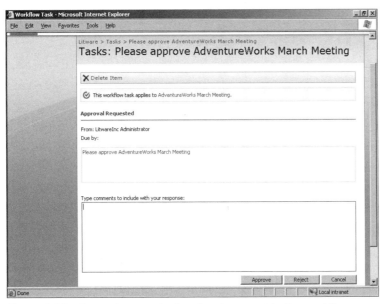

Figure 1-19   Approving or rejecting the document in the workflow

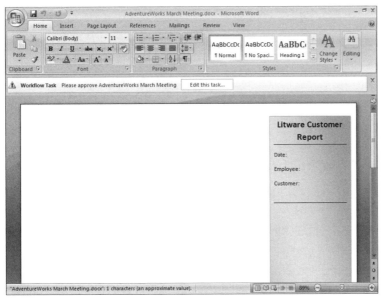

Figure 1-20   Microsoft Word 2007 displaying a panel with a task to complete for this document

When Tracy clicks on the Edit Task button, she'll see the same Microsoft InfoPath 2007 form that Mike saw in the browser, but now it is rendered in a dialog box as shown in Figure 1-21. Therefore, Tracy doesn't need to leave her comfort zone and can complete her workflow task without an extra navigation to the browser.

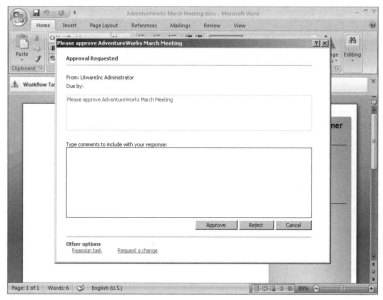

Figure 1-21   The Microsoft InfoPath 2007 form rendered in the Office 2007 client

Going back to the workflow status page, you'll now see that both players in the workflow have completed their respective task, and the workflow status is *Complete*.

This also completes the first walkthrough describing the different steps for associating, starting, and completing a workflow both in the browser as well as in the Microsoft Office 2007 smart clients.

Summary

The key to understanding Microsoft Office SharePoint Server 2007 is that it delivers additional services (shared services), solutions, new site definitions, Features, extensions, Web Parts, and more, above and beyond the solutions platform delivered with Windows SharePoint Services 3.0. This first chapter gave you a broad overview of these additions, and we finished with a demonstration of an approval workflow. If you continue reading, you'll get an inside view of each of the discussed services and solutions from a developer's perspective with plenty of additional walkthroughs illustrating the rich out-of-the-box features and the various customization and extensibility scenarios.

Chapter 2

Collaboration Portals and People Management

- Understand the architecture and the provisioning flow of a collaboration portal.

- Learn about the different options you have for customizing and branding collaboration portals: master pages, Cascading Style Sheet (CSS) files, and navigation.

- Understand the page model and the publishing cycle in portals.

- Learn how to create custom page layouts.

- Discover the *Microsoft.Office.Server.UserProfiles* namespace and the support in the object model for working with user profiles, audiences, and the social networking integration in the Microsoft Office SharePoint Server 2007.

The Collaboration Portal Architecture

A *collaboration portal* is a collection of sites within one single site collection. It is a hub for accessing and aggregating information at a higher level than the level of the Windows SharePoint Services team sites. Typically, a collaboration portal is a dedicated place for managing content and supporting collaboration at the level of a department, division, or the entire enterprise. Figure 2-1 displays the result of going through the steps of provisioning a collaboration portal. These steps are detailed in the walkthrough later on.

Site Hierarchy

A collaboration portal is thus not limited to one site. Different types of sites are created, each with their own goals. Figure 2-2 shows the site hierarchy for an out-of-the-box collaboration portal. Every one of these sites is provisioned based on a specific site definition physically located in the \12\Template\SiteTemplates folder.

Figure 2-1   The result of provisioning a collaboration portal

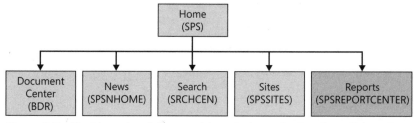

Figure 2-2   The hierarchy of sites provisioned when selecting the collaboration portal site template

At the top, there is a site called *Home* that is provisioned based on the SPS site definition. A number of important Features are activated for the site collection and the site itself, such as the different workflows that can be used, Features supporting the publishing cycle (see later for more details), a set of common Web Parts, and much more. As subsites, there are the Document Center, the News, the Search Center, and the Sites Directory. If you have an Enterprise CAL for the Microsoft Office SharePoint Server 2007, you'll get an additional subsite called the Report Center.

The *Document Center* is a site based on the site definition named BDR in the file system, providing a large-scale authoring environment for documents. It contains a document library optimized for storing large numbers of documents. All of the document management Features are turned on, including versioning and forced check-in and check-out of the documents, and multiple content types are enabled by default. The News subsite is based on the SPSNHOME site definition and is basically a publishing site tuned to author, manage, and deliver news items in the form of pages to the visitors of the collaboration portal. There is also a place by default in the collaboration portal where users can execute search queries and review the results returned by the search service. The site is called *Search* and is based on the SRCHCEN site definition. Chapter 3, "Customizing and Extending the Microsoft Office SharePoint 2007 Search," discusses the Search Center in full detail. The Sites subsite is also referred to as the Sites Directory and is meant to be a place to organize the possibly many subsites that are living under the portal or are linked to it. The site is provisioned based on the SPSSITES site definition. If you have experience with Microsoft SharePoint Portal Server 2003, you'll probably recognize it.

There is one big difference you should know about when comparing against the previous version. The creation of a new site using the Create Site link, at the top-right corner in Figure 2-3, does not result in the creation of a new site collection as was the case with Microsoft Share-Point Portal Server 2003. By default, the newly created site becomes part of the site collection you created when provisioning the portal. The benefits of this approach are that you automatically inherit all of the user administration settings as well as the other configurations (for example, the Features) done at the level of the site collection. If needed, you can revert back to the old approach and have the users create new site collections from the Sites Directory. You first have to turn on the Self-Service Site Creation option for the IIS Web Application that hosts your portal in the SharePoint 3.0 Central Administration. In the Site Collection Administration, you'll find the Site Directory Settings link that brings you to the page where you can enable the option to have new site collections created from the site directory.

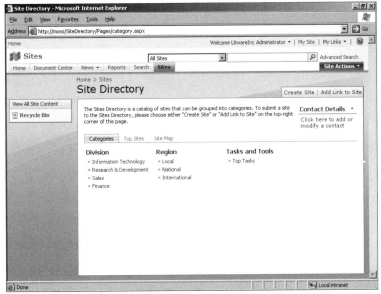

Figure 2-3   The Sites Directory allowing you to either create sites in the same site collection of the portal or link existing sites

The final subsite shown in Figures 2-1 and 2-2 is called *Reports*, and, as mentioned previously, is only when you have the standard CAL of the Microsoft Office SharePoint Server 2007. The Report Center is based on the SPSREPORTCENTER site definition and is discussed in full in Chapter 7, "Integrating with Excel Services."

The Provisioning Flow

Let's discuss in more detail the mechanism that drives the provisioning of both the collaboration and the publishing portals. It's important to understand the whole process because insight to how portals are provisioned opens doors to new ways of extending and customizing the process. In this chapter, I'll only discuss the different components that play a role in the flow. In Chapter 6, "Customizing and Branding Publishing Portals," I'll go a step further and guide you through the steps of actually customizing the provisioning flow.

Figure 2-4 shows the different players involved. To start, when you decide to create a new site in an existing or new site collection, SharePoint displays the list of available templates. The items in this list are defined by a collection of small XML files that all start with a prefix WEBTEMP located in the \12\Template\1033\XML folder. Notice that these are stored in a folder using the locale 1033, and thus you can have other folders and translations of these files when working with non-English SharePoint language packs. In the directory, a number of these WEBTEMP-prefixed files are already there, including the one that is used during the provisioning process of the portals: webtempsps.xml.

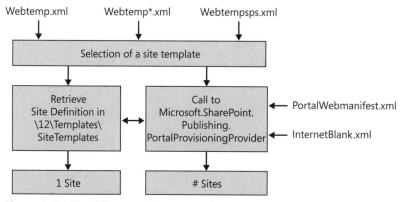

Figure 2-4 The different components playing a role in the provisioning of SharePoint sites

In that XML file, there are different templates defined, each corresponding with a possible site template displayed in the Create Site or Create Site Collection page. Interesting to us here is the template named SPSPORTAL that corresponds to the Collaboration Portal entry in that list.

```
<Template Name="SPSPORTAL" ID="47">
 <Configuration ID="0" Title="Collaboration Portal" Type="0"
 Hidden="FALSE" ImageUrl="/_layouts/1033/images/template_corp_intranet.png"
 Description="A starter site hierarchy for an intranet divisional portal.
```

```
It includes a home page, a News site, a Site Directory, a Document Center,
and a Search Center with Tabs. Typically, this site has nearly as many
contributors as readers and is used to host team sites."
 ProvisionAssembly="Microsoft.SharePoint.Publishing, Version=12.0.0.0,
Culture=neutral, PublicKeyToken=71e9bce111e9429c"
 ProvisionClass="Microsoft.SharePoint.Publishing.PortalProvisioningProvider"
 ProvisionData="SiteTemplates\\WebManifest\\PortalWebManifest.xml"
 RootWebOnly="TRUE" DisplayCategory="Publishing"
 VisibilityFeatureDependency="97A2485F-EF4B-401f-9167-FA4FE177C6F6">
 </Configuration>
 </Template>
```

Notice that the SPSPORTAL template is not pointing to a subfolder in the \12\Template\ SiteTemplates folder as is the case with many of the other template configurations you'll find in webtempsps.xml and other webtemp*.xml files. For portals, the provisioning engine actually gets the help from a .NET assembly defined by the *ProvisionAssembly* attribute in the XML and a class within that assembly set as the value of the *ProvisionClass* attribute. The assembly wrapping the provisioning engine is the *Microsoft.SharePoint.Publishing.dll*, and the class that is used by the provisioning engine is the *PortalProvisioningProvider*. How does the provisioning engine know what to create if we don't point to a site definition folder? The answer can be found in a small XML file, PortalWebManifest.xml, located in the \12\Template\ SiteTemplates\WebManifest folder. The location of this file is included in the template configuration definition as the value of the *ProvisionData* attribute. The publishing portal uses another file called InternetBlank.xml, located in the \12\Template\XML folder. Here is the content of PortalWebManifest.xml:

```
<portal xmlns="PortalTemplate.xsd">
 <web name="Home" siteDefinition="SPS"
  displayName="$Resources:spscore,PortalManifest_Home_DisplayName;"
  description="$Resources:spscore,PortalManifest_Home_Description;">
  <webs>
   <web name="News" siteDefinition="SPSNHOME"
    displayName="$Resources:spscore,PortalManifest_News_DisplayName;"
    description="$Resources:spscore,PortalManifest_News_Description;" />
   <web name="SiteDirectory" siteDefinition="SPSSITES"
   displayName="$Resources:spscore,PortalManifest_SiteDirectory_DisplayName;"
   description="$Resources:spscore,PortalManifest_SiteDirectory_Description;" />
   <web name="SearchCenter" siteDefinition="SRCHCEN"
    displayName="$Resources:spscore,PortalManifest_SearchCenter_DisplayName;"
    description="$Resources:spscore,PortalManifest_SearchCenter_Description;" />
     <web name="Docs" siteDefinition="BDR"
      displayName="$Resources:spscore,PortalManifest_DocumentCenter_DisplayName;"
      description="$Resources:spscore,PortalManifest_DocumentCenter_Description;" />
   </webs>
  </web>
 </portal>
```

The above XML block is essentially a script for the provisioning engine containing the site hierarchy to create. The site hierarchy is defined using nested Web XML elements that contain attributes for the name, the display name, a description, and, very important, the site definition that has to be used by the provisioning engine. You can identify a root-level site called *Home* based on the SPS site definition together with four subsites: News, Site Directory, Document Center, and Search. So your end result, the provisioned sites, is actually defined by the small script in these XML files. And, yes, you can make your own scripts. Chapter 6 contains a small walkthrough demonstrating this.

Walkthrough: Creating a Collaboration Portal

The steps involved in the creation of a collaboration portal are not very different from the ones you have to follow when creating other types of SharePoint sites. By default, collaboration portals can only be root-level sites in a site collection. This site collection can be hosted on a fresh IIS Web Application or one that has already been extended. The creation and extension of an IIS Web Application is a process you can start from the SharePoint 3.0 Central Administration. In the Application Management page, there is the Create or Extend Web application link under the SharePoint Web Application Management group. Figure 2-5 displays the page with the two options available.

Figure 2-5   Creating or extending an IIS Web Application

The first option is to create and extend a new IIS Web Application. The second option can be used to support a scenario where the SharePoint sites hosted on one IIS Web Application have to be accessed by users within a different authentication zone. For example, the collaboration portal is available on the intranet, and the authentication is done via integrated Windows authentication defined at the level of the first IIS Web application. Additionally, there is the request to provide access to partners or customers via an extranet possibly using an HTTPS connection. This last option is to extend a second IIS Web Application pointing to the same SharePoint content and configuring that IIS Web Application for HTTPS.

Assume you start from scratch and your plan is to host your first collaboration portal. The first option on the page displayed in Figure 2-5 is therefore the most appropriate. A page opens where you'll enter some details. First of all, when you haven't previously done any preparation work in the IIS Management Console, you have to select the option to create a new IIS Web site. The description of the new site can be something like *LitwareInc Portal*. If you have done some additional preparation work and created a DNS alias name up front, such as *portal.litwareinc.com*, you'll be able to use port 80 and differentiate from the other IIS Web Applications listening to the same port via the host header *portal.litwareinc.com*. If you cannot configure a new DNS alias, use a different port number, such as port 8000, and leave the host header blank. The physical folder that will be associated with your new IIS Web site is by default created in the C:\Inetpub\wwwroot\wss\VirtualDirectories folder. It is possible, of course, to make a change here and point to another folder in the file system. Figure 2-6 shows the configuration for the new IIS Web site.

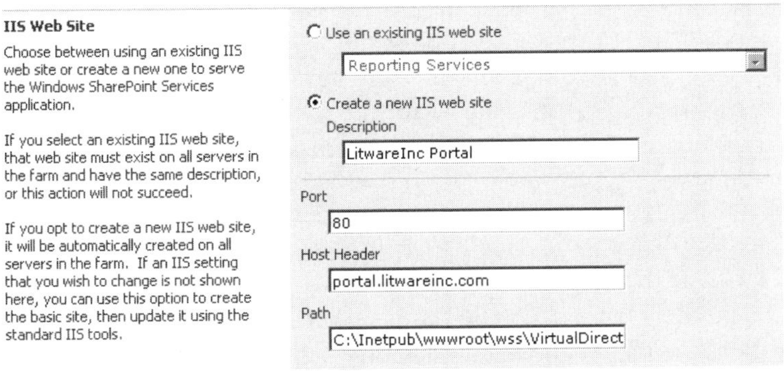

Figure 2-6   The settings for a new IIS Web site

Next, you have the security configuration settings at the level of IIS. Options here are Kerberos and NTLM. Enabling Kerberos as your authentication provider involves extra work in Active Directory configuring a *Service Principal Name* for the account configured to run the worker process hosting the portal. NTLM is the default option. No need for anonymous access here. I'll come back to this in Chapter 6 and take you through the steps for configuring a SharePoint portal for anonymous access.

The next section in the configuration is quite important. SharePoint sites run in their own worker process, isolated from the IIS process. This worker process runs with an account known as the Application Pool Identity. The account is very crucial to SharePoint because it is the account used to communicate with the different databases that store the configuration and content data. It's a best practice to create a domain account with just the required privileges and use this to be the Application Pool Identity for all of the SharePoint-related worker processes. Figure 2-7 displays the configuration with the *sp_workerprocess* account.

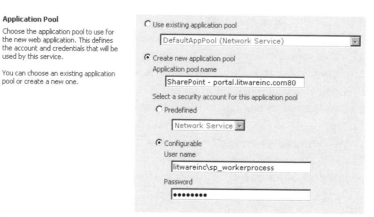

Figure 2-7   Configuration of the IIS application pool

The last section to consider includes the details regarding the content database created during the whole process. Every site in your site collections will drop their content by default in this content database. It is not a bad idea to change the name of the database to better represent the purpose. This way, in SQL Server, you'll be able to differentiate better between the various SharePoint-related databases. When all of the details are supplied, you can start the job of creating and extending the IIS Web site.

After the successful execution of the job, there is the option of navigating to the Create Site Collection page. It is here that you'll make the decision to create a collaboration portal by selecting the corresponding template in the Template Selection list under the Publishing tab, shown in Figure 2-8. To complete the required data, you'll have to enter a title (for example, *LitwareInc Portal*) and provide an account for the primary and/or secondary site collection administrator.

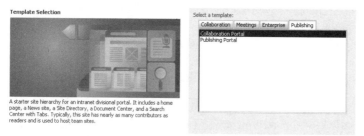

Figure 2-8   Selecting the collaboration portal template for the top-level site

After SharePoint completes the process of provisioning the site collection and the top-level site, you'll be able to browse to the brand new intranet portal. Figure 2-1 displays the result of the out-of-the-box template for the collaboration portal.

Customizing and Branding Portals

In the real world, there will often be the need to customize and brand the two types of portals available with the Microsoft Office SharePoint Server 2007. The work typically involves modifying the master pages that are used—the various cascading style sheets for the general look and feel—and maybe there will be the need to tune the navigation options for the users in the portal. I'll discuss each of these to some degree in this chapter and continue the story in Chapter 6, where I'll cover more options.

Master Pages

Master pages play an important role in customizing and branding sites because they make available the various controls that are responsible for rendering the common elements shared across all of the pages within a site. These common elements include:

- Top and left navigation menus
- Logos
- Search fields
- Page editing controls
- Login controls
- Any other custom controls you decide to create and intend to make available on the pages in a site

Master pages also contain CSS references that define the chrome, or overall look and feel of the page. Typically, many (if not all) of the pages in your site collection will use the same master page in order to preserve a consistent branding all over the portal. There are scenarios, however, where within one site collection you'll want to employ multiple master pages for different areas within the collection. For example, a company's portal may have one section for the marketing division and another one for the human resources division, and both may require a different look and feel from the rest of the site. In that scenario, it may be wise to create a new master page or customize an existing one in order to distinguish the pages from the other sites.

Different master pages are available out-of-the-box, and if you work in a portal, you'll be able to very easily switch between different master pages. The place where you actually do this is the Site Master Page Settings page (displayed in Figure 2-9), accessible via the Master Page link under the Look and Feel section in the Site Settings page. Here, you'll be able to see the list of available candidates and will have the opportunity to select one and apply it to a site. You can also push the change to all of the subsites. At the level of the subsites, it is possible to break the inheritance and associate the site with its own personal master page.

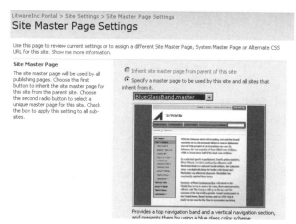

Figure 2-9   Changing to another master page using the Site Master Page Settings page

As a result of the action, the collaboration portal will look similar to a publishing portal, as displayed in Figure 2-10.

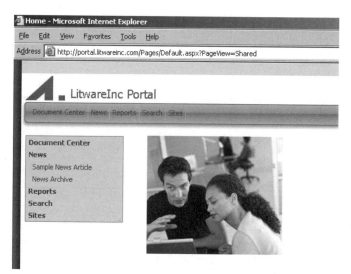

Figure 2-10   A collaboration portal with the BlueGlassBand master page activated

The Master Page Gallery

Master pages are stored in the *Master Page Gallery*, a standard document library at the level of the site collection. There is one per site collection. The Master Page Gallery provides all of the functionality of a typical Windows SharePoint Services 3.0 document library including versioning, page creation based on multiple content types, check-in/check-out control, and workflow. Note that every site in the site collection will show the link to the Master Page Gallery in the Site Settings administration page. Clicking on this link will always bring you to the Master Page Gallery at the level of the site collection. Figure 2-11 shows the Master Page Gallery for the collaboration portal.

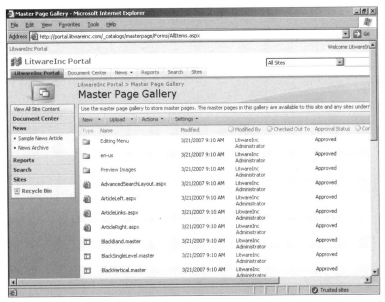

Figure 2-11   The Master Page Gallery at the level of the site collection where you store the master pages along with the page layout files

In a SharePoint site with the publishing Features enabled, as is the case with the publishing and the collaboration portals, there are two types of master pages stored in the Master Page Gallery (each identified by a unique icon as displayed in Figure 2-12):

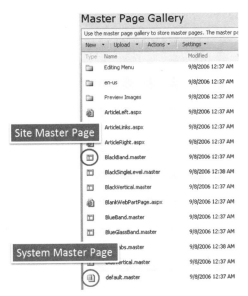

Figure 2-12   Two types of master pages are available for the portal: the System Master Pages and the Site Master Pages

- *System master pages* define the look and feel of the administration pages associated with the site: the list and library form pages, and the views and Web Part pages. For example, when opening the page to consult the contents of the Master Page Gallery, you will notice that it has a more traditional SharePoint look and feel compared to the home page of the publishing portal.

- *Site master pages* define the look and feel of the pages published within the site. These pages, which are based on page layouts or templates, are the ones the visitors of the site will see, and therefore they are more important to customize than the system master pages.

A Closer Look at the *default.master*

Let's have a look at the internals of the *default.master* before we start doing any customization work. Chapter 6 contains a full description of the internals of the other master pages that are available in the Master Page Gallery.

The Microsoft Office SharePoint Designer 2007 is the place to be if you want to explore the various elements that make up a master page. You open the product and then use the File menu to open the portal. The folder list displays the complete structure and all of the individual pieces that make up the publishing portal. You can review the contents of the Master Page Gallery by expanding the *_catalogs* node and then selecting the *masterpage* node. Figure 2-13 shows the contents of the gallery for the portal.

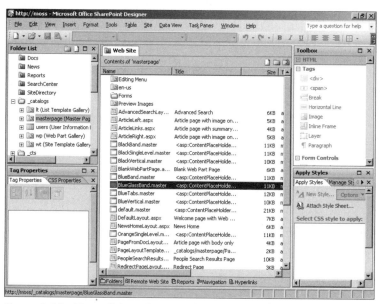

Figure 2-13   The collaboration portal ready for customization work in the Microsoft Office SharePoint Designer 2007

By default, the collaboration portal uses the *default.master* as the active master page. In the Microsoft Office SharePoint Designer, you open the master page in the designer by double-clicking the *default.master* file and confirming that you want to check it out. You may want to switch to split mode so that you have the designer and the code editor visible as illustrated in Figure 2-14.

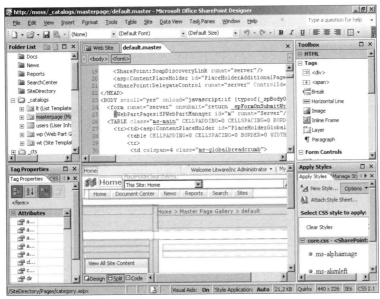

Figure 2-14   Designing the *default.master* in the Microsoft Office SharePoint Designer 2007

Important   The *contributor settings* are a layer of security in the Microsoft Office SharePoint Designer 2007 that enables administrators to assign specific authoring rights to people working in the product. By creating contributor groups, there is the option of defining permissions to perform certain operations on pages in the site at a very fine level.

There are a number of ASP.NET server and user controls included in the master page, and several .NET assemblies deliver the necessary code-behind logic. In the *default.master*, most of these controls are part of the SharePoint framework and are prefixed with *SharePoint* or *WebPartPages*. They are the Web controls or Web Parts delivered with the *Microsoft.SharePoint.dll*. You'll find these controls in most of the SharePoint sites, even those that are not enabled with the publishing Feature. Table 2-1 summarizes the important controls found in the *default.master* for the collaboration portal. Later in the book, I'll present a description of the controls and assemblies used by the other master pages available in the Master Page Gallery.

Table 2-1   SharePoint Framework Controls in the *default.master*

Control	Description
CssLink	Links to the various CSS files retrieved from the \12\Template\ Layouts\locale-id\styles folder.
ScriptLink	Links to the JavaScript files in the \12\Template\Layouts folder responsible for the client-side user experience.
DelegateControl	Delegate controls are at rendering time populated by other controls.
AspMenu	ASP.NET navigation control rendering a menu-driven interaction with the sites and pages in the site collection.
SPWebPartManager	Control that behind the scenes coordinates the work for Web Parts on Web Part pages.
SiteActions	The definition of the different items displayed by the Site Actions menu (overridden with the definition of new menu items when working in a portal).
SPSecurityTrimmedControl	The control that renders the View All Site Content link just above the Quick Launch.
SPNavigationManager	The control rendering the Quick Launch.
SiteLogoImage	The control rendering the image containing the logo as it is defined for the site.

In addition to the ASP.NET server controls, you'll also find two ASP.NET user controls (ASCX files) implanted in the *default.master* page. Both are physically stored in the \12\Template\ Controltemplates folder:

■ The *Welcome.ascx* is a user control displayed at the top of a page welcoming the visitor and allowing him or her to modify the personal settings. This user control appears on all of the SharePoint sites.

■ The *DesignModeConsole.ascx* is a small user control displaying some status information for the page.

The ASP.NET *ContentPlaceHolder* controls is the last set of controls in the master pages. The most important one is the *PlaceHolderMain*. The body of this control will hold the actual content page.

The *DelegateControl* on the Master Page

If you look in detail to the structure of the *default.master*, you'll notice a number of definitions for the *DelegateControl* in the page. The *DelegateControl* is able to populate itself at runtime with any control you ask it to render. Take for example the inclusion of the search box:

```
<SharePoint:DelegateControl runat="server"
ControlId="SmallSearchInputBox"/>
```

The control that the *DelegateControl* has to pick up at runtime is set via the *ControlID* attribute. In the sample above, it has the value *SmallSearchInputBox*. The details regarding that control are contained within a Feature. By default, there are three Features that contain a definition for the *SmallSearchInputBox*: OSearchBasicFeature, OSearchEnhancedFeature, and ContentLightUp. Each of these Features has a SearchArea.xml file that you can open. Here is the one for the OSearchBasicFeature:

```xml
<?xml version="1.0" encoding="utf-8" ?>
<Elements xmlns="http://schemas.microsoft.com/sharepoint/">
    <Control
        Id="SmallSearchInputBox"
        Sequence="50"
        ControlClass="Microsoft.SharePoint.Portal.WebControls.SearchBoxEx"
        ControlAssembly="Microsoft.SharePoint.Portal, Version=12.0.0.0,
Culture=neutral, PublicKeyToken=71e9bce111e9429c">
        <Property Name="GoImageUrl">/_layouts/images/gosearch.gif</Property>
        <Property Name="GoImageUrlRTL">/_layouts/images/goRTL.gif</Property>
        <Property Name="GoImageActiveUrl">
          /_layouts/images/gosearch.gif</Property>
        <Property Name="GoImageActiveUrlRTL">
          /_layouts/images/goRTL.gif</Property>
        <Property Name="DropDownMode">ShowDD</Property>
        <Property Name="SearchResultPageURL">
          /_layouts/osssearchresults.aspx</Property>
        <Property Name="ScopeDisplayGroupName"></Property>
        <Property Name="FrameType">None</Property>
    </Control>
</Elements>
```

Here is the one for the OSearchEnhancedFeature:

```xml
<?xml version="1.0" encoding="utf-8" ?>
<Elements xmlns="http://schemas.microsoft.com/sharepoint/">
  <Control
    Id="SmallSearchInputBox"
    Sequence="25"
    ControlClass="Microsoft.SharePoint.Portal.WebControls.SearchBoxEx"
    ControlAssembly="Microsoft.SharePoint.Portal, Version=12.0.0.0,
Culture=neutral, PublicKeyToken=71e9bce111e9429c">
      <Property Name="GoImageUrl">/_layouts/images/gosearch.gif</Property>
      <Property Name="GoImageUrlRTL">/_layouts/images/goRTL.gif</Property>
      <Property Name="GoImageActiveUrl">
          /_layouts/images/gosearch.gif</Property>
      <Property Name="GoImageActiveUrlRTL">
          /_layouts/images/goRTL.gif</Property>
      <Property Name="UseSiteDefaults">true</Property>
      <Property Name="FrameType">None</Property>
      <Property Name="ShowAdvancedSearch">true</Property>
  </Control>
</Elements>
```

The third one, the ContentLightUp, contains the following XML:

```xml
<?xml version="1.0" encoding="utf-8"?>
<Elements xmlns="http://schemas.microsoft.com/sharepoint/">
  <Control
     Id="SmallSearchInputBox"
     Sequence="100"
     ControlSrc="~/_controltemplates/searcharea.ascx">
  </Control>
</Elements>
```

Now what's the difference between all of them? The first two definitions tell the *DelegateControl* to show an instance of the *SearchBoxEx* control, while the last one points to an ASP.NET user control, *searcharea.ascx*, available in the \12\Templates\ControlTemplates folder. Another difference is the value for the *Sequence*, ranging from 25 to 100. And that is now exactly the important information for the *DelegateControl* introducing a new level of flexibility in SharePoint. The *DelegateControl* always goes for the control defined in the activate Features with the lowest sequence number.

All of this is interesting, such as with the following scenario. Let's say you have thousands of sites, each using a master page working with this *DelegateControl*. Perhaps there is a requirement to have a new type of search experience delivered to these sites. With the creation, installation, and activation of one simple Feature containing the new search experience and, very important, a sequence number that is lower than any of those previously mentioned, the update will be directly visible in all of the sites.

Walkthrough: Customizing a Master Page

In Chapter 6, you'll step through a tutorial to create a master page from scratch. In this chapter, you'll perform a small customization to the *default.master*: change the logo of the portal. Start by opening the Microsoft Office SharePoint Designer 2007 and open the collaboration portal. As said, the Master Page Gallery is located under the *_catalogs* node in the folder list. After checking out the *default.master*, the designer renders the page and it's ready for the alterations.

First, make sure that you copy a logo to the \12\Template\Images folder. For example, you can take the litware_logo.jpg that is available from the companion Web site. Next, in the Microsoft Office SharePoint Designer 2007, remove the *<SharePoint:SiteLogoImage* element and replace it with:

```
<asp:image ImageUrl="/_layouts/images/litware/litware_logo.jpg"
 runat="server"/>
```

Save your work, and navigate to the top-level site in your site collection. You'll see the change in the logo. It may be necessary to use the Site Master Page Settings page to apply the changes to the subsites. Figure 2-15 displays the result of your work.

Figure 2-15   Customizing the *default.master* with a new logo

Changes to the master page are saved in the Master Page Gallery, and after customizations are checked in and subsequently approved, visitors to the site will see the new logo on all pages in the site where the master page is active.

Styling the Portal

The look and feel of the collaboration portal is, for the biggest part, defined by a number of cascading style sheets that are linked by the master page. Windows SharePoint Services 3.0 and the Microsoft Office SharePoint Server 2007 use a standards-based CSS rendering engine, which basically provides you with the same powerful support as pure ASP.NET applications. Table 2-2 describes the different cascading style sheets that define the look and feel for pages that use the *default.master*.

Table 2-2   CSS Files for *default.master*

CSS File	Description
Core.css	Contains the core CSS classes linked to the master page at runtime by the *CssLink* control. Located in \12\Template\Layouts\1033\Styles.
HtmlEditorCustom-Styles.css	Defines the formatting for custom styles in the *HTML Editor* control. Located in \12\Template\Layouts\1033\Styles.
HtmlEditorTable-Formats.css	Defines the formatting for tables in the *HTML Editor* control. Located in \12\Template\Layouts\1033\Styles.

It is possible to override the *core.css* by specifying an alternate CSS URL in the Site Master Page Settings page, as displayed in Figure 2-16. You can upload your own custom *core.css* to the Style Library and, as a result, the *CSSLink* control will link this one instead of the default *core.css*.

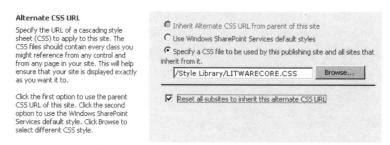

Alternate CSS URL

Specify the URL of a cascading style sheet (CSS) to apply to this site. The CSS files should contain every class you might reference from any control and from any page in your site. This will help ensure that your site is displayed exactly as you want it to.

Click the first option to use the parent CSS URL of this site. Click the second option to use the Windows SharePoint Services default style. Click Browse to select different CSS style.

Figure 2-16 Specifying an alternative CSS URL for the core CSS styles

Navigation in the Portal

The navigation in a portal, as well as in other SharePoint sites, is fully based on the ASP.NET 2.0 provider model—a layered, loosely coupled, and pluggable architecture of different components that work together to drive the SharePoint navigation.

The *PortalSiteMapProvider*

The *PortalSiteMapProvider* is the provider class for the Microsoft Office SharePoint Server 2007. The class is part of the *Microsoft.SharePoint.Publishing.dll* and inherits from the ASP.NET 2.0 *SiteMapProvider* class. The role of a *SiteMapProvider* class is to take care of the retrieval of the site hierarchy data from the underlying data source. In the Microsoft Office SharePoint Server 2007, that data source is the SQL Server database, the *PortalSiteMapProvider* understands exactly how to do this. The class is also enhanced with SharePoint-specific security trimming and caching. Four different configurations for the *PortalSiteMapProvider* are registered in the *web.config* associated with the IIS Web application. Each of them builds up a tree of *SiteMapNode* objects in a slightly different way, tuned for a specific type of navigation control. These configurations are also exposed as properties of the *PortalSiteMapProvider* class.

```
<add name="GlobalNavSiteMapProvider"
  description="CMS provider for Global navigation"
  type="Microsoft.SharePoint.Publishing.Navigation.PortalSiteMapProvider,
Microsoft.SharePoint.Publishing, Version=12.0.0.0, Culture=neutral,
PublicKeyToken=71e9bce111e9429c" NavigationType="Global"
  EncodeOutput="true" />
<add name="CombinedNavSiteMapProvider"
  description="CMS provider for Combined navigation"
  type="Microsoft.SharePoint.Publishing.Navigation.PortalSiteMapProvider,
Microsoft.SharePoint.Publishing, Version=12.0.0.0, Culture=neutral,
PublicKeyToken=71e9bce111e9429c" NavigationType="Combined"
  EncodeOutput="true" />
<add name="CurrentNavSiteMapProvider"
  description="CMS provider for Current navigation"
  type="Microsoft.SharePoint.Publishing.Navigation.PortalSiteMapProvider,
```

```
Microsoft.SharePoint.Publishing, Version=12.0.0.0, Culture=neutral,
PublicKeyToken=71e9bce111e9429c" NavigationType="Current"
  EncodeOutput="true" />
<add name="CurrentNavSiteMapProviderNoEncode"
  description="CMS provider for Current navigation, no encoding of output"
  type="Microsoft.SharePoint.Publishing.Navigation.PortalSiteMapProvider,
Microsoft.SharePoint.Publishing, Version=12.0.0.0, Culture=neutral,
PublicKeyToken=71e9bce111e9429c" NavigationType="Current"
  EncodeOutput="false" />
```

The *PortalSiteMapDataSource* Controls

These controls are embedded in the master page, and they link the navigation controls with one of the *PortalSiteMapProvider* configurations. The *PortalSiteMapDataSource* controls allow for a specific view through the setting of various attributes on the tree of nodes built up by the *PortalSiteMapProvider*.

Navigation Controls

The last type of component in the navigation architecture is the *Navigation* controls. For the top navigation, the *default.master* uses the *AspMenu* control, linking it via the *DataSourceID* attribute to the one of the *PortalSiteMapDataSource* controls. You'll notice that again a *DelegateControl* ensures that the appropriate controls are in place.

The Publishing Cycle

Pages in a collaboration or publishing portal are delivered in the browser in a very different manner than pages that are part of a pure Windows SharePoint Services 3.0 team site. The difference is the page model. In short, pages in a site with the publishing Feature active are based on page layouts (also often referred to as templates). The pages are not physical files but items stored in a document library: the Pages library. The pages aren't published immediately for everybody. Before getting published, there are publishing rules, workflows, and policies to follow. These are typically at the level of the content type associated with the page layout; they can also be defined at the Pages library for all of the pages stored in it.

Authoring Content for a Collaboration Portal

Before talking about the options for customizing and extending the page model, I'll quickly cover the steps a content author has to take to get new content delivered in the portal, such as a new news item. The new page is created by opening the Site Actions menu and selecting the Create Page link. This opens the page to enter the name and description of the news item. And, very important, the page lists the available page layouts, each of them defining the type of content that can be entered and the way it will be visualized. Figure 2-17 illustrates all of this.

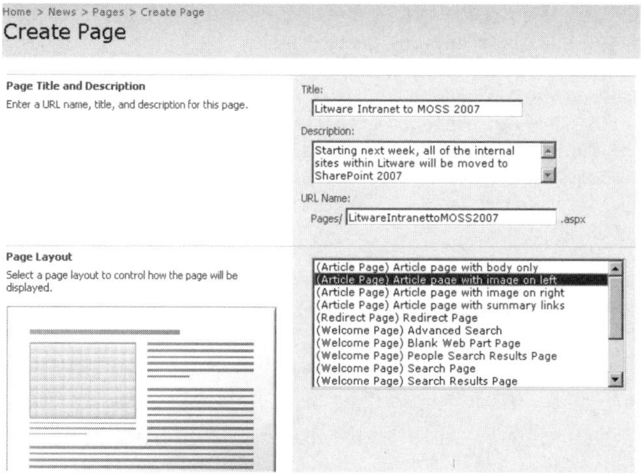

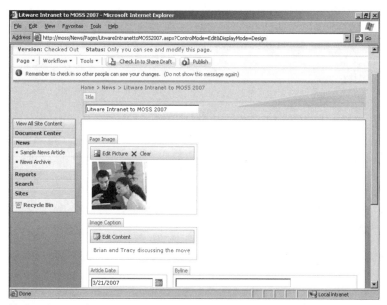

Figure 2-17   A content author creating a new page based on one of the available page layouts

The page itself is now presented in the browser and, via the various controls on the page, it can be populated with content, as shown in Figure 2-18.

Figure 2-18   The news item ready to be checked in by the content author

After it is checked in, the news item will have a minor version number assigned to it, and only users with specific permissions will be able to read it. To publish it to a major version, a workflow can be loaded and started, or, as is the case by default, users who have the appropriate permission can simply click the Publish button on the toolbar. This will raise the version number of the news item to *1.0*, making it a published page, as displayed in Figure 2-19.

Figure 2-19   A user approving the page created by a content author

Page Layouts

All of the publishing pages in a collaboration and publishing portal are based on a certain page layout (a.k.a. a template for readers who have experience with the Microsoft Content Management Server 2002 product). A *page layout* controls what content is displayed and how that content is laid out for site visitors. It is the basis for a rich and flexible content management system where IT and developers make use of page layouts to set up the infrastructure and then leave the content creation and management up to the business users or information workers.

More in detail, a page layout is an ASP.NET page stored in the Master Page Gallery along with the master pages. They are associated with a content type used to store the definition of what data is captured and made available via field controls. How about some hands-on experience?

Walkthrough: Creating Custom Page Layouts

Of course, the best way to learn what a page layout is all about is to create one yourself. In this walkthrough, I'll guide you through the steps for creating a custom page layout. You'll do all of the work in the browser. Later in the book, I'll explain how to deliver custom page layouts using a Feature, a far better approach.

Assume that the LitwareInc portal contains a subsite called *Travel Stories*, based on the News site template. The requirement is to create a page layout that everybody can use to write a travel story for publishing on the intranet.

The Site Columns   After long hours of discussion with the boss, you've identified five different pieces of content that make up a travel story page. All of these will end up as new site columns, as shown in Figure 2-20.

Figure 2-20   The site columns used to store the content for a travel story page

Open the top-level site of the portal in the browser and sign in with an account that has administrative rights. Use the Site Actions menu and the Modify All Site Settings to open up the Site Columns Gallery. Click on the link under the Galleries group. Notice that many columns are already available in this gallery. These are columns that are provisioned via the Fields Feature. Click the Create button on the toolbar to add the fields to this list one by one:

- **Travel Story Title**   Single line of text

- **Travel Story Author**   Single line of text

- **Travel Story Summary**   Multiple lines of text

- **Travel Story Body**   Publishing HTML

- **Travel Story Picture**   Publishing image

No additional options need to be set. You will probably want to create your own group to differentiate from the existing groups. A good candidate for the group name is *Travel Story Columns*.

The Content Type   Your next step is the creation of a content type. *Content types* are packaged definitions of what you want to store in SharePoint. In many cases, content types will define specific types of documents or list items, but in our scenario here, the content type will define what a travel story page is all about. This includes the metadata associated with a travel story, the data managed by the content author and displayed to the page, and the various other configurations such as a workflow and information management policy associated with the content type. In your case, you only have to add the site columns created in the previous step.

Where do you create a custom content type? Again, it's created at the top-level site in the site collection, where you click the Site Content Types link under the Galleries section in the Site Settings page. Numerous types are already stored in the gallery. Many of them, if not all, are provisioned via the ctypes Feature. Use the Create link on the toolbar to navigate to the page where you enter the name and description of the new content type. In addition, you have to select your parent content type. Content types inherit from one another with the System content type being the root of this hierarchy. The goal of your content is to package the definition of a new page layout. Therefore, select the Publishing Content Types group and the Page content type in that group. If you inherit from the Page content type, Windows Share-Point Services 3.0 will hook up your new content type with the Pages document library in the site. Remember that this Pages document library is the container where your created Travel Story pages will actually end up being stored. As shown in Figure 2-21, the custom group is a last setting on the page you can create to distinguish your content types from the other content types.

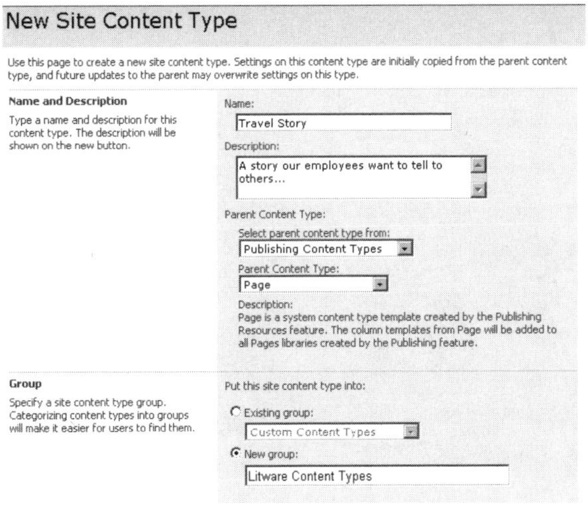

Figure 2-21   The travel story content type

Looking at the associated columns for your new content type, you'll already have a number of the columns or fields because you inherit from the Page content type. Now add your own columns to this list. They have been created before, so click on Add from the available site columns, select the Travel Story Columns group, and add all of the five columns of that group to your content type, as shown in Figure 2-22.

The Page Layout   Next, you will create the ASPX page that will be the physical represen-tation of the Travel Story page layout. Page layouts are stored in the Master Page and Page Layouts Gallery at the level of your site collection. Navigate to the Site Settings page at the level of the site collection and click the Master Page and Page Layout Gallery. Notice in Figure 2-23 how you can click the New button on the toolbar to create a new page layout.

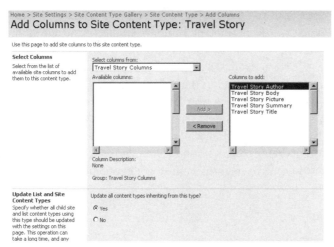

Figure 2-22   Adding the travel story columns to the content type

Figure 2-23   Creating a new page layout in the Master Page and Page Layouts Gallery

But wait, there is another option to create your new page layout. You can do all of the work using the Microsoft Office SharePoint Designer 2007. And let's do this not only because it's more fun but also because you need to go into the product anyway to finish the final steps for the page layout. Open the Microsoft Office SharePoint Designer 2007 and use the File menu to open the site you are working on. The complete site collection is now represented in the Folder List. Create a new page layout file using the File menu and open the dialog box that enables you to create new SharePoint content. The page layout is one of the things you can create from here. The page layout must be associated with the content type created in the previous step since it defines what data will be made available with the template. Figure 2-24 shows the settings to complete. Select your content type group and then the content type itself. A name for the page and a title are the last pieces of information to provide before clicking the OK button.

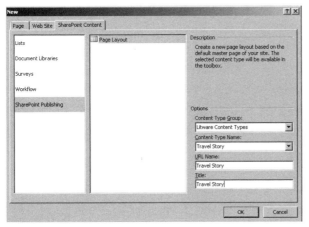

Figure 2-24   Creating a new page layout using the Microsoft Office SharePoint Designer 2007

The page is created in the proper place, the Master Page and Page Layouts Gallery. You can verify this by expanding the _catalogs and *masterpage* nodes in the Folder List. The page itself is rendered in design mode where you can see the attached master page and the empty *PlaceHolderMain*. That placeholder is where you will do your layout work. The Microsoft Office SharePoint Designer 2007 also prepares the toolbox where you'll find the field controls you can add to the page. Figure 2-25 gives a complete overview of your design environment. The toolbox contains all of the controls that can be dropped on the page layout. All of the field controls mapping to the columns associated with the Page content type are under the *Page Fields* node. The custom columns you created for the custom content type are available under the *Content Fields* node.

You're ready now to lay out the controls on the page. The best thing to do first is to create a layout structure using either a *TABLE* element or a couple of *DIV* elements. Remember, do all of this work within the boundaries of the *PlaceHolderMain*. Next, drag and drop the field controls one by one in the layout structure. Figure 2-26 shows one possible layout you can use.

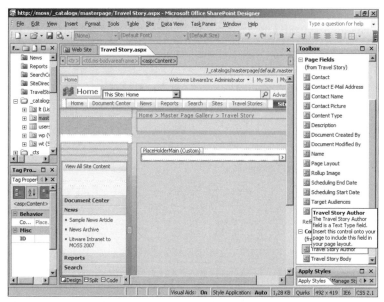

Figure 2-25 The designer experience when creating a new page layout in the Microsoft Office SharePoint Designer 2007

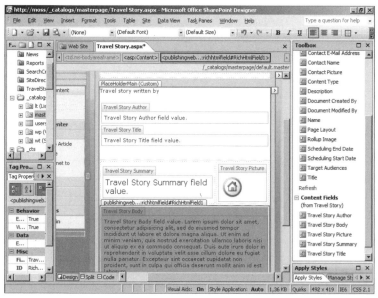

Figure 2-26 Lay out the field controls within the boundaries of the *PlaceHolderMain*

Each of the field controls exposes multiple properties that can be set using the Tag Properties panel. Typically, you apply some styling for the controls in edit mode using the *CssClass* property pointing to one of the *CSS* classes defined in the attached CSS files. You also can style the controls in display mode by adding *DIV* or *SPAN* elements in the HTML and again applying *CSS* classes to these elements. Use the Apply Styles pane to get an impression of the style.

Other properties can be modified for the *RichHtmlField* and the *RichImageField* if needed. For example, you may want to avoid having content authors add images to the product descriptions. This can be enforced simply by setting the *AllowImages* property of the *RichHtmlField* control to *false*.

When finished, save the page layout. It is still in draft mode because the Master Page and Page Layouts Gallery is a managed document library—versioning is enabled, and content approval is turned on to transition an item from a minor version to a major or published version. However, you should be able to test it without going through these steps right now: In the browser, choose Create a Page from the Site Actions menu. Notice that your new page layout is part of the list of available options, as shown in Figure 2-27.

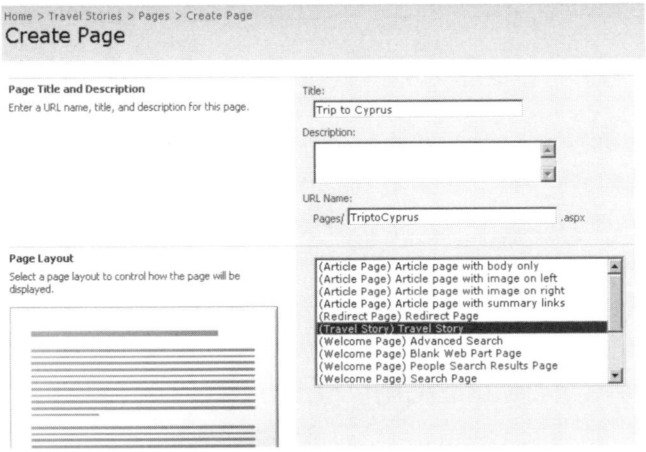

Figure 2-27   Creating a travel story page based on the new page layout

Figure 2-28 shows the page in edit mode, and each of the field controls is displayed in edit mode so that you can enter the values.

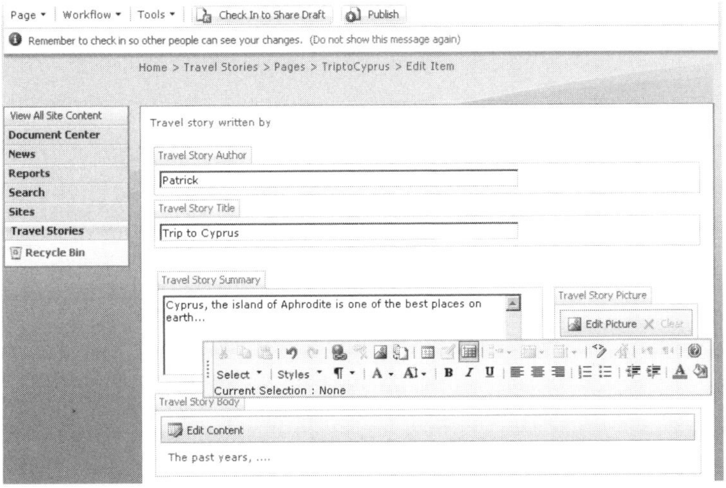

Figure 2-28   Populating the travel story page with data

After adding some sample data, the page can be checked in and published to all of the users that have access to the portal.

User Profiles and Audiences

Now let's cover something completely different but still very much related to collaboration portals. Remember that these types of portals become places on the intranet used by company employees. The Microsoft Office SharePoint Server 2007 can maintain more information than just the name, account information, and e-mail addresses of these employees. It is possible to associate a user profile with a user storing a lot more information. Many of the placeholders, or properties, for maintaining this information are already in place and can be synchronized with external data sources like an LDAP-story such as Active Directory or stores that are connected to the Business Data Catalog. Once the user profiles are in place, they can be used for grouping users together in audiences. You can have, for example, all of the developers older than 30 years grouped together in the audience *Senior Developers* while the younger ones are members of the *Junior Developers* audience. Audiences can be used to adapt the experience in the portal—for example, showing or hiding Web Parts—and to target information. In the next couple of pages, I won't directly focus on how to manage and configure the user profiles and audiences as an administrator in the administration site of the Shared Services Provider. The focus will instead be on how, as a developer, you can manipulate the people management Features programmatically.

Programmatic Access to the User Profile Store

User profile information is stored in a database under the control of the Shared Services Provider. But just like with any other store in SharePoint, you can code the access to that user profile store either directly via the object model or by consuming a Web Service called *UserProfileService.asmx*. A developer may perform administrative operations as well as retrieve and update user profiles.

Note   The Web Service does not really support administrative tasks. You'll have to embed the calls to the object model in your own custom Web Service if you want to support remote administration of the user profile store.

User Profile Administration Object Model

The different types used for connecting to and administrating the user profile store are delivered with the *Microsoft.Office.Server.dll*, and there is a new namespace grouping the various classes: the *Microsoft.Office.Server.UserProfiles*.

The *UserProfileConfigManager* Class   The administrative tasks can be divided into two categories. First, you have the operations you can do on the store itself, and these are done by instantiating an object of the *UserProfileConfigManager* class. The following lines of code show you how to do this:

```
ServerContext ctx = ServerContext.GetContext(nameSSP);
UserProfileConfigManager mngr = new UserProfileConfigManager(ctx);
```

I'll explain the *ServerContext* type in more detail in the next chapter. In short, it allows you to get a reference to the context of the Shared Services Provider. There are different ways of getting the instance. An easy one is just giving it the name of the Shared Services Provider. Once you have the instance, you can provide it as an input parameter for the constructor of the *UserProfileConfigManager*.

One task the *UserProfileConfigManager* supports is to import the user profiles and user profile information from an external store, an LDAP store, or a store that is connected to SharePoint through the Business Data Catalog. In a server farm with an Active Directory, you'll see one already in place, as displayed in Figure 2-29.

Figure 2-29   A connection to the *litwareinc* domain used to import user profiles from Active Directory accounts

The list of defined connections is exposed in the object model with the *DataSource* property of the *UserProfileConfigManager* instance. Here is how you access it:

```
DataSource ds = mngr.GetDataSource();
```

The *Connections* property of the *DataSource* instance can be used to list all of the connections, and it is possible to create a new connection by using the *Add* method at the level of the *DataSource* instance. You provide an instance that derives from the abstract *Connection* type. Possible candidates are an instance of the *LDAPConnection* class or one of the *Application-RegistryConnection* class. The first type can be used for connecting to a second Active Directory, the second type can be used to connect to an application definition in the Business Data Catalog. The following lines of code show you how to create a new connection to the *contoso* domain in order to import the user profiles and use the connection to map profile properties:

```
LDAPConnection conn = new LDAPConnection(ds);
conn.ConnectionName = "contoso";
conn.DomainName = "contoso";
conn.LeverageServerIncremental = true;
conn.AutoDiscover = false;
conn.Server = "internal.contoso.com";
conn.SearchBase = "DC=contoso,DC=com";
conn.SearchFilter = "(&(objectCategory=Person)(objectClass=User))";
conn.SearchScope = System.DirectoryServices.SearchScope.Subtree;
ds.Add(conn);
ds.Commit();
```

The importing of the user profiles can be started and managed by a number of methods and properties such as the *StartImport*, *StopImport*, *GetImportStatus*, and *IsImportInProgress*.

A user profile is basically a set of properties. There are properties directly available and you have the option of creating custom ones. Here is the code that retrieves the list of properties:

```
PropertyCollection props = mngr.GetProperties();
foreach (Property prop in props)
{
  Display property
}
```

The *Microsoft.Office.Server.UserProfiles* namespace contains a type *Property* that represents each individual user profile property. Basically, all of the information that is displayed in the browser concerning the user profile property can be retrieved and changed. And of course new ones can be created by first instantiating a new *Property* object, setting the properties, adding the instance to the *PropertyCollection*, and committing the whole process. The following lines illustrate how you can create a custom property called *company* and map it to the *company* attribute in the Active Directory that is connected via the *litwareinc* import connection:

```
Property newprop = props.Create(false);
newprop.Name = "company";
newprop.DisplayName = "company";
newprop.Type = PropertyDataType.String;
newprop.Length = 255;
newprop.IsUserEditable = true;
newprop.IsVisibleOnEditor = true;
newprop.IsVisibleOnViewer = true;
newprop.IsAlias = false;
props.Add(newprop);
PropertyMapCollection pmc = ds.PropertyMapping;
pmc.Add(newprop.Name, "company", "litwareinc");
```

The *UserProfileManager* Class   The second type of administrative task has more to do with the creation and management of the user profiles themselves. The main entry class here is the *UserProfileManager* class. We'll have a closer look at this one using a sample application, *UserProfileManagerDemo*, available on the companion Web site.

With the *UserProfileManager* class, you have access to the contents of the user profile store. The class allows members to create and manage the profiles. Members may also simply access the data in order to use the information in, for example, a custom Web Part, delivering a more personalized user experience. You are using the same process as discussed with the *UserProfileConfigManager*, in that you are first getting a reference to the context of the Shared Services Provider. If you are running your code in the context of a SharePoint site, this first line is not required. In the sample application, clicking the Connect button will execute these lines of code:

```
private ServerContext context = null;
private UserProfileManager profileManager = null;

private void buttonConnect_Click(object sender, EventArgs e)
{
  try
  {
    this.context = ServerContext.GetContext(textBoxSSP.Text);
    this.profileManager = new UserProfileManager(this.context);
    MessageBox.Show(this.profileManager.Count.ToString() +
                    " profiles found!");
  }
  catch (Exception ex)
  {
    MessageBox.Show
      ("Problem occurred when connecting to the user profile store!");
  }
}
```

There is no member available at the level of the *UserProfileManager* instance to directly retrieve the list of existing user profiles that are stored in the database. However, there is support to create, modify, and remove single user profile instances.

To create a new user profile, you use the *CreateUserProfile* method, which in most cases just passes the account name of the user. The return value is an instance of the *UserProfile* class. The following line of code creates a user in the sample application:

```
UserProfile profile =
    this.profileManager.CreateUserProfile(textBoxAccount.Text);
```

Removing a user profile from the profile store is accomplished by using the *RemoveUserProfile* method, passing either the ID of the user profile expressed as a GUID or, more friendly, the account name of the user.

The other thing you can do is get a reference to an existing user profile and get or set the values of the various user profile properties. Following is a block of code that retrieves the user profile information for Mike Fitzmaurice, performs an update to the value of the department property, and then commits the change:

```
UserProfile profile = this.profileManager.GetUserProfile(@"litwareinc\mikef");
profile["Department"].Value = "SharePoint Team";
profile.Commit();
```

All of the above code samples work directly with the object model and therefore your code must run on a server running SharePoint. What if you want to work remotely with the user profiles? Working remotely is possible with the Web Service that exposes a number of the operations you can do with user profiles. Let's see this in action with a small walkthrough.

Walkthrough: Populating User Profiles Remotely

In this walkthrough, you'll learn how to communicate with the Web Services that expose and let you manipulate user profile information from a remote client.

Before you start the coding, create a new user profile property that stores the favorite color for a SharePoint user. For simplicity, let's do this in the browser. Open the SharePoint 3.0 Central Administration site and navigate via the quick launch to the administration site of the Shared Services Provider you want to work with. I'll assume that you have one called *SharedServices1*. Under the User Profiles and My Site section, there is a link to navigate to the User Profiles and Properties page. The property can be created in the Add User Profile Property page. Use *FavoriteColor* as the name and *Favorite Color* as the display name for the new property. You can set the length to 250 and then change a couple of settings. In the Policy Settings section, enable the option for the user to override whatever the value is going to be. Next, turn on the option for the user to edit the value of the property and have the value displayed in the profiles property section in the user's profile page. Figure 2-30 displays the entry for the *FavoriteColor* property.

The application, shown in Figure 2-31, is a simple Windows application with a basic user experience. If you would like to try it, there is a starter project called *FavoritesManagerApp* on the companion Web site.

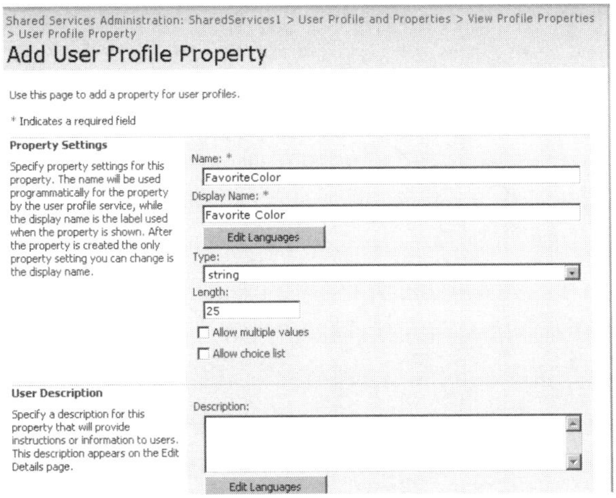

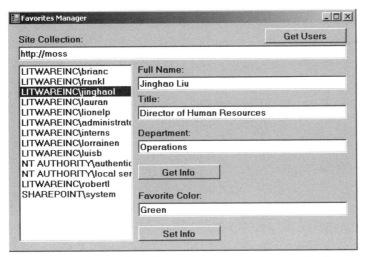

Shared Services Administration: SharedServices1 > User Profile and Properties > View Profile Properties
> User Profile Property

Add User Profile Property

Use this page to add a property for user profiles.

* Indicates a required field

Property Settings

Specify property settings for this property. The name will be used programmatically for the property by the user profile service, while the display name is the label used when the property is shown. After the property is created the only property setting you can change is the display name.

Name: *

FavoriteColor

Display Name: *

Favorite Color

Edit Languages

Type:

string

Length:

25

☐ Allow multiple values

☐ Allow choice list

User Description

Specify a description for this property that will provide instructions or information to users. This description appears on the Edit Details page.

Description:

Edit Languages

Figure 2-30   Creating a new user profile property called *FavoriteColor*

Figure 2-31   The user interface of the small Windows application communicating with the user profile store in SharePoint

The first Web Service to communicate with is the *UserGroup.asmx*. Using this service, you'll be able to grab all of the users that are known within a site collection. In Visual Studio.NET 2005, use the *Add Web Reference* dialog box to point to the .asmx file using the URL of one of the site collections you have in your farm. Don't worry about the URL since you can override it in your code if needed. Click the Add Reference button to generate the proxy class that encapsulates all of the communication with the Web Service. It is not a bad idea to change the namespace to *UserGroup*, for example, to make the distinction later with the second proxy you'll generate.

When done, you're ready to implement the code for the *Click* event handler of the button used for retrieving all of the users with access to the specified site collection. The code is the following:

```
UserGroup.UserGroup ws = new UserGroup.UserGroup();
ws.Url = textBoxSiteCollection.Text + @"/_vti_bin/usergroup.asmx";
ws.Credentials = CredentialCache.DefaultCredentials;
XmlNode nodes = ws.GetAllUserCollectionFromWeb();
```

First, an instance of the proxy class is created. You can set the *URL* property so that the communication is done with the site collection entered in the text box. Next, credentials are passed to SharePoint and the method *GetAllUserCollectionFromWeb* is called. This method does the work without the need for input parameters and returns the following XML:

```
<GetAllUserCollectionFromWeb
 xmlns="http://schemas.microsoft.com/sharepoint/soap/directory/">
  <Users>
    <User ID="15" Sid="S-1-5-21-2939933348-92754331-1621104545-1136"
    Name="Brian Cox" LoginName="LITWAREINC\brianc"
    Email="BrianC@litwareinc.com" Notes="" IsSiteAdmin="False"
    IsDomainGroup="False" />
    <User ID="1" Sid="S-1-5-21-2939933348-92754331-1621104545-500"
    Name="LitwareInc Administrator" LoginName="LITWAREINC\administrator"
    Email="Administrator@litwareinc.com" Notes="" IsSiteAdmin="True"
    IsDomainGroup="False" />
    <User ID="13" Sid="S-1-5-19" Name="NT AUTHORITY\local service"
    LoginName="NT AUTHORITY\local service" Email="" Notes=""
    IsSiteAdmin="False" IsDomainGroup="False" />
    <User ID="1073741823" Sid="S-1-0-0" Name="System Account"
    LoginName="SHAREPOINT\system" Email="" Notes="" IsSiteAdmin="False"
    IsDomainGroup="False" />
  </Users>
</GetAllUserCollectionFromWeb>
```

Each user is represented by a *User* element, and various attributes provide us with the necessary additional information. For now, let's just drop all of the users in the list box with the following snippet of code added in the event handler for the button:

```
foreach (XmlNode node in nodes.FirstChild.ChildNodes)
{
  listBoxUsers.Items.Add(node.Attributes.GetNamedItem("LoginName").Value);
}
```

You may want to filter out the SharePoint System account and perhaps other accounts that are not useful for the scenario here. To get the full user profile details, you'll have to pass the login name of the user.

Remote access to the user profile information is achieved by connecting to a second Web Service that you have to add as a reference: the *UserProfileService.asmx*. Generate the proxy by using basically the same steps as before except perhaps using a different namespace.

In addition to the custom property created before, there are three more properties to display in the application: the *full name*, the *department*, and the *title of the user*. Let's first retrieve those values with a call to one of the methods exposed by the Web Service. Double click the Get Info button and then write the following code:

```
UserProfile.UserProfileService ws = new UserProfile.UserProfileService();
ws.Url = textBoxSiteCollection.Text + @"/_vti_bin/userprofileservice.asmx";
ws.Credentials = CredentialCache.DefaultCredentials;
```

The first lines are pretty much the same as before: creating the instance, changing the *URL* property, and passing the credentials. Next, there is a call to the *GetUserProfileByName* method that passes the selected account name from the list box. The return value is an array of *PropertyData* objects. Declare a couple of class-level variables to store a reference to this array and the one item from it that corresponds to the *Favorite Color User Profile* property. You need that later when writing the code to update the property value. Here are the variable declarations:

```
private UserProfile.PropertyData[] props = null;
private UserProfile.PropertyData propFavoriteColor = null;
```

Here is the call to the method of the Web Service:

```
this.props = ws.GetUserProfileByName(listBoxUsers.SelectedItem.ToString());
```

There is no immediate access to the value of a certain property using the name of the property, so you'll have to write a small loop to get the ones you're interested in (*preferredName, title, and department*):

```
foreach (UserProfile.PropertyData prop in props)
{
  switch (prop.Name)
  {
    case "PreferredName":
    {
      if(prop.Values.Length != 0)
        textBoxFullName.Text = prop.Values[0].Value.ToString();
      break;
    }
```

```
        case "Title":
        {
          if (prop.Values.Length != 0)
            textBoxTitle.Text = prop.Values[0].Value.ToString();
          break;
        }
        case "Department":
        {
          if (prop.Values.Length != 0)
            textBoxDepartment.Text = prop.Values[0].Value.ToString();
          break;
        }
        case "FavoriteColor":
        {
          if (prop.Values.Length != 0)
            textBoxFavoriteColor.Text = prop.Values[0].Value.ToString();
          this.propFavoriteColor = prop;
          break;
        }
        default:
          break;
    }
}
```

The last action to support in the application is to modify the favorite color value and communicate the change back to the user profile store. There is a Set Info button for which you'll implement the *Click* event now. The first lines of code are again the creation of the instance of the proxy class and the settings of the needed property values:

```
UserProfile.UserProfileService ws = new UserProfile.UserProfileService();
ws.Url = textBoxSiteCollection.Text + @"/_vti_bin/userprofileservice.asmx";
ws.Credentials = CredentialCache.DefaultCredentials;
```

Earlier, you stored a reference for the property that has to be updated in a class level variable. The first step is to tell SharePoint that you have changed that value. Do this by setting the *IsValueChanged* property to *true*.

```
this.propFavoriteColor.IsValueChanged = true;
```

It's possible that this is the first time a value has been assigned to this user profile property. If so, you'll have to initialize the *ValueData* array. In our sample here, room needs to be reserved for one item in the array: the *ValueData* type. The *Value* property of this type can be set to the value the user entered in the text box. If the array is already available, you only need to set the value of the first item.

```
if (this.propFavoriteColor.Values.Length == 0)
{
  UserProfile.ValueData[] values = new UserProfile.ValueData[1];
  values[0] = new UserProfile.ValueData();
  values[0].Value = textBoxFavoriteColor.Text;
  this.propFavoriteColor.Values = values;
}
else
{
  this.propFavoriteColor.Values[0].Value = textBoxFavoriteColor.Text;
}
```

The last line of code is the call to the *ModifyUserPropertyByAccountName* method of the *UserProfileService.asmx*. You have to pass both the account name of the user and the array of user profile properties. You might want to wrap all of this in an exception handler so that you can show the user any problems that may occur. Here is the call to the method:

```
ws.ModifyUserPropertyByAccountName
    (listBoxUsers.SelectedItem.ToString(),this.props);
```

At the time of writing, there is a problem with the Web Service throwing a cast exception for the first user profile property in the *PropertyData* array. You can work around this problem by adding the following line of code just before the actual call to the method of the Web Service:

```
this.props[0].Values[0].Value = this.props[0].Values[0].Value.ToString();
```

When done, the user profile data store has been updated, and the profile of the selected user now contains a value for the *Favorite Color* property.

Audience Targeting

Users with a similar user profile can be grouped together in an audience. The object model contains a number of classes that help you target content to specific types of audiences. There is also support for performing administrative tasks such as creating audiences and adding rules. However, you won't find any support for programmatically compiling the audiences.

> **More Info**   *Global audiences* are created in the administration site of the Shared Services Provider. It's easy to do. Simply create one or more rules that tell SharePoint the conditions that have to be met for the user profiles to become a member of the audience. When an audience is created, you have to compile it so that the membership information is immediately available at run time for SharePoint. Note also that in addition to the global audiences, you can also target content based on two other types of audiences that are immediately available out-of-the-box. SharePoint groups, distribution lists, and security groups can also be used as audiences in the SharePoint sites.

The classes to use are part of the *Microsoft.Office.Server.dll* and are located in the *Microsoft.Office.Server.Audience* namespace. The companion Web site contains a sample Web Part that illustrates how to retrieve the membership information for an audience and how to use that information to personalize the rendering of the Web Part.

The *AudienceManager* class is your entry class. Again, if you are running your code outside of the context of SharePoint, you'll have to create an instance of the *ServerContext* class and provide it as the value for the parameter in the constructor of the class. For the Web Part example, the code runs in the context of SharePoint, so with a single line of code you can create your instance:

```
AudienceManager mgr = new AudienceManager();
```

The class has an *Audiences* that can be used to loop over all of the defined audiences, and there are various methods you can call to get one single audience. The Web Part uses an *IsMember-OfAudience* method to verify whether the logged-on user is part of a specific audience. In the Web Part, the method is used to branch the code and output a different string to the user. But of course you can do a lot more with this type of logic in the real world.

```
if (mgr.IsMemberOfAudience
        (SPContext.Current.Web.CurrentUser.LoginName,
         "SharePoint Team Members"))
{
  writer.Write("You are part of the SharePoint team! Congrats!");
}
else
{
  writer.Write("I see you are not part of SharePoint team. Too bad!");
}
```

My Site

Typically, in an intranet scenario, identified users will have a My Site provisioned. My Site is a place where users can store their personal information, share it with other SharePoint visitors, maintain a blog site, and access personal applications such as their mailbox, calendar, and so on. My Site can be accessed in the object model through the *UserProfile* object. Once you have retrieved the *UserProfile* instance representing a specific user, you can create a personal site for that user using the following code:

```
profile.CreatePersonalSite();
```

The result of this code is shown in Figure 2-32. Mike Fitzmaurice now has his own My Site. This is a normal Windows SharePoint Services 3.0 site, and Mike can therefore start adding subsites, lists, and document libraries together with pages that are linked in the Profile page (the public page of My Site) for visitors.

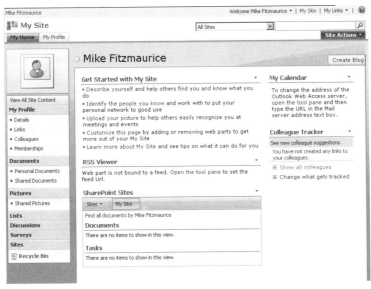

Figure 2-32   Mike Fitzmaurice's My Site

The Profile page, discussed previously and displayed in Figure 2-33, is the public view of My Site where users can share information with other users that have access to the portal. All of the user profiles that have been marked as *public* are displayed on the Profile page, and there is also a Web Part on the page that displays the most recently shared documents. As we will see in a moment, there is a lot of functionality in Microsoft Office SharePoint Server 2007 for colleagues and social networking. For example, users are able to see the public properties of their colleagues and memberships to distribution lists, among other things, on the Profile page, and they can also see what they have in common with the user connected to the Profile page.

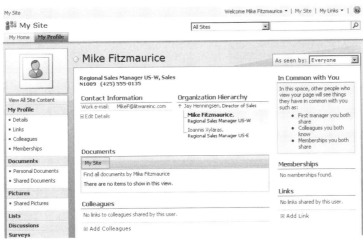

Figure 2-33   Mike's Profile page, displaying the public properties of his user profile, colleagues, membership information, shared documents, links to interesting pages he created as part of his site, and more

Colleagues and Social Networking

A last topic I'd like to discuss is the support we have for social networking in this version of SharePoint. Looking at the bottom of Figure 2-33, you'll see a Web Part that lists the names of Mike's colleagues. SharePoint tries to ascertain as much of this information as possible, consulting Mike's local Microsoft Messenger as well as his Microsoft Office Outlook e-mails. Of course, there is a manual intervention that allows Mike to maintain his social network himself. All of the social networking is exposed in the object model via the *ColleagueManager* and the *Colleague* class, part of the *Microsoft.Office.Server.UserProfiles* in the *Microsoft.Office.Server.dll*. At the level of the *UserProfile* class, you can consult the *Colleagues* property to return an instance of the *ColleagueManager* so that you can use this information for a specific scenario, such as in a custom Web Part.

Summary

This chapter consisted of two major sections. The first section covered the various options for customizing and branding collaboration portals. Although this is targeted to intranets, there will definitely be demands for performing customizations at this level. We talked about master pages, some of the styling options, navigation and optional customization, and a publishing cycle that takes your pages step-by-step from a draft version to a published version. As mentioned before, if you are interested in learning a bit more about all of this, Chapter 6 will cover more about customization and branding operations when the publishing portal is discussed.

The second section discussed the support for social networking and the options developers have to communicate with the user profiles and audiences. As demonstrated in a number of practical examples, there is a lot of exposure in the object model for these types of programmatic scenarios. We have seen the fundamentals, but refer to the Software Development Kit for a full review of the different classes involved.

Chapter 3

Customizing and Extending the Microsoft Office SharePoint 2007 Search

- Understand the basic components that make up the index and search architecture.
- Learn the different classes in the new search administration object model and work through some practical examples.
- Learn how to customize the Search Center, a new site definition aimed at providing a rich and customizable search experience to the users.
- Learn how to programmatically construct queries using the different syntax languages and the classes required to prepare and execute the queries.
- Learn how to work with the Query Web Service and execute Enterprise search queries remotely.
- Understand the additional security trimming layer that supports scenarios for filtering search results based on custom business logic or security rules.

The index and search engines are two major components of the Microsoft Office SharePoint Server 2007. Together, they form the infrastructure for supporting the ability to crawl pretty much any content in any location. They also deliver a rich and powerful search experience for users visiting the SharePoint sites that leverage the indexes created.

In this chapter, I'll start with a discussion of the architecture that makes it all happen behind the scenes and will continue with topics that will give you an understanding of how, as a developer, you can start customizing and extending the different features involved. I also refer to the *Microsoft Office SharePoint Server 2007 Administrator's Companion* (Microsoft Press), written by Bill English, for more detail of the topics related to the administration and configuration of the index and search engines.

Overview of the Search Architecture

Today, Microsoft invests a lot in search, whether it's at the desktop, Internet, or intranet level. Each of these search modes has its own specifics; however, the goal is to make the underlying architecture for all of them similar and common. Figure 3-1 summarizes the different building blocks of the Enterprise search architecture. Let's discuss this architecture in a bit more detail and focus only on the search supported in a Microsoft Office SharePoint Server 2007 server farm. But keep in mind that a similar architecture is also in place for the desktop and the Internet search.

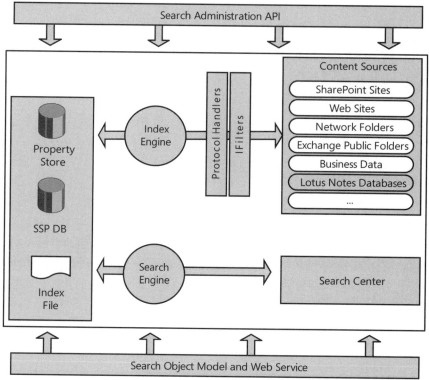

Figure 3-1 The common Enterprise search architecture

At the right side of Figure 3-1, there are the various repositories, also referred to as content sources, that can be accessed and crawled out-of-the-box. In the list, you'll find external Web sites, SharePoint sites, public Microsoft Exchange folders, any line-of-business data you are able to connect to via the Business Data Catalog, network shares, Lotus Notes databases (require a post-installation step)—and the dots can be replaced with any type of data store for which you have correctly installed the required protocol handlers and IFilters. Protocol handlers open the door to the location of an arbitrary repository for the crawler, and IFilters make it possible to open the rich resources (such as Office documents) stored within the location and index their content.

As a result of all of this crawling, an index file is built up and data is stored in the search database. The index file is a physical file stored in the file system. A big difference from SharePoint Portal Server 2003 is that, per Shared Services Provider, there is only one index file possible. The index file is continuously propagated to the different search servers rather than waiting until it is completely created and then starting the copy process. All of the metadata collected during the crawling, such as the values of the custom columns for the documents in SharePoint document libraries, is stored in the property store and will help users build more complex search queries, as I'll discuss later in the chapter.

There are numerous pieces that make up the configuration data. In the case of SharePoint, all of this data is stored in the database under the control of the Shared Services Provider. This data includes: the configuration data for the ranking algorithm, the keywords and best bets that administrators can set, the schema elements used for defining the queries and other XML that is involved when indexing and searching, the scopes for limiting the results users see in the search results pages, the logs created during the crawling, and the configuration data for the content sources themselves. Most of these will be explained later.

There are two search API's for developers. The first one, the search administration API at the top of Figure 3-1, is a brand new one. It allows developers to programmatically perform the tasks administrators are doing in the administration site of the Shared Services Provider. At the bottom of Figure 3-1 is the search API, probably the most interesting part of the picture for developers. This API is fully managed and consists of a rich object model that allows you to execute the queries in different ways. Parts of the API are exposed by a Web Service so that external applications, such as remote smart clients, are able to perform search queries and display the results to users.

Managing the Index and Search Engine

Microsoft Office SharePoint Server 2007 introduces a new object model that enables developers to programmatically support many of the search administration tasks that are typically done in the browser. The search administration object model is physically contained within a new .NET assembly called the *Microsoft.Office.Server.Search.dll*, and all of the classes related to the search administration (the major ones are displayed in Figure 3-2) are defined in the *Microsoft.Office.Server.Search.Administration* namespace. I'll review some of the major administration and configuration steps administrators can perform in the browser, and I'll describe how you can use all of the classes to programmatically accomplish the same tasks.

There is a sample application called *SearchAdminSample* on the companion Web site that I'll use to illustrate many of the techniques. I recommend that you load the project in Visual Studio.NET 2005 and frequently switch to the source code while reading through the following pages.

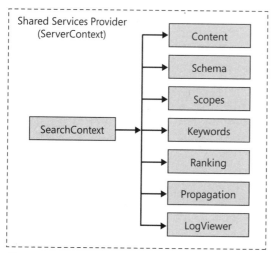

Figure 3-2 The major classes in the Microsoft Office SharePoint Server 2007 search administration object model

The *SearchContext* Class

To begin, let me explain something important. As discussed in Chapter 1, the indexing and search capabilities delivered with Microsoft Office SharePoint Server 2007 are under the control of the Shared Services Provider (SSP). As a result, whatever you do programmatically related to indexing and search will have to begin with retrieving a reference to the context of the Shared Services Provider. The *ServerContext* class defined in the *Microsoft.Office.Server* namespace and part of the *Microsoft.Office.Server.dll* is designed to do this.

The *ServerContext* class has two static members to get the reference of the context of the Shared Services Provider. The first one, the *Current* property, can be used to get the context while already running in a SharePoint context. A second member is the *GetContext* method, which accepts the name of the Shared Service Provider. The latter is the member to use when your code runs outside of the context of SharePoint, such as the case in the sample application. The following line of code is executed after providing the name of the Shared Services Provider in the text box:

```
ServerContext context = ServerContext.GetContext(name)
```

The other reference is the *SearchContext* object part of the *Microsoft.Office.Server.Search.Administration* namespace. This is the entry object within the search administration object model, and it exposes nearly the same interface as the *ServerContext* object described previously. Again, two static members are important: the *Current* property and the *GetContext* method. The former can only be used when your code runs in the context of SharePoint; the latter is the one to use outside of the context. The *GetContext* method accepts three possible arguments: One is the name of the search application (only if running in the context of one of the portals), a second one is a reference to the *ServerContext* object, and a final one is a reference to an *SPSite* object, used internally to retrieve the reference to the context of the Shared Services Provider with which the IIS Web application hosting the site collection is associated. Here is a typical call to retrieve the *SearchContext* reference:

```
SearchContext searchcontext = SearchContext.GetContext(context);
```

Now that you have the instance, you have different methods you can use within the code. They are summarized in Table 3-1.

Table 3-1   *SearchContext* Instance Methods

Member	Description
Reset	Call this method with utmost care since it will clean up the entire index and all of the metadata that has been collected and stored in the search database. However, the search admin configuration, such as the list of the already defined content sources, will be preserved.
UpdateDiacriticSensitive	This method sets the *DiacriticSensitive* property, a setting that is used for configuring the search engine so it accounts for accents, such as with the French language.
UpdateQueryLoggingEnabled	Turns the query logging on or off. Don't forget that logging each of the queries performed by the users can be an expensive operation.
UpdateAlertNotificationFormat	Updates the formats of the alert notifications users get when they create an alert for the search results.

Once you have a reference to the *SearchContext* object, you'll have access to the other classes in the API required for the different configuration tasks discussed in the following pages.

Working with Content Sources

As an administrator of a SharePoint server farm, one of your duties will probably be to create content sources and configure one or more crawl rules for them. These tasks can be done by navigating to the administration site of the Shared Services Provider. Also, there is full support in the object model to finalize the steps in a programmatic way.

Creating Content Sources Using the Browser

Creating a content source is a very clear-cut task. In the *Search* section of the Shared Services Provider administration site, there is an option to navigate to the Configure Search Settings page. Here, you'll find the link to drill down to the Manage Content Sources page, displayed in Figure 3-3. By default, there is only one content source available. This content source, called Local Office Sharepoint Server Sites, indexes all of the SharePoint sites that are available after the installation or upgrade of the server.

Figure 3-3   The listing of content sources that are crawled and their status

Figure 3-4 displays the five possible types of content sources you can create in the browser: SharePoint sites, normal Web sites, file shares, Microsoft Exchange public folders, and any data store that is connected to the Shared Services Provider using the Business Data Catalog middle layer (fully discussed in Chapter 4, "Working with the Business Data Catalog"). In Figure 3-4, a file share, *SharePointLabs*, is ready to be created as a content source.

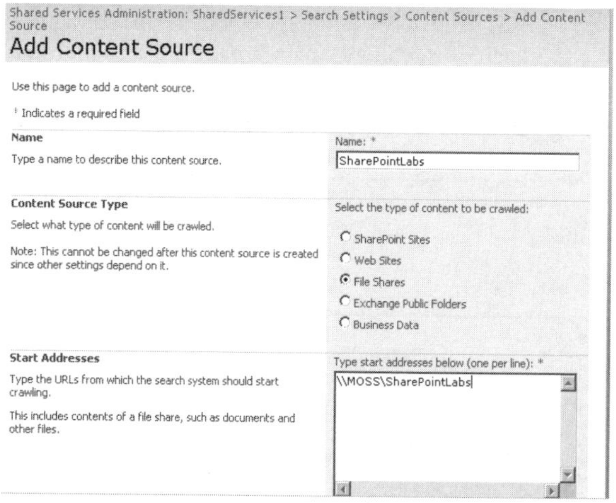

Figure 3-4   The configuration of a shared folder as a new content source

There are specific settings to complete for each of the content source types. I again refer you to *Microsoft Office SharePoint Server 2007 Administrator's Companion* by Bill English for details. In addition to the settings, there are the configuration of the crawl rules and the scheduling of the actual crawling itself.

Managing Content Sources Programmatically

Now, this is all great, but what if you want to programmatically perform all of these steps? Earlier, we discussed the necessary starter object, the *SearchContext*. Let's now have a look at the .NET types involved in the process of listing, creating, and configuring content sources. All of the classes reviewed are part of the *Microsoft.Office.Server.Search.Administration* namespace.

The first class to consider is the *Content* class, a required class before getting access to the different classes at the lower level that represents each of the possible types of content sources. The *Content* class is also the one to start with for the other types of configurations you want to perform, such as the search scopes, the crawl rules, and crawl settings. The argument for the constructor is a reference to the *SearchContext* object. The following code shows how to get to a reference to a *Content* object:

```
Content content = new Content(searchcontext);
```

In the sample application, after connecting to the Shared Services Provider, there is a button to populate the treeview control with all of the content sources defined. Take a look at the code associated with the *Click* event of this button. After the creation of the instance of a Content type, the list of content sources is retrieved via the *ContentSources* property. The property gives you access to all of the defined content sources with, of course, all of the methods in place to manipulate this collection. Following is the code for listing all of the content sources and creating a node for them in the treeview with sub-nodes for the different addresses that are crawled (accessible via the *StartAddresses* property of the ContentSource type):

```
if (this.searchContext != null)
{
  Content content = new Content(this.searchContext);
  foreach (ContentSource contentsource in content.ContentSources)
  {
    TreeNode node = treeViewIndexSearch.Nodes.Add(contentsource.Name);
    node.Tag = contentsource;
    foreach (object startaddress in contentsource.StartAddresses)
    {
       node.Nodes.Add(startaddress.ToString());
    }
  }
}
```

The various types of content sources are represented by their own SharePoint class, as shown in Figure 3-5.

The *ContentSource* class is the base class for a content source defined as an abstract class. It encapsulates the common operations inherited by each of the underlying child classes. Table 3-2 summarizes the members:

Table 3-2   *ContentSource* Members

Member	Description
Delete	Deletes a content source.
PauseCrawl	Pauses the crawling for the content source.
ResumeCrawl	Resumes the crawling for the content source.
StartFullCrawl	Starts a full crawl for the content source.
StartIncrementalCrawl	Starts an incremental crawl for the content source.
StopCrawl	Stops the crawling for the content source.
Update	Updates any changes made to the content source.

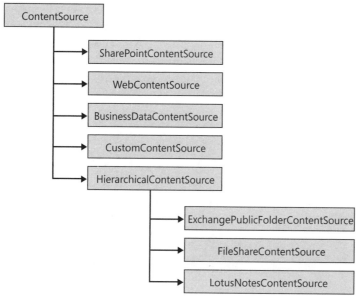

Figure 3-5 The classes in the search administration object model representing each of the possible types of content sources

The sample application shows you the details of the crawl status for a selected content source. There is also the option of starting a full crawl or an incremental crawl.

Let's return to the different types of content sources. The following are defined as direct children of the *ContentSource* class: the *SharePointContentSource*, the *WebContentSource*, and the *BusinessDataContentSource* types. Indexing SharePoint sites is done by creating a *SharePoint* content source, an object of type *SharePointContentSource*. There is one additional property exposed at this level: the *SharePointCrawlBehavior*. It enables you to specify whether all of the sites on the IIS Web application need to be crawled (the *CrawlVirtual-Servers* value) or only particular site collections (the *CrawlSites* value). A content source for a normal Web site is exposed as a *WebContentSource* object. The class has two specific properties to control the number of site-hops the crawler can take from the start address to a content item: the *MaxPageEnumerationDepth* and the *MaxPageEnumerationDepth* properties. Microsoft Office SharePoint Server 2007 also allows you to index business data when selecting the new Business Data Catalog protocol handler. All of the business applications are internally defined by the *BusinessDataContentSource* type. Two static methods are available at this level on top of the inherited members for detailing the business data application to be indexed: *ConstructStartAddress* and *ParseStartAddress*. Later in the book, I'll discuss the indexing of business applications in more detail.

An additional intermediate layer, the *HierarchicalContentSource* class, is added under the *ContentSource* class to provide the necessary abstraction for the remaining types of content sources: the *ExchangePublicFolderContentSource*, the *FileShareContentSource*, and the *Lotus-NotesContentSource* class. All three of them inherit the *FollowDirectories* property as an extra member on top of the ones inherited from the base *ContentSource* class. The *FollowDirectories* property provides you with the means to tell the crawler whether it should include subdirectories in the crawl.

There is one final child class of the *ContentSource* class that we've not yet discussed: the *CustomContentSource* class. In addition to the six types of content sources that are immediately creatable out-of-the-box, you can basically let the crawler access any other type of location. The condition is that you provide the index engine with all of the required plumbing for accessing that location. The required information is made available and registered in the form of a custom protocol handler. Once done, additional content sources can be created that leverage the custom protocol handler. Creating custom protocol handlers are out-of-scope for this book.

In the sample application, you have the option to create a new content source of type *Share-Point*. The code is the following:

```
try
{
  Content content = new Content(this.searchContext);
  SharePointContentSource contentsource =
      (SharePointContentSource)
          content.ContentSources.Create(typeof(SharePointContentSource),
                                    textBoxContentSourceName.Text);
  contentsource.StartAddresses.Add(new Uri(textBoxSharePointURL.Text));
  contentsource.Update();
  MessageBox.Show("Content source created!");
}
catch (Exception ex)
{
  MessageBox.Show(ex.ToString());
}
```

After you've created the content source, you can start the full crawl.

Working with Search Scopes

A second important concept when discussing the search administration is the whole notion of search scopes. From an administrator's perspective, a search scope is a subdivision of the index built up by the crawler. The items in the index will be matched against one or more rules created by the administrator. From a user's perspective, a search scope is a means to limit the amount of search results returned after a search query to only those that match the rules contained within the search scope. Examples can be: get me only the search results for one specific content source, or get me only the documents authored by Brian Cox.

Managing Search Scopes in the Browser

Administrators have two levels where they can create the search scopes. A first level is the Shared Services Provider, also referred to as the *global level*. The search scope instances created at this level are called *shared search scopes* because, once defined, they are re-usable anywhere within the server farm—that is, for the SharePoint sites that are associated with the Shared Service Provider in question. The second level is the site-collection level. Site collection administrators can limit the search scope to be used only within one specific site collection.

For both types, however, the steps are the same. Figure 3-6 shows the View Scopes page for a site collection containing a collaboration portal. This page is where you can start maintaining the search scopes and also create new ones.

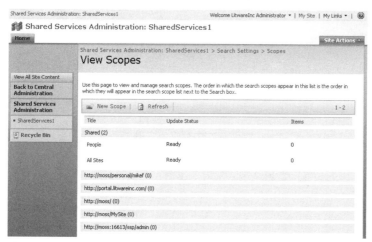

Figure 3-6   The list of search scopes and display groups defined for a site collection

Creating a new search scope starts by simply specifying a title and description, as shown in Figure 3-7. You also have to associate the search scope with one of the existing display groups. A *display group* is a layer between the actual search scopes and the dropdown control that displays the search scopes to the user. A search scope, defined either at the global or site collection level, will not be displayed in the dropdown controls in the SharePoint pages unless they are associated to the corresponding display group.

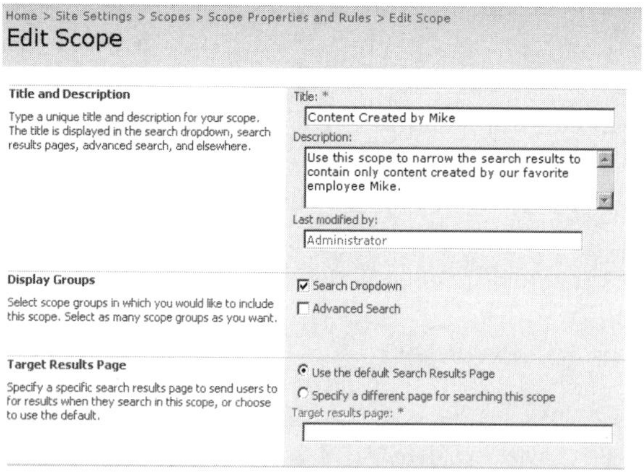

Figure 3-7   Providing the details for a new search scope at the level of the site collection

The final step is to create one or more rules defining the conditions for the search results in the search scope. There are three types of rules possible. For the first, the scope is a URL. The second is an arbitrary property-based rule, and the third is a rule scoped to one of the content sources. Figure 3-8 displays how you can construct a rule defining that users can only see content or documents created by Mike.

Home > Site Settings > Scopes > Scope Properties and Rules > Add Scope Rule
Add Scope Rule

Scope Rule Type Scope rules define what is in or not in a scope. Use different types of rules to match items in various ways	◯ Web Address (http://server/site) ⦿ Property Query (Author = John Doe) ◯ All Content
Property Query Enter the property restriction as a comparison of property to a value. All items matching the property query will be added to the scope. To make additional properties available for use in scopes, navigate to the managed properties list and select "Allow this property to be used in scopes" for the desired managed properties.	Add property restrictions: Author = Mike Example: Author = John Doe
Behavior Decide how this rule should be applied to the overall scope. The scope-wide filter is used when combining the items matching all rules to determine what is in the	⦿ Include - Any item that matches this rule will be included, unless the item is excluded by another rule ◯ Require - Every item in the scope must match this rule ◯ Exclude - Items matching this rule will be excluded from the scope

Figure 3-8   Filtering the search results for only the content or documents created by Mike

Once the search scope is created, updated, and associated with one of the display groups, users will see it listed in the scopes dropdown box, as displayed in Figure 3-9. Executing a search with this search scope will limit the results to only those matching the rules.

Figure 3-9   A new search scope presented to the users in the scopes dropdown box in the Search Center

Working with Search Scopes in a Programmatic Way

Again, all of the administrative steps performed above in the browser can be done programmatically. The sample application illustrates some of the things you can do with search scopes.

This time, the entry object to start with is the *Scopes* object. Just as with the *Content* object discussed previously, the *Scopes* constructor needs an instance of the *SearchContext* class as a parameter:

```
Scopes scopes = new Scopes(searchcontext);
```

Numerous members are available to perform the various administrative operations. One example is the *StartCompilation* method. In Microsoft Office SharePoint Server 2007, search scopes are actually subsets of an index file and, therefore, when changes are done either at the level of the index file itself or the search scopes, you need to run a compilation of the search scopes to again mark the different subsets in the index file that match up with the active search scopes.

Table 3-3 summarizes a number of the important methods that you'll work with to get a hold of either the display groups or the search scopes at any of the levels: global or local.

Table 3-3 *Scopes* Methods

Method	Description
GetDisplayGroup	Based on the provided URL of a site collection and the name of a display group, it returns a reference to the corresponding *ScopeDisplayGroup* object.
GetDisplayGroupsForSite	Returns an enumerator you can use to loop through all of the *ScopeDisplayGroup* instances defined for a provided site collection URL.
GetScope	Returns an instance of the *Scope* class for a specified URL of a site collection and a name.
GetScopesForSite	Returns an enumerator for looping through all the search scopes defined at the level of a specific site collection.
GetSharedScope	Returns a global search scope in the form of an instance of the *Scope* class based on a name.
GetSharedScopes	Returns an enumerator for looping through all of the shared search scopes.
GetUnusedScopesForSite	Returns an enumerator you can use to loop through all of the search scopes defined at the level of a site collection but that are not connected to any of the display groups.

If you return to the sample application, you'll be able to display all of the search scopes in the treeview. The code behind the button to create the nodes looks like this:

```
//-- loop over all shared search scopes
TreeNode sharedScopesNode = treeViewIndexSearch.Nodes.Add("Shared Search Scopes");
foreach (Scope scope in scopes.GetSharedScopes())
{
    TreeNode node = sharedScopesNode.Nodes.Add(scope.Name);
    node.Tag = scope;
}
```

```
//-- loop over all scopes but filter on only local search scopes
TreeNode localScopesNode = treeViewIndexSearch.Nodes.Add("Local Search Scopes");
foreach (Scope scope in scopes.AllScopes)
{
    if (scope.OwningSite != null)
    {
        TreeNode node = localScopesNode.Nodes.Add(scope.Name);
        node.Text += " (" + scope.OwningSite.Url + ")";
        node.Tag = scope;
    }
}
```

It is also possible to loop over all of the display groups and show the individual scopes that are members:

```
//-- loop over all display groups
TreeNode displaygroupNode = treeViewIndexSearch.Nodes.Add("Display Groups");
foreach (ScopeDisplayGroup group in scopes.AllDisplayGroups)
{
    TreeNode node = displaygroupNode.Nodes.Add(group.Name);
    if (group.OwningSite != null)
        node.Text += " (" + group.OwningSite.Url + ")";
    node.Tag = group;

    foreach (Scope scope in group)
    {
        node.Nodes.Add(scope.Name);
    }
}
```

You'll work with either an instance of a *ScopeDisplayGroup* class or an instance of the *Scope* class. The former is a type that internally maintains a collection of *Scope* instances that is of course maintainable using the traditional collection operations. The latter, the *Scope* class, represents an individual search scope with numerous methods to perform operations on the scope, such as the addition of one or more *ScopeRule* instances that make up the logic for creating the subset of matching items in the index.

Let's have a look at the code that enables you to create a shared search scope:

```
Scopes scopes = new Scopes(this.searchContext);
scopes.AllScopes.Create
    (textBoxSharedSearchScopeName.Text,
     textBoxScopeDescription.Text, null, true,
     "results.aspx", ScopeCompilationType.AlwaysCompile);
```

The new *Scope* instance is created by calling the *Create* method at the level of the *ScopeCollection* that is returned by the *AllScopes* method. The first argument for which to provide a value is the name of the new scope. Secondly, you can give a value for the description and then the value for the *OwningSite* property. If you want to end up with a shared search scope, you have to pass the null value here. Of course, you can also provide a URL, but then you are creating a local search scope. The boolean indicates whether you want to have the scope displayed in the user interface for the administrators: yes or no. The next parameter is the page for showing the results of the query and the type of compilation you desire. There is an option to choose a conditional compilation, which would be used in the rare case that the number of scope rules exceeds 24.

But simply creating the scope is not enough. You'll have to create the rules too. Before doing that, review the following block of code:

```
private void PopulateWithRules(Scope scope, TreeNode node)
{
    foreach (ScopeRule rule in scope.Rules)
    {
        if (rule is PropertyQueryScopeRule)
        {
            PropertyQueryScopeRule prule = (PropertyQueryScopeRule)rule;
            TreeNode childnode = node.Nodes.Add("Property Query Rule: ");
            childnode.Text += prule.Property.Name + " = " + prule.Value;
        }

        if (rule is AllContentScopeRule)
        {
            AllContentScopeRule arule = (AllContentScopeRule)rule;
            node.Nodes.Add("All Content Rule");
        }

        if (rule is UrlScopeRule)
        {
            UrlScopeRule urule = (UrlScopeRule)rule;
            TreeNode childnode = node.Nodes.Add("URL Rule: ");
            childnode.Text += urule.MatchingString;
        }
    }
}
```

There are three different types of rules, each represented by its own class inheriting from the general *ScopeRule* class: The *PropertyQueryScopeRule* type is used when creating a rule that performs a property query and also when associating with a content source. The *AllContent-ScopeRule* covers all of the content sources, and the last type is *UrlScopeRule*, which accepts a URL as the condition.

Once you've created a new search scope, you'll create one or more rules. The *Scope* class exposes a *Rules* property with three methods you can call for the creation of the three different types of rules: the *CreatePropertyQueryRule*, the *CreateAllContentRule*, and the *CreateUrlRule*. Here is the code that creates a *URL* rule for one of the scopes:

```
scope.Rules.CreateUrlRule
    (ScopeRuleFilterBehavior.Include,
     UrlScopeRuleType.HostName, textBoxURLRule.Text);
```

The first parameter is the *ScopeRuleFilterBehavior*. Three options are valid here: *Exclude*, *Include*, and *Required*. *Exclude* means that any matching items are excluded from the search results. *Include* is of course the reverse, and *Required* means that the content items included in the search results must match the defined rule. Next you have the value for the *UrlScopeRule-Type*. Possibilities here are *Domain*, *Folder*, or *HostName*. For a Web site, you select *HostName*. If you are going for a file share, you select *Folder*.

As previously mentioned, a search scope is actually a subset identified for the index, and it also becomes part of the index itself. That's why you have to compile your search scopes so that this subset can be created. The start of the compilation is done by calling the *Start-Compilation* method at the level of the *Scopes* type:

```
Scopes scopes = new Scopes(this.searchContext);
scopes.StartCompilation();
```

Schema Management

While crawling the content as defined by the different content sources, the crawler collects all of the metadata associated with the different resources found. The metadata is stored in the *Search* database, a database created by and under the control of the Shared Services Provider. Don't underestimate the amount of information this can be. A typical crawl in a medium-sized company can involve hundreds of thousands of documents, and many, many different aggregated properties can end up in the database. It is the administrator's job to organize all of this metadata and make properties available for the user in the advanced search user interface. This can be a very challenging task. However, Microsoft Office SharePoint Server 2007 has a number of improvements that will facilitate it. One important change is the introduction of a new layer called managed properties.

Creating and Using Managed Properties in the Browser

Managed properties map to one or more of the crawled properties. They group together the related crawled properties and expose them to the user. For example, after a crawl, you can end up with three different properties, *Product Code*, *ProductCode*, and *Product Number*. All of them basically have the same meaning, but users responsible for creating and maintaining lists and document libraries do not always work in the same consistent manner. However, as an administrator, you can create managed properties and apply some level of consistency in the advanced search page for users who need to create more complex search queries involving the crawled metadata in the WHERE clauses.

The Search Settings in the administrative site of the Shared Services Provider has a Metadata Property Mappings link. Clicking on it brings you to the Metadata Property Mappings page, shown in Figure 3-10.

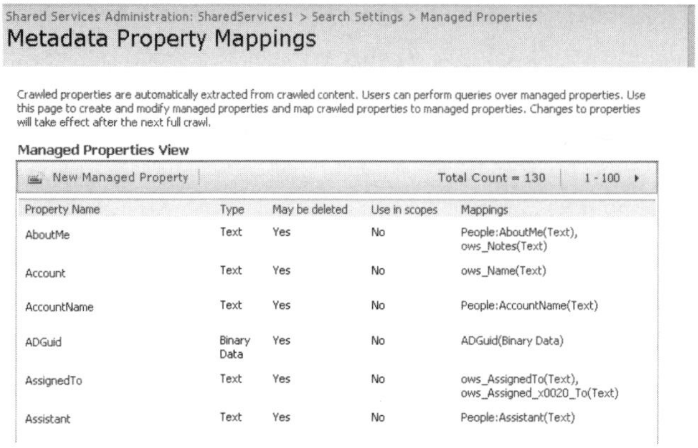

Figure 3-10   The list of managed properties, properties that map to one or more crawled properties

Creating a new managed property involves two simple steps, illustrated in Figure 3-11. First, provide a name for the property, enter a description, and specify the type of the property.

Figure 3-11   Creating a new managed property and mapping it to the crawled properties, *Product Code, ProductCode,* and *Product Number*

The second step is to map to the crawled properties. The Add Mapping button pops up a dialog box where you can navigate through all of the crawled properties and select the ones you want to map to the managed property. Figure 3-12 shows the three crawled properties: *ows_Product_x0020_Code, ows_Product_x0020_Number,* and *ows_ProductCode.* You have to add them one by one to the list of mapped properties.

But, how do you make the new managed property available in the advanced search page of the Search Center? That job cannot be done in the administration site of the Shared Services Provider. For this, you have to go to the Advanced Search page of the Search Center itself and switch the page to edit mode. The page contains the Advanced Search Web Part, and by using the properties tool pane, you can tweak and configure a lot of the configuration settings, as depicted in Figure 3-13.

Figure 3-12   The three crawled properties to use for mapping with the managed property *ProductCode*

Figure 3-13   The Advanced Search Box in edit mode with the properties pane for the configuration of the numerous settings

If you expand the *Properties* node in the tool pane, you'll be able to modify the XML that defines the list of properties the Web Part knows about. In the XML, an element called *PropertyDefs* contains the entries for all of the managed properties that should be displayed to the user as possible criteria for the WHERE parts of their search queries.

```
<PropertyDefs>
  <PropertyDef Name="Path" DataType="text" DisplayName="URL"/>
  <PropertyDef Name="Size" DataType="integer" DisplayName="Size"/>
  <PropertyDef Name="Write" DataType="datetime" DisplayName="Last Modified Date"/>
  <PropertyDef Name="FileName" DataType="text" DisplayName="Name"/>
  <PropertyDef Name="Description" DataType="text" DisplayName="Description"/>
  <PropertyDef Name="Title" DataType="text" DisplayName="Title"/>
  <PropertyDef Name="Author" DataType="text" DisplayName="Author"/>
  <PropertyDef Name="DocSubject" DataType="text" DisplayName="Subject"/>
  <PropertyDef Name="DocKeywords" DataType="text" DisplayName="Keywords"/>
```

```
    <PropertyDef Name="DocComments" DataType="text" DisplayName="Comments"/>
    <PropertyDef Name="Manager" DataType="text" DisplayName="Manager"/>
    <PropertyDef Name="Company" DataType="text" DisplayName="Company"/>
    <PropertyDef Name="Created" DataType="datetime" DisplayName="Created Date"/>
    <PropertyDef Name="CreatedBy" DataType="text" DisplayName="Created By"/>
    <PropertyDef Name="ModifiedBy" DataType="text" DisplayName="Last Modified By"/>
</PropertyDefs>
```

Take the following *PropertyDef* element for example. It defines an entry for the new *Product-Code* managed property:

```
<PropertyDef Name="ProductCode" DataType="text" DisplayName="Product Code"/>
```

Before this entry will appear in the dropdown menu in the *Advanced Search* Web Part, you'll also have to add a *PropertyRef* element as a child to the *ResultType* element.

```
<ResultTypes>
  <ResultType DisplayName="All Results" Name="default">
    <Query/>
    <PropertyRef Name="Author" />
    <PropertyRef Name="Description" />
    <PropertyRef Name="FileName" />
    <PropertyRef Name="Size" />
    <PropertyRef Name="Path" />
    <PropertyRef Name="Created" />
    <PropertyRef Name="Write" />
    <PropertyRef Name="CreatedBy" />
    <PropertyRef Name="ModifiedBy" />
    <PropertyRef Name="ProductCode" />
  </ResultType>
<ResultTypes>
```

As Figure 3-14 shows, the *Product Code* property will be included in the list of properties to use for a selected result type only if you perform this last step.

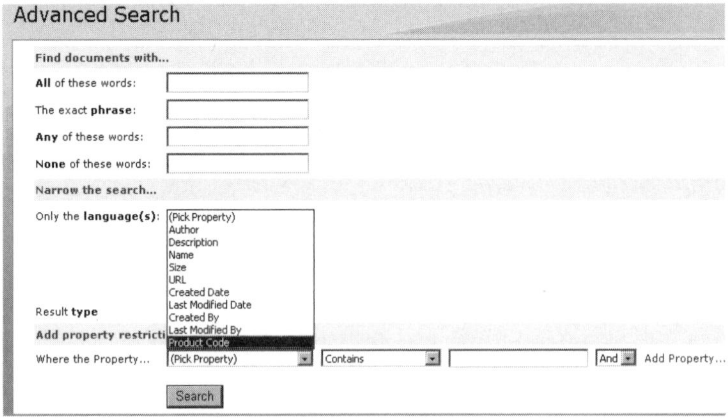

Figure 3-14   The new managed property available in the dropdown in the Advanced Search box

Managed Properties in the Object Model

How is all of this exposed in the search administration object model? Your entry point this time is the *Schema* object that is created with a *SearchContext* instance as the parameter.

```
Schema schema = new Schema(searchcontext);
```

The *Schema* class has a property called *AllManagedProperties,* an instance of the *ManagedPropertyCollection* class. With this collection, you can loop over all of the managed properties, and you edit the settings one by one. The following code shows how the treeview is populated in the sample application:

```
foreach (ManagedProperty prop in schema.AllManagedProperties)
{
    TreeNode node = treeViewManagedProperties.Nodes.Add(prop.Name);
    node.Tag = prop;
    foreach (Mapping mapping in prop.GetMappings())
    {
        TreeNode mappingnode = node.Nodes.Add(mapping.CrawledPropertyName);
    }
}
```

Creating a new managed property is done by calling the *Create* method at the level of the *ManagedProperties* collection and giving it the name of the property and then the type, as illustrated by the following lines of code:

```
Schema schema = new Schema(this.searchContext);
schema.AllManagedProperties.Create
    (textBoxManagedPropertyName.Text, ManagedDataType.Text);
```

The *Schema* class exposes a method, *QueryCrawledProperties*, that returns the list of crawled properties. The method accepts a number of parameters you can use to filter the, possibly very large, list of crawled properties. Here is the call that returns them and adds them to the list box in the sample application:

```
foreach (CrawledProperty cprop in schema.QueryCrawledProperties
    (string.Empty, 1000, Guid.NewGuid(), string.Empty, true))
{
    listBoxCrawledProperties.Items.Add(cprop);
}
```

Creating a mapping between one or more crawled properties and a managed property is not necessarily straightforward. Review the following code block with the different steps that have to be done:

```
ManagedProperty prop =
    (ManagedProperty)treeViewManagedProperties.SelectedNode.Tag;
MappingCollection mappings = new MappingCollection();
foreach (CrawledProperty cprop in listBoxCrawledProperties.SelectedItems)
```

```
{
    mappings.Add(new Mapping(cprop.Propset,
                             cprop.Name, cprop.VariantType, prop.PID));
}
```

```
prop.SetMappings(mappings);
```

To start, you have to create a new instance of the type *MappingCollection*. This collection has to be populated with instances of type *Mapping*, each of them representing one mapping with a crawled property. The information identifying the crawled property is something you provide during the creation of the instance with the constructor. After all of the crawled properties you intend to map are collected in the *MappingCollection* instance, you just have to call the *SetMappings* method of the *ManagedProperty* instance in question and assign it the new *MappingCollection*.

There is a lot more to discuss regarding the new search administration object model. I refer to the MOSS 2007 Software Developer Kit (SDK) that contains a full description of all of the classes that are part of the object model as well as some additional code samples.

Customizing the Search Center

The Search Center is a new type of site delivered with Microsoft Office SharePoint Server 2007 and is by default a subsite of the collaboration portal. Actually, you have two versions of the Search Center:

■ *Search Center Lite* is a version of the Search Center that does not require the Publishing Feature activated at the level of the site collection. You can therefore very quickly add Search Center Lite to a site collection that only contains team sites and provide a place within the site collection where users can execute a search query against the index file that's under the control of the Shared Services Provider, with which the IIS Web application hosting the site collection is associated. Figure 3-15 displays such a scenario. Search Center Lite is a version of the Search Center without the tabs and thus does not allow full customization.

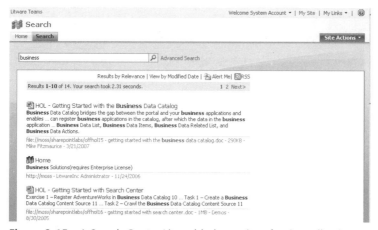

Figure 3-15 A Search Center Lite added as a site of a site collection containing only SharePoint team sites

- *Search Center with Tabs* is the full version of the Search Center. It requires the Microsoft Office SharePoint Server Publishing Infrastructure Feature to be activated and comes with a tab-based interface, as shown in Figure 3-16, that is fully customizable, as you'll see in the next couple of pages.

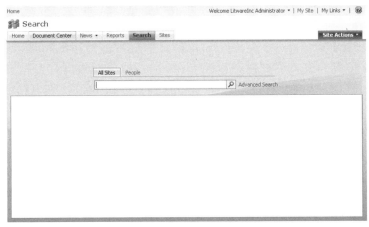

Figure 3-16   A Search Center with Tabs, by default a subsite of the collaboration portal

For the rest of the chapter, I'll concentrate only on the Search Center with Tabs version since it provides the full customization options.

Architecture of the Search Center

The Search Center is a normal SharePoint site built on the same fundamentals as any other site. Thus, we have a master page associated with the site that defines the overall look and feel, the chrome, the navigation, and other types of SharePoint controls you'll see on many other types of sites. Content pages are displayed that are connected to this master page and, as discussed in Chapter 2, "Collaboration Portals and People Management," these pages are stored in the Pages document library. The pages are based on page layouts that are provisioned along with the site. After the site has been created, you have four of these page layouts available. Table 3-4 summarizes them:

Table 3-4   Search Center Page Layouts

Page Layout	Description
Search Page	Pages based on this page layout are connected to the various tabs. By default, they contain the *Search Box* Web Part.
Search Results Page	This page layout defines the layout and functionality for the pages that show the search results. In addition to the *Search Box* Web Part, you'll find about seven more Web Parts on the page that delivers the search results experience. I'll detail them later.
Advanced Search Page	The page layout for the advanced search page with the *Advanced Search Box* as a Web Part on the page.
People Search Results Page	This is the page layout that defines the page for displaying the search results when making use of the *People* tab. It contains about eight Web Parts that display a part of the search results.

One major component of the Search Center is the tab-based user interface. By default, you have two tabs: *All Sites* which is the standard scope and *People* for a people-oriented search operation. Behind the scenes, the tabs are items stored in two lists. One is the Tabs in Search Pages list that contains the tabs for the pages based on the Search Page and the Advanced Search Page page layouts. The second list is the Tabs in Search Results, which contains the tabs for the Search Results Page and the People Search Results Page page layouts.

The tabs are actually rendered by the *ListBoundTabStrip* control contained within the *Microsoft.SharePoint.Portal.dll* and defined in the *Microsoft.SharePoint.Portal.WebControls* namespace. If you open one of the page layouts in Microsoft Office SharePoint Designer 2007, you'll notice the following element representing this control:

```
<SPSWC:ListBoundTabStrip runat="server" id="Tab" persistQueryString="true"
  cssClassNamePrefix="ms-sctab"
  ListName="<%$Resources:sps,SearchCenterOnet_SearchResultsListName%>"
  UnselectedTabTrimLength="-1" IgnoredQueryStringParameters="s,start1">
</SPSWC:ListBoundTabStrip>
```

So, everything is pretty much in place to customize the user's experience when working within the Search Center. Let's have a look at what you can accomplish.

Custom Tabs with Custom Search and Search Results Pages

Figure 3-17 shows an overview of the different page layouts that are involved in the tab-based user interface. The All Sites tab is associated with a page based on the Search Page page layout. The button that executes the search query is associated with a page based on the Search Results Page page layout, and you also have a page based on the Advanced Page page layout associated with the Advanced Search link. The People tab follows the same approach. The difference is that the People Search Results Page page layout replaces the Search Results Page page layout.

Figure 3-17   The various page layouts used in the Search Center

In the walkthrough later on, I'll guide you through all of the steps for customizing the Search Center with a custom tab and customized search and search results pages. In short, first, you'll create the pages you need based on the corresponding page layout, and next you'll add a new tab and connect both artifacts with each other and customize the various Web Parts included in the different pages. But before that, let's have a closer look at each of the different Web Parts that are available for the search-related pages.

Overview of the Search Web Parts

In total, you have nine Search Web Parts, and each of them exposes a wide variety of properties you can change to offer your users the search experience you have in mind. Many of these properties have to do with formatting, but there are also many options for configuring the actual execution of the search query itself. There is also the option of replacing the XSL used to transform the XML that contains the search results into the HTML presentation displayed in the Search Results page. All of the Search Web Parts are connected to one another, and there is a hidden control in charge of executing the search query, wrapping it into an XML block and sharing it with all of the other Web Parts available on the page.

The Search Box Web Part

The Search Box Web Part is used by the user to enter the query string. It can display the Scopes DropDown and the Query Text Box, a button to execute the query, and a link to the Advanced Search page. Each of these components is customizable by opening the Properties tool pane for the Web Part.

Table 3-5 describes the various modes in which you can make the Scopes Dropdown appear within the Search Box.

Table 3-5   Scopes DropDown Modes

Mode	Description
Do not show scopes dropdown	Hides the scopes dropdown.
Show scopes dropdown	Shows the scopes dropdown with both the contextual scopes and the ones that are active for the display group that is associated with the scopes dropdown.
Show, and default to 's' URL parameter	Same as the previous mode but the scope that is passed as the value of the 's' parameter in the query string is set as the default.
Show and default to contextual scope	Show the scopes defaulting to the contextual scope, that is, *This Site*.
Show, do not include contextual scopes	Excludes the contextual scopes out of the list of available scopes.
Show, do not include contextual scopes, and default to 's' URL parameter	Same as previous, but again takes the value of the 's' parameter out of the query string as the default scope.

In addition to the display mode, you can also set a label for the scopes dropdown and set the width to a fixed size.

The Query Text Box exposes properties that allow you to set a label, fix the width of the text box, and have additional query terms appended to the query string inputted by the user. An example of these additional query terms is shown in Figure 3-18. It shows how you can limit the scope of the search results to only contain documents by automatically adding the query term *isDocument:1* to every query.

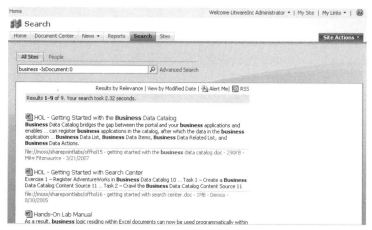

Figure 3-18   The search results only contain documents because the search box has been configured to append the *isDocument:1* query term to every query string entered by the user.

A last group of exposed properties is under the *Miscellaneous* node. There are properties that allow you to replace any of the default images used in the Search Box with your own custom ones. There is also the option to specify a URL for the custom advanced search page and the search results page you may have created. A last important property is the name of the display group that is connected to the scopes dropdown and used to populate the dropdown with the available search scopes.

The Search Summary Web Part

This Web Part can show the summary of the search query and offer to correct the user if needed by displaying the Did You Mean... Feature, displayed in Figure 3-19. The content of the summary can be displayed in compact or extended mode, and there is also the option to hide or display messages to the user.

Figure 3-19   The Search Summary Web Part showing the correction for the entered search query string

The Search Action Links Web Part

With the Search Action Links Web Part, the user is able to perform certain actions on the returned search results. The operations supported are: sorting of the results based on the relevance ranking or the modified date, creating alerts on the search results, and navigating to the RSS feed generated. Each of these operations can be turned on or off. There is also the option to modify the XSL that is being used to display the different action links. However, there is no option here for adding custom action links.

The Search Best Bets Web Part

The Search Best Bets Web Part shows the results that match up with a keyword, a best bet, or high-confidence results. For all, you can configure properties that have an effect on how the results are displayed. For example, you can turn on or off the display of the title and the description, and you can limit the amount of results displayed by the Web Part. Again, the XSL that transforms the results in an HTML block displayed within the Web Part can be customized or replaced with your own custom XSL.

The Search Statistics Web Part

The Search Statistics Web Part displays statistics such as the number of results shown on the page, the total amount of results, and the time it took to execute the search query. There's nothing really exciting to configure other than the option of displaying the text on one line or two and another option for hiding or displaying individual items.

The Search Paging Web Part

The Search Paging Web Part shows the links for navigation between the different pages showing the search results. You can tune how many links are being shown before and after the current page link as well as what the link looks like. You can have plain text or replace the text with an image. The amount of results for a page is not defined in this Web Part.

The Search High Confidence Results Web Part

The Search High Confidence Results Web Part has pretty much the same goal as the Search Best Bets Web Part, and, as you'll see, it even exposes the same type of properties. But this Web Part, by default, displays only the high confidence results, while the Search Best Bets Web Part only shows the results for the best bets and keywords.

The Search Core Results Web Part

This is definitely the most important Web Part on the Search Results page; it's responsible for displaying results to the user. First, you have properties to configure the paging and the default sorting. Next, you have some options for tuning the results query. Duplicate results can be displayed or hidden from the user. By default, search term stemming is not enabled.

Stemming is a method of mapping a linguistic stem to all matching words to increase the number of relevant results. For example, the stem *buy* matches *bought, buying*, and *buys*. Another option is to enable or disable noise word queries. It is turned on by default, which means that users are able to input a search string containing only noise words, such as *the, or*, and *a*.

An interesting property is *Selected Columns*, which contains an XML string that defines all of the columns that are to be displayed in the search results. The following is the default list of columns shown in the search results:

```
<root xmlns:xsi="http://www.w3.org/2001/XMLSchema-instance">
 <Columns>
  <Column Name="WorkId"/>
  <Column Name="Rank"/>
  <Column Name="Title"/>
  <Column Name="Author"/>
  <Column Name="Size"/>
  <Column Name="Path"/>
  <Column Name="Description"/>
  <Column Name="Write"/>
  <Column Name="SiteName"/>
  <Column Name="CollapsingStatus"/>
  <Column Name="HitHighlightedSummary"/>
  <Column Name="HitHighlightedProperties"/>
  <Column Name="ContentClass"/>
  <Column Name="IsDocument"/>
  <Column Name="PictureThumbnailURL"/>
 </Columns>
</root>
```

Adding a column is simply adding a *Column* element with the proper name. But it does not mean that you'll get to see it in the search results. There is the additional step of modifying the XSL associated with the Web Part and inserting the XSL block to pick up the additional property and display it to the user.

Instead of displaying the search results based on a query string entered by the user in the Search TextBox, you also have the option of configuring the Search Core Results Web Part to show the results of a fixed query string, as displayed in Figure 3-20.

This is an interesting process to follow if, for example, you need to display on a home page a list of the five most recent documents that contain the word *Business*. Figure 3-21 shows the Search Core Results Web Part on the home page of a team site displaying just that. The configuration is pretty simple. Set the *Fixed Query* property to your query string, for example *Business -isDocument:0*, and don't forget to set the Cross-Web Part query ID to something other than *User Query*.

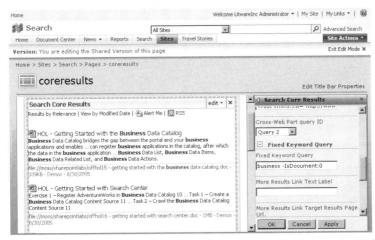

Figure 3-20   Configuring the properties of the Search Core Results Web Part

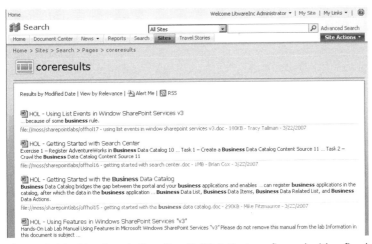

Figure 3-21   The Search Core Results Web Part configured with a fixed query on a home page of a SharePoint team site

The most important customization option for the Search Core Results Web Part is of course the XSLT that you can either customize or completely replace with one of your one. Before we detail this further, let's just review exactly how the search results end up in the body of the Web Part. Figure 3-22 shows the different steps.

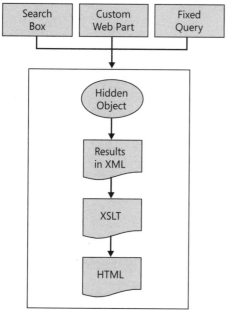

Search Core Results Web Part

Figure 3-22   The path followed to end up with the search results displayed to the user as the body of the Search Core Results Web Part

A query expressed as a string is passed to the Search Core Results Web Part by one of three ways: the user entering a query in the Search Box Web Part, a custom Web Part connected to it, or the internal fixed query property itself. An internal hidden object coordinates the execution of the query and returns the search results as an XML string. The XSL transformation performed on the XML results in the view users see in the Web Part. The XML that is the input for the transformation looks like this:

```
<All_Results>
  <Result>
    <id>1</id>
    <rank>713</rank>
    <title>Microsoft.SharePoint Namespace</title>
    <author />
    <size>39058</size>
    <url>http://msdn.microsoft.com/library/SV01017995.asp</url>
    <description>Microsoft.SharePoint Namespace</description>
    <sitename> http://msdn.microsoft.com/library</sitename>
    <collapsingstatus>0</collapsingstatus>
    <hithighlightedsummary>
      <...>
    </hithighlightedsummary>
    <hithighlightedproperties>
      <...>
    </hithighlightedproperties>
```

```
   <...>
   </Result>
   <Result>
   <...>
   <...>
   </Result>
</All_Results>
```

It is possible to have additional properties included in this XML, for example by adding more *Column* elements to the *Selected Columns* property as previously discussed.

One way to visualize the raw XML in the browser is by replacing the XSLT with the following:

```
<?xml version="1.0" encoding="UTF-8"?>
<xsl:stylesheet version="1.0" xmlns:xsl="http://www.w3.org/1999/XSL/Transform">
<xsl:output method="xml" version="1.0" encoding="UTF-8" indent="yes"/>
<xsl:template match="/">
<xmp><xsl:copy-of select="*"/></xmp>
</xsl:template>
</xsl:stylesheet>
```

With a full understanding of the structure of the raw XML, you're ready to start creating your own custom XSLT. You'll work out an example in the walkthrough, but for now, let's just have a look at the different sections within the XSLT that you should include in your custom XSLT.

A first block is the definition of various configuration parameters that can be passed to the transformation at run-time. A lot of these are used to branch the XSLT at some point.

```
<xsl:param name="ResultsBy" />
<xsl:param name="ViewByUrl" />
<xsl:param name="ViewByValue" />
<xsl:param name="IsNoKeyword" />
<xsl:param name="IsFixedQuery" />
<...>
```

The first pattern-matching rule, found at the bottom of the XSLT, is the one that matches with the root-node of the XML to be transformed. This is the one that initiates the whole process:

```
<!-- XSL transformation starts here -->
<xsl:template match="/">
  <xsl:if test="$AlertMeLink">
     <input type="hidden" name="P_Query" />
     <input type="hidden" name="P_LastNotificationTime" />
  </xsl:if>
  <xsl:choose>
     <xsl:when test="$IsNoKeyword = 'True'" >
        <xsl:call-template name="dvt_1.noKeyword" />
     </xsl:when>
     <xsl:when test="$ShowMessage = 'True'">
        <xsl:call-template name="dvt_1.empty" />
     </xsl:when>
```

```
        <xsl:otherwise>
            <xsl:call-template name="dvt_1.body"/>
        </xsl:otherwise>
    </xsl:choose>
</xsl:template>
```

In the template, the values of the incoming parameters are checked and used to jump to one of the other templates. If there is no keyword filled in by the user and the fixed query property is not set, the user will see a message indicating that something is wrong.

```
<!-- When there is keyword to issue the search -->
<xsl:template name="dvt_1.noKeyword">
  <span class="srch-description">
    <xsl:choose>
      <xsl:when test="$IsFixedQuery">
          Please set the 'Fixed Query' property for the webpart.
      </xsl:when>
      <xsl:otherwise>
          Enter one or more words to search for in the search box.
      </xsl:otherwise>
    </xsl:choose>
  </span>
</xsl:template>
```

It is also possible that no search results are returned for the inputted search query string. In that scenario, the action links are displayed along with a message telling the user that nothing was found.

```
<!-- When empty result set is returned from search -->
<xsl:template name="dvt_1.empty">
  <div class="srch-sort">
    <xsl:if test="$AlertMeLink and $ShowActionLinks">
        <span class="srch-alertme" >
          <a href ="{$AlertMeLink}" id="CSR_AM1" title="{$AlertMeText}">
            <img style="vertical-align: middle;"
                src="/_layouts/images/bell.gif" alt="" border="0"/>
            <xsl:text disable-output-escaping="yes"> </xsl:text>
            <xsl:value-of select="$AlertMeText" />
          </a>
        </span>
    </xsl:if>

    <xsl:if test="string-length($SrchRSSLink) &gt; 0 and $ShowActionLinks">
      <xsl:if test="$AlertMeLink">
          |
      </xsl:if>
      <a type="application/rss+xml" href ="{$SrchRSSLink}"
         title="{$SrchRSSText}" id="SRCHRSSL">
```

```
            <img style="vertical-align: middle;" border="0"
                src="/_layouts/images/rss.gif" alt=""/>
            <xsl:text disable-output-escaping="yes"> </xsl:text>
            <xsl:value-of select="$SrchRSSText"/>
          </a>
        </xsl:if>
      </div>
      <br/><br/>
      <span class="srch-description" id="CSR_NO_RESULTS">
      No results matching your search were found.
      <ol>
        <li>Check your spelling. Are the words in your query
           spelled correctly?</li>
        <li>Try using synonyms. Maybe what you're looking for uses
           slightly different words.</li>
        <li>Make your search more general. Try more general terms in
           place of specific ones.</li>
        <li>Try your search in a different scope. Different scopes can
           have different results.</li>
      </ol>
    </span>
  </xsl:template>
```

Of course, the most interesting part of the XSLT is the part that is called when search services return search results. You'll find a first block to render the action links:

```
<!-- Main body template. Sets the Results view (Relevance or date) options -->
<xsl:template name="dvt_1.body">
  <div class="srch-results">
    <...> XSLT for the action links - see above <...>
    <xsl:apply-templates />
  </div>
  <xsl:call-template name="DisplayMoreResultsAnchor" />
</xsl:template>
```

But then the real fun starts with the template that matches the *Result* node. One by one, the *Result* elements in the XML are transformed into *SPAN* and *DIV* elements. First, the icon is rendered:

```
<!-- This template is called for each result -->
<xsl:template match="Result">
  <xsl:variable name="id" select="id"/>
  <xsl:variable name="url" select="url"/>
  <span class="srch-Icon">
    <a href="{$url}" id="{concat('CSR_IMG_',$id)}" title="{$url}">
      <img align="absmiddle" src="{imageurl}" border="0"
      alt="{imageurl/@imageurldescription}" />
    </a>
  </span>
```

Next, there is a block that transforms the title of the search result. This one is a bit more complicated because of highlighting of the possible keyword entered by the user in the query string:

```
<span class="srch-Title">
  <a href="{$url}" id="{concat('CSR_',$id)}" title="{$url}">
    <xsl:choose>
      <xsl:when test="hithighlightedproperties/HHTitle[. != '']">
        <xsl:call-template name="HitHighlighting">
          <xsl:with-param name="hh" select="hithighlightedproperties/HHTitle" />
        </xsl:call-template>
      </xsl:when>
      <xsl:otherwise>
        <xsl:value-of select="title"/>
      </xsl:otherwise>
    </xsl:choose>
  </a>
  <br/>
</span>
```

The highlighting itself is delegated to a couple of additional templates that abstract the whole process. Continuing with processing the result, there is the rendering of the description, again calling the template for highlighting the keywords in the description if needed:

```
<div class="srch-Description">
  <xsl:choose>
    <xsl:when test="hithighlightedsummary[. != '']">
      <xsl:call-template name="HitHighlighting">
        <xsl:with-param name="hh" select="hithighlightedsummary" />
      </xsl:call-template>
    </xsl:when>
    <xsl:when test="description[. != '']">
      <xsl:value-of select="description"/>
    </xsl:when>
  </xsl:choose>
</div >
```

The same processing is basically applied to the URL of the search results:

```
<p class="srch-Metadata">
  <span class="srch-URL">
    <a href="{$url}" id="{concat('CSR_U_',$id)}" title="{$url}" dir="ltr">
      <xsl:choose>
        <xsl:when test="hithighlightedproperties/HHUrl[. != '']">
          <xsl:call-template name="HitHighlighting">
            <xsl:with-param name="hh"
                select="hithighlightedproperties/HHUrl" />
          </xsl:call-template>
```

```
      </xsl:when>
      <xsl:otherwise>
         <xsl:value-of select="url"/>
      </xsl:otherwise>
    </xsl:choose>
   </a>
 </span>
```

To conclude, there is the processing of the other properties of the search result, the size, and the author.

```
    <xsl:call-template name="DisplaySize">
       <xsl:with-param name="size" select="size" />
    </xsl:call-template>
    <xsl:call-template name="DisplayString">
       <xsl:with-param name="str" select="author" />
    </xsl:call-template>
    <xsl:call-template name="DisplayString">
       <xsl:with-param name="str" select="write" />
    </xsl:call-template>
    <xsl:call-template name="DisplayCollapsingStatusLink">
       <xsl:with-param name="status" select="collapsingstatus"/>
          <xsl:with-param name="urlEncoded" select="urlEncoded"/>
          <xsl:with-param name="id" select="concat('CSR_CS_',$id)"/>
       </xsl:call-template>
    </p>
  </xsl:template>
```

If you have additional properties that need to be displayed, you can add them here following the same pattern and action. The rendering of the size and author is done with two generic templates:

```
<!-- The size attribute for each result is prepared here -->
<xsl:template name="DisplaySize">
  <xsl:param name="size" />
    <xsl:if test='string-length($size) &gt; 0'>
    <xsl:if test="number($size) &gt; 0">
      -
    <xsl:choose>
      <xsl:when test="round($size div 1024) &lt; 1">
          <xsl:value-of select="$size" /> Bytes
       </xsl:when>
       <xsl:when test="round($size div (1024 *1024)) &lt; 1">
          <xsl:value-of select="round($size div 1024)" />KB
       </xsl:when>
       <xsl:otherwise>
          <xsl:value-of select="round($size div (1024 * 1024))"/>MB
       </xsl:otherwise>
     </xsl:choose>
   </xsl:if>
```

```
  </xsl:if>
</xsl:template>

<!-- A generic template to display string with non 0 string length
    (used for author and lastmodified time -->
<xsl:template name="DisplayString">
  <xsl:param name="str" />
    <xsl:if test='string-length($str) &gt; 0'>
      -
      <xsl:value-of select="$str" />
    </xsl:if>
</xsl:template>
```

There is more in the XSLT, but what I have described above is enough to give you a basic understanding of how the transformation is organized, and a key message to take away is that all of this is, of course, very customizable. The template that matches with the *Result* element is a part in the XSLT you'll probably focus on often.

The Advanced Search Box Web Part

The last Web Part we'll discuss is the Advanced Search Box Web Part, which provides plenty of configuration options. First of all, instead of just one search text box, you have a few: the *All Words*, *Exact Phrase*, *Any Words*, and *None Of These Words* search boxes. For each of them, you can decide whether to display the Web Part to the user or not.

Next, there is the section for the scopes that is configured so that the No Scopes Drop Down is displayed by default. But, with a single click, you can display one for the user. When deciding to do that, you'll also have to connect the scopes drop down to one of the existing display groups. Within the same section, there is also the language picker and the results type picker—again with the option to hide or display.

The property picker and the possible extension with custom additional managed properties has been discussed previously. In the Miscellaneous section, you'll find the place to redirect the user to one of the custom search results pages you may have created.

Walkthrough: Customizing the Search Center

Let's practice all of this with a walkthrough for three major goals: to show you how to add a custom tab in the Search Center, to demonstrate how to replace the search and the search results page with your own custom pages, and to show you a technique for replacing the XSLT that transforms the XML containing the search results with a custom one.

Assume that within the collaboration portal there is the need to deliver a customized search experience for the employees within the organization. The users should be able to visit the Search Center, navigate to their own search page, and then enter a search query with the results containing only documents. The results page needs a different look and feel and some additional customizations. To follow the walkthrough, you'll need a collaboration portal that is up and running.

Custom Tabs and Search Pages

Since there is the need for both a customized search and a search results page, let's start by navigating to the Search Center of this collaboration portal. Using the Site Actions, open the Create Page page and select the Search Page page layout. Enter **SharePoint Training Search Page** as the name and URL. Figure 3-23 shows the page ready to be created.

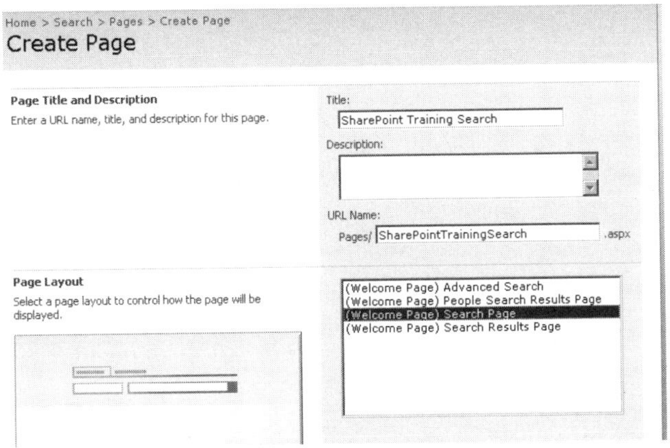

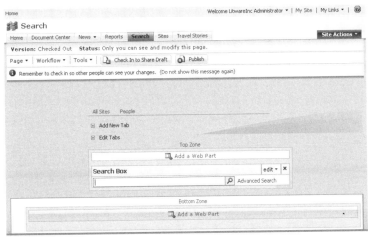

Figure 3-23   Creating a custom page based on the Search Page page layout

Just publish the page for now. You'll make some customizations later. Follow the same steps as before, but now create the SharePoint Training Search Results page based on the Search Results Page page layout. Again, just publish the page without any customizations.

You now have the two pages the users need for the customized search. Now, navigate back to the Search Center home page and use the Site Actions menu to switch to edit mode. The page is now ready to be customized, as displayed in Figure 3-24.

Figure 3-24   The home page of the Search Center ready to be populated with a new tab

Create a new tab by clicking the Add New Tab link. Remember that you are just creating a new list item with the details for the new tab. Figure 3-25 shows the New Item page where a Tab Name, such as *Training*, is entered along with the name of the custom search page, *SharePointTrainingSearch.aspx*, which is associated with the new tab. Publish the changes you've made to the Search Center home page.

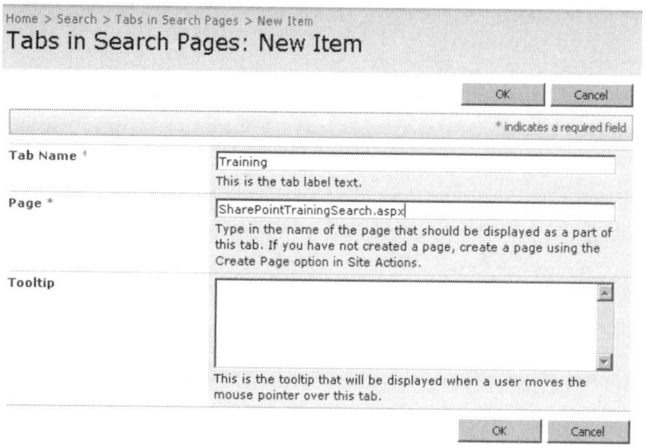

Figure 3-25 Creating a custom tab called Training connected to the custom search page

You can test your work by clicking on the Training tab. The *SharePointTrainingSearch.aspx* is now displayed. Your next step is to make sure that when users enter a search query and execute it, they'll be directed to the custom Search Results page that was previously created. On the *SharePointTrainingSearch.aspx*, use the Site Actions to switch the page to edit mode. Now, you'll configure a couple of the properties for the Search Box. Use the Modify Shared Web Part menu item to open the tool pane. Here, configure the option to show the scopes dropdown. Expand the *Query Text Box* node and add the string *-isDocument:0* as the value for the *Additional Query Terms* property. This string will be appended to every search query entered by the user and will apply an additional filter that forces only documents to be returned in the search results. The last configuration to finish the job is the specification of the URL to the custom Search Results page. Expand the *Miscellaneous* node and find the *Target search results page URL* property. Here you'll enter the name of the custom page previously created: *SharePointTrainingResults.aspx*. This concludes the configuration, and you can save and publish everything.

If you have followed all of the steps up to now, you should be able to enter a query string. Click on the Execute button and see the results for your custom Search Results page, as displayed in Figure 3-26.

Notice that the page displays both of the out-of-the-box tabs, but it does not display the Training tab you just created. What happened? The answer is very simple. The custom tab you created ended up in the SharePoint list that is not used by the pages that are based on the Search Results Page page layout. Those pages use a second list for the definition of the tabs. So, if you want to have the Training tab appear in the results pages, then you'll have to add it to the Tabs in the Search Results list. There are a couple of ways to accomplish this: One way is to navigate to the Tabs in the Search Results list and just create a new item—no different from the steps you take to create items in other lists. You provide the same name and the same value for the search page as with the previously created list item for the first tab. Now, if you repeat the steps to test out your work, you'll see the Training tab in the Search Results page.

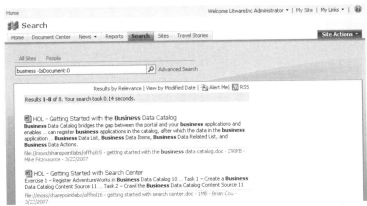

Figure 3-26   The search results displayed in the custom search results page

Displaying the Search Results with Custom XSLT

Let's focus our attention now on customizing the Search Results page. We'll change some properties for the Search Core Results Web Part, and let's say your company also needs to replace part of the XSLT with some custom rendering, such as grouping the results by the author of the document. It is possible to create the required XSLT from scratch in Notepad if you are really into the XSLT language, but a better option may be to use a professional XSLT editor from a third-party provider. There are numerous products that can help you with this. For this book, I'll stick with the Microsoft products, and I'll show you how you can leverage the DataView Web Part and Microsoft Office SharePoint Designer 2007 to accomplish what your company needs for the search results customization.

The first thing you'll need is the XML that is returned by the search engine. As previously discussed, a quick way to get these results is to replace the XSLT of the Search Core Results Web Part with the following:

```xml
<?xml version="1.0" encoding="UTF-8"?>
<xsl:stylesheet version="1.0" xmlns:xsl="http://www.w3.org/1999/XSL/Transform">
<xsl:output method="xml" version="1.0" encoding="UTF-8" indent="yes"/>
<xsl:template match="/">
<xmp><xsl:copy-of select="*"/></xmp>
</xsl:template>
</xsl:stylesheet>
```

Switch the *SharePointTrainingResults.aspx* to edit mode, and choose Modify Shared Web Part from the Search Core Results Web Part menu to find the XSLT button in the tool pane. In the dialog box, replace the XSLT with the snippet that returns the raw XML. Apply all of your changes, and then test a search query. The Web Part now shows the XML with all of the search results. Isolate all of this XML in a file.

Next, open Microsoft Office SharePoint Designer 2007 and open one of your SharePoint sites. It really doesn't matter which one—a SharePoint team site with a blank home page, for example. Create a new ASPX page and proceed with the steps for creating a data source that makes the XML for the search results available. Use the Data View menu and click on Manage Data Sources. The Data Source Library tool pane is opened as a result, and now you can expand the *XML Files* node, adding your XML file using the link available. Confirm that you want to include the XML file as a file in your SharePoint site, though it's not important. Figure 3-27 shows what you should have in the tool pane at this point.

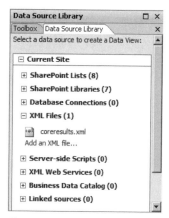

Figure 3-27   The XML containing the search results defined as data source in Microsoft Office SharePoint Designer 2007 and ready as input for the DataView Web Part

Everything is in place now for creating the Data View Web Part. In the tool pane, use the context menu of the new data source and select the option to show the data. A new tab in the tool pane is opened with the list of nodes that are part of the XML data source. No need here to select all of the nodes. The users only have to see the file type image, the title, the description, and the size of the document. Therefore, select the following nodes in the list: *title*, *size*, *write*, and *author*. Drag and drop all of the selected nodes to one of the Web Part zones available on the page in the designer. The result will be a default rendering of the Data View Web Part as displayed in Figure 3-28.

There is some tuning to do now. If you move the cursor over the Data View Web Part, you'll see a small button with an arrow giving you access to a pane displaying the configuration options. The first thing to do is click on the Edit Columns link. Then you have to rearrange the order of the columns, as shown in Figure 3-29. The first column is the title, followed by the author, write, and finally the size of the document.

Proceed again in the Common Data View Tasks dialog box by clicking on the Sort and Group link to define how you want the grouping to be done. The grouping is based on the author field. Therefore, move it to the Sort Order list box. Under the Group Properties section, select the option to show the group header and then click OK to save the configuration. Figure 3-30 shows the work process for the grouping.

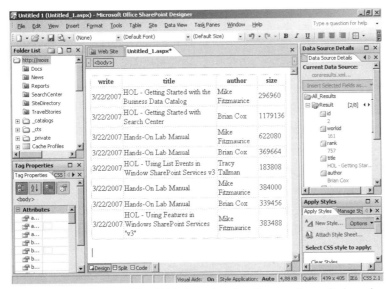

Figure 3-28   The DataView Web Part showing the search results based on the selection of nodes from the XML data source using the default XSLT

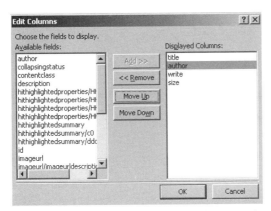

Figure 3-29   Editing the columns in the Data View Web Part

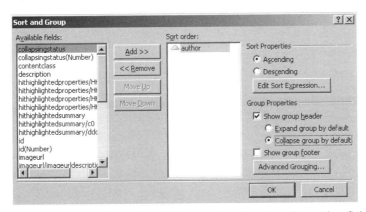

Figure 3-30   Configuration of the grouping based on the author field

In the designer, you should already see the results of your work. There is one last configuration you'll have to do. The user should be able to click on the title of the search result and open the document with it. This is formatting you'll have to do at the column level. Use the smart tag and select *hyperlink* as the format. A dialog is shown where you can configure what the hyperlink needs to show as text and what the address is. For the text to display, enter the value *{title}*, and for the address enter the value *{url}*, as shown in Figure 3-31.

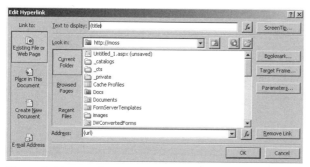

Figure 3-31   Configuration of the hyperlink that will show the title of the document and let the user jump to the document itself with the value of the *url* field

There are a lot more things you can do for the configuration of the Data View Web Part, and I invite you to explore more options. But we gotta move on. If you switch to the page code, you'll find the XSLT that is responsible for the view in the Web Part. It is contained as the body of the *XSL* element within the page. As a starter, you can simply drop this XSLT as the replacement of the default XSLT for the Search Core Results Web Part. Before you do this, copy the default XSLT to a new XML file in an editor such as Visual Studio.NET 2005. You'll need it in a moment. After applying and publishing the page, the search results should be nicely grouped by author, as displayed in Figure 3-32.

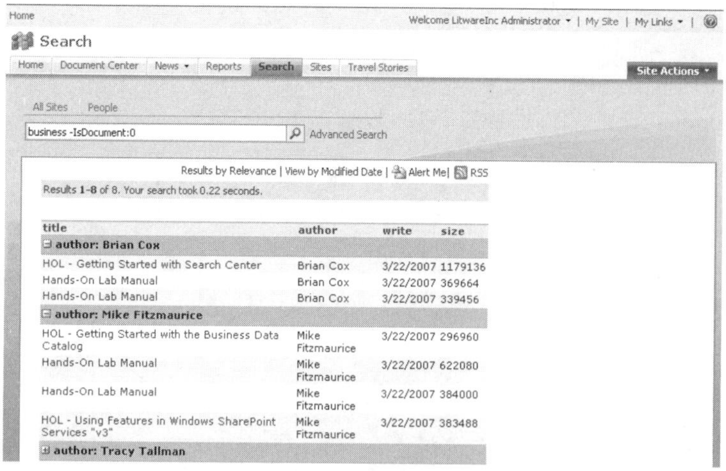

Figure 3-32   The search results now displayed using the XSLT built up behind the Data View Web Part in Microsoft Office SharePoint Designer 2007

This is a good start. Now, you need to finish it. The best thing to do is open your favorite XML editor again and load the generated XSLT in a new XML file. You should now have the two XSLT files in there: the custom one and the default XSLT of the Search Core Results Web Part. It is a good idea to copy all of the *param* elements from the latter and paste them at the top of your custom XSLT just before the *root template* element since you will need all of this for branching logic in the XSLT. Next, copy the templates named *dvt_1.noKeyword* and *dvt_1.empty* to the custom XSLT. In case there are no keyword or search results found, these templates will render the appropriate messages to the user.

The root template with the match attribute set to "/" has to be modified to make use of the copied templates. Again, you can just copy from the default XSLT and replace the body of the root template. There is one change you'll have to do: The call-template at the end must point to the *dvt_1* instead of the *dvt_1.body* template. The full root template looks like this:

```
<xsl:template match="/">
    <xsl:if test="$AlertMeLink">
        <input type="hidden" name="P_Query" />
        <input type="hidden" name="P_LastNotificationTime" />
    </xsl:if>
    <xsl:choose>
        <xsl:when test="$IsNoKeyword = 'True'" >
            <xsl:call-template name="dvt_1.noKeyword" />
        </xsl:when>
        <xsl:when test="$ShowMessage = 'True'">
            <xsl:call-template name="dvt_1.empty" />
        </xsl:when>
        <xsl:otherwise>
            <xsl:call-template name="dvt_1"/>
        </xsl:otherwise>
    </xsl:choose>
</xsl:template>
```

If there is a need for the action links to be displayed within the Search Core Results Web Part, you'll have to copy and paste another block of XSLT. But, let's ignore this and do one additional configuration. The size of the document has to be formatted appropriately. Copy the following template from the default XSLT to the custom XSLT:

```
<!-- The size attribute for each result is prepared here -->
<xsl:template name="DisplaySize">
    <xsl:param name="size" />
    <xsl:if test='string-length($size) &gt; 0'>
        <xsl:if test="number($size) &gt; 0">
            <xsl:choose>
                <xsl:when test="round($size div 1024) &lt; 1">
                    <xsl:value-of select="$size" /> Bytes
                </xsl:when>
                <xsl:when test="round($size div (1024 *1024)) &lt; 1">
                    <xsl:value-of select="round($size div 1024)" />KB
```

```
                </xsl:when>
                <xsl:otherwise>
                    <xsl:value-of select="round($size div (1024 * 1024))"/>MB
                </xsl:otherwise>
            </xsl:choose>
        </xsl:if>
    </xsl:if>
</xsl:template>
```

The only thing to do now is to make sure that the size of the document is formatted using the algorithm defined in the body of the above template. Look for the place in the custom XSLT where the size is rendered: the *dvt_1.rowview* template. At the bottom, you'll find a *<xsl:value-of ...* statement for inserting the value of the *size* field. Replace that one with the following:

```
<td class="ms-vb">
    <xsl:call-template name="DisplaySize">
        <xsl:with-param name="size" select="size" />
    </xsl:call-template>
</td>
```

There is a bit more work to do if you also want to include highlighting for the keywords in the title and the description. Again, this can be achieved by copying the corresponding XSLT snippets from the default XSLT into your custom XSLT and by calling the template at the places where the functionality is needed. For our walkthrough, however, what you've done is more than enough. Just save everything and publish it. Figure 3-33 displays the result for a typical query.

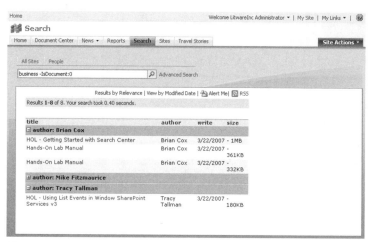

Figure 3-33   The search results displayed using a custom XSLT

This concludes our walkthrough. Don't forget that the technique for using the Data View Web Part to generate the custom XSLT is only one approach you can take—one that has to be used with care, but it can be a starter for those of you who are not familiar with XSLT language. You can also build your XSLT completely from scratch by using any of the professional XML/XSLT editors available in the market.

The Search Query Object Model

Microsoft Office SharePoint Server 2007 introduces a brand new object model to support developers who need to programmatically prepare and execute a search query. Before describing these new classes, I'll quickly discuss the two ways to express the query. At the end, there is a walkthrough showing how to execute a search via a custom Web Part that can be dropped on SharePoint sites.

Keyword Syntax versus Enterprise SQL Search Query Syntax

A search query can be expressed by building a simple string consisting of keywords or by making use of the powerful, but more complex, Enterprise SQL Search query language that extends the standard SQL-92 and SQL-99 database query syntax and is tuned for compiling full-text search queries.

Keyword Syntax

The keyword syntax is a new query syntax introduced with Microsoft Office SharePoint Server 2007 that greatly reduces the complexity of formulating a search query. Of course, reducing complexity in the syntax also has as a catch: Search queries using the keyword syntax do not fully leverage the power of the search engine. However, as this is often not required, keyword syntax is quickly becoming a popular query language that targets not only the end user but also the developer that builds custom search experiences for the end user. It is also a query language that is consistently used for executing Office, Windows, and Microsoft Live searches.

The core of this query syntax are of course the keywords. There are three possible options:

- The query consists of the keyword expressed as a word including one or more characters without spaces or punctuation.

- Multiple keywords can be combined into a phrase separated by spaces, but the words must be enclosed in quotation marks.

- The last option is to use a prefix, including a part of a word, from the beginning of the word.

There is support for required and excluded terms. To include a required term, you simply use the "+" in front of the keyword. To exclude a term, you use the "-" in front of the keyword. Here is an example of a query trying to find everything that contains the keyword *business* but excluding the results where business is used in the phrase Business Data Catalog:

```
business -"Business Data Catalog"
```

A last option is the use of property filters. These can narrow the focus of the keyword search based on the inclusion or exclusion of managed properties, scopes, and/or collapsed results. Here is an example of how to search for all of the documents created by Mike Fitzmaurice that contain the keyword *business*:

```
business +author:fitzmaurice +isDocument:1
```

Enterprise SQL Search Query Syntax

This syntax allows for more complex search queries and is therefore also used in more advanced search solutions. The basic skeleton of a SQL search query is:

```
SELECT <columns>
FROM <content source>
WHERE <conditions>
ORDER BY <columns>
```

The SDK contains a detailed description of what your options are for the artifacts available for each of the different parts of the query. I'll just be brief here and discuss the most important ones you need for the rest of the chapter.

Within the *SELECT* part, you specify the columns you want to include in the search results. The *FROM* part can only contain the *SCOPE()* statement in Microsoft Office Share-Point Server 2007. The name of the scope is then further defined in the *WHERE* part as follows:

```
SELECT title, author, rank FROM scope() WHERE "scope"='All Sites'
```

Using the scope as a possible condition in the *WHERE* part is not the only option. The *WHERE* part is also the place where you include the columns and the possible conditions they have to match to. All types of predicates can be used starting with the traditional ones everybody knows ("=","!=","<",">", ...) to very specific ones such as *LIKE, DATEADD, NULL*, and the full-text predicates *FREETEXT* and *CONTAINS*. The *CONTAINS* predicate performs comparisons on columns that contain text. Based on the proximity of the search terms, matching can be performed on single words or phrases. In comparison, the *FREETEXT* predicate is tuned to match the meaning of the search phrases against text columns.

An example of a query using all of these options follows:

```
SELECT URL, Title, Description FROM SCOPE() WHERE "scope"='All Sites'
    AND FREETEXT('gallery hinges') AND SITE = "http://supportdesk"
    AND NOT CONTAINS('brass')
```

The last part of the SQL statement is the *ORDER BY*, which gives you the option to sort the query results based on the value of one or more columns specified.

The New Search Query Classes

The new managed API to support the execution of an Enterprise search query is encapsulated within the *Microsoft.Office.Server.Search.dll* and defined within the *Microsoft.Office.Server.Search.Query* namespace. Two classes are important here. Both inherit from the *Query* class, an abstract class that is not intended to be used directly in code. The two classes are:

- **KeywordQuery**   dedicated to executing a query defined with the keyword syntax
- **FullTextSqlQuery**   used when the search query is defined using the Enterprise SQL search query syntax

Important to note is that both classes use the same flow for the execution of the query. They both expose properties to assign possible configurations of options and the query that has to be executed. The *Execute* method executes the query and returns the search results in the same manner as a set of *IDataReader* objects. All the members required to support this flow are defined at the level of the *Query* class. I'll quickly discuss the most important members of this class.

Query Class

Most of the properties at the level of the *Query* class, summarized in Table 3-8, are there to help you prepare the execution of the search query.

Table 3-8   *Query* Class Properties

Property	Description
Culture	The culture to use for things such as stemming, noise words, thesaurus, and more.
EnableStemming	Turn stemming on or off.
IgnoreAllNoiseQuery	Allow or do not allow a query consisting only of noise words.
KeywordInclusion	Indicates whether the query results contain all or any of the specified search terms.
QueryText	The most important property since this is the one used to assign the query string to be executed.
ResultTypes	Defines the result types to be included in the search results.
RowLimit	The maximum number of rows returned in the search results.
StartRow	Gets or sets first row included in the search results.
TrimDuplicates	Gets or sets a Boolean value that specifies whether duplicate items should be removed from the search results.

The *Execute* method is used to execute the query assigned to the *QueryText* property. The results of the query are returned as an object of type *ResultTableCollection*, a collection of *IDataReader* objects to be processed one by one.

KeywordQuery and *FullTextSqlQuery* Class

Both classes are instantiated in the same manner. Since the objects execute a query against the search service, and the search service is part of the shared services, it is necessary to provide information about the Shared Services Provider you'll want to connect to. The constructor accepts an instance of the *ServerContext* object, an instance of an *SPSite* object, or the string of the search application name. The following code illustrates how to start with the *KeywordQuery* class:

```
ServerContext context = ServerContext.GetContext("SharedServices1");
KeywordQuery kwq = new KeywordQuery(context);
```

After this, it is a matter of assigning the values for one or more properties that prepare the query and that the classes inherit from the *Query* class. One of them, the *ResultTypes*, is set to indicate what types of result you are interested in. There are a few options here, summarized in Table 3-9.

Table 3-9 *ResultType* Values

Value	Description
DefinitionResults	Definitions for keywords matching the search query.
HighConfidenceResults	High confidence results matching the search query.
None	No result type specified.
RelevantResults	The main search results from the content index matching the search query.
SpecialTermResults	Best bets matching the search query.

The *QueryText* property is of course a very important one to set. When you are working with a *KeywordQuery* class, the query is just a string containing the keywords. If you work with the *FullTextSqlQuery* class, it is a full-blown SQL statement. Here is an example of the first scenario:

```
kwq.ResultTypes = ResultType.RelevantResults;
kwq.EnableStemming = true;
kwq.TrimDuplicates = true;
kwq.QueryText = "business +isDocument:1";
```

Next, the *Execute* method is called, which returns an instance of the *ResultTableCollection* object.

```
ResultTableCollection results = kwq.Execute();
```

You can extract the type of results you'd like to process further. In the following sample, all of the relevant results are retrieved in the form of an individual instance of the *ResultTable* type.

```
ResultTable resultTable = results[ResultType.RelevantResults];
```

The rest of the process is, of course, dependent on what you want to do with the results. Here is an example that takes the *ResultTable* object, implements the *IDataReader* interface, and drops it into a *DataTable* that is then bound to a *DataGrid*:

```
DataTable tbl = new DataTable();
tbl.Load(resultTable, LoadOption.OverwriteChanges);
dataGridView1.DataSource = tbl;
```

If you use all of this code in a small Windows application, such as what's shown in Figure 3-34, you can let the users formulate a search query, execute it, and have the results displayed in a *DataGrid*. Don't forget to add a reference to the *System.Web.dll*, *Microsoft.Office.Server.dll*, *Microsoft.Office.Server.Search.dll*, and *Microsoft.SharePoint.dll*.

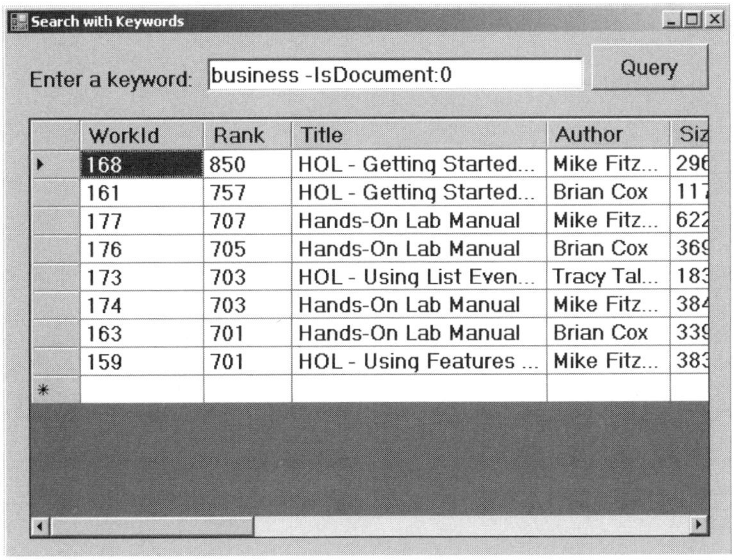

WorkId	Rank	Title	Author	Siz
168	850	HOL - Getting Started...	Mike Fitz...	296
161	757	HOL - Getting Started...	Brian Cox	117
177	707	Hands-On Lab Manual	Mike Fitz...	622
176	705	Hands-On Lab Manual	Brian Cox	369
173	703	HOL - Using List Even...	Tracy Tal...	183
174	703	Hands-On Lab Manual	Mike Fitz...	384
163	701	Hands-On Lab Manual	Brian Cox	339
159	701	HOL - Using Features ...	Mike Fitz...	383

Enter a keyword: business -IsDocument:0   Query

Figure 3-34   Executing a keyword syntax query in a Windows application

Walkthrough: Building a Custom Search Web Part

There are many possible opportunities for using the *KeywordQuery* and *FullTextSqlQuery* classes in custom Web Parts. Since you've been exposed to the *KeywordQuery* class in the previous section, I'll focus now on the *FullTextSqlQuery* class. The walkthrough will describe the steps for building a Web Part that can be dropped on a site home page and show all the documents that have been added to SharePoint sites and indexed within the past week. Instead of building the Web Part the traditional way, you'll encapsulate all of the logic into an ASP.NET 2.0 user control and use SmartPart to make the user control available as a Web Part on a SharePoint page.

More Info   *SmartPart* is a free community tool developed by Jan Tielens, who works for U2U. It is a generic Web Part that you can use to load ASP.NET 2.0 user controls and have them rendered as a Web Part. SmartPart is available for download on *http://www.smartpart.info*. The installation is pretty simple and is documented on the site.

You can start by creating an ASP.NET 2.0 Web Site using Visual Studio.NET 2005. In the project, you'll need one additional item on top of the *default.aspx*, which is already available. The additional item is a Web user control, an ASCX file named *ThisWeeksDocuments.ascx*. The only control needed is a Label named *labelResults*. We'll not bother much with the aesthetics.

There are three references that you'll have to add to the project: one for *Microsoft.SharePoint.dll*, another one for *Microsoft.Office.Server.Search.dll*, and a third for *Microsoft.Office.Server.dll*. Continue now by opening the code-behind class for the user control. The following *using* statements for the namespaces that you'll use in the code have to be added in addition to the ones already there:

```
using System.Text;
using Microsoft.Office.Server;
using Microsoft.Office.Server.Search.Query;
```

All of your code will be written in the *Page_Load* procedure that is already available. First, there is the declaration of a couple of variables that will be needed later. One of them contains the SQL query that will be executed:

```
string item = "<A href='{0}' />{1}</A> (authored by {2})<BR>";
StringBuilder sb = new StringBuilder();

string query = "SELECT url, title, author " +
               "FROM Scope() " +
               "WHERE \"scope\" = 'All Sites' AND " +
               "isDocument=1 AND write > DATEADD(Day, -7, GetGMTDate())";
```

The process for executing the query has been previously discussed. To start, you need an object of the type *FullTextSqlQuery*. It is possible that the ASP.NET 2.0 user control is used outside of the SharePoint context, such as on a traditional ASP.NET Web site. Therefore, you cannot assume that you'll have immediate access to the context, and you need to first create an object of type *ServerContext* and pass this instance as parameter during the construction of the *FullTextSqlQuery* object. Here is the code for it:

```
ServerContext context = ServerContext.GetContext("SharedServices1");
FullTextSqlQuery qry = new FullTextSqlQuery(context);
```

Next, there is the preparation of the query. You have to assign values for a number of properties. The query string is set as the value for the *QueryText* property.

```
qry.ResultTypes = ResultType.RelevantResults;
qry.EnableStemming = true;
qry.TrimDuplicates = true;
qry.QueryText = query;
```

After the preparation step, it is time to execute the query. Call the *Execute* method and store the results in a variable of type *ResultTableCollection* as shown in the following code:

```
ResultTableCollection results = qry.Execute();
```

Again, you're only interested in the actual search results and therefore you'll isolate these and extract them as follows:

```
ResultTable resultTable = results[ResultType.RelevantResults];
```

The rest of the code is all about processing the results. Remember that the *ResultTable* implements the *IDataReader* interface. The processing can be done by looping through all of the search results one by one and building up the string to be displayed in the label. Add the following code as the final piece of the user control:

```
if (resultTable.RowCount == 0)
{
    labelResults.Text = "No documents that were created today have been found";
}
else
{
    while (resultTable.Read())
    {
        sb.AppendFormat(item, resultTable.GetString(0),
            resultTable.GetString(1), resultTable.GetString(2));
    }
}

labelResults.Text = sb.ToString();

qry.Dispose();
```

It is possible to test out the code without running it in the context of SharePoint. Just drop the user control from the solution explorer on the *default.aspx* in design mode and browse this page. The result, as shown in Figure 3-35, is not really fancy, but you should get the list of all of the documents added within the week to the SharePoint site crawled by the index engine.

Figure 3-35   The list of documents added to a SharePoint site in the past week

Now take the following steps to make this ASP.NET 2.0 user control available as a Web Part on a SharePoint site. First, copy both the *ascx* and the code-behind file in a folder called UserControls in the directory that is associated with the IIS Web Application that hosts the SharePoint site and where the SmartPart is installed. If the UserControls folder is not there, you'll have to create it. Because you are not deploying the ASP.NET user control as a pre-compiled .NET assembly, you also have to add the following two elements as child elements of the *assemblies* element in the *web.config* of the IIS Web Application:

```
<add assembly="Microsoft.Office.Server, Version=12.0.0.0,
    Culture=neutral, PublicKeyToken=71E9BCE111E9429C"/>
<add assembly="Microsoft.Office.Server.Search, Version=12.0.0.0,
    Culture=neutral, PublicKeyToken=71E9BCE111E9429C"/>
```

Next on the SharePoint site, add the SmartPart on a page. If it is installed properly, you'll see it in the list of available Web Parts when you click the Add a Web Part button, as shown in Figure 3-36.

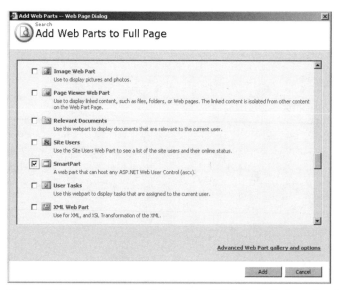

Figure 3-36   The SmartPart in the list of Web Parts that can be dropped on the SharePoint page

Open the tool pane that shows the properties exposed by the SmartPart. At the top, there is a dropdown that is populated with all of the ASCX files that the SmartPart has found in the UserControls folder. Select the one that you've copied to the folder and, after applying this setting, the user control will be displayed as a Web Part on the page. Figure 3-37 displays the end result.

Figure 3-37   The ASP.NET user control showing the search results, now in a SharePoint page hosted by SmartPart

The Query Web Service

Talking to the search service remotely is done by consuming the Query Web Service that's exposed by Microsoft Office SharePoint Server 2007. When starting a new Visual Studio.NET 2005 project, the first thing to do is to generate a proxy class. You accomplish this by adding a *Web Reference* pointing to the following URL:

```
http://Server_Name/[sites/][Site_Name/]_vti_bin/search.asmx
```

The proxy class facilitates the communication with the Web Service by encapsulating all of the low-level plumbing such as the required SOAP packaging of your requests.

Table 3-10 lists all of the methods that can be called for the Query Web Service. On the companion Web site, you'll find a Windows application called MOSSQueryWebServiceDemo that illustrates most of the calls you can do with the Query Web Service. Figure 3-38 shows the user interface of the application.

Table 3-10   Query Web Service Methods

Method	Description
GetPortalSearchInfo	Returns all of the search scopes.
GetSearchMetaData	Returns all of the managed properties and the search scopes.
Query	Returns a set of results in an XML string for the specified query.
QueryEx	Returns a set of results in a Microsoft ADO.NET *DataSet* object for the specified query.
Registration	Method used to register the Query Web Service as a Research service in the Microsoft Office clients and Internet Explorer.
Status	Returns availability of the search service.

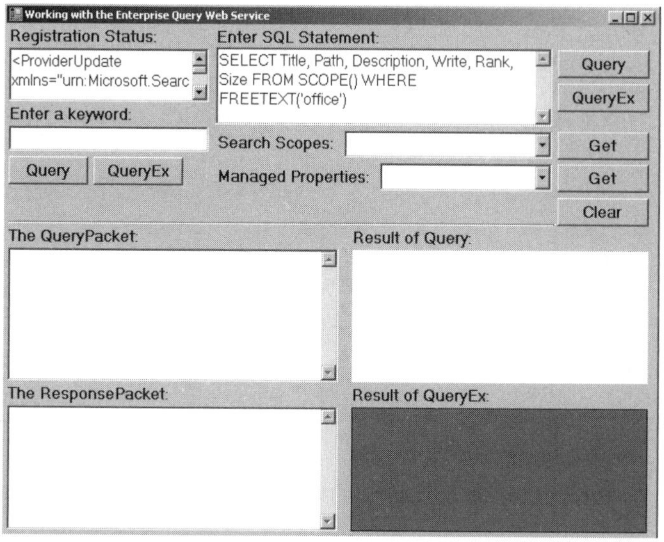

Figure 3-38 An example of a smart client executing search queries via the Query Web Service

The moment you start the application, it connects to the Web Service sending the credentials of the currently logged on user.

```
searchService = new SearchService.QueryService();
searchService.Credentials = System.Net.CredentialCache.DefaultCredentials;
```

You may want to verify that the search service is up and running before attempting to execute queries. There is a method called *Registration* that returns an XML response containing the status information. Here is the call to that method:

```
string result = searchService.Registration(registrationString);
```

If all is well, you'll receive a status *SUCCESS* along with other information regarding the provider that delivers the search results. This information is used by, for example, Microsoft Office smart clients when you register the Query Web Service as a Research Service.

```
<ProviderUpdate xmlns="urn:Microsoft.Search.Registration.Response">
  <Status>SUCCESS</Status>
  <Providers>
    <Provider>
     <Id>{86051521-13de-4dac-80d1-231406b51b57}</Id>
     <Name>Microsoft Office SharePoint Server 2007 Search</Name>
     <QueryPath>http://moss/_vti_bin/search.asmx</QueryPath>
     <Type>SOAP</Type>
     <Services>
        <Service>
         <Id>{86051521-13de-4dac-80d1-231406b51b57}</Id>
         <Name>Home</Name>
         <Category>INTRANET_GENERAL</Category>
```

```
                <Description>This service allows you to search the site :
                        Home</Description>
                <Copyright>Microsoft® Office SharePoint® Server 2007 Search</Copyright>
                <Display>On</Display>
            </Service>
          </Services>
        </Provider>
      </Providers>
    </ProviderUpdate>
```

The most important methods are the *Query* method and the *QueryEx* method. The input you have to give for both is very similar: It is an XML string starting with the *QueryText* element containing the query formulated either with the keyword syntax or with the Enterprise SQL Search Query syntax. In the application, you can test a keyword syntax query with both methods. As you'll notice, the *QueryText* element is nicely wrapped into a *QueryPacket* element so that it can be interpreted correctly by the Web Service. Here is the full XML that is submitted to the Web Service when executing a keyword syntax query:

```
<QueryPacket xmlns="urn:Microsoft.Search.Query" Revision="1000">
  <Query domain="QDomain">
    <SupportedFormats>
      <Format>urn:Microsoft.Search.Response.Document.Document</Format>
    </SupportedFormats>
    <Context>
      <QueryText language="en-US" type="STRING">sharepoint</QueryText>
    </Context>
  </Query>
</QueryPacket>
```

The XML compiled when you execute a query using the Enterprise SQL Search Query syntax is only different at the level of the value for the *type* attribute of the *QueryText* element and of course the value of the *QueryText* element itself:

```
<QueryPacket xmlns="urn:Microsoft.Search.Query" Revision="1000">
  <Query domain="QDomain">
    <SupportedFormats>
      <Format>urn:Microsoft.Search.Response.Document.Document</Format>
    </SupportedFormats>
    <Context>
      <QueryText language="en-US" type="MSSQLFT">
        SELECT Title, Path, Description, Write, Rank, Size FROM SCOPE() WHERE
        FREETEXT('office')
      </QueryText>
    </Context>
  </Query>
</QueryPacket>
```

The code for executing the queries is as follows:

```
// executing with Query method and getting the results in XML format back
string queryResults = searchService.Query(query);
// executing the query with the QueryEx method and getting an ADO.NET DataSet back
DataSet resultDataset = searchService.QueryEx(query);
```

With the *Query* call, you'll receive a *ResponsePacket* containing the search results in XML format. There is a difference between a query created with the keyword syntax and a query created with a SQL statement. Using the keyword syntax, you do not have the option to specify what columns need to be included in the results. You also do not have the option to make use of the search scopes to limit the results or filter the results based on some kind of condition formulated with a search predicate. Here is the XML that's returned when executing a keyword syntax query:

```xml
<ResponsePacket xmlns="urn:Microsoft.Search.Response">
  <Response domain="QDomain">
    <Range>
      <StartAt>1</StartAt>
      <Count>10</Count>
      <TotalAvailable>83</TotalAvailable>
      <Results>
        <Document relevance="893" xmlns="urn:Microsoft.Search.Response.Document">
          <Title>Home</Title>
          <Action>
            <LinkUrl size="0">http://moss</LinkUrl>
          </Action>
          <Description />
          <Date>2006-12-27T16:10:22-08:00</Date>
        </Document>

        <more elements of Document type>

      </Results>
    </Range>
    <Status>SUCCESS</Status>
  </Response>
</ResponsePacket>
```

The *QueryEx* call returns an ADO.NET *DataSet* serialized as an XML block. The proxy class immediately wraps this into an ADO.NET *DataSet* object so that you can bind it, for example, to a *DataGrid*. The *ResponsePacket* for the *QueryEx* method has a number of additional properties that are returned, such as the information you'll be able to use for displaying the keywords highlighted in the description. Also, all types of search results are returned, such as the relevant results, keyword matches, and best bets. The XML typically looks like this:

```xml
<Results>
  <RelevantResults>
    <WorkId>72</WorkId>
    <Rank>893</Rank>
    <Title>Home</Title>
    <Author>LitwareInc Administrator</Author>
```

```
    <Size>0</Size>
    <Path>http://moss</Path>
    <Write>2006-12-27T16:10:22-08:00</Write>
    <SiteName>http://moss</SiteName>
    <CollapsingStatus>0</CollapsingStatus>
    <HitHighlightedSummary>Welcome to Microsoft®
        &lt;c0&gt;Office&lt;/c0&gt; SharePoint®
        Server 2007  &lt;ddd/&gt; Get started with the new
        version of Microsoft
        &lt;c0&gt;Office&lt;/c0&gt; SharePoint Server 2007:
    </HitHighlightedSummary>
    <HitHighlightedProperties>&lt;HHTitle&gt;Home&lt;/HHTitle&gt;&lt;HHUrl&gt;
        http://moss&lt;/HHUrl&gt;
    </HitHighlightedProperties>
    <ContentClass>STS_Site</ContentClass>
    <IsDocument>0</IsDocument>
  </RelevantResults>
</Results>
```

Executing a query using the full SQL syntax allows you to specify exactly what you want to have returned; you also have the option to use search scopes and conditions for filtering the search results. The *ResponsePacket* for a query executed with the *Query* method therefore includes—on top of the default elements that are returned—the various properties defined in the SELECT part of the SQL statement. For each of these, there is a *Property* element containing the name, type, and value of the property. Here is an extract from it:

```
<ResponsePacket xmlns="urn:Microsoft.Search.Response">
  <Response domain="QDomain">
    <Range>
      <StartAt>1</StartAt>
      <Count>10</Count>
      <TotalAvailable>77</TotalAvailable>
      <Results>
        <Document xmlns="urn:Microsoft.Search.Response.Document">
        <Action>
          <LinkUrl>http://moss</LinkUrl>
        </Action>
        <Properties xmlns="urn:Microsoft.Search.Response.Document.Document">
          <Property>
            <Name>TITLE</Name>
            <Type>String</Type>
            <Value>Home</Value>
          </Property>
          <Property>
            <Name>PATH</Name>
            <Type>String</Type>
            <Value>http://moss</Value>
          </Property>
        </Document>
      </Results>
    </Range>
    <Status>SUCCESS</Status>
  </Response>
</ResponsePacket>
```

Executing queries is not the only option you have with the Query Web Service. There are two methods for returning metadata information that can be used when creating the query. This one returns the most information:

```
DataSet results = searchService.GetSearchMetadata();
```

The *GetSearchMetaData* returns an ADO.NET *DataSet* with two tables in it. One contains the list of search scopes, and the other contains the list of managed properties.

A second method, the *GetPortalSearchInfo*, returns an XML string that only contains the search scopes:

```
string results = searchService.GetPortalSearchInfo();
```

Take some time to experiment with the sample application, executing all kinds of queries and seeing the results either in the *DataGrid* or the Web Browser.

Custom Security Trimming

A last topic for this chapter is the creation of custom security trimmers that can act on the search results before they are displayed to the user. By default, a user will not see the search results originating from the SharePoint sites or shared folders for which he or she does not have the appropriate permissions. The index engine, while crawling, collects and stores the information out of the Access Control List (ACL) defined for the resource or container where the resource is stored. While searching, this information is being used by the search service, thus filtering the search results. But this is not the case for all of the different types of content sources administrators can create. For example, there is no security trimming for the results coming out of normal, non-SharePoint Web sites or for the business data indexed. It may also be a business requirement to execute more than what the index engine does by default. In the walkthrough, for example, you'll work out a scenario where administrators can store GUIDs of list instances that they do not want to appear in the search results for a specific user. The list of excluded list instances can be part of the profile of the user. You can think of many other types of specific business rules that may need to be applied before the search results are displayed to the user. That's exactly what a custom security trimmer allows you to do. We'll first have a look at some of the basics and then proceed to the walkthrough.

The *ISecurityTrimmer* Interface

The *ISecurityTrimmer* interface is defined in the *Microsoft.Office.Server.Search.Query* namespace and located in the *Microsoft.Office.Server.Search.dll*. There are two methods that have to be implemented: the *Initialize* method and the *CheckAccess* method.

The *Initialize* Method

This method is called at the time that the .NET assembly is loaded into the worker process. This means that the code written here is executed only once. It is typically the place where you specify values for some of the configuration properties that are defined at the time you register the custom security trimmer using the *stsadm* command line utility (discussed more later). These properties can then be used in the *CheckAccess* method that is called for each of the search results. For example, for performance reasons, you may want to limit the amount of crawled URLs to be processed by your custom security trimming code. Think of it— when performing a search query, thousands, even millions, of search results can be returned. If you are going to apply custom business logic for each of these search results before they get displayed to the user, you'll risk slowing down the whole process. You may want to let the administrator set a limit on the amount of URLs that need to be checked and then use that information before you execute the business logic. If there are too many URLs to check, you may want to notify the user that the search query needs to be refined.

The *CheckAccess* Method

This method is where all of your business logic that will trim the search results ends up. It is typically called each time a query is performed. All of the crawled URLs are passed as an instance of a *System.Collections.Generic.IList*. It is possible that the method is called multiple times per search session depending on the amount of search results returned. This is why you may want to limit the amount of results, as discussed previously. The second parameter that is passed to the method contains information that can be used to track information across multiple *CheckAccess* method calls for the same search query.

A typical flow within the method is to first retrieve information about the currently logged on user and any additional information as needed, such as the associated user profile values. All of this can be used while the search results are processing, and you have to tell SharePoint to display the result, *yes* or *no*, in the results page. For that reason, you'll notice a return value of type *System.Collections.BitArray* that contains a *true* or *false* value for every search result. Your job is to set this flag in the loop based on the outcome of your business logic.

Let's see all this in action.

Walkthrough: Building a Custom Security Trimmer

The goal of this walkthrough is to show the steps for building a small custom security trimmer that filters the search results before they are displayed, excluding the results of a list for which the GUID has been defined as part of the profile of the user performing the search. You can start by building a new class library project called *CustomSecurityTrimmerDemo* in Visual Studio.NET 2005. *InsideMOSS.Samples* is the namespace I'll be using for all of the types included in the assembly. Next, you'll need a couple of references to .NET assemblies that are required for the execution logic. The first one is the *Microsoft.Office.Server.dll*, because you're going to access the user profiles programmatically, and the second one is the *Microsoft.Office.Server.Search.dll.* There are a couple of *using* statements that are needed in addition to the ones already there for the class in this project:

```
using System.Collections.Specialized;
using System.Security.Principal;
using Microsoft.Office.Server;
using Microsoft.Office.Server.Search.Query;
using Microsoft.Office.Server.Search.Administration;
using Microsoft.Office.Server.UserProfiles;
```

A custom security trimmer class has to implement the *ISecurityTrimmer* interface with two methods: the *CheckAccess* method and the *Initialize* method. You'll use only the first one, but you have to make sure that the *Initialize* method returns something else instead of an exception. Here is the full class ready for the business logic that makes up the custom security trimming:

```
namespace InsideMOSS.Samples
{
    public class CustomTrimmer : ISecurityTrimmer
    {
        public System.Collections.BitArray CheckAccess
            (IList<string> documentCrawlUrls,
             IDictionary<string, object> sessionProperties)
        {
        }

        public void Initialize(NameValueCollection staticProperties,
            SearchContext searchContext)
        {
        }
    }
}
```

The *CheckAccess* method returns an instance of a *BitArray* type that simply contains a *true* or *false* value per search result that is returned by the search service. *True* means that it will be displayed to the user, while *false* means, of course, that it will be hidden from display. It is your job now to code your business rule and toggle these flags *on* or *off* depending on your scenario. Let's prepare the return value:

```
BitArray retArray = new BitArray(documentCrawlUrls.Count);
for (int x = 0; x < documentCrawlUrls.Count; x++)
  {
      retArray[x] = true;
  }
return retArray;
```

At this point, all of the results will be displayed. Inside the loop however, you'll first find out who the user is and retrieve his or her user profile. The following code shows how to do this:

```
string user = WindowsIdentity.GetCurrent().Name;
UserProfileManager profileManager = new UserProfileManager(ServerContext.Current);
UserProfile profile = profileManager.GetUserProfile(user);
```

The user profile can be extended with one additional custom property called *ExcludedListsFrom-SearchResults* that will store one or more GUIDs that identify the lists and the content inside that you want excluded from the search results. You'll have to use the administration site of your Shared Services Provider to create that user profile property. Refer back to Chapter 2 for an explanation of how to do this. Once the property is there, you can retrieve the value. If this is a multi-valued property, you'll have to write a small loop to process the array of GUIDs:

```
if (profile["ExcludedListsFromSearchResults"].Value != null)
{
    string[] excludedLists =
        profile["ExcludedListsFromSearchResults"].ToString().Split(';');
}
```

The search results are processed one by one within the main loop, and each of them is accessed by the first incoming parameter called *documentCrawlUrls*. This parameter contains an array built up out of strings, each of them representing the information concerning one of the search results. For a result indexed with the *sts3* protocol handler, that is, the Windows SharePoint Services 3.0 protocol handler, the string resembles the following:

```
sts3://moss/siteurl=/siteid={86051521-13de-4dac-80d1-231406b51b57}
/weburl=/webid={e67908fc-024b-4689-b854-4837d0d32abb}
/listid={30dc794a-c5b6-4c86-97f6-2ed65133149d}/viewid={efc86211-
96e2-4443-9dfc-5d8e42daf285}
```

The string is not delimited, but you can retrieve the *listid* out of the string using the following lines of code:

```
if (documentCrawlUrls[x].StartsWith("sts3") &&
    documentCrawlUrls[x].Contains("/listid="))
{
    int pos = documentCrawlUrls[x].IndexOf("/listid=");
    string listID = documentCrawlUrls[x].Substring(pos + 8, 38);
}
```

The only task left to finish the job is to check whether the GUID of the list in the *listID* variable is part of the list of GUIDs in the custom user profile property. Add these lines of code after the *listID* variable declaration:

```
foreach (string item in excludedLists)
{
  if (item.ToUpper() == listID.ToUpper())
  {
    retArray[x] = false;
  }
}
```

If there is a match, it means you do not want SharePoint to display the search results. There-fore, set the flag for that processed search result to *false*. In the real world, you'll probably add more meat to this code by encapsulating all of it in the proper exception handlers and perhaps adding more business logic to it. But for this walkthrough, we've done enough.

Now, let's prepare the .NET assembly for deployment. Since the *dll* has to be deployed in the Global Assembly Cache (GAC), you'll have to sign it. Adding the assembly to the GAC can be done by utilizing the *gacutil* command line utility after you've built the assembly:

```
gacutil /i CustomSecurityTrimmerDemo.dll
```

You have to register the .NET assembly as a custom security trimmer in order for SharePoint to take custom security trimmers into consideration. Before doing that, make sure you have a crawl rule defined that covers one or more of the content sources that are indexed. The following is the call to the *stsadm* command line utility that will register the trimmer:

```
stsadm -o registersecuritytrimmer -ssp SharedServices1 -id 1
  -typeName InsideMOSS.Samples.CustomTrimmer, CustomSecurityTrimmerDemo,
Version=1.0.0.0,Culture=Neutral, PublicKeyToken=4c04f619a71116ef"
-rulepath http://moss/*
```

Nothing really happens unless you restart IIS with a call to *IISRESET* from the command line and—don't forget—a full crawl for the content sources that the security trimmer is targeting and the crawl rule(s) for which the trimmer has been activated.

Test your trimmer by making sure you have a GUID of a SharePoint list as a value of the user profile property. When searching, none of the search results should contain resources from that list.

Summary

In this chapter, I've discussed plenty of topics that should have interested you if you enjoy search functionality. First, there was the discussion of the new search administration object model with plenty of opportunities to automate certain tasks that administrators normally perform while managing the Shared Services Provider Web site. You've also learned about options for customizing the Search Center and about the different Web Parts that, together, deliver the search experience to the user. I've also described the new classes to use when you want to programmatically execute the Enterprise search queries either directly on the machine where SharePoint is installed or remotely by using the Query Search Web Service. In the final part of the chapter, I explained the new additional security trimming layer that enables you to filter the search results based on custom business logic or security restrictions that you want to enable for a specific user or a group of users.

Chapter 4
Working with the Business Data Catalog

- Understand the architecture of the Business Data Catalog.
- Learn about the core elements of an application definition file.
- Learn the administration and configuration tasks involved.
- Learn about the out-of-the-box Business Data Web Parts, the search integration, and the Business Data field type.
- Learn how to programmatically create application definition files and how to build your own custom applications that consume business data.

Introducing the Business Data Catalog

A major job for many IT managers is the integration of numerous disparate systems and data islands that exist within an organization. As depicted in Figure 4-1, on the one hand, you have information workers that spend most of their time in personal productivity zones, such as the Microsoft Office client products and the different types of collaboration workspaces provisioned by Windows SharePoint Services. In these zones, people work with and handle unstructured data stored in places such as Office documents. On the other hand, many organizations have back-end systems that are designed to store information such as human resource data and sales or customer relationship data in a very structured way. These back-end systems also often sustain complete business processes that support the interaction with that data. We often refer to these systems as line-of-business (LOB) systems since they are usually extremely crucial to the proper functioning of the business as a whole. Examples of LOB systems include the various SAP systems, Siebel, PeopleSoft, the Microsoft CRM system, and many others.

Figure 4-1   The often wide gap between the unstructured world of the information workers and the structured world of the line-of-business systems

Integrating the unstructured world of the information workers and the structured world of the LOB systems is often a challenge for IT, always looking for better ways to integrate the two. Unlocking the data stored in the LOB systems is an important means for increasing the effectiveness and productivity of the business as a whole. In the past, solutions were commonly sought in custom development, and for SharePoint, we see a lot of companies building custom Web Parts that extend SharePoint pages to deliver the LOB data in the collaboration workspaces in a point-to-point way. Typically, the development of these Web Parts is an expensive effort because developers have to learn both sides of the integration (the SharePoint APIs and the LOB system APIs) to develop this type of solution. And whenever something changes, a lot of rework has to be done. Point-to-point connections are not popular as a model anymore, and there is a push in many companies today to deliver integration with more service-oriented architectures that work in layers and communicate in a more loosely coupled and declarative way.

Meet the Business Data Catalog (BDC). The Business Data Catalog is best described as a middle-layer software that bridges the gap between information workers and LOB systems in a very declarative, XML-based way. Figure 4-2 depicts this relationship.

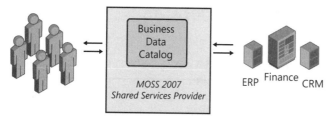

Figure 4-2   The BDC bridging the gap between the unstructured world and the structured world

That is to say, connecting the two ends using the Business Data Catalog enables IT to define an interface to the LOB system in one central place and unlock data to a lot of people in the collaborative workspaces and portals built with the new Windows SharePoint Services 3.0 and Microsoft Office SharePoint Server 2007. Out-of-the-box, a number of front-end Features are available, such as Web Parts and a new field type for the lists and document libraries, allowing power users within SharePoint sites to connect immediately to any of the LOB systems IT has interfaced with the BDC. No coding is involved at all. No knowledge required of how the external systems are working. Once an LOB system is integrated with the BDC, developers have the option to write custom code to access the data via the BDC object model. This means developers can access data in SAP, Siebel, etc. via the BDC API rather than having to learn different, non-consistent interfaces.

This chapter first discusses the architecture of the Business Data Catalog by explaining all of the different components that are involved. You'll learn how to create application definition files, work with the out-of-the-box Web Parts, enable your business application for search, and work with the lookups in your lists and document libraries. We'll conclude with an overview of how to connect to the Business Data Catalog in a programmatic—that is custom—way.

Business Data Catalog Architecture

Figure 4-3 summarizes the architecture behind the Business Data Catalog mapping out the many different components, each playing their own role in the story.

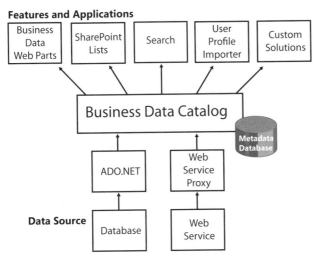

Figure 4-3   The BDC architecture

To start with, you have the connection layer to the external data sources. We sometimes also refer to the external data source as *the system*. Two options are available to connect to a system with the Business Data Catalog:

- An ADO.NET interface connects you to any traditional data store that supports a connection of type OLE-DB or ODBC. Examples are the Microsoft SQL Server database, a Microsoft Access database, and non-Microsoft databases such as Oracle.

- Data sources that are not reachable with an ADO.NET type of connection are accessible via a SOAP interface, meaning one or more Web Services that interact with the system and expose the data. Examples where you will be accessing the business data with Web Services are SAP, Siebel, or a Microsoft CRM type of system. The BDC generates a Web Service proxy based on information you supply in the metadata and uses an instance of it at run-time to interact with the Web Services.

The description of the business data you want to pull in via the Business Data Catalog can be stored in an XML file we refer to as the application definition file. We'll have a look at the internals later. But briefly, by means of a set of pre-defined XML elements, an *application definition file* describes the connection details to the external data source and the list of entities (for example *product, customer, order*) to work with. Additionally, it contains all of the details to get to this data, find the data, and enumerate it. And to conclude, in the application definition file you'll find actions that can be performed with the entity instances and the possible associations between the various entities.

Once the system has been modeled, the application definition file is imported in the Business Data Catalog metadata database. Since the BDC is delivered as a shared service, the place where administrators can get this done is the administration site of the Shared Services Provider (SSP). The metadata repository is part of the databases that are created and used by the Shared Services Provider.

Once the application definition file is imported, all of the artifacts are represented as database records, and it is possible for administrators to do some configuration and administration work around it as we will discuss later. The business applications made available in the BDC are exposed by a runtime API that is internally used to drive the BDC engine, but the API is also exposed to the developers that build front-ends for integrating the business data into the SharePoint pages and custom applications. With the runtime API, one can browse the metadata, execute methods, retrieve instances, and traverse the relationships that have been set up between the entities in the application definition file. An explanation and scenarios for using this runtime API along with the administration API are discussed at the end of the chapter.

Application Definition Files

Application definition files are your starting point when designing an integration with an external system—be it a traditional database or a line-of-business (LOB) system. These XML-based files follow a schema, the *bdcmetadata.xsd*, that can be found in the C:\Program Files\Microsoft Office Servers\12.0\Bin folder.

> **Note**   At the time of this writing, there are very few designers available to help with the design of the application definition file. One community project, the *MetaData Manager for the Microsoft Office SharePoint Server Business Data Catalog* (http://www.bdcmetaman.com), is headed in the right direction. The schema itself, though, can help you in Microsoft Visual Studio.NET 2005 to enable Intellisense in the XML editor. To get Intellisense to work, drag-and-drop the .xsd in the designer and in the root node of the XML hook up with the schema.

The Microsoft Office SharePoint Server 2007 software developer kit (SDK) contains a full description of every XML element you can use within the application definition file along with the various attributes associated with each of the elements. It's not my goal to duplicate all of that information here in the book. What I'll do is cover the core metadata elements using two sample application definition files that you can find on the companion Web site that accompanies the book. The first application definition file, called *AdventureWorks_HumanResources.xml*, is an illustration of how to connect to data stored in a SQL Server database. The second, *SampleWebServiceMetadata.xml*, deals with customers and orders and follows the Web Service approach—useful in scenarios where you connect to an LOB system such as SAP or Microsoft CRM.

The *LobSystem* Element

The root element of an application definition file is the *LobSystem* element. This element identifies the business application or the system you want to model within the metadata file. Here is an example of the element being the root of the application definition file working with the AdventureWorks human resource data:

```
<LobSystem xmlns:xsi="http://www.w3.org/2001/XMLSchema-instance"
xsi:schemaLocation="http://schemas.microsoft.com/office/2006/03/
BusinessDataCatalog BDCMetadata.xsd" Type="Database" Version="1.0.0.0"
  Name="Human Resources Data"
  xmlns="http://schemas.microsoft.com/office/2006/03/BusinessDataCatalog">
...
</LobSystem>
```

The *Type* attribute above has the value *Database*, which basically tells the Business Data Catalog that it has to use the ADO.NET interface to connect to the external system. Giving *WebService* as the value of the *Type* attribute makes a connection to the business data via a generated Web Service proxy. Other attributes for the *LobSystem* element are the *Name* and *Version*.

The *LobSystem* Properties

Property elements are used all over the place in the application definition file. Properties are a means to define in a dynamic way the parameters and values for the parent elements in which they are nested. So, for example, at the level of the *LobSystem* element, *Property* elements can be nested under the *Properties* element and provide needed additional metadata. A property you can create is one called *WildcardCharacter*:

```
<Properties>
 <Property Name="WildcardCharacter" Type="System.String">%</Property>
</Properties>
```

When requesting data from the system, users are able to use wildcards for the values of the filters defined later in the application definition file. The above property is recognized by the BDC and orders it to replace the traditional * character with the %, the one required by Microsoft SQL Server.

In case you are working with a Web Service, two additional properties are declared:

```
<Property Name="WebServiceProxyNamespace" Type="System.String">
  ProxyName
</Property>
<Property Name="WsdlFetchUrl" Type="System.String">
  AsmxOrWSDLurl
</Property>
```

The Business Data Catalog creates a Web Service proxy at runtime, connecting it to the Web Service that exposes the business data. This proxy is a .NET class that is going to live in a certain namespace whose name is specified by the *WebServiceProxyNamespace* property in the application definition file. The second property, the *WsdlFetchUrl*, points the Business Data Catalog to the Web Service itself (the asmx file) or the Web Service Description Language (WSDL) file. Both are used in the generation of the Web Service proxy. The SDK documents a number of additional properties that can be included here.

The *LobSystemInstance* Element

The next element is a child element of the *LobSystem* root element. The *LobSystemInstances* element contains one or more *LobSystemInstance* elements. With these elements, you'll get a bit more physical with the system modeled in the application definition file. That is to say, again using a collection of *Property* elements, you're going to provide the specific security and authentication settings and parameters to allow the BDC to actually connect to the system. For a database type of application definition, it can be as follows:

```
<LobSystemInstances>
 <LobSystemInstance Name="HR">
  <Properties>
    <Property Name="AuthenticationMode" Type="Microsoft.Office.
Server.ApplicationRegistry.SystemSpecific.Db.DbAuthenticationMode">
      PassThrough</Property>
    <Property Name="DatabaseAccessProvider" Type="Microsoft.Office.Server.
ApplicationRegistry.SystemSpecific.Db.DbAccessProvider">
      SqlServer</Property>
    <Property Name="RdbConnection Data Source" Type="System.String">
      MOSSDB
    </Property>
  <Property Name="RdbConnection Initial Catalog" Type="System.String">
    AdventureWorks</Property>
  <Property Name="RdbConnection Integrated Security"
    Type="System.String">SSPI</Property>
 </Properties>
 </LobSystemInstance>
</LobSystemInstances>
```

The properties used simply define a connection to the AdventureWorks SQL Server 2005 database running on a server named *MOSSDB*. The authentication is done using the *PassThrough* option, indicating to the BDC to take the account of the currently logged-on user and use that account to authenticate against the SQL Server. It is also possible to pass explicit credentials by setting the *AuthenticationMode* property to *Credentials* or use single sign-on (SSO) to drive the authentication by setting the *AuthenticationMode* property to *Windows-Credentials*. The *PassThrough* and the *SSO* options are the recommended approach. Here is an example of the SSO approach:

```
<LobSystemInstances>
    <LobSystemInstance Name="AdventureWorksSampleSSO">
      <Properties>
        <Property Name="AuthenticationMode"
            Type="System.String">WindowsCredentials</Property>
        <Property Name="DatabaseAccessProvider"
            Type="System.String">SqlServer</Property>
```

```
         <Property Name="RdbConnection Data Source"
              Type="System.String">
              YourAdventureWorks2000ServerNameHere
         </Property>
         <Property Name="RdbConnection Initial Catalog"
              Type="System.String">
              AdventureWorks2000
         </Property>
         <Property Name="RdbConnection Integrated Security"
              Type="System.String">SSPI</Property>
         <Property Name="RdbConnection Pooling"
              Type="System.String">false</Property>
         <Property Name="SsoApplicationId"
              Type="System.String">AdventureWorks</Property>
         <Property Name="SsoProviderImplementation"
              Type="System.String">Microsoft.SharePoint.Portal.
              SingleSignon.SpsSsoProvider,
              Microsoft.SharePoint.Portal.SingleSignon,
              Version=12.0.0.0, Culture=neutral,
              PublicKeyToken=71e9bce111e9429c</Property>
      </Properties>
   </LobSystemInstance>
 </LobSystemInstances>
```

For a Web Service, the connection details are defined at the level of the properties associated directly with the *LobSystem* element. So, for the *LobSystemInstance* element, you only have to optionally provide the authentication mode to be used. This is done using the *WebService-AuthenticationMode* property, which can basically receive the same values as discussed previously with the properties for the database connection. Here is an example:

```
<LobSystemInstance Name="SampleWebServiceInstance">
   <Properties>
    <Property Name="WebServiceAuthenticationMode"
         Type="System.String">PassThrough</Property>
   </Properties>
</LobSystemInstance>
```

The *Entity* Element

One of the core elements within the application definition file is definitely the *Entity* element. As a child element of the *LobSystem* root element, the *Entities* element can contain one or more *Entity* elements, each of them mapping to the business objects you want to work with. Here is an example definition of the *Employee* and *Department* entities:

```
<Entities>
   <Entity Name="Employee"></Entity>
   <Entity Name="Department"></Entity>
</Entities>
```

Entities contain identifiers, methods, and actions. And as we will see later, you can also associate entities with other related entities.

The Entity Identifier

Identifier elements are required in order to be able to connect to the business data and have the front-ends (for example the Business Data Web Parts) search and find and perform actions on the entity instances. Typically, in a database-driven system, the identifier points to a primary key. Here is how you define an *Identifier* element:

```
<Entity Name="Employee">
  <Identifiers>
    <Identifier Name="EmployeeID" TypeName="System.Int32" />
  </Identifiers>
</Entity>
```

For the *Employee* entity in this case, the identifier is the *EmployeeID* of type *System.Int32* because it is defined as type *int* in the SQL Server database.

The *Method* Element

The *Methods* element is the one to add as a child element of the *Entity*, containing one or more *Method* elements. Each of these *Method* elements store the definition of a possible operation one can do with the entity.

```
<Entity Name="Employee">
...
  <Methods>
    <Method Name="GetEmployees"></Method>
  </Methods>
</Entity>
```

The methods for the entities will typically be retrieving data, but it is possible to also define methods for updating data. However, very often, updating data involves some kind of validation and business logic to be executed, and therefore the best place for users to perform update operations is outside of the BDC with custom front-ends accessible with actions defined at the level of the entity.

If you look in the *AdventureWorks_HumanResources.xml*, you'll find the *Employee* entity with one method defining how to retrieve the employees, possibly with some filtering applied to it. For the *Department* entity, we have pretty much the same type of operation, one to retrieve the departments again with a possible filtering value. A second method for the *Department* entity is the *GetEmployeesForDepartment*. This is the method that will be called when a user follows the association between the *Department* and the *Employee* entity, which we'll define later.

In the *SampleWebServicesMetadata.xml*, there are methods such as *GetCustomers*, *GetCustomerByID*, *GetOrdersForCustomerAndRegion*, and more. The definition at the level of the *Method* element is the same as with the database-type of application definition file, but of course we map here to the Web Methods exposed by the Web Service.

The *Method* Properties

Property elements are used again here at the level of the *Method* element to provide the dynamic type of information for the Business Data Catalog. For a system of type *Database*, add the *RdbCommandType* and the *RdbCommandText* properties. Together, both map the method to the SQL statement or stored procedure that the BDC must execute to get to the data. The first one is the definition of the type of query, *Text* or *StoredProcedure,* and the second one is the actual statement or name of the stored procedure.

For the *GetEmployees* method, the SQL statement is as follows:

```
<Method Name="GetEmployees">
 <Properties>
   <Property Name="RdbCommandText" Type="System.String">
     SELECT  *
       FROM   HumanResources.vEmployee
       WHERE ( EmployeeID &gt;= @MinEmployeeID AND
               EmployeeID &lt;= @MaxEmployeeID)
               AND LastName LIKE @LastName
   </Property>
   <Property Name="RdbCommandType" Type="System.Data.CommandType">
     Text</Property>
 </Properties>
</Method>
```

At first glance, the above SQL can be a little confusing because of the many parameters. The goal, however, is to retrieve employees, one or many, using the *EmployeeID* and/or the *Last-Name* as a filter. All of these options are possible with this SQL statement. Later on, we'll explain the details of all of these parameters.

The *Department* entity has a method *GetDepartments* that basically follows the same approach.

```
<Method Name="GetDepartments">
 <Properties>
  <Property Name="RdbCommandText" Type="System.String">
    SELECT DepartmentID, Name
    FROM HumanResources.Department
    WHERE (DepartmentID &gt;= @MinDepartmentID AND
           DepartmentID &lt;= @MaxDepartmentID)
           AND Name LIKE @Name
  </Property>
  <Property Name="RdbCommandType" Type="System.Data.CommandType">
     Text</Property>
 </Properties>
</Method>
```

The final method to map to a SQL statement is the *GetEmployeesForDepartment.* The statement to execute is a bit more complex since there are some joins that have to be performed. The only parameter used here is the *DepartmentID.* This method is called by the BDC when there is a request for retrieving all of the employees working in a particular department—that is a request working with the *Association,* and I'll explain in a moment. It is not meant to be a method that is directly called by users.

```
<Method Name="GetEmployeesForDepartment">
 <Properties>
   <Property Name="RdbCommandText" Type="System.String">
    SELECT  e.EmployeeID, c.FirstName, c.LastName,
            e.Title AS JobTitle, d.Name AS Department
    FROM    HumanResources.Employee AS e INNER JOIN
            Person.Contact AS c ON c.ContactID = e.ContactID INNER JOIN
            HumanResources.EmployeeDepartmentHistory AS edh
            ON e.EmployeeID = edh.EmployeeID
            INNER JOIN HumanResources.Department AS d
            ON edh.DepartmentID = d.DepartmentID
    WHERE   (GETDATE() BETWEEN edh.StartDate AND
            ISNULL(edh.EndDate, GETDATE()))
            AND (d.DepartmentID = @DepartmentID)
   </Property>
   <Property Name="RdbCommandType" Type="System.Data.CommandType">
      Text</Property>
 </Properties>
</Method>
```

For the application definition file describing the business data retrieved through the Web Service, you do not find any *Property* elements since the name of the *Method* element maps to the name of the Web Method as defined in the Web Service WSDL.

The *FilterDescriptor* Element

We've talked about the filters for the methods. Each of them must now be further detailed in the application definition file using *FilterDescriptor* elements. All of the *FilterDescriptor* elements are collected in a *FilterDescriptors* element, a child element of the *Method* element. Here is the list of *FilterDescriptor* elements for the *GetEmployees* method of the *Employee* entity.

```
<Method Name="GetEmployees">
 …
 <FilterDescriptors>
  <FilterDescriptor Type="Comparison" Name="EmployeeID" />
  <FilterDescriptor Type="Wildcard" Name="LastName">
    <Properties>
     <Property Name="UsedForDisambiguation" Type="System.Boolean">
      true</Property>
    </Properties>
  </FilterDescriptor>
 </FilterDescriptors>
</Method>
```

You give each of the filters a name as it will appear to the users in the Business Data Web Parts (see later). The *UsedForDisambiguation* property, a property of the *FilterDescriptor* with the name *LastName* above, is used by the Business Data Picker control and the Business Data Web Parts to generate the list of matching candidates to the filter.

The value for the *Type* attribute is very important in the definition of the *FilterDescriptor*. You have two categories of filtering patterns as an option.

User Filters   *User filters* are filters that can be set by the user. Most of the Business Data Web parts can display controls that accept values for the filters. Examples of user filters include the *wildcard, comparison,* and *limit* filters. The *wildcard* is a type of filtering pattern that gives users filters such as *starts with* and *contains.* For the *Employee* entity, the application definition contains a *FilterDescriptor* of this type to enable a *wildcard* filter on the last name of the employee. The *comparison* filter can be used to define a condition restraining the number of instances returned for the entity. SQL supports it with the WHERE clause. This is the filter to use when looking for an exact match, such as *EmployeeID = 1.* And finally, the *limit* filter is a useful filtering pattern if you want to limit the number of instances returned. SQL supports it with the SELECT TOP clause.

System Filters   *System Filters* are set by the Business Data Catalog and retrieve context information that is used either for a filter value or some security setting. Examples of the former type are the *UserContext* and the *UserProfile* type of filters. The *UserContext* is a filtering pattern that can limit the instances with the current user's context, appending the current Microsoft Windows user's domain/username to the method call. The *UserProfile* filter is a simple filter type you can specify in the *FilterDescriptor* definition to connect to a user profile property. You have to add a *System.String* property with the name *UserProfilePropertyName,* whose value is the name of a user profile property. The Business Data Catalog will look up the current user's profile, read the value of the property with this name, and plumb that through to the back-end invocation. Other system filters work with security information. Examples are the *UserName, Password,* and *SSOTicket* filter. The *UserName* filter limits the instances by a single sign-on (SSO) user name. This filter tells the Business Data Catalog to pass the user name from SSO as part of a parameter to the method call. The *Password* filter works in association with the *UserName* filter and tells the Business Data Catalog to pass the password from SSO as part of a parameter to the method call. The last one, the *SSOTicket* filter, tells the Business Data Catalog to pass the SSO ticket from SSO as part of a parameter to the method call.

The *FilterDescriptor* elements for the *GetDepartments* method of the *Department* entity look similar to the ones previously discussed.

```
<Method Name="GetDepartments">
...
<FilterDescriptors>
  <FilterDescriptor Type="Comparison" Name="DepartmentID" />
   <FilterDescriptor Type="Wildcard" Name="Name">
    <Properties>
     <Property Name="UsedForDisambiguation" Type="System.Boolean">
       true</Property>
    </Properties>
   </FilterDescriptor>
</FilterDescriptors>
</Method>
```

We do not have any *FilterDescriptor* elements for the last method, the *GetEmployeesForDepartment* of the *Department* entity, since this method is not supposed to be called by the users directly.

For the Web Service, you'll find similar definitions of *FilterDescriptor* elements. This is the one for the *GetCustomers* method at the level of the *Customer* entity:

```
<Method Name="GetCustomers">
  <FilterDescriptors>
    <FilterDescriptor Type="Wildcard" Name="Name" />
    <FilterDescriptor Type="Limit" Name="Limit" />
  </FilterDescriptors>
```

The *Parameter* Element

The next metadata definition blocks are all fairly large. They are the definitions of the parameters describing the *In*, *Out*, and *Return* details for each of the methods. The *Parameter* element itself is a child of the *Parameters* element, by itself a child element of the *Entity* element. Here is the definition of the *in* parameters for the *GetEmployees* method of the *Employee* entity:

```
<Method Name="GetEmployees">
...
 <Parameters>
  <Parameter Direction="In" Name="@MinEmployeeID">
   <TypeDescriptor TypeName="System.Int32" IdentifierName="EmployeeID"
       AssociatedFilter="EmployeeID" Name="MinEmployeeID">
    <DefaultValues>
     <DefaultValue MethodInstanceName="EmployeeFinderInstance"
     Type="System.Int32">0</DefaultValue>
    </DefaultValues>
   </TypeDescriptor>
  </Parameter>
  <Parameter Direction="In" Name="@MaxEmployeeID">
   <TypeDescriptor TypeName="System.Int32" IdentifierName="EmployeeID"
    AssociatedFilter="EmployeeID" Name="MaxEmployeeID">
    <DefaultValues>
      <DefaultValue MethodInstanceName="EmployeeFinderInstance"
      Type="System.Int32">99999</DefaultValue>
    </DefaultValues>
   </TypeDescriptor>
  </Parameter>
  <Parameter Direction="In" Name="@LastName">
    <TypeDescriptor TypeName="System.String"
     AssociatedFilter="LastName" Name="LastName">
    <DefaultValues>
      <DefaultValue MethodInstanceName="EmployeeFinderInstance"
      Type="System.String">%</DefaultValue>
      <DefaultValue MethodInstanceName="EmployeeSpecificFinderInstance"
      Type="System.String">%</DefaultValue>
    </DefaultValues>
   </TypeDescriptor>
  </Parameter>
```

For the first three *Parameter* elements, the *Direction* attribute is set to the value *In* indicating that they are the definitions for the input parameters. Each of them gets a value for the *Name* attribute, the same as the parameter name in the SQL statement, for example @*LastName*. The details of the parameter are provided by inserting a child element of type *TypeDescriptor*. This element has a *Name* attribute that must exactly match the name of the column in the

SQL Server table. In addition, you have the type of the parameter and a link to the *Identifier* element. In the case that the parameter represents the unique key of the entity, there is the attribute *IdentifierName* that points to the corresponding *Identifier* element. The last attribute of the *Parameter* element is the *AssociatedFilter* attribute that links the parameter with the *FilterDescriptor* element defined for the entity. A set of *DefaultValue* elements are added as child elements of the *FilterDescriptor* element. These values are linked to the *MethodInstance* elements, which will be explained in a moment. The default values are used for the execution of the method if no value is supplied by the user.

Next, you have the definition of the *Return* parameter:

```
<Parameter Direction="Return" Name="Employees">
  <TypeDescriptor TypeName="System.Data.IDataReader, System.Data,
Version=2.0.3600.0, Culture=neutral, PublicKeyToken=b77a5c561934e089"
    IsCollection="true" Name="EmployeeDataReader">
      <TypeDescriptors>
        <TypeDescriptor TypeName="System.Data.IDataRecord, System.Data,
Version=2.0.3600.0, Culture=neutral, PublicKeyToken=b77a5c561934e089"
          Name="EmployeeDataRecord">
        <TypeDescriptors>
          <TypeDescriptor TypeName="System.Int32"
            IdentifierName="EmployeeID" Name="EmployeeID">
            <LocalizedDisplayNames>
             <LocalizedDisplayName LCID="1033">
                 Employee ID</LocalizedDisplayName>
            </LocalizedDisplayNames>
          </TypeDescriptor>
          <TypeDescriptor TypeName="System.String" Name="FirstName">
            <LocalizedDisplayNames>
               <LocalizedDisplayName LCID="1033">
                 First Name</LocalizedDisplayName>
            </LocalizedDisplayNames>
            <Properties>
             <Property Name="DisplayByDefault" Type="System.Boolean">
              true</Property>
            </Properties>
          </TypeDescriptor>
          <TypeDescriptor TypeName="System.String" Name="LastName">
          <LocalizedDisplayNames>
             <LocalizedDisplayName LCID="1033">
               Last Name</LocalizedDisplayName>
          </LocalizedDisplayNames>
          <Properties>
             <Property Name="DisplayByDefault" Type="System.Boolean">
              true</Property>
            </Properties>
          </TypeDescriptor>
          <TypeDescriptor TypeName="System.String" Name="JobTitle">
           <LocalizedDisplayNames>
             <LocalizedDisplayName LCID="1033">
               Job Title</LocalizedDisplayName>
            </LocalizedDisplayNames>
            <Properties>
             <Property Name="DisplayByDefault" Type="System.Boolean">
              true</Property>
```

```
            </Properties>
          </TypeDescriptor>
          <TypeDescriptor TypeName="System.String" Name="Phone">
           <LocalizedDisplayNames>
            <LocalizedDisplayName LCID="1033">
             Phone</LocalizedDisplayName>
           </LocalizedDisplayNames>
           <Properties>
            <Property Name="DisplayByDefault" Type="System.Boolean">
             true</Property>
           </Properties>
          </TypeDescriptor>
          <TypeDescriptor TypeName="System.String" Name="EmailAddress">
           <LocalizedDisplayNames>
            <LocalizedDisplayName LCID="1033">
              Email</LocalizedDisplayName>
           </LocalizedDisplayNames>
           <Properties>
            <Property Name="DisplayByDefault" Type="System.Boolean">
             true</Property>
           </Properties>
          </TypeDescriptor>
         </TypeDescriptors>
        </TypeDescriptor>
       </TypeDescriptors>
      </TypeDescriptor>
    </Parameter>
   </Parameters>
</Method>
```

The second type of *Parameter* element is the element with the *Direction* attribute set to *Return*. For this element, we define what will be returned as fields of the entity instances to the Business Data Catalog. As a first child element, a *TypeDescriptor* indicates to the BDC in what form it will receive the data. If connecting directly to a Microsoft SQL Server database, this is typically set to an object of the type *IDataReader*, a conventional ADO.NET interface object. With the stream, one by one, the BDC will receive objects of type *IDataRecord*. What you'll find as the bulk of the body of the *Parameter* element is the definition of an *IDataRecord* object and how it is built up with columns and localized labels. For every column, a *TypeDescriptor* element is used with the option to localize the display name of the column with the *LocalizedDisplayName* element and the *DisplayByDefault* property indicating to the BDC to always show this column by default.

The definition of the parameters for the *GetDepartments* method of the *Department* entity is basically the same:

```
<Method Name="GetDepartments">
...
 <Parameters>
  <Parameter Direction="In" Name="@MinDepartmentID">
    <TypeDescriptor TypeName="System.Int16" IdentifierName="DepartmentID"
      AssociatedFilter="DepartmentID" Name="MinDepartmentID">
      <DefaultValues>
        <DefaultValue MethodInstanceName="DepartmentFinderInstance"
         Type="System.Int16">0</DefaultValue>
```

```xml
          </DefaultValues>
        </TypeDescriptor>
      </Parameter>
      <Parameter Direction="In" Name="@MaxDepartmentID">
        <TypeDescriptor TypeName="System.Int16" IdentifierName="DepartmentID"
            AssociatedFilter="DepartmentID" Name="MaxDepartmentID">
          <DefaultValues>
            <DefaultValue MethodInstanceName="DepartmentFinderInstance"
              Type="System.Int16">999</DefaultValue>
          </DefaultValues>
        </TypeDescriptor>
      </Parameter>
      <Parameter Direction="In" Name="@Name">
        <TypeDescriptor TypeName="System.String" AssociatedFilter="Name"
          Name="Name">
         <DefaultValues>
           <DefaultValue MethodInstanceName="DepartmentFinderInstance"
             Type="System.String">%</DefaultValue>
           <DefaultValue MethodInstanceName="DepartmentSpecificFinderInstance"
             Type="System.String">%</DefaultValue>
         </DefaultValues>
        </TypeDescriptor>
      </Parameter>
      <Parameter Direction="Return" Name="Departments">
        <TypeDescriptor TypeName="System.Data.IDataReader, System.Data,
Version=2.0.3600.0, Culture=neutral, PublicKeyToken=b77a5c561934e089"
          IsCollection="true" Name="DepartmentDataReader">
         <TypeDescriptors>
           <TypeDescriptor TypeName="System.Data.IDataRecord, System.Data,
Version=2.0.3600.0, Culture=neutral, PublicKeyToken=b77a5c561934e089"
             Name="DepartmentDataRecord">
            <TypeDescriptors>
              <TypeDescriptor TypeName="System.Int16"
                IdentifierName="DepartmentID" Name="DepartmentID">
                <LocalizedDisplayNames>
                  <LocalizedDisplayName LCID="1033">
                     Department ID</LocalizedDisplayName>
                </LocalizedDisplayNames>
              </TypeDescriptor>
              <TypeDescriptor TypeName="System.String" Name="Name">
               <LocalizedDisplayNames>
                 <LocalizedDisplayName LCID="1033">
                    Department</LocalizedDisplayName>
               </LocalizedDisplayNames>
               <Properties>
                 <Property Name="DisplayByDefault" Type="System.Boolean">
                    true</Property>
               </Properties>
              </TypeDescriptor>
             </TypeDescriptors>
            </TypeDescriptor>
          </TypeDescriptors>
         </TypeDescriptor>
      </Parameter>
    </Parameters>
  </Method>
```

For the last method, the *GetEmployeesForDepartment* of the *Department* entity, the *Parameter* elements are almost the same except that we have no *FilterDescriptor* associations here.

```xml
<Method Name="GetDepartments">
…
 <Parameters>
   <Parameter Direction="In" Name="@DepartmentID">
     <TypeDescriptor TypeName="System.Int16"
      IdentifierName="DepartmentID" Name="DepartmentID" />
   </Parameter>
   <Parameter Direction="Return" Name="EmployeesForDepartment">
     <TypeDescriptor TypeName="System.Data.IDataReader, System.Data,
Version=2.0.3600.0, Culture=neutral, PublicKeyToken=b77a5c561934e089"
      IsCollection="true" Name="EmployeesForDepartmentDataReader">
     <TypeDescriptors>
     <TypeDescriptor TypeName="System.Data.IDataRecord, System.Data,
Version=2.0.3600.0, Culture=neutral, PublicKeyToken=b77a5c561934e089"
       Name="EmployeesForDepartmentDataRecord">
      <TypeDescriptors>
        <TypeDescriptor TypeName="System.Int32"
          IdentifierEntityName="Employee" IdentifierName="EmployeeID"
          Name="EmployeeID">
         <LocalizedDisplayNames>
           <LocalizedDisplayName LCID="1033">
             Employee ID</LocalizedDisplayName>
         </LocalizedDisplayNames>
        </TypeDescriptor>
        <TypeDescriptor TypeName="System.String" Name="FirstName">
         <LocalizedDisplayNames>
          <LocalizedDisplayName LCID="1033">
            First Name</LocalizedDisplayName>
         </LocalizedDisplayNames>
         <Properties>
          <Property Name="DisplayByDefault" Type="System.Boolean">
            true</Property>
         </Properties>
        </TypeDescriptor>
        <TypeDescriptor TypeName="System.String" Name="LastName">
         <LocalizedDisplayNames>
          <LocalizedDisplayName LCID="1033">Last Name</LocalizedDisplayName>
         </LocalizedDisplayNames>
         <Properties>
          <Property Name="DisplayByDefault" Type="System.Boolean">
            true</Property>
         </Properties>
        </TypeDescriptor>
        <TypeDescriptor TypeName="System.String" Name="JobTitle">
          <LocalizedDisplayNames>
           <LocalizedDisplayName LCID="1033">
             Job Title</LocalizedDisplayName>
          </LocalizedDisplayNames>
         <Properties>
          <Property Name="DisplayByDefault" Type="System.Boolean">
             true</Property>
         </Properties>
```

```
        </TypeDescriptor>
        <TypeDescriptor TypeName="System.String" Name="Department">
          <LocalizedDisplayNames>
           <LocalizedDisplayName LCID="1033">
              Department</LocalizedDisplayName>
          </LocalizedDisplayNames>
          <Properties>
           <Property Name="DisplayByDefault" Type="System.Boolean">
            true</Property>
          </Properties>
         </TypeDescriptor>
        </TypeDescriptors>
       </TypeDescriptor>
      </TypeDescriptors>
     </TypeDescriptor>
   </Parameter>
   </Parameters>
</Method>
```

For the first *TypeDescriptor* element of the *Parameter* defining the structure of the return values, there is one attribute we've not used before. The *EmployeeID* parameter is an identifier of the *Employee* entity, not an identifier of the *Department* entity. So you must switch to another *Entity* element here in the definition. The *IdentifierEntityName* attribute enables you to tell the BDC to use the identifier information from the entity that is set as the value.

The application definition file for the business data coming in via the Web Service follows pretty much the same flow. Here is the definition of the *Parameter* elements for the *GetCustomers* method:

```
<Parameters>
   <Parameter Direction="In" Name="name">
   <TypeDescriptor TypeName="System.String"
     AssociatedFilter="Name" Name="name" />
   </Parameter>
   <Parameter Direction="In" Name="limit">
    <TypeDescriptor TypeName="System.Int32"
      AssociatedFilter="Limit" Name="limit" />
   </Parameter>
   <Parameter Direction="Return" Name="Customers">
     <TypeDescriptor TypeName="SampleWebServiceProxy.Customer[],
       SampleWebService" IsCollection="true" Name="ArrayOfCustomer">
       <TypeDescriptors>
         <TypeDescriptor TypeName="SampleWebServiceProxy.Customer,
         SampleWebService" Name="Customer">
          <TypeDescriptors>
            <TypeDescriptor TypeName="System.String"
              IdentifierName="CustomerID" Name="CustomerID" />
            <TypeDescriptor TypeName="System.String" Name="Name" />
            <TypeDescriptor TypeName="System.Int64"
                Name="WorkPhoneNumber" />
            <TypeDescriptor TypeName="System.Int64"
                Name="MobilePhoneNumber" />
            <TypeDescriptor TypeName="System.String" Name="Industry" />
```

```
          <TypeDescriptor TypeName="System.String" Name="WebSite" />
        </TypeDescriptors>
      </TypeDescriptor>
    </TypeDescriptors>
  </TypeDescriptor>
  </Parameter>
</Parameters>
```

The difference is the definition of the *TypeDescriptor* elements for the return parameter. As mentioned at the beginning of this section, the Business Data Catalog generates a Web Service proxy to access the Web Service. Here, the first *TypeDescriptor* defines the type that will be returned, in this case an array of customers: *SampleWebServiceProxy.Customer[]*. The second *TypeDescriptor* element defines what each object in that array is all about; in our case, each object is of type *SampleWebServiceProxy.Customer*. The remaining *TypeDescriptor* elements just detail each of the fields of a *Customer* instance.

The *MethodInstance* Element

MethodInstance elements are added to the application definition file to define how the *Method* objects are to be used by the Business Data Catalog. For example, you can have multiple *MethodInstance* elements for one method, each defining a possible call with supplied default values.

The *MethodInstance* elements found in the first application definition file are immediately identified by the Business Data Catalog as specific methods that can be called when the user performs certain operations within the front-end user interface components that interact with the BDC.

```
<Method Name="GetEmployees">
...

  <MethodInstances>
    <MethodInstance Name="EmployeeFinderInstance" Type="Finder"
     ReturnParameterName="Employees" />
   <MethodInstance Name="EmployeeSpecificFinderInstance"
     Type="SpecificFinder" ReturnParameterName="Employees" />
  </MethodInstances>
</Method>

<Method Name="GetDepartments">
...

  <MethodInstances>
   <MethodInstance Name="DepartmentFinderInstance" Type="Finder"
     ReturnParameterName="Departments" />
   <MethodInstance Name="DepartmentSpecificFinderInstance"
     Type="SpecificFinder" ReturnParameterName="Departments" />
  </MethodInstances>
</Method>
```

The *MethodInstance* elements of type *Finder* are needed by the Business Data List Web Part in order to return the results for a query that users execute or administrators prepare with a view.

In the case of the *GetDepartments* method, for example, you associate this method with the *MethodInstance* named *DepartmentFinderInstance* for the input parameter called *@Name*.

MethodInstance elements of type *SpecificFinder* return one instance and are typically associated with the *Parameter* elements that are connected with *FilterDescriptors* of type *Comparison*.

The *Association* Element

The next block of metadata you can add to the application definition file is the definition of associations between entities. For example, in the database-type of application definition file, you can find an association between the *Employee* and the *Department* entity:

```
<Associations>
  <Association AssociationMethodEntityName="Department"
   AssociationMethodName="GetEmployeesForDepartment"
   AssociationMethodReturnParameterName="EmployeesForDepartment"
   Name="DepartmentToEmployees" IsCached="true">
    <SourceEntity Name="Department" />
    <DestinationEntity Name="Employee" />
  </Association>
</Associations>
```

An *Associations* element can be added directly as a child element under the *LobSystem* element. You can add an *Association* element for each association you want between entities. Different attributes are used to detail the association. The *AssociationMethodEntityName* attribute tells the BDC where it can find the method to be executed when the associated entity instances are requested. The method name itself is defined as a value of the *AssociationMethodName* and uses the *AssociationMethodReturnParameterName* to point to the parameter of type *Return*, which further defines the details of the entity instances to be retrieved. As child elements of the *Association* element, you have the two players in the association: the *SourceEntity* and the *DestinationEntity*. In our example, we describe a relation between the *Department* towards the *Employee* entity. The *Department* entity is thus the source entity, and the *Employee* is the destination.

Importing Application Definition Files

Application definition files created as XML files have to be imported in the Business Data Catalog metadata repository. As we'll see at the end of the chapter, you can also programmatically communicate to the metadata repository and build up the metadata objects one by one in a custom application.

The place to be is the Shared Services Provider administration site where you have the Business Data Catalog section with the links to the various administration pages. One of these links is the Import Application Definition, displayed in Figure 4-4.

Figure 4-4   The administration site of the Shared Services Provider with the administration links for the Business Data Catalog

The process of importing the application definition file is very straightforward. Using the page shown in Figure 4-5, you browse to the XML file you want to import. Now instead of application definition files containing the full metadata of a business application, you can also have files that contain only resources, for example localized names for the parameters or security information. Uploading these files requires that you first set the *File Type* option to *Resource* and then detail the type of resources you want to import under it.

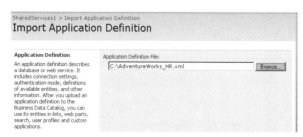

Figure 4-5   Importing the AdventureWorks_HumanResources application definition file

During the import process, SharePoint uses the *bdcmetadata.xsd* to validate the XML inside the application definition files. Any violations will be reported immediately.

Configuration and Management of BDC Applications

After a successful import of the application definition file, all of the defined metadata elements are translated into metadata objects stored in the repository. There are a couple of configurations possible. Let's have a quick look at your options.

Review the Metadata

You can drill down and review the metadata objects that are imported. Just navigate to the home page of the administration site for the Shared Services Provider and click on the View Applications link. You end up in a page where you see all of the imported and available business applications. As shown in Figure 4-6, clicking on one of them opens up the page where you see the list of entities. Figure 4-7 displays the pages that show all of the metadata associated with a selected entity.

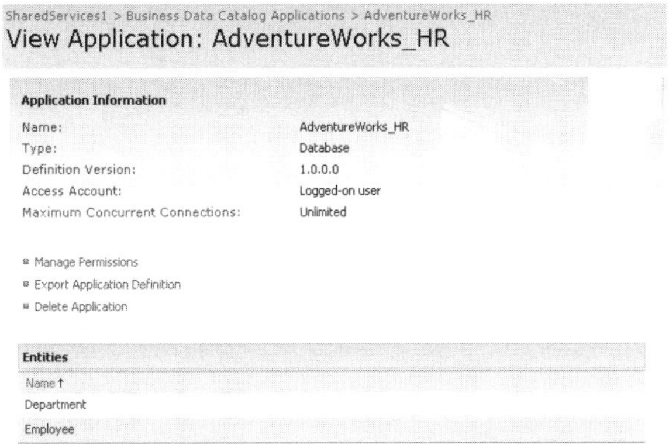

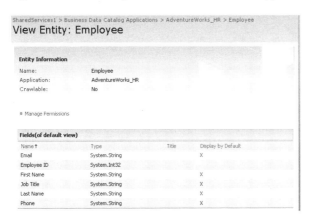

Figure 4-6   Reviewing the entities as a business application

Figure 4-7   Reviewing the details of an entity

Adding Actions

Another option is to add actions for an entity. Every entity that supports a *MethodInstance* of type *SpecificFinder* gets one action by default during the importing of the application definition file. This action allows users to navigate to the full details of the entity using a profile page. This profile page is by default located in the Shared Services Provider administration site, and it contains just an instance of the Business Data Item Web Part. Later we'll have a closer look at it. You have an option to modify the template to be used for all of the profile pages. To do this, go back to the home page of the administration site and click on the Edit Profile Page Template link.

Additional actions are easy to create by clicking on the Add Action link in the *View Entity* page. You can support all kinds of scenarios with additional actions. One thing you might need to do is allow users to open one of the pages or screens of the back-end application where the business data regarding the entity is stored. Here, the user can make modifications to the business data. The page for adding an action, displayed in Figure 4-8, invites you to give a name for the action and the URL to the page or screen that users can navigate to. Along with the new request, data can travel as part of the querystring of the HTTP request. You have the option to map one or more of the fields of the entity to parameters in the querystring.

SharedServices1 > Business Data Catalog Applications > AdventureWorks_HR > Employee > Add Action
Add Action

Name	
Type a name for the action.	Action Name:
	Update Employee

URL	
Type the URL to navigate to when you click on the action. If you want the URL to vary depending on the item to which it applies, add one or more parameters, then assign a property to each parameter below. Type a number in braces such as {0} where you want to insert a parameter in the URL	Navigate to this URL:
	http://www.foo.com/update?id={0}
	Example: http://example.com/edit.aspx?id={0}
	Launch the action in a new browser window:
	○ Yes ● No

URL Parameters	
Assign a property to each parameter in the URL	Parameter Property
	0 EmployeeID ▾ Remove
	Add Parameter

Figure 4-8 Adding extra actions to the entity

Configuring Security

There are three topics we need to discuss here. A first one is authentication. In short, the authentication for BDC applications can be supported in two ways. When connecting to an external system, such as SAP, the administrator of that external system can prepare an account that can be used by the BDC for making the connection. This approach is what is referred to as the *Trusted Subsystem* model. A second model to support authentication is the *Impersonation and Delegation* model. This is typically useful if you connect to a traditional data store, such as Microsoft SQL Server, and use the account of the client to perform the authentication.

After authentication comes authorization, with again the support for two types of models. When you decide to opt for the *Impersonation and Delegation* authentication model, it means that the back-end system has knowledge about the account used to access the business data. The authorization, which grants permissions to access and work with the data, can be a result of the responsibility of the back-end system. If you opt for the *Trusted Subsystem* model, the authorization is totally done at the level of the business application since everybody is authenticated with the same account in the back-end system. The authorization can be included in the metadata of the application file where at the level of different elements (*LobSystem*, *Entity*, *Method*, and *MethodInstance*) you have the option to define Access Control Lists (ACLs). With the ACL, you specify which principals have which rights on the object. For example, the following definition of the *Employee* entity includes one *AccessControlEntry* element indicating that a certain principal (can be an individual user or a group) has a number of rights (*Edit*, *Execute*, *SetPermissions*, *SelectableInClients*).

```
<Entity EstimatedInstanceCount="10000" Name="Employee">
  <AccessControlList>
    <AccessControlEntry Principal="LITWAREINC\administrator">
      <Right BdcRight="Edit" />
      <Right BdcRight="Execute" />
      <Right BdcRight="SetPermissions" />
      <Right BdcRight="SelectableInClients" />
    </AccessControlEntry>
  </AccessControlList>
```

Instead of including the authorization information in the application definition files, administrators can also go to the Shared Services Provider administration site, navigate to an entity, and configure the authorization directly in the browser. Figure 4-9 shows the page where you can set the permissions.

Figure 4-9   Setting permissions at the level of the entity in a business data application

A last option we have to discuss regarding security is the *Business Data Catalog Security Trimmer*. Security trimming is useful in scenarios where you want to apply additional security layers in a dynamic way at the level of the entity instances. Note that this mechanism ties in very closely with the Enterprise Search Query Processing engine, which provides a framework for plugging in dynamic query time security trimming modules where the specific results of a single user query can be security-trimmed before being displayed in Search Results. I've discussed custom security trimming in Chapter 3, "Customizing and Extending the Microsoft Office SharePoint 2007 Search."

The Business Data Web Parts

Microsoft Office SharePoint Server 2007 comes with a number of Web Parts that immediately let you connect to the business data defined and managed within the Business Data Catalog. These Web Parts are referred to as the Business Data Web Parts, and you have five of them that are advertised in the Add Web Parts dialog box, shown in Figure 4-10, for SharePoint sites that are part of a site collection with the Office SharePoint Server Enterprise Site Collection features Feature activated.

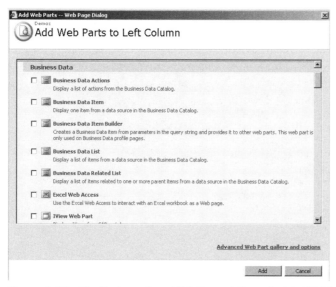

Figure 4-10   The Business Data Web Parts delivered with MOSS 2007

Let's have a closer look at each of them and connect them to one of the entities that is available in the BDC metadata repository. All of these definitions are there because of the two application definition files that were previously created and imported.

Business Data List Web Part

The Business Data List Web Part is probably the one most used on SharePoint pages. It can display a list of instances of one of the entities registered in the Business Data Catalog. The link with the entity, as shown in Figure 4-11, is done via the properties tool pane where you will work with the Business Data Picker control and/or the Business Data Picker dialog box. Note that users must have permission to connect to the Business Data Catalog in order for the Web Part to be functional on the page.

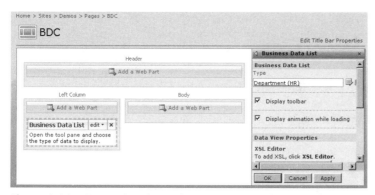

Figure 4-11   Connecting the Business Data List Web Part with the *Department* entity via the tool pane

Along with the other Business Data Web Parts, the Business Data List Web Part is actually built on top of the Data View Web Part infrastructure. Data View Web Parts are Web parts that can be created in Microsoft Office SharePoint Designer 2007. They allow for a very flexible way of connecting to a data source, in this case the business data catalog application, and bring in this data in XML format and then apply an XSL transformation on the data in order to turn it into the HTML that makes up the body of the Web Part. Via the tool pane, you have the option to replace the default XSLT with your own custom one. On top of that, you have the option to control the parameters that are delivered to the XSLT and possibly add more values that are used within the XSLT to slice the incoming data.

If you simply connect to an entity and apply the changes, the users visiting the page with the Business Data List Web Part on it will be able to make use of the filters defined in the metadata. For example, Figure 4-12 shows the Business Data List Web Part associated with the *Department* entity and showing the two filters.

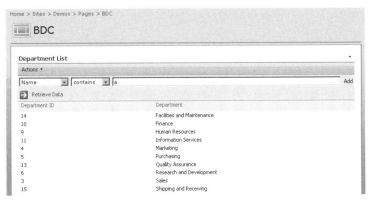

Figure 4-12   Using the Business Data List Web part with the filters defined in the BDC application definition

This, however, is only one possible mode in which you can deliver the Business Data List Web Part to users. There is also the option to prepare a view for the Web Part to show. This is done by first switching the page to edit mode and then clicking on the Edit View link in the toolbar. A page allows you to fine-tune the view you want to give to the users. There is an option to define a custom query and disable the option for users to change the criteria. The query can be based on the criteria or the filters as the user sees them in the Business Data List Web Part, shown in Figure 4-12. Administrators also have the option to create a condition that matches one of the filters in a more dynamic way to one of the properties of the user profile for the currently logged-on user. Figure 4-13 illustrates the creation of the view. For the rest, you have other settings for sorting, filtering, and paging the results.

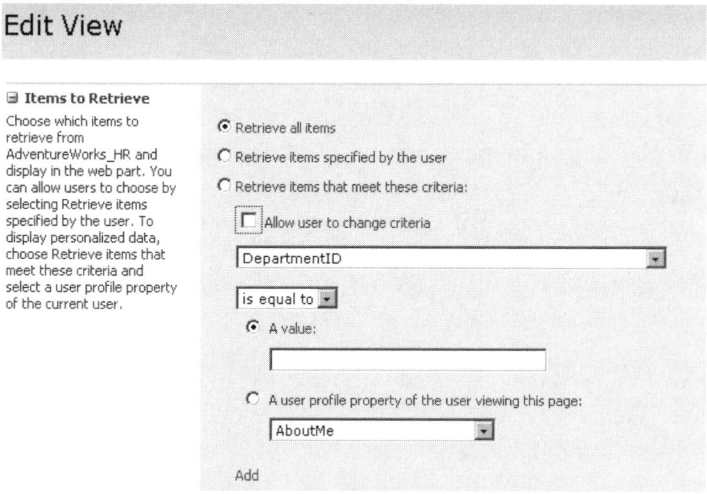

Edit View
Items to Retrieve
Choose which items to retrieve from AdventureWorks_HR and display in the web part. You can allow users to choose by selecting Retrieve items specified by the user. To display personalized data, choose Retrieve items that meet these criteria and select a user profile property of the current user.
Retrieve all items
Retrieve items specified by the user
Retrieve items that meet these criteria:
Allow user to change criteria
DepartmentID
is equal to
A value:
A user profile property of the user viewing this page:
AboutMe
Add

Figure 4-13 Creating a view for the Business Data List Web Part

Business Data Related List Web Part

This Web Part is useful if you have created associations between entities in the Business Data Catalog. The Business Data Related List Web Part is not one that can live on its own. You have to add it to a page where you have already placed the Business Data List Web Part. Next, via the tool pane, you configure the relationship you want to have visualized by the Web Part, as shown in Figure 4-14.

Home > Sites > Demos > Pages > BDC
BDC
Edit Title Bar Properties
Add a Web Part
Add a Web Part
Department List
Actions
Edit View
Department ID
Department
1 Engineering
2 Tool Design
3 Sales
4 Marketing
5 Purchasing
6 Research and Development
7 Production
8 Production
Business Data Related List
Open the tool pane and choose the type of data to display.
Business Data Related List
Business Data Related List
Type
Employee (HR)
Relationship
DepartmentToEmployees
Display toolbar
Display animation while loading
OK
Cancel
Apply

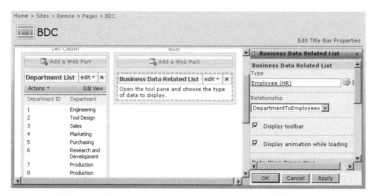

Figure 4-14 Configuring the Business Data Related List Web Part to display the employees working in a selected department

Once the configuration is done, you connect the Business Data List Web Part with the Business Data Related List Web Part, portrayed in Figure 4-15.

Figure 4-15   Connecting the Web Part showing the departments to the Business Data Related List Web Part in order for it to display the employees working in that department

The result of the work is that users can now select a department, and the Business Data Related List Web Part immediately picks up the choice and retrieves the associated entity instances. Figure 4-16 shows this master-detail scenario.

Figure 4-16   Listing the employees working in a selected department

Note that the Web Part also allows for the configuration of a view and the options to replace the default XSL transformation with a custom one.

Business Data Item Web Part

The details of an individual entity instance, such as an employee, can be delivered via the Business Data Item Web Part. After adding an instance to the page, you configure it to connect to one of the entities in the BDC with the option to either display an entity instance in a static way or display the details of a selected entity in one of the other Business Data Web Parts that can send the entity key value to the Business Data Item Web Part. In Figure 4-17, you can see how the Business Data Related List Web Part allows a user to select an employee, starting the process of sending the employee ID to the Business Data Item Web Part, which then retrieves all of the details for the employee and displays it again with a default XSL transformation.

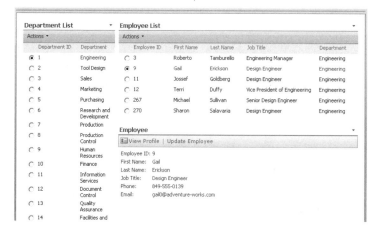

Figure 4-17   The Business Data Item Web Part showing the details of the selected employee

Business Data Actions Web Part

This Web Part can show all of the actions the user can perform for a specific entity instance. You typically connect the Business Data Actions Web Part with one of the other Business Data Web Parts, linking an employee entity instance, for example, with the possible actions that can be performed on it.

Business Data Item Builder Web Part

The last Web Part is one that you only can use on the so-called profile pages. These are basically normal SharePoint pages that you navigate to, attaching identifier information in the querystring regarding a specific entity instance so that the Business Data Item Builder Web Part can pick it up and display the details of the entity in question.

Search and the BDC

In Chapter 3, we discussed the various options for customizing the search experience and programmatically executing search queries. We worked mainly with content sources of type SharePoint site and the file system. There is one other type of content source administrators can define: a content source of type Business Data. Before the index engine is able to crawl your business data, you must, however, add the necessary metadata elements to the application definition file to support the whole process. We'll cover this extra metadata first, and then we'll walk through the quick steps for creating and configuring a Business Data type of content source.

Metadata to Support Search

First of all, if you want entity instances to get crawled, you have to add unique identifiers and support the *SpecificFinder MethodInstance*. Going back to the first application definition file, the *AdventureWorks_HumanResources.xml*, you can verify that those conditions have been fulfilled. But there is more. You also have to add a special type of *MethodInstance* element called *IDEnumerator* in your metadata. The *IDEnumerator* method returns a searchable list of IDs (unique key) for the entity in question, and it is this list that enables the indexing of the details of the entities included.

The following shows the new method for the *Employee* entity that basically just returns a list of *EmployeeIDs* and then makes that method accessible via a *MethodInstance* of type *idEnumerator*.

```
<Method Name="EmployeeIDEnumerator">
  <Properties>
    <Property Name="RdbCommandText" Type="System.String">
    SELECT EmployeeID FROM HumanResources.Employee</Property>
    <Property Name="RdbCommandType" Type="System.String">Text</Property>
  </Properties>
  <Parameters>
   <Parameter Name="EmployeeIDs" Direction="Return">
     <TypeDescriptor TypeName="System.Data.IDataReader, System.Data,
Version=2.0.3600.0, Culture=neutral, PublicKeyToken=b77a5c561934e089"
      IsCollection="true" Name="Employees">
       <TypeDescriptors>
       <TypeDescriptor TypeName="System.Data.IDataRecord, System.Data,
Version=2.0.3600.0, Culture=neutral, PublicKeyToken=b77a5c561934e089"
        Name="Employee">
        <TypeDescriptors>
          <TypeDescriptor TypeName="System.Int32"
            IdentifierName="EmployeeID" Name="EmployeeID">
            <LocalizedDisplayNames>
             <LocalizedDisplayName LCID="1033">ID</LocalizedDisplayName>
            </LocalizedDisplayNames>
          </TypeDescriptor>
        </TypeDescriptors>
       </TypeDescriptor>
      </TypeDescriptors>
     </TypeDescriptor>
   </Parameter>
  </Parameters>
  <MethodInstances>
   <MethodInstance Name="EmployeeIDEnumeratorInstance"
     Type="IdEnumerator" ReturnParameterName="EmployeeIDs" />
  </MethodInstances>
</Method>
```

This is the necessary support for a full crawl, but if you also want to support the incremental crawl mode, then you have to make sure that one of the return fields in the *IDEnumerator* for the entity represents the time the entity instance was last updated in the line-of-business (LOB) application. You should then set the *__BdcLastModifiedTimeStamp* property of the entity with the name of the *TypeDescriptor* object in the return value of the *IDEnumerator* method that represents the last modified date.

Creating New Business Data Content Source

Let's now walk through the steps for configuring a new content source that tells the index engine to crawl our AdventureWorks human resources data. As a starter, you have to import the *AdventureWorks_HumanResources.xml* application definition file into the Business Data Catalog.

The addition of a new content source is done in the administration site of the Shared Services Provider you are working with. Go to the search settings page where you have the option to create a new content source by clicking on the Content sources and crawl schedules link. As shown in Figure 4-18, you select the type Business Data and then select the business data application or go for all of them.

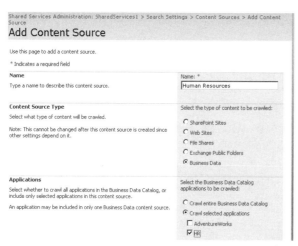

Figure 4-18   Configuring a new content source for indexing business data

To finalize the work here in the Shared Services Provider administration site, make sure a crawl is started—a full crawl to start with. When done, you are ready to search the business data.

Business Data Lookups

Business objects that are identified as entities in the Business Data Catalog can also be delivered as possible values for the columns that are part of a list or a document library. The *Business Data* field type is part of the Office SharePoint Server Enterprise Site features Feature, a Feature that has to be activated at the level of the individual site within a site collection.

Take for example a list in a SharePoint team site based on the *Contacts* template to store colleagues. Figure 4-19 illustrates how as an administrator of this list, you have the option to create an additional column of type *Business Data*.

Home > Sites > Demos > Colleagues > Settings > Create Column

Create Column: Colleagues

Use this page to add a column to this list.

Name and Type

Type a name for this column, and select the type of information you want to store in the column.

Column name:

[Department]

The type of information in this column is:

- ○ Single line of text
- ○ Multiple lines of text
- ○ Choice (menu to choose from)
- ○ Number (1, 1.0, 100)
- ○ Currency ($, ¥, €)
- ○ Date and Time
- ○ Lookup (information already on this site)
- ○ Yes/No (check box)
- ○ Person or Group
- ○ Hyperlink or Picture
- ○ Calculated (calculation based on other columns)
- ● Business data

Additional Column Settings

Specify detailed options for the type of information you selected.

Description:

[   ]

Require that this column contains information:

○ Yes ● No

Type:

[Department (HR)]

Display this field of the selected type:

[Department]

- ☑ Display the actions menu
- ☑ Link this column to the profile page

Add a column to show each of these additional fields:

- ☐ Department
- ☐ Department ID
- ☑ Add to default view

Figure 4-19   Adding a column of type Business Data to a list

The *Business Data Picker* provides you with the means to select the entity you want to connect to and then finish the job. Select one or more of the fields of the entity to add as columns to the list. After applying the addition to the list schema, users are able to use the *Business Data Picker* control when creating or modifying an item in the list. Figure 4-20 shows that the *Business Data Picker* control can be used to select a department for a new colleague.

Figure 4-20   Using the Business Data Picker to enter a department for a new colleague

Building a Custom Application with the Business Data Catalog

The scenarios to work with the LOB application definitions stored in the Business Data Catalog do not stop with the Business Data Web Parts, the Business Data field type, the option to index and search external business data, or the integration with the user profiles. Nope! There are many other scenarios you can go for because there is a rich object model exposed by the Microsoft Office SharePoint Server 2007, and a number of classes in that object model have to do with BDC functionality. This entails that as a developer, you can build your own custom applications that talk to the Business Data Catalog.

There are two main .NET assemblies that encapsulate all of the BDC-related classes: the *Microsoft.SharePoint.Portal.dll* and the *Microsoft.Office.Server.dll*. I'll quickly describe the most important namespaces you will encounter while coding against the Business Data Catalog:

- The *Microsoft.Office.Server.Administration* namespace is not the namespace you'll work with directly. Most of the classes are reserved for internal use. However, you will find a couple of the general exception classes.

- The *Microsoft.Office.Server.ApplicationRegistry.Administration* contains the classes that can be used when building administrative type of applications for the BDC. Using these classes, you can create, update, read, and delete all of the application definition metadata along with the related configuration and management information such as the security data.

- The *Microsoft.Office.Server.ApplicationRegistry.Infrastructure* is the namespace that provides all of the necessary classes to create and manage connections to the Business Data Catalog next to classes that are needed when dealing with the security services for the BDC clients.

- The *Microsoft.Office.Server.ApplicationRegistry.MetadataModel* contains the classes that represent the metadata of an application defined in the Business Data Catalog and that are used in applications to read from and execute the business logic described in the metadatabase. These classes are optimized to make full usage of the BDC caching mechanisms and should be used in favor of the classes in the *Microsoft.Office.Server.Application-Registry.Administration* to work with the BDC metadata from a client perspective.

- The *Microsoft.Office.Server.ApplicationRegistry.Runtime* is the namespace that contains the classes and base classes that are used to access the BDC client application functionality. Examples are the different classes that have to do with the filters defined in the metadata.

In short, all of the available classes allow developers to programmatically perform the following type of operations:

- Create application definitions using code. Tools and designers can be created that can replace the creation of an XML-based application definition file and immediately create the necessary BDC artifacts in the metadata repository.

- Administer, configure, and manage existing application definitions with the support for importing and exporting application definition files.

- Build new front-ends that consume business data from external LOB-systems via the BDC engine. Examples can be custom Web Parts and Web pages that integrate within SharePoint sites, but other examples include applications that are completely independent from SharePoint such as Windows applications, add-ins that extend the Microsoft Office clients, mobile applications, and lots more.

First, we'll cover all of the major classes that will have to be addressed in these three scenarios, and then we'll go through a couple of walkthroughs to get you started.

Connecting to the Shared Services Provider Database

Within your server farm, you'll have one or more Shared Services Providers up and running that can deliver Business Data Catalog services. As a first step, building a custom application that connects to a Business Data Catalog involves setting up a connection to the Shared Services Provider database associated with one of these providers.

The *SqlSessionProvider* class, defined in the *Microsoft.Office.Server.ApplicationRegistry.Infrastructure* namespace is the key class to use here. It is implemented as a singleton with the connection details of the provider exposed through the *Instance()* method. The *SetSharedResourceProviderToUse* method is called to make changes to the provider details by giving either an instance of the *ServerContext* or simply a string representing the name of the Shared Services Provider you want to connect to. The former is an option if your code is executed in a place such as a Web Part sitting in one of the SharePoint WebPart pages. Setting the provider details by using the name of the provider is the option you have when the code runs outside the context of SharePoint. You use the following syntax to connect to a Shared Services Provider with the name *SharedServices1*:

```
SqlSessionProvider.Instance().SetSharedResourceProviderToUse
  ("SharedServices1");
```

The *ApplicationRegistry*

The *ApplicationRegistry* is the top-level object in the Business Data Catalog's object model. It gives you access to all of the objects representing the individual metadata elements you want to work with.

More Info   Application Registry was actually the original name given to the Business Data Catalog. The name survives in the object model.

Administration versus MetadataModel   The *ApplicationRegistry* class can be found in two namespaces: *Microsoft.Office.Server.ApplicationRegistry.Administration* and *Microsoft.Office.Server.ApplicationRegistry.MetadataModel*. Depending on the type of work you want to perform in your custom application, you will select one. Select the last one, the *Microsoft.Office.Server.ApplicationRegistry.MetadataModel*, if you prefer only a "read" operation on the metadata that is building, as one example, a tool that represents all of the artifacts that make up an application definition or, as another example, an application where you execute the business logic contained within the application definition. If you are going to work with the metadata in a more administrative mode—that is, creating, modifying, deleting, importing, and exporting—then you opt for the first namespace. The difference is performance. The

Microsoft.Office.Server.ApplicationRegistry.MetadataModel uses the BDC caching and is optimized to give you the best performance. The *Microsoft.Office.Server.ApplicationRegistry.Administration* is not optimized and therefore is only to be used when really doing administrative work on the BDC metadata.

Exporting and Importing Packages   One type of operation you can perform immediately at the level of the *Microsoft.Office.Server.ApplicationRegistry.Administration.ApplicationRegistry* class is the exporting and importing of application definition packages. Exporting a package is done by calling the *ExportPackage* method with the name of the existing application definition, a *System.IO .Stream* type of object, and the type of information you want to export via the *PackageContents* enumeration. In case you want to export the complete package, select the *PackageContents .Model*. Other options are to export only the *LocalizedNames* in case you want to add multilinguality to the application definition, the *Permissions*, or access control lists or the *Properties*. The following code exports an application definition called *Human Resources Data* to file:

```
FileStream file = new FileStream
    (@"C:\HumanResourcesData.xml",System.IO.FileMode.Create);
ApplicationRegistry.Instance.ExportPackage
    ("Human Resources Data", file, PackageContents.Model);
file.Flush();
file.Close();
```

Importing is also a fairly straightforward operation. You call the *ImportPackage* method that delivers the content as a *System.IO.Stream*, also providing an object of type *ParseContext* (part of the same namespace as the *ApplicationRegistry* class) that is used to store possible state information and errors gathered during the parsing. As a last parameter, again call the type of content you want to import using the *PackageContents* enumeration. The return value is of type *LobSystem*. Here is code illustrating the import of an application definition file defining the access to data stored in a CRM system:

```
System.IO.FileStream file =
    new System.IO.FileStream(@"C:\crm.xml",System.IO.FileMode.Open);
ParseContext pc = new ParseContext();
LobSystem lobsystem =
    ApplicationRegistry.Instance.ImportPackage(file, pc, PackageContents.Model);
```

Getting *LobSystem* and *LobSystemInstance* Objects   Both the *ApplicationRegistry* classes in the *Microsoft.Office.Server.ApplicationRegistry.Administration* as well as the *Microsoft.Office .Server.ApplicationRegistry.MetadataModel* namespace give you access points to start working with the metadata objects part of the application definition. Note that you keep working in the same namespace once you start with a specific *ApplicationRegistry* class.

The following code gives an idea of how you can connect to the *LobSystemInstance* in the Human Resources Data application definition and retrieve all of the entities available (working here with the Administration namespace):

```
SqlSessionProvider.Instance().SetSharedResourceProviderToUse
    ("SharedServices1");
foreach (LobSystem sys in ApplicationRegistry.Instance.LobSystems)
```

```
{
    foreach (Entity entity in sys.Entities)
        listBoxEntities.Items.Add(entity.Name + " (" + sys.Name + ")");
}
```

Once you have a reference to the *LobSystem* object within your application definition, you are ready to explore the complete tree of metadata objects by either doing administrative work on them or executing the methods that are defined for them.

Walkthrough: Creating an Application Definition Programmatically

In this first walkthrough, we'll go through the steps for recreating the application definition for working with the human resources data that is part of the AdventureWorks SQL Server database. In the beginning of this chapter, we went through the XML elements; now we'll work through the different steps using C# to build a reduced version of the same application definition file. To refresh your memory, the human resources department wants to get access to the employees and the department information in a SharePoint environment. For this walkthrough, to keep it simple, we'll only worry about creation of the necessary metadata objects to retrieve all of the employee data.

Let's use a small Windows application to drive this walkthrough and not keep ourselves busy with the details of the UI composition, just one button on a form that is ready to be implemented.

The first thing to do is make sure you have the references to the various assemblies needed for the code. The first reference is the *Microsoft Office Server* component, the *Microsoft.Office.Server.dll*, and the second one is the *Microsoft.Office.SharePoint.Server* component, the *Microsoft.Share-Point.Portal.dll*.

Once they are part of the project, continue with writing the *using* statements that we need for the rest of the coding. Here is the list you have to put at the top of the code-behind class of the form:

```
using Microsoft.Office.Server.ApplicationRegistry.Administration;
using Microsoft.Office.Server.ApplicationRegistry.Infrastructure;
using Microsoft.Office.Server.ApplicationRegistry.SystemSpecific.Db;
```

Next, you implement the *Click* event handler of the button and insert the statements to connect to the Shared Services Provider database as discussed previously:

```
SqlSessionProvider.Instance().SetSharedResourceProviderToUse("SharedServices1");
```

Since you start from scratch in this walkthrough, you first have to create a *LobSystem* object, representing your business application, in the database. The top-level object, *Application-Registry*, has a collection of type *LobSystemCollection* that you can access via the *LobSystems* property of the currently initialized *SqlSessionProvider* instance. A call to the *Create* method creates the needed object, and some values for the parameters have to be provided. The first one is the name of the *LobSystem*. The second one is simply a flag indicating whether you want to support caching or not. And the final three parameters indicate what type of *LobSystem* you want to create.

```
LobSystem lobsystem = ApplicationRegistry.Instance.LobSystems.Create
    ("Mini Human Resources Data", true,
     "Microsoft.Office.Server.ApplicationRegistry.SystemSpecific.
Db.DbSystemUtility","Microsoft.Office.Server.ApplicationRegistry.
SystemSpecific.Db.DbConnectionManager","Microsoft.Office.Server.
ApplicationRegistry.SystemSpecific.Db.DbEntityInstance");
```

In the above call, you are using the parameters that define that you are going to connect to a database system. If you need to connect to the external data source via one or more Web Service calls, then use the following values for the last three parameters:

```
LobSystem lobsystem = ApplicationRegistry.Instance.LobSystems.Create
    ("Human Resources Data", true, "Microsoft.Office.Server.
ApplicationRegistry.SystemSpecific.WebService.WSSystemUtility",
"Microsoft.Office.Server.ApplicationRegistry.SystemSpecific.
WebService.WSConnectionManager","Microsoft.Office.Server.
ApplicationRegistry.SystemSpecific.WebService.WSEntityInstance");
```

Let's also add a property defining the character % that will be replacing the * wildcard entered by the users.

```
lobsystem.Properties.Add("WildcardCharacter", "%");
lobsystem.Update();
```

Now that you have the *LobSystem* object, you're ready to create one instance providing all of the details necessary for the Business Data Catalog to be able to connect to the external data source—in our case, the local SQL Server and the AdventureWorks database. The *LobSystem-Instance* is created by calling the *Create* method on the *LobSystemInstances* property of the *LobSystem* object created previously. The connection details are defined using properties added to the *Properties* collection of the *LobSystemInstance* object.

```
LobSystemInstance sysInstance =
    lobsystem.LobSystemInstances.Create("Mini Human Resources Data", true);
sysInstance.Properties.Add
    ("AuthenticationMode", DbAuthenticationMode.PassThrough);
sysInstance.Properties.Add("DatabaseAccessProvider",
    DbAccessProvider.SqlServer);
sysInstance.Properties.Add("RdbConnection Data Source", "MOSS");
sysInstance.Properties.Add("RdbConnection Initial Catalog",
    "AdventureWorks");
sysInstance.Properties.Add("RdbConnection Integrated Security", "SSPI");
sysInstance.Update();
```

For the authentication mode, you can again just use the *PassThrough* option indicating that the connection has to be done using the account of the currently logged-on user.

> **Note**   At any time during the walkthrough, you can test your code by executing it and verifying the results in the *Business Data Catalog Applications* page, which is accessible from the View Applications link at the administration site of the Shared Services Provider. Don't forget to delete the application definition before you execute the code again.

Your next assignment is to create the *Employee* entity. The *LobSystem* object has an *Entities-Collection* exposed via the *Entities* property where you can add new *Entity* objects to use the *Create* method. The only parameter values needed are the name of the entity along with the boolean for including the entity in the caching mechanism. The return value is an *Entity* object.

```
Entity entity = lobsystem.Entities.Create("Employee", true);
```

Entity objects need to have at least one identifier defined for them. This is important, otherwise you will not be able to search for or locate the entity instances. The *IdentifiersCollection*, exposed with the *Identifiers* property, can be populated with one or more *Identifier* objects providing just the name, the caching flag value, and then the type of the identifier as it is known in the SQL Server database.

```
Identifier identifier =
    entity.Identifiers.Create("EmployeeID", true, "System.Int32");
```

Entities have one or more methods that pull the data from the external data stores into the SharePoint environment. In our example here, we have one method for the *Employee* entity, and that is the *GetEmployees* method. The metadata object that represents the method is created by using the *Create* method at the level of the *MethodCollection* exposed as the *Methods* property of the *Entity* object. Once you have the *Method* object, your task is to tell the BDC what the mapping is to either a Web Service call or a SQL statement. In our case, we go for the latter because our data comes out of the local SQL Server AdventureWorks database. The SQL statement is very general, allowing for the retrieval of one employee, all employees, or a filtered set based on criteria. All of this information is again defined with a set of *Property* objects you add to the *PropertyCollection* of the *Method* object.

```
Method method = entity.Methods.Create("GetEmployees", true, true);
method.Properties.Add("RdbCommandText",
  "SELECT  * FROM HumanResources.vEmployee " +
  "WHERE (EmployeeID >= @MinEmployeeID AND EmployeeID <= @MaxEmployeeID) "
  + " AND LastName LIKE @LastName");
method.Properties.Add("RdbCommandType", CommandType.Text);
```

The next step is to create the two filters that the BDC front ends can show to the users, such as the Business Data Web Parts. You have two filters for the *GetEmployees* method. Users will be able to tell the BDC to return one employee using the *EmployeeID* as the criteria. So the first *FilterDescriptor*, the metadata objects representing the filters that appear in the UI, is for the *EmployeeID*, and you have to provide the type of filter as the last parameter value. For the first one, we have the type set to the *ComparisonFilter* defined in the *Microsoft.Office.Server.Application-Registry.Runtime* namespace. The second filter is a *WildcardFilter* named *LastName*.

```
FilterDescriptor filterDescID =
   method.FilterDescriptors.Create("EmployeeID", true,
  "Microsoft.Office.Server.ApplicationRegistry.Runtime.ComparisonFilter");

FilterDescriptor filterDescName =
   method.FilterDescriptors.Create("LastName", true,
  "Microsoft.Office.Server.ApplicationRegistry.Runtime.WildcardFilter");
```

Looking back at the SQL statement you've mapped to the *GetEmployees* method, you see a number of parameters that are embedded in the SQL. Your job now is to define what they are one by one and the type they represent and connect them to *Identifier* and/or *FilterDescriptor* objects you have already created. In addition, you need to create a *Parameter* object defining what to expect as output from a call to the method. The *Method* object has a *ParameterCollection* exposed by the *Parameters* property. You again populate this collection one by one using the *Create* method. The important parameter other than the name of the parameter is the direction. An enum called *DirectionType* can be used to specify whether the parameter is an *In* or *Return* parameter. Other options for the enum are *InOut* and *Out*. Parameters with type *Out* allow you to pass the parameter to the BDC, which will populate it with a value so that after the execution of the method you can retrieve the updated value and process it further.

```
Parameter parMinID = method.Parameters.Create("@MinEmployeeID", true,
Microsoft.Office.Server.ApplicationRegistry.MetadataModel.DirectionType.In,
"Microsoft.Office.Server.ApplicationRegistry.
Infrastructure.DotNetTypeReflector");

Parameter parMaxID = method.Parameters.Create("@MaxEmployeeID", true,
Microsoft.Office.Server.ApplicationRegistry.MetadataModel.DirectionType.In,
"Microsoft.Office.Server.ApplicationRegistry.Infrastructure.
DotNetTypeReflector");

Parameter parName = method.Parameters.Create("@LastName", true,
Microsoft.Office.Server.ApplicationRegistry.MetadataModel.DirectionType.In,
"Microsoft.Office.Server.ApplicationRegistry.Infrastructure.
DotNetTypeReflector");

Parameter parEmployees = method.Parameters.Create("Employees", true,
Microsoft.Office.Server.ApplicationRegistry.MetadataModel.
DirectionType.Return, "Microsoft.Office.Server.ApplicationRegistry.
Infrastructure.DotNetTypeReflector");
```

Defining just the name and direction of every *Parameter* object is not enough. You also have to tell the BDC about the data type of the parameter. This is done by creating *TypeDescriptor* objects for the *Parameter* objects. For the first three parameters, this is pretty straightforward. You use the *CreateRootTypeDescriptor* method of the *Parameter* object again with a string value for the name of *TypeDescriptor* object, the caching flag, and the data type as it is known in the external data source. If the parameter is mappable to an identifier, you provide the reference to the *Identifier* object. As last values, you give the reference to the matching *FilterDescriptor* object—in order to map the *Parameter* with the filter in the UI—and conclude with a flag to tell the BDC whether the parameter will contain a collection of values or one single value.

```
TypeDescriptor typedescMinID = parMinID.CreateRootTypeDescriptor
 ("@MinEmployeeID", true, "System.Int32", identifier, filterDescID, false);

TypeDescriptor typedescMaxID = parMaxID.CreateRootTypeDescriptor
 ("@MaxEmployeeID", true, "System.Int32", identifier, filterDescID, false);

TypeDescriptor typedescName = parName.CreateRootTypeDescriptor
 ("@LastName", true, "System.String", null, filterDescName, false);
```

The process is a bit more complicated for the *Parameter* object that is defined as the return parameter. First, you have to create a *TypeDescriptor* object with the definition of the .NET object that will be used to return the data. In our example, since we are connecting to a SQL Server database, you can opt for a traditional ADO.NET *IDataReader* object. Every incoming entity instance will be of type *IDataRecord* within that stream. Next, you define one by one what the fields are of that *IDataRecord* matching the names and the type exactly with the corresponding columns in the database table. If appropriate, you can connect the *TypeDescriptor* with either an *Identifier* or a *FilterDescriptor* object. There is some extra information you can provide for the *TypeDescriptor* object. For instance, you can set a value for the *Localized-DisplayName* property, replacing the actual table column name with a friendlier name that will be displayed in the user interface. You can also localize these strings by adding *Localized-DisplayName* objects to the *LocalizedDisplayNames* collection that associates a string with an LCID (Localized Display Name ID). Property objects can also provide dynamic information such as the *DisplayByDefault* property that tells the Business Data Web Parts, for example, to pick up the output field value and display it by default in the user interface.

```
TypeDescriptor typedescEmployees =
  parEmployees.CreateRootTypeDescriptor("EmployeeDataReader", true,
  "System.Data.IDataReader, System.Data, Version=2.0.3600.0,
Culture=neutral, PublicKeyToken=b77a5c561934e089", null, null, true);

TypeDescriptor typedescEmployees1 =
  typedescEmployees.ChildTypeDescriptors.Create("EmployeeDataRecord", true,
  "System.Data.IDataRecord, System.Data, Version=2.0.3600.0,
Culture=neutral, PublicKeyToken=b77a5c561934e089", null, null, false);

TypeDescriptor typedescEmployees11 =
  typedescEmployees1.ChildTypeDescriptors.Create
  ("EmployeeID", true, "System.Int32", identifier, filterDescID, false);
typedescEmployees11.LocalizedDisplayName = "Employee ID";

TypeDescriptor typedescEmployees12 =
  typedescEmployees1.ChildTypeDescriptors.Create
  ("FirstName", true, "System.String", null, null, false);
typedescEmployees12.LocalizedDisplayName = "First Name";
typedescEmployees12.Properties.Add("DisplayByDefault", true);
typedescEmployees12.Update();

TypeDescriptor typedescEmployees13 =
  typedescEmployees1.ChildTypeDescriptors.Create
  ("LastName", true, "System.String", null, filterDescName, false);
typedescEmployees13.LocalizedDisplayName = "Last Name";
```

```
typedescEmployees13.Properties.Add("DisplayByDefault", true);
typedescEmployees13.Update();

TypeDescriptor typedescEmployees14 =
   typedescEmployees1.ChildTypeDescriptors.Create
   ("JobTitle", true, "System.String", null, null, false);
typedescEmployees14.LocalizedDisplayName = "Job Title";

TypeDescriptor typedescEmployees15 =
   typedescEmployees1.ChildTypeDescriptors.Create
   ("Phone", true, "System.String", null, null, false);
typedescEmployees15.LocalizedDisplayName = "Phone";

TypeDescriptor typedescEmployees16 =
   typedescEmployees1.ChildTypeDescriptors.Create
   ("EmailAddress", true, "System.String", null, null, false);
typedescEmployees16.LocalizedDisplayName = "Email";
```

You're almost finished. The last step is the definition of the *MethodInstance* objects. These objects describe how one can call a method pointing to the metadata object itself that defines the method as well as possible default values for the input parameters. The Business Data Web Parts along with the Business Data Picker control expect to find two *MethodInstance* objects—one of type *Finder* and one of type *SpecificFinder*. The first one returns a collection of entity instances while the last one returns one single entity instance.

```
MethodInstance methInstance1 = method.MethodInstances.Create
      ("EmployeeFinderInstance", true, typedescEmployees,
       Microsoft.Office.Server.ApplicationRegistry.MetadataModel.
MethodInstanceType.Finder);

MethodInstance methInstance2 = method.MethodInstances.Create
      ("EmployeeSpecificFinderInstance", true, typedescEmployees,
       Microsoft.Office.Server.ApplicationRegistry.MetadataModel.
MethodInstanceType.SpecificFinder);
```

To finish, you associate some of these *MethodInstance* objects to the *TypeDescriptor* objects specifying some default values that can be picked up by the BDC.

```
typedescMinID.SetDefaultValue(methInstance2.Id, 0);
typedescMaxID.SetDefaultValue(methInstance2.Id, 99999);
typedescName.SetDefaultValue(methInstance1.Id, "%");
typedescName.SetDefaultValue(methInstance2.Id, "%");
```

Running all of this code results in a new business data application registration in the Business Data Catalog. You can explore the different objects created in code by drilling down in the *Employee* entity and verifying the work done. You can also go to any of your SharePoint sites and add the Business Data List Web Part on the page to try out the new application definition you have created.

Walkthrough: Custom Web Part Connecting to the Business Data Catalog

The second example we'll work out together is a custom Web Part that basically mimics what the Business Data List Web Part is doing in combination with the Business Data Related List Web Part. The Web Part connects to the AdventureWorks human resources data business application imported at the beginning of this chapter, executes the method to retrieve the collection of department entity instances, and then uses the association that is defined in the metadata to show the employees working for the selected department in a small data grid. The result is shown in Figure 4-21.

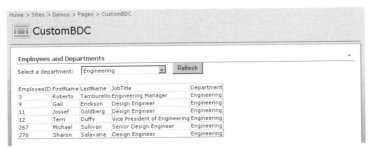

Figure 4-21   A custom Web Part connecting programmatically to the BDC application

Figure 4-22 shows how you start by opening Microsoft Visual Studio.NET 2005 and creating a new Web Part project. Let's just call it *HRWebParts*–the name does not really matter. As you will see after confirming your choices, a new project is waiting for you in Visual Studio.NET with all of the necessary infrastructural pieces in place regarding the Web Part.

Note   I am assuming here that you have installed the Visual Studio.NET Extensions for Windows SharePoint Services 3.0 downloadable from the Microsoft MSDN site.

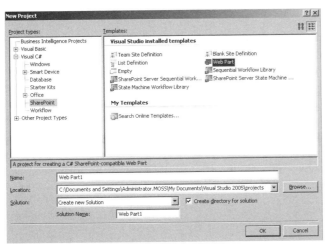

Figure 4-22   Creating a Web Part project in Visual Studio.NET 2005

There are a couple of things you have to do before you program the access to the Business Data Catalog. A set of steps simply have to do with the fact that you are building a Web Part and that this needs to be deployed at the end to a SharePoint site collection. Therefore, right-click the project and navigate to the tab named SharePoint Solutions, as displayed in Figure 4-23. This opens up the details of the Feature that will make the Web Part available within the targeted site collection, illustrated in Figure 4-24. If you feel like it, you can make changes to the title and the description. Staying in the pane for the properties of the project, activate the Debug tab and fill in the URL of the site collection you want to target with your Web Part. That's all you need to do to configure the deployment of your Web Part.

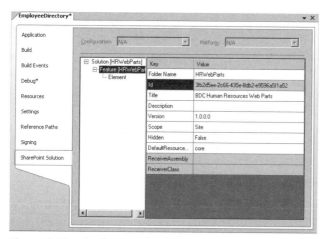

Figure 4-23   Configuring the Feature that will make the Web Part available within a SharePoint site collection

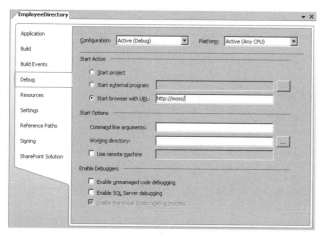

Figure 4-24   Targeting a specific site collection with the Web Part

As discussed in the previous walkthrough, there are a number of .NET assemblies that encapsulate the classes you need to work with when programming against the Business Data Catalog. Using the Solution Explorer, add the references to the *Microsoft.Office.Server.dll* and the

Microsoft.SharePoint.Portal.dll. The first one is identified with the component name *Microsoft Office Server* and the last one as *Microsoft Office SharePoint Server*. While you are here, also select the *System.Data.dll* assembly since you will work with an ADO.NET *DataTable* later on.

Now focus on the class that is already available—the *WebPart1.cs*. Optionally, change the name of the class and the file. You might also want to modify the namespace. The namespaces required in addition to what's already there are:

```
using System.Web.UI.WebControls;
using System.Data;
using Microsoft.Office.Server.ApplicationRegistry.Infrastructure;
using Microsoft.Office.Server.ApplicationRegistry.MetadataModel;
using Microsoft.Office.Server.ApplicationRegistry.SystemSpecific.Db;
using Microsoft.Office.Server.ApplicationRegistry.Runtime;
```

Note that we'll work now primarily with the *Microsoft.Office.Server.ApplicationRegistry .MetadataModel* namespace and the classes defined within it—this instead of the *Microsoft.Office .Server.ApplicationRegistry.Administration* namespace you've used in the previous walkthrough. This is because we want to fully leverage the caching mechanism provided by the Business Data Catalog, giving us the maximum performance for our access to the business data.

The Web Part needs a couple of user interface elements: a *Label*, a *DropDownList*, a *Button*, and a *DataGrid*. For each of them, declare a class-level variable of the correct type and initialize them to null:

```
private Label labelDepartment = null;
private DropDownList listDepartments = null;
private Button buttonRefresh = null;
private DataGrid gridEmployees = null;
```

The controls are created one by one at run-time in the *CreateChildControls* method of your parent—the *System.Web.UI.WebControls.WebParts.WebPart* class—that you override within your custom Web Part class. After the creation of the child controls, add them to the *Controls* collection of your Web Part. There's also some initialization work to do for some of the control properties, and you have to create an event handler for the *Click* event of the button.

```
protected override void CreateChildControls()
{
    this.labelDepartment = new Label();
    this.listDepartments = new DropDownList();
    this.buttonRefresh = new Button();
    this.gridEmployees = new DataGrid();
    this.labelDepartment.Text = "Select a department: ";
    this.buttonRefresh.Text = "Refresh";
    this.buttonRefresh.Click += new EventHandler(buttonRefresh_Click);
    this.Controls.Add(this.labelDepartment);
    this.Controls.Add(this.listDepartments);
    this.Controls.Add(this.buttonRefresh);
    this.Controls.Add(this.gridEmployees);
    base.CreateChildControls();
}
```

To finalize the basic work on the Web Part, drop the code responsible for the rendering of all the child controls in the *Render* method that is already available, which contains some commented code in your Web Part class. The following lines simply build up the user interface for the Web Part:

```
protected override void Render(HtmlTextWriter writer)
{
    writer.RenderBeginTag(HtmlTextWriterTag.P);
    this.labelDepartment.RenderControl(writer);
    writer.Write("   ");
    this.listDepartments.RenderControl(writer);
    writer.Write("   ");
    this.buttonRefresh.RenderControl(writer);
    writer.RenderEndTag();
    this.gridEmployees.RenderControl(writer);
}
```

If you are curious about the result of the work done so far, just press F5 and Visual Studio.NET 2005 will start the building and deployment process. When successful, navigate to the home page of the top-level site of the site collection you targeted with the deployment and you'll find your custom Web Part in the Add Web Part dialog box, ready to be dropped on the page. Nothing really exciting will happen yet since you still have to write all of the code to populate the controls. Let's get started with those steps.

The first thing to do is create a small private procedure, called *FillUpDepartments*, that will populate the *DropDownList* with all of the departments. In it, you first connect to the *LobSystemInstance* that represents the AdventureWorks human resource data business application in the BDC. Notice that you do not have to set the Shared Resource Provider to be used as with the first walkthrough because you're not working in a Windows application anymore; you're working now in the context of SharePoint, and all of your code—and thus also the BDC connections—will be done within the current SharePoint context. But you do have to connect to your *LobSystemInstance*, and here is the code to do this:

```
private void FillUpDepartments()
{
    NamedLobSystemInstanceDictionary instances =
        ApplicationRegistry.GetLobSystemInstances();
    LobSystemInstance instance = instances["Human Resources Data"];
}
```

The top-level *ApplicationRegistry* class has the option to return a *NamedLobSystemInstance-Dictionary* object by calling the *GetLobSystemInstances* method. The only thing to do after that is to use the name of the *LobSystemInstance* to get the instance itself.

Remember that the goal is to populate the *DropDownList* with all of the departments. Therefore, connect to the *Department* entity using the following code:

```
Entity entity = instance.GetEntities()["Department"];
```

The *LobSystemInstance* exposes a method *GetEntities* you can call to have a *NamedEntity-Dictionary* returned from which you can retrieve the *Entity* instance you need for the rest of the work.

The list of all of the departments—or better said, the list of all entity instances representing the departments—is retrieved by calling an instance of the *Method* that is defined in the metadata at the level of the *Entity*. In our case, this is the *GetDepartments* method, and there are two *MethodInstances* defined you can work with. Since you don't want to retrieve one specific instance, opt for the *DepartmentFinderInstance*, a *MethodInstance* of type *Finder*. Here is the code that executes that method and collects the results in a *DbEntityInstanceEnumerator*:

```
Method method = entity.GetMethods()["GetDepartments"];
MethodInstance methodinstance =
        method.GetMethodInstances()["DepartmentFinderInstance"];
DbEntityInstanceEnumerator departments =
        (DbEntityInstanceEnumerator)entity.Execute(methodinstance, instance);
```

So, you first get the reference to the *Method* itself and then the *MethodInstance* you want. At the level of the *Entity*, you have the *Execute* method you can call with the parameters being the reference to the *MethodInstance* object and the *LobSystemInstance* you're working with. The return value of the *Execute* method is of type *Object*, which you cast to the proper type to work with: the *DbEntityInstanceEnumerator* type.

The last steps have to do with using the enumerator to loop through all of the returned *Entity* instances, populating the *DropDown* List with the name of the department, and storing the ID of the department for later use as the value of the *ListItem*.

```
while (departments.MoveNext())
{
    DbEntityInstance department = (DbEntityInstance)departments.Current;
    this.listDepartments.Items.Add
        (new ListItem(department.GetFormatted("Name").ToString(),
                    department.GetFormatted("DepartmentID").ToString()));
}
```

The *DbEntityInstance* object is an adapter-specific database interface to the contents of the entity instance, and it has a number of properties that are useful for further processing. One of them is the *GetFormatted* method you can call to retrieve the values of the fields of a specific entity instance.

Before you test out this work by pressing F5 again, make sure you call this *FillUpDepartments* procedure somewhere in the *CreateChildControls* method after the lines where you have created the controls.

```
FillUpDepartments()
```

Now let's finish the Web Part by adding the code to the *Click* event handler of the one button we have in the UI. A user selects a department and expects to see the employees that work for that department. So you need the ID of the department as a starter. The ID can be retrieved as the value of the selected item of the *DropDownList* converted to its proper type:

```
void buttonRefresh_Click(object sender, EventArgs e)
{
    Int16 depID = Int16.Parse(this.listDepartments.SelectedItem.Value);
}
```

Next, you need the *Entity* instance that represents the selected department. You basically perform the same steps as the ones you started with when populating the *DropDownList* except that now you call the *SpecificFinder MethodInstance*. You want one *Entity* instance as a return value: the one that matches up with the supplied ID of the department.

```
NamedLobSystemInstanceDictionary instances =
        ApplicationRegistry.GetLobSystemInstances();
LobSystemInstance instance = instances["HR"];
Entity entity = instance.GetEntities()["Department"];
IEntityInstance department = entity.FindSpecific(depID, instance);
```

The *Entity* object has a method called *FindSpecific* that internally maps to the *SpecificFinder* and accepts the unique identifier as a first parameter. Note that if you do not have defined *Identifier* metadata objects within your application definition file, you'll not be able to call this method. The return value now is an object of type *IEntityInstance*. This represents the interface that you can use to again access to the contents of the returned *Entity* instance. But you don't really want to show anything more of the department; you want the employees that are working for that department. Remember that in the application definition file we built up in the beginning of this chapter for the AdventureWorks human resources data business application, we defined an association between *Department* and *Employee*. This association is called *DepartmentToEmployees* and is mapped to the *GetEmployeesForDepartment* method defined at the level of the *Department* entity. You cannot call this method directly since it does not have any *MethodInstances* associated with it. The following code allows you to retrieve the employees working for the selected department:

```
IEntityInstanceEnumerator employees =
        department.GetAssociatedInstances("DepartmentToEmployees");
```

At the level of the *IEntityInstance* object, there is a method called *GetAssociatedInstances* that needs information about the association you want to follow. This can be delivered as an object of the *Association* class itself or simply by providing the name of the association. The return value is again an enumerator, now of type *IEntityInstanceEnumerator*.

Let's process all of the returned employees now. They need to be displayed in a *DataGrid*, a control that is completely ready to be bound to ADO.NET objects such as a *DataTable*. The following code populates such an object and binds it to the *DataGrid*:

```
DataTable tbl = null;
while (employees.MoveNext())
{
    if (tbl == null)
```

```
        tbl = employees.Current.EntityAsDataTable;
    else
        employees.Current.EntityAsDataRow(tbl);
}
this.gridEmployees.DataSource = tbl;
this.gridEmployees.DataBind();
```

The *IEntityInstance* object has one property that is useful here: the *EntityAsDataTable* property that returns a *DataTable* containing both the schema and the contents as a *DataRow* of all of the field values for the instance. Once the structure of the *DataTable* is known, you can just continue populating it with the values of the remaining *IEntityInstance* objects by calling the *EntityAsDataRow* method. This method needs a *DataTable* following the schema of the *Entity* as an input argument. The rest of the code is simply databinding.

To test your work, use the magic of pressing F5 again, and Visual Studio.NET 2005 will build and deploy your new Web Part to the targeted site. After adding the Web Part to the page, you should be able to select departments and see the associated employees, just like in Figure 4-21.

Summary

In this chapter, we've had a look at the various components that are involved when adding support to the SharePoint sites in order to integrate with external data stored in standard non-SharePoint databases and line-of-business systems.

As a starter, the external system has to be modeled using metadata that can either be manually created in an XML file (or generated by designer tools) or programmatically created directly in the metadata repository of the Business Data Catalog. Application definition files provided as XML files have to be imported using one of the Shared Services Provider administration pages. Once all of this was done, we discussed the other side of the story: the front ends such as the Business Data Web Parts, the search, and the Business Data field type. All of them give us an excellent out-of-the-box experience when working with the Business Data Catalog. However, in the real world, this often will not be enough, and there is the need to create custom code to integrate with the Business Data Catalog. A number of scenarios have been discussed along with an explanation of the major classes and coding techniques to get you started. Further details on all of this can be found in the SDK of the Microsoft Office SharePoint Server 2007.

Chapter 5
InfoPath Forms Services

- Learn the different configuration and administration options developers should know about.
- Learn how to make use of the Data Connection Library.
- Understand the different scenarios for publishing InfoPath templates to a SharePoint environment.
- Understand the role of InfoPath forms in the workflow story.
- Learn how you can embed InfoPath forms within SharePoint pages.

Configuration and Administration of the InfoPath Forms Services

There are a number of configuration and administration tasks involved with the InfoPath Forms Services that you should know about as a developer since they will impact the solutions you build.

General Tasks

Since InfoPath Forms Services are not part of the Shared Services, you won't find the configuration and administration pages on the Shared Services Provider administration site. You simply have to open the SharePoint 3.0 Central Administration and navigate to the Application Management page.

From the Application Management page, go to the Configure InfoPath Forms Services page. There are some important settings to review. The first set are options that enable or disable the rendering of the InfoPath forms in the browser. By default, they are turned on and you probably want to leave them on since we'll be going through the steps for deploying a browser-enabled InfoPath form and using it in a SharePoint site. Other settings are more important since they can have an impact on your solutions. They concern the various options administrators can turn on or off:

- A first setting is *Require SSL for HTTP authentication to data sources*. This is on by default, and it can be used by administrators to enforce SSL whenever authentication is required, such as in the case of your InfoPath forms consuming Web Services.

- Another setting, *allow embedded SQL authentication*, can prevent you from storing connection details for accessing SQL Server databases stored in the InfoPath template. Embedding connections in your template is actually not a good practice anymore since, as you'll learn later, the Data Connection Library serves the purpose. This should be where you store the different data connection files.

■ Administrators can use the *Allow user form templates to use authentication information contained in data connection files option* setting to prevent the use of hard-coded user credentials in the connection files.

■ And the last setting, *Allow cross-domain data access for user form templates that use connection settings in a data connection file*, is very important in scenarios where your InfoPath forms connect to external data sources such as SharePoint lists or document libraries residing in other IIS Web Applications within your server farm. By default, this option is turned off. In case the InfoPath forms have these types of connections, administrators have to turn it on to prevent nasty errors from being shown to the users.

A last option to discuss is the configuration of the user session that will be created and used by InfoPath Forms Services. Two options are possible here. You may use the Session State Service, a farm-level service that uses a SQL Server database to store the session state. Use this option with care if you have a lot of users connecting to your InfoPath forms because it will stress the machine hosting the SQL Server database. But it is the choice to make if you target users that have a low bandwidth. If they don't, you may want to consider the second option, which stores the data for the user session in the Form View. So the data is sent back and forth between the client and the server and thus has an impact on the bandwidth, but if you can, select Form View as the recommended choice.

The Data Connection Library

I mentioned earlier that embedding connection details in the InfoPath templates is no longer a good practice. Template designers had no other option with Microsoft InfoPath 2003, and it caused a lot of problems when deploying and maintaining the InfoPath templates in the real world. Think of it, a template designer creates a data connection to a SQL Server database that grabs data out of a table and deploys the template to 50 locations. After a while, the database administrator decides to move the database to another machine, which immediately breaks all of the deployed templates because they use embedded data connection details to connect to the SQL Server.

All of the real-world problems regarding embedded data connections can now be resolved by using InfoPath templates in combination with a new type of library, the Data Connection Library, part of Microsoft Office SharePoint Server 2007. These libraries can store Office Data Connection files (with an .odc extension) as well as the newer type of connection files, the Universal Data Connection files (with a .udcx extension). InfoPath 2007 supports these new types of files and is your best choice since the connection details are stored as XML and you have a more powerful way of defining the parameters. The biggest benefit of using a Data Connection Library is that you only have to go to one place when updates need to be done to the connection details. Later in the book, you'll also learn that Excel Services uses these types of libraries. Unlike with Excel Services, the libraries accessed by InfoPath do not have to be defined as trusted libraries. However, smart administrators will be tempted to enforce the use of the Data Connection Library as the only possibility for InfoPath template designers to access their external data sources such as a SQL Server database.

Walkthrough: Working with the Data Connection Library

Let's work out a little scenario as a walkthrough. Assume you are responsible for making an expense report template available with one of the controls populated with the list of employees stored and retrieved from the SQL Server database. You are asked not to embed these connection details in the InfoPath template.

Before you do any work with InfoPath, you have to prepare a SharePoint site with a new Data Connection Library. You can pick any type of site you have available. Note that there is also the option to make use of the Data Connection Library already available in SharePoint 3.0 Central Administration. Let's create a new one dedicated for use by all of the InfoPath templates deployed within the site collection. The Data Connection Library, named InfoPath Connections in Figure 5-1, is created within the site like any other container using the Site Actions menu and the Create page.

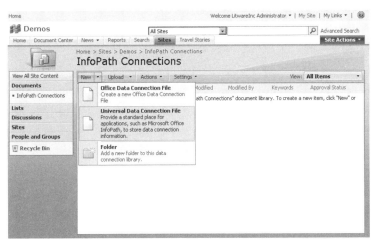

Figure 5-1   A Data Connection Library ready to store connection files used by InfoPath 2007

If you look at Figure 5-1, two content types are associated with the Data Connection Library: one to upload an existing Office Data Connection File and one to upload the newer type, the Universal Data Connection File. Let's now proceed and create a connection file this way since it requires that you have the file already available. Instead, I'll describe the steps to let InfoPath 2007 do all of the work for us. First, you'll create a data connection the traditional way (that is the embedded way) and then convert the connection details to a .udcx file that immediately stores the connection file in the new Data Connection Library.

Open Microsoft InfoPath 2007. In the Getting Started dialog box, select the Expense Report sample. No need to create a new template. There is only one small change to make in the template. There is a text box control bound to the *name* field. Right-click it and change the type to dropdown list box. It will be populated by a data connection retrieving employee names from the *AdventureWorks* sample database in SQL Server 2005.

The new data connection can be created by opening the Data Connections dialog box from the Tools menu in the design environment. Clicking on the Add button will start a wizard that shows the options for where the connection details will be stored. By default, searching for a connection on the Microsoft Office SharePoint Server is the active selection, as shown in Figure 5-2. This is the best choice, and you'll come back to it in a moment. However, there probably aren't any connections yet available in the Data Connection Library. As said, you'll use InfoPath to create an entry in the Data Connection Library. So, first create the connection the traditional way by selecting the option in the dialog box to create a new connection to receive data, as shown in Figure 5-2. Proceed by selecting Database as the source of the data and via the Select Database button, create an .odc file storing the details to connect to the Employee view found in the AdventureWorks database.

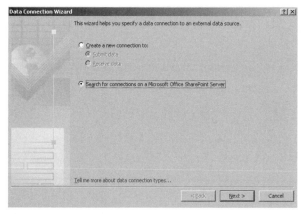

Figure 5-2   Creating a new data connection using the Data Connection wizard in Microsoft InfoPath 2007

Now, you won't leave it like this. This is the old way of connecting to the data store, and perhaps the SharePoint administrator has forbidden the use of embedded SQL connections. Use the Convert button in the Data Connections dialog box to change this. The Convert Data Connection dialog box, as shown in Figure 5-3, can be used to enter the URL to the Data Connection Library where you'll drop the converted .odc file.

Figure 5-3   Converting an embedded .odc file to a .udcx file and immediately storing this new file in the Data Connection Library

Here is the path to enter:

```
http://moss/SiteDirectory/AdventureWorks/InfoPath Connections
/employees.udcx
```

For the Connection link type, you'll stay with the option to work with a path relative to the site collection. The result of your work is that a new item is added to the Data Connection Library. It is still in pending mode, so you'll have to approve it. Figure 5-4 shows the newly created item.

Figure 5-4   A Data Connection Library ready to store connection files used by InfoPath 2007

Now start over again. Delete the connection you have just created and pretend that you are starting from zero again. Select the suggested option to search for a connection. Before InfoPath will be able to show you the newly created .udcx file, you'll have to add the URL of the site to the dropdown via the Manage Sites button. When selecting it now, there will be an option to select the employees.udcx file, as illustrated in Figure 5-5.

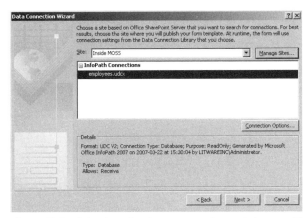

Figure 5-5   Selecting the data connection as it is stored in the Data Connection Library

To finalize this walkthrough, you just have to double-click the dropdown that is bound to the name field and configure it to look up the values from your newly created data source. Select one of the fields to be displayed to the user and probably the same one to store in the XML that will be saved. You can use the Preview button to check out the work you have done.

Publishing InfoPath Templates

InfoPath templates can be packaged as a Microsoft Installer (MSI) file or published to many places: a SharePoint server with or without InfoPath Forms Services, e-mail recipients, or a network location. Since this book is all about Microsoft Office SharePoint Server 2007, I'll concentrate solely on the first option.

Publishing to Document Library

InfoPath templates that do not contain any code can be directly published by the template designer as templates of document libraries in a SharePoint site. The publishing wizard starts guiding you through the steps by asking for the input of the URL to the SharePoint site where you want to create the document library. The next step, shown in Figure 5-6, is important. Here, you have to make the decision whether or not you are going to enable the InfoPath template for a browser-based scenario. It is also the place where you select the option for creating a document library.

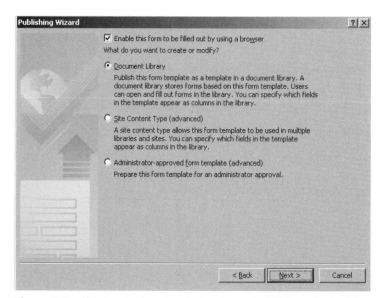

Figure 5-6   The step in the wizard where you decide how the template will be published

The wizard continues asking for the name of the document library and the columns it needs to create. Each of these columns can expose the value of an XML node that is part of the InfoPath form submitted. A very important change compared to the previous version is that these columns can now be updated by the SharePoint user, and the changes will also be automatically applied to the corresponding XML nodes in the InfoPath form. This is very useful since when you now want to programmatically access and modify values of the forms, you do not have to write code to load the XML document, which parses the XML in search of the XML node you want to modify and pushes that back with a save into the XML document. A quick call to the *SPListItem* object and the column is enough for now.

Warning   When updating the values of the XML form via the mapped columns, all of the validation code, formulas, scripts, and rules will not run anymore. Be aware of this when making use of this new option.

When finished with the wizard, you'll end up with a document library in the SharePoint site ready for accepting new InfoPath forms.

Deploying as a Content Type

The Publishing Wizard also gives you the option of publishing the InfoPath template as a SharePoint content type. This is always a better option if you intend to re-use the template in many places within the site collection. After making the choice in the wizard as shown in Figure 5-7, you have to point to the site where you want to have the content type created.

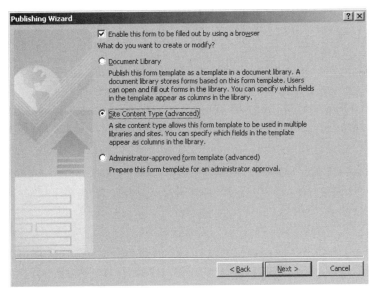

Figure 5-7   Making the decision to publish the InfoPath template as a content type instead of directly connecting it to a document library

The content type is made available in the Site Content Types gallery. Via the Advanced Settings of a new or existing document library, there is an option to then add it as a content type for the container.

Preparing and Deploying Advanced InfoPath Templates

Advanced InfoPath templates are templates that contain code. You can no longer simply finish the wizard when preparing and deploying advanced InfoPath templates. The options for deploying the InfoPath template directly to a document library or as a content type will be disabled.

Personally, I recommend this type of deployment even for designing simple InfoPath templates because it provides the best support for management. Let me explain this a bit further. If you perform an administrative deployment of the template, it will be dropped in a document library that is part of the SharePoint 3.0 Central Administration. From there, administrators can manage the template and, when needed, activate it for a specific site collection. On that site collection, it will then be available as a content type that can be associated with any of the document libraries made available through this site collection. Administrators can maintain and version the templates from one central location, giving them more control over their lifecycle. When needed, they can be upgraded, de-activated from the site collection, or quiesced from it. The last option is interesting when you know that there are still users actively busy with the InfoPath template. The template will be removed quietly without users even knowing it. A small walkthrough will show the steps for performing an administrative deployment of an InfoPath template.

Walkthrough: Deploying InfoPath Templates (advanced mode)

In this walkthrough, you'll learn the various steps to take when you decide to make your InfoPath template available in the SharePoint environment using the so-called advanced mode in the publishing wizard. Note that in many cases this is the preferred mode even for the simple type of InfoPath templates, and it is the necessary road to take when your InfoPath template contains code. Describing the extensibility of InfoPath templates with managed code is out of scope for this book. Therefore, the InfoPath template you'll use is a simple one—a sample that comes with the product.

Open Microsoft InfoPath 2007 and select one of the out-of-the-box sample templates, such as the Travel Request template. You might want to use the Design Checker to verify the compatibility with the InfoPath Forms Services. Before you start with the Publishing Wizard, save the template somewhere on your local drive.

The wizard starts with the selection of the type of location you want to target for your InfoPath template. Select the first option: *To a SharePoint Server with or without InfoPath Forms Services*. Next, the wizard asks you for the URL of the SharePoint site. The URL entered is actually not very important since you'll not deploy directly to the site. More important is the next step, shown in Figure 5-8, where you select the last option: *Administrator-approved form template (advanced)*.

In the next step, enter a location that is a shared network folder reachable by the SharePoint administrator or that allows you to work directly on the SharePoint server folder on the drive. After this, just complete the wizard by accepting the defaults. You don't need Microsoft InfoPath anymore.

Administrators who have access to the SharePoint 3.0 Central Administration can now use the Upload Form Template link in the Application Management page under the InfoPath Forms Services group. Here, enter the path to the network folder and the InfoPath template that is stored and click the Verify button to check whether the template is compatible with the InfoPath Forms Services. No need to check the upgrade option if this is the first time you have done this. Figure 5-9 displays the page where all of the action occurs.

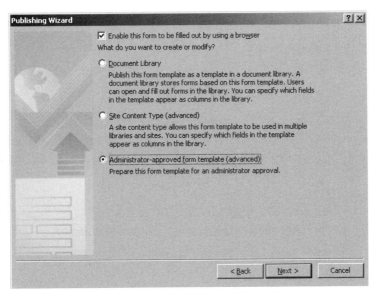

Figure 5-8 Making the decision in the Publishing Wizard to select the advanced mode of deploying the Microsoft InfoPath template

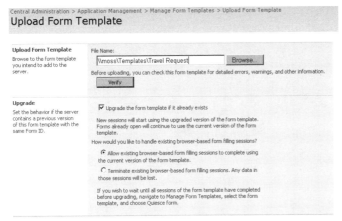

Figure 5-9 The administrator of the SharePoint 3.0 Central Administration uploading the Microsoft InfoPath template

If all goes well, a confirmation page will be displayed and you will be ready to make the template available on one or more site collections. Press the OK button in the confirmation page to go to the Manage Form Templates page where you'll see the InfoPath template stored along with other templates deployed this way, as illustrated in Figure 5-10.

Central Administration > Application Management > Manage Form Templates

Manage Form Templates

📤 Upload form template

Type	Name	Version	Modified	Category	Status	Workflow En
📄	Travel Request.xsn	1.0.0.7	3/22/2007		Ready	No
📄	CollectSignatures_Sign_1033.xsn	12.0.0.1	11/17/2006	Workflow	Ready	Yes
📄	Expiration_Complete_1033.xsn	12.0.0.1	11/17/2006	Workflow	Ready	Yes
📄	RR_OOB_WrapItUp_1033.xsn	12.0.0.1	11/17/2006	Workflow	Ready	Yes
📄	ReviewRouting_Assoc_1033.xsn	12.0.0.1	11/17/2006	Workflow	Ready	Yes
📄	ReviewRouting_Init_1033.xsn	12.0.0.1	11/17/2006	Workflow	Ready	Yes
📄	ReviewRouting_Modify_1033.xsn	12.0.0.1	11/17/2006	Workflow	Ready	Yes
📄	ReviewRouting_Review_1033.xsn	12.0.0.1	11/17/2006	Workflow	Ready	Yes
📄	ReviewRouting_UpdateTasks_1033.xsn	12.0.0.1	11/17/2006	Workflow	Ready	Yes
📄	Xlate_Complete_1033.xsn	12.0.0.1	11/17/2006	Workflow	Ready	Yes
📄	Xlate_Init_1033.xsn	12.0.0.1	11/17/2006	Workflow	Ready	Yes

Figure 5-10   The centrally managed library storing all of the InfoPath templates deployed using the advanced mode

This will be the only place where administrators go to maintain the InfoPath template. You can push the template from here to one or more site collections by using the Activate to a Site Collection option in the context menu for the template. As shown in Figure 5-11, select the site collection and just hit the OK button. Behind the scenes, the InfoPath template will be packaged as a content type and activated as a site collection feature in the targeted site collection.

Central Administration > Application Management > Manage Form Templates > Activate to a Site Collection

Activate Form Template: Travel Request

Form Template Properties

Form name:
Travel Request

Description:

Category name:

Status:
Ready

Form ID:
urn:schemas-microsoft-com:office:infopath:Travel-Request:-myXSD-2005-10-21T21-12-27

Activation Location
Choose a site collection where you want to activate the form template.

Site Collection: **http://moss** ▼

OK   Cancel

Figure 5-11   Activating the InfoPath template for a site collection

There are other actions you can perform on the InfoPath template. You can deactivate it from a site collection, quiesce the form template, or completely remove it. The first option has direct consequences for anybody working with the template. They will get exceptions and will be rudely interrupted in their work. The second option is the more elegant approach where you let SharePoint deactivate the template from the site collection after everybody has finished working with it.

Now open a browser session and navigate to the site collection you used to target the InfoPath template. At the level of the site collection, you'll see in the Site Collection Features page the Travel Request Feature activated and ready to be associated with one of the form or document libraries.

The Role of InfoPath in Workflows

InfoPath forms can take care of communication with users involved in a workflow instead of the traditional ASP.NET pages. The benefits of using InfoPath forms instead of ASP.NET pages are the ease of developing these forms, the quick access to the data in XML format, and definitely the support for displaying these InfoPath forms that are part of the workflow within the Office 2007 clients. In Chapter 1, "Introducing the Microsoft Office SharePoint Server 2007," if you go back to the walkthrough that discusses the steps to use the out-of-the-box approval workflow, you'll see how Office 2007 clients can let the information workers start and complete the workflow tasks directly from within familiar products such as Word 2007 and Outlook 2007.

Building custom workflows is discussed in *Inside Microsoft® Windows® SharePoint® Services 3.0* (Microsoft Press), authored by Ted Patisson and Daniel Larson. Microsoft Office SharePoint Server 2007 adds a couple of ready-to-use workflows such as the approval workflow to Share-Point sites, but the Windows Workflow Foundation support is basically part of the Windows SharePoint Services platform. Thanks to the Microsoft Office Forms Server 2007, however, you'll be able to leverage the InfoPath forms as communication pages in the browser as well as in the Office 2007 clients.

Important   Building custom workflows can be done using third-party tools, the Microsoft Office SharePoint Designer 2007, and the extensions that can be added to the Microsoft Visual Studio.NET development environment. If you stick with the Microsoft products, only the last option provides you with the opportunity to work with InfoPath forms as the means of communication with the users involved in the workflow. The SharePoint Designer is capable of generating only ASP.NET pages.

Embedding InfoPath Forms in SharePoint Pages

Rendering the InfoPath form in the browser is handled by the *XmlFormView* ASP.NET control, embedded in the FormServer.aspx page. This is one of the pages located in the \12\Template\Layouts folder and is therefore common to all the SharePoint sites running on the machine. Figure 5-12 shows one of the InfoPath sample templates rendered in the browser using the FormServer.aspx page.

Now, an advantage for you is that you can also use this ASP.NET control with your own SharePoint pages or even with custom Web pages. A requirement for the custom pages is that they run within the context of SharePoint, that is, on the same IIS Web Application as the one used to host the SharePoint sites. The story becomes even more interesting for SharePoint users because the ASP.NET control also exposes the necessary infrastructure for it to become a Web Part on one of the pages. And that's what you'll learn if you go through the steps of the last walkthrough for this chapter.

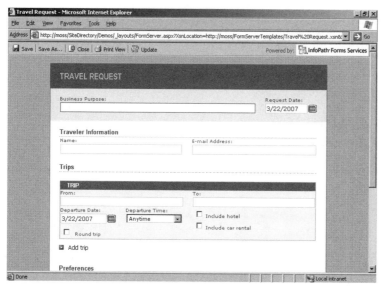

Figure 5-12   The FormServer.aspx page displaying the InfoPath form in the browser using the *XmlFormView* ASP.NET control

Note   Embedding InfoPath forms within Web pages is not your only option. Windows developers can also use a Windows control (the *FormControl* control) within smart clients. This way, they can accomplish pretty much the same thing as their colleagues, the Web developers. The desktops running these smart clients that embed InfoPath forms must have the full Microsoft InfoPath 2007 product installed locally.

Walkthrough: Embedding InfoPath Forms in a SharePoint WebPart Page

To conclude this chapter, I'll explain the steps for making an InfoPath form part of a SharePoint page instead of the form taking over the browser as you saw previously in Figure 5-12. This can be necessary in the real world where a company, such as *Litwareinc*, offers trainings and workshops internally for employees. These employees can visit the intranet portal and browse through the catalog with the different courses. When a good training is found, they can register for it using an InfoPath form. The InfoPath form should follow the site's look and feel and therefore be embedded within one of the pages. So, let's get started by first working on the InfoPath template.

Keep the InfoPath template simple by capturing just the basic information concerning the registration for a course. Figure 5-13 shows the sample you can grab from the companion Web site. Of course, you may construct your own InfoPath template, possibly connecting some of the controls to data sources such as a list of possible courses to follow. Remember that working with Data Connection Libraries is the best practice when creating connections to external data sources.

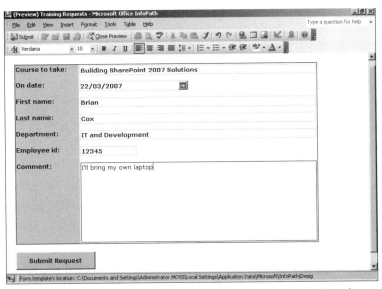

Figure 5-13   A small InfoPath form used by employees to register for a training

If you take the template from the companion Web site, you'll notice that there is a second view defined showing some text that will be displayed when the user submits the training request. I'll come back to it in a moment.

Before you publish the template, you have to configure some of the form options. Use the Tools menu and select Form Options to open the dialog box where you can do this. One thing you probably don't want to see in the page displaying the InfoPath form are the toolbars in the header and the footer. You can turn these off by clicking on the Browser category and then clearing the checkboxes for displaying the toolbars. You may want to turn off options in the Open and Save category too since your InfoPath template contains a Submit button that will take care of submitting the data back to SharePoint. No explicit saving must be made available.

Your next step is to publish this template to a SharePoint site and make it available as the template for a form library. Just use the publishing wizard and follow the steps previously discussed. Nothing fancy here, just make sure that you are enabling the template for Web browser-based access. In order for the Submit button on the form to function properly, that is to submit the data entered by the user back to the form library just created, you'll have to edit the InfoPath template again and create a new data connection. Editing the uploaded template is possible if you go via the Settings menu in the form library to the Form Library Settings page. Here you'll find the Advanced Settings to click on. There is a small link under the field containing the template URL. Click on it, and your InfoPath client will load the template again, allowing you to proceed with the requested changes.

Double-click the Submit Request button and then click the Rules button. Add a rule that has two actions and no conditions. The first action to add to the rule is Submit Using A Data

Connection. Via the Add button, you're able to go through the steps for defining a connection back to the form library. For simplicity, you can use an embedded connection by selecting the option to create a new connection to submit data, as shown in Figure 5-14.

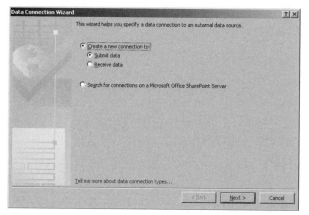

Figure 5-14 Creating a new data connection to submit the data back to the form library

Next, select the option To A Document Library On A Sharepoint Site and provide the URL to the form library previously created. It is a good idea to insert a formula to compile a unique file name for the submitted form. Click the Insert Formula button and use a *concat* function to construct the following formula:

```
concat("TRAINING-"; EmpID;"-"; Date;"-",Course)
```

Press OK and finish the wizard. There is a second action to include, one that switches to the second view showing the Thank You message. The complete rule is shown in Figure 5-15.

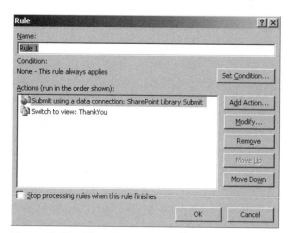

Figure 5-15 The rule to submit the data back to the form library

Close all of the open dialog boxes. After saving the template locally on your machine, go through the publishing wizard again and accept all of the defaults. When finished, the template in the form library is updated with your new changes.

There is one last thing you want to do before testing all of this. By default, the InfoPath smart client is used for working with the InfoPath form. However, there is a setting you can use to force SharePoint to display the InfoPath form in the browser, ignoring the smart client. This can be done by using the Settings menu in the form library to go to the Form Library Settings page and then Advanced Settings. Here, select the option to open browser-enabled documents in a Web page all the time.

Now go ahead and try out your work. Figure 5-16 illustrates how by default the InfoPath form fills up a complete browser window. This is not exactly what your users like to see, but you'll fix that in a moment. However, you can try out the form by filling in some data and testing your Submit button.

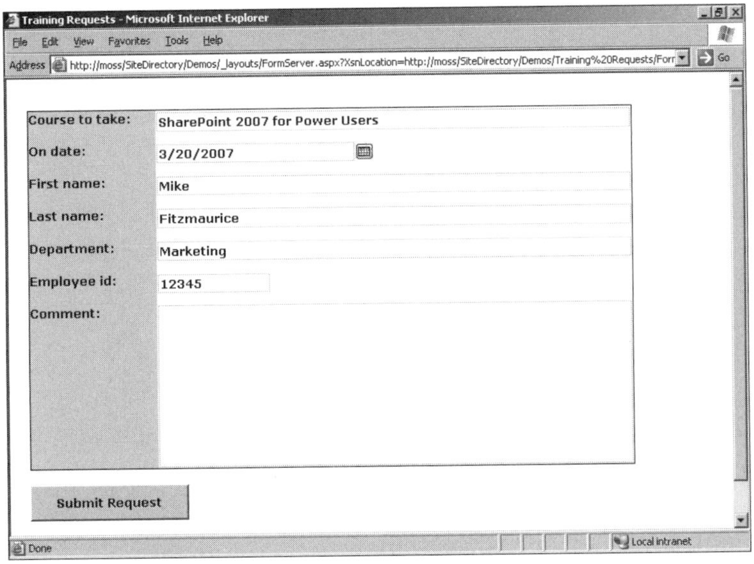

Figure 5-16   Displayed in the browser, the form for reserving a seat in a training

So now you can embed this form as part of a page instead of letting it completely take over your browser. The good news is that with a few steps, you are able to advertise a Web Part capable of delivering this experience. The Web Part is delivered as part of the *Microsoft.Office.InfoPath.Server.dll*. This .NET assembly is stored in the *C:\Program Files\Microsoft Office Servers\12.0\Bin* folder.

You'll first have to insert the *web.config* of the IIS Web Application that is hosting your site as an entry in the SafeControls section. Typically, the *web.config* is found in a subfolder of the C:\Inetpub\wwwroot\wss\VirtualDirectories folder. Open the *web.config* in Visual Studio.NET, locate the *SafeControls* element, and add the following entry as either the first one or the last one:

```
<SafeControl Assembly="Microsoft.Office.InfoPath.Server, Version=12.0.0.0,
 Culture=neutral, PublicKeyToken=71e9bce111e9429c"
 Namespace="Microsoft.Office.InfoPath.Server.Controls"
 TypeName="XmlFormView" Safe="True" />
```

Save the *web.config* and return to the browser and open the Web Part Gallery. This gallery can be found at the level of the root site within your site collection in the Site Settings page. Click the New button. In the list of available Web Parts, an entry for the XmlFormView Web Part should be available, as shown in Figure 5-17. Click the Populate Gallery button at the top of the page to add this Web Part to the list shown in the Add Web Part dialog box.

This list displays all available Web Parts for this gallery. Select each Web Part you want to add, and then click Populate Gallery.

| Populate Gallery |

☐ Overwrite if file already exists?

☐ Web Part Type Name	File Name
☐ AdventureWorksWebParts.EmployeeHumanResourcesDetail	EmployeeHumanResour
☐ AdventureWorksWebParts.EmployeeList	EmployeeList
☐ InsideMOSS.Samples.EmployeeDirectoryWebPart	EmployeeDirectoryWebF
☐ Microsoft.Office.Excel.WebUI.ExcelWebRenderer	ExcelWebRenderer
☐ Microsoft.Office.Excel.WebUI.InternalEwr	InternalEwr
☑ Microsoft.Office.InfoPath.Server.Controls.XmlFormView	XmlFormView

Figure 5-17   The XmlFormView can be added as one of the Web Parts in the Web Part Gallery.

The Web Part must be added to a Web Part page in your SharePoint site. This can be the home page but is not recommended. There are a couple of ways you can make such a page available, and it depends on whether you are working in a normal team site or in one of the portals. The difference is that by default in the portals, the Office SharePoint Server Publishing Feature is activated and the page model is very different than the one used to deliver the pages in a normal team site. You may want to refer back to Chapter 2, "Collaboration Portals and People Management." I assume here that you are working in a portal but within a team site created under the portal. So the Office SharePoint Server Publishing Feature is not turned on, and you do not work with pages that are stored in the Pages library and that are based on page layouts. Create a new document library called Pages and use the Web Part Page as the template. This will be the container where you can store your own pages, including the one that will be used to show the InfoPath form to the users, as shown in Figure 5-18.

On the page, in edit mode, you can now click the Add a Web Part button and select the XmlFormView Web Part that is available under the Miscellaneous section. An InfoPath Forms Services error will be shown but you can simply close it. It is generated because you need to configure a couple of properties for this Web Part. Open up the properties panel via the Edit menu at the Web Part level and select the Modify Shared Web Part option. You'll notice at the bottom a section called Features. Expand it and don't worry about the options for displaying the header and footer. You have disabled them already in the template itself. The EditingStatus has to be set to *Editing* if you intend to display new or existing InfoPath forms in the Web Part. Expand the DataBinding section to find three fields to fill in the paths to either a template (the *XsnLocation*) when displaying a blank form, the path to an existing form (the *XmlLocation*), and the possible path of the container where you want to save the completed form. For this walkthrough, I'll assume that you are going to display blank forms that are ready to be populated. So the configuration should look like the one displayed in Figure 5-19. The *XsnLocation* field contains the full path to the *template.xsn* stored in the form library created earlier.

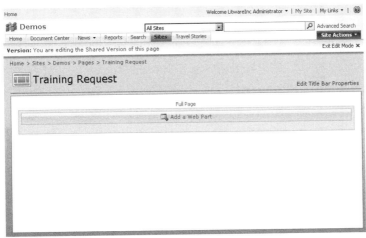

Figure 5-18   A page stored in a document library called Pages, part of a team site and ready to host the Web Part displaying the InfoPath form

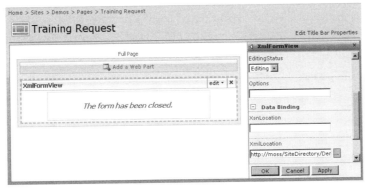

Figure 5-19   Configuring the properties of the XmlFormView Web Part telling it to display an empty form based on a template

Apply your changes and switch the page back to view mode. The page now shows an empty XML form and is ready for the user, as shown in Figure 5-20.

Fill in some data and click the Submit button. Behind the scenes, the form has been saved in the form library with the appropriate name, and the second view is displayed showing the Thank You message.

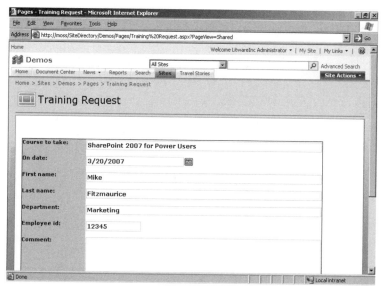

Figure 5-20 The page with the XmlFormView Web Part displaying a blank InfoPath form ready to be filled in

Summary

A key message to remember from this chapter is that the combination of InfoPath 2007, InfoPath Forms Services, and Microsoft Office SharePoint Server 2007 represents a very rich and powerful trio of technologies for creating, publishing, displaying, and managing electronic forms. Forms target not only people within your company, but, thanks to the ability to render the forms in the browser, they also target users outside of your company.

Chapter 6

Customizing and Branding Publishing Portals

- Learn how to create publishing portals and configure them for anonymous access and forms-based authentication.

- Understand the page model involved and the out-of-the-box publishing features.

- Learn more options in addition to those in Chapter 2, "Collaboration Portals and People Management," for how to customize and extend the publishing features.

- Learn about the *Microsoft.SharePoint.Publishing.dll* and the different classes involved that allow you to programmatically access the publishing features.

- Understand your options for customizing the Page Editing toolbar.

- Configure the site to support multiple languages for the published pages.

- Understand the document conversions framework and how it can be leveraged in a publishing portal.

Introducing Publishing Portals

On television, you often see advertisements where one interviews the man or woman on the street asking questions like "Have you heard about product X?" or "How do you use product Y?" If you were to ask an IT professional what SharePoint is and how it is used in businesses, you would probably get a reply such as: SharePoint is used for setting up a collaboration space and a document store inside a controlled setting called the intranet. To some degree, there is exposure to the outside world via extranets with partners or customers. And yes, occasionally you see SharePoint sites also as public sites on the Internet (typically in the blogging community). But the majority of the people asked the question will answer that SharePoint is typically used within the confines of the company network.

In the past, creating Internet-facing sites in the Microsoft world was done by using the ASP.NET framework in a direct way or by using additional layers on top of it provided by products such as Microsoft Content Management Server (CMS) or Microsoft Commerce Server (CS). The ASP.NET 2.0 framework offers all of the necessary APIs for a developer to create rich and compelling sites meeting most, if not all, of the requirements many customers have for a public site. There are plenty of examples available on the Web today demonstrating this. However, in many cases, people have additional requirements that involve a lot of work when purely working with ASP.NET 2.0. There may be a need for very dynamic branding capabilities where one must be able to make changes to the look and feel, the navigation infrastructure, and the branding of sites without having to go into development or a modification of the HTML in the pages directly. In many organizations, there are skilled people dedicated to constructing Web sites and all of the infrastructure involved. But very often, the responsibility for the content of those sites lies with a different group of professionals who don't have these same skills. Rather than knocking at the door of the IT department to deliver the site content, business users and content owners have moved to requesting a more decentralized authoring framework. They like to see an environment where they can take control of the content. They want to author and maintain the content using easy, flexible, but rich out-of-the-box features without having to touch the internals that make up a site or a page on that site.

If you want your public site to attract a lot of visitors, you need to frequently update it with new content. In today's business world, it's important, sometimes even a requirement, to get content published quickly and in an easy but highly controlled way. Transformation of draft content into published content usually involves one or more workflow steps, by which a draft page becomes a published page.

Finally, because in the work world today compliance to rules and regulations is more and more important, many organizations want to impose strict guidelines, policies, and rules on the content delivered as well as the process for creating and publishing that content. Adding all of the pieces to meet these requirements purely with ASP.NET 2.0 is possible but will involve a lot of extra work and time.

Microsoft Content Management Server 2002 (CMS) delivers a platform and toolset that addresses most, if not all, of the requirements for a content management system. For the new version, Microsoft decided to integrate the CMS product into Microsoft Office SharePoint Server 2007 in order to deliver one consistent and unified process for content management, for both the internal portals as well as the external portals. The publishing portal is a new site definition available following a successful installation of Microsoft Office SharePoint Server 2007. The goal of this template is to give you a starter site for the delivery of a public site. The site has all of the rich publishing features activated and, as a result, you can address all of the business requirements for a content management infrastructure.

Important   It is important to understand that all of the topics in this chapter discussing the publishing features are also valid for the collaboration portal or any SharePoint site where administrators have activated the publishing features. If you skipped Chapter 2, I advise you to return and read the first part of it since a lot of the basic concepts and terminologies are explained in that chapter. For this chapter, I'll only focus on the publishing portal and go a step further to explain both the concepts as well as the options for customizing and branding the publishing portals.

So, maybe you're new to this and your company decides to deliver an Internet site using Microsoft Office SharePoint Server 2007. What follows is a list of typical steps for the creation and design of publishing portals. Some of these steps are explained in Chapter 2, while others will be explained in this chapter:

- Prepare and extend an IIS Web application to host the publishing portal and all of the subsites.

- Provision the site collection and the top-level site based on the publishing portal site definition.

- Configure the publishing portal for anonymous access and forms-based authentication if there is the need to work with users that are not known or are not allowed as accounts in the domain.

- Invite users and assign roles within the site.

- Set up a site hierarchy, configuring and tuning the navigation and often incorporating the need for varying the sites and pages to deliver a multi-lingual or multi-device type of rendering.

- Brand the publishing portal with the company's look and feel.

- Create page layouts or templates that content owners can use for creating pages in a structured and controlled way.

- Configure the publishing cycle and the workflow involved.

- Enable smart client authoring and document conversion options for content owners who prefer to create and maintain content in a more familiar environment (such as Microsoft Word) instead of the browser.

- Set up an infrastructure for versioning and archiving content.

- Put in place the procedures and the mechanics for staging or deploying content from an authoring or staging environment to a production environment.

Creating Publishing Portals

Chapter 2 includes a walkthrough for extending an IIS Web application and provisioning a collaboration portal hosted on it. Exactly the same steps can be followed for provisioning a publishing portal. If you are unfamiliar with the process, return to Chapter 2 and review the steps in the walkthrough. The only alteration in the flow can be the anonymous access that can be turned on at the level of IIS while in the page for extending the IIS Web application. Figure 6-1 displays the *AdventureWorks* publishing portal as an example of the provisioning process.

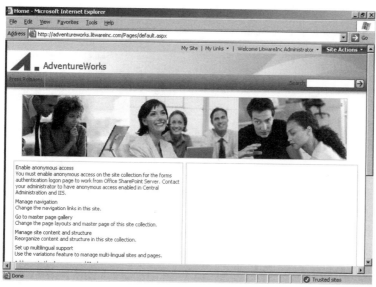

Figure 6-1 The new publishing portal in the browser

The Provisioning Flow

SharePoint has provisioned the publishing portal, and all of this has been very straight-forward, but, as explained in Chapter 2, the underlying mechanisms are a bit different from the provisioning of a Windows SharePoint Services 3.0 team site. Let's have a look again at the various players, summarized in Figure 6-2, since an understanding of the flow can open doors to new ways of extending and customizing the provisioning of publishing portals.

Every available template for a site is delivered by means of a *Template* element in one of the WEBTEMP* files located in the \12\Template\1033\XML folder. This folder is localized per language. The one that is used during the provisioning process of a publishing portal (and also the collaboration portal) is the *webtempsps.xml*. The following *Template* element contains the definition for the publishing portal:

```
<Template Name="BLANKINTERNETCONTAINER" ID="52">
    <Configuration ID="0" Title="Publishing Portal"
    Hidden="FALSE" ImageUrl="/_layouts/1033/images/IPPT.gif"
    Description="A starter site hierarchy for an Internet-facing site or
a large intranet portal. This site can be customized easily with
 distinctive branding. It includes a home page, a sample press releases
subsite, a Search Center, and a login page. Typically, this site has many
more readers than contributors, and it is used to publish Web pages with
approval workflows."
        ProvisionAssembly="Microsoft.SharePoint.Publishing,
Version=12.0.0.0, Culture=neutral, PublicKeyToken=71e9bce111e9429c"
        ProvisionClass="Microsoft.SharePoint.Publishing.
```

```
PortalProvisioningProvider"
        ProvisionData="xml\\InternetBlank.xml"
        RootWebOnly="TRUE" DisplayCategory="Publishing"
        VisibilityFeatureDependency="97A2485F-EF4B-401f-9167-FA4FE177C6F6">
    </Configuration>
  </Template>
```

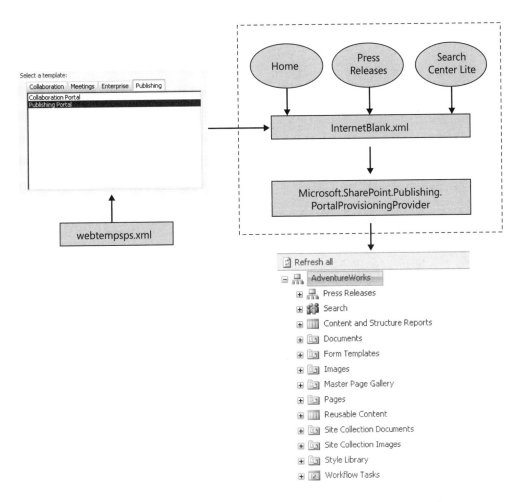

Figure 6-2   The different players in the provisioning process of a publishing portal

Portals are provisioned by means of a class in the *Microsoft.SharePoint.Publishing.dll*. The strong name of the .NET assembly is assigned as a value for the *ProvisionAssembly* attribute. The *PortalProvisioningProvider* class does the hard work and is set as the value for the *ProvisionClass* attribute. The script executed by the provisioning engine is the *Internet-Blank.xml* located in the \12\Template\XML folder. The location of this file is included in the template configuration definition as the value of the *ProvisionData* attribute. The content of that file is the following XML by default:

```
<portal xmlns="PortalTemplate.xsd">
  <web name="Home" siteDefinition="BLANKINTERNET#0"
    displayName="$Resources:cmscore,IPPT_Portal_Root_DisplayName;"
    description="$Resources:cmscore,IPPT_Portal_Root_Description;" >
    <webs>
      <web name="PressReleases" siteDefinition="BLANKINTERNET#1"
      displayName=
              "$Resources:cmscore,IPPT_Portal_PressRelease_DisplayName;"
      description="" />
      <web name="Search"
        siteDefinition="SRCHCENTERLITE#1"
        displayName=
          "$Resources:cmscore,IPPT_Portal_SearchCenterLite_DisplayName;"
        description="" />
    </webs>
  </web>
</portal>
```

The provisioning flow can be customized so that administrators can have portals that contain fully populated site hierarchies instead of only the Home, Press Releases, and the hidden Search Center Lite that are defined by default in *InternetBlank.xml*. That's exactly what you'll learn in the next walkthrough.

Walkthrough: Creating a Provisioning Script

Assume that you have to create many portals with a similar site hierarchy—let's say a top-level site, four subsites (Products, Services, News, Job Postings), two subsites under News (Press Releases and Announcements), and Search. Instead of creating these sites in the browser, one by one, you'll learn the steps to create a custom version of *InternetBlank.xml* and feed that to the provisioning engine.

Since you typically don't want to customize the out-of-the-box definitions, start by copying the *webtempsps.xml* to a new *webtemp_litware.xml* file in the \12\Template\1033\XML folder. Remove everything except the Template block for the *BLANKINTERNETCONTAINER*. Next, make some changes like the *name*, *title*, and *description*. It is important to also change the *ProvisionData* attribute value pointing to your own custom script, a copy of the *InternetBlank.xml*.

```
<Templates xmlns:ows="Microsoft SharePoint">
  <Template Name="LITWAREINTERNETCONTAINER" ID="1000">
    <Configuration ID="0"
    Title="Litware Internet Starter Kit" Hidden="FALSE"
    ImageUrl="/_layouts/1033/images/IPPT.gif"
    Description="This template can be used to create a starter internet
```

```
site for our customers."
    ProvisionAssembly="Microsoft.SharePoint.Publishing, Version=12.0.0.0,
Culture=neutral, PublicKeyToken=71e9bce111e9429c"
    ProvisionClass="Microsoft.SharePoint.Publishing.
PortalProvisioningProvider"
    ProvisionData="xml\\Litware\\InternetBlank.xml"
    RootWebOnly="TRUE" DisplayCategory="Publishing"
    VisibilityFeatureDependency="97A2485F-EF4B-401f-9167-FA4FE177C6F6">
    </Configuration>
    </Template>
</Templates>
```

It is a good idea to create this new script for the provision engine in a custom folder of \12\Template\XML, such as *Litware*. Make a copy of the original *InternetBlank.xml* and make the changes below to outline the custom site hierarchy.

More Info   For simplicity, you can hard-code any of the strings used, but in a real-world scenario you'd want to use resource files to localize the strings used in the XML. The resource files are created in the \12\Resources folder. Within your XML, replace a hard-coded string with something like $Resources:litware,key. The first part (litware) is the name of the resource file, while the key is used to get to the value to be inserted in the XML.

```xml
<portal xmlns="PortalTemplate.xsd">
  <web name="Home" siteDefinition="BLANKINTERNET#0"
    displayName="Home" description="Home" >
    <webs>
      <web name="JobPostings" siteDefinition="BLANKINTERNET#1"
        displayName="Job Postings" description="" />
      <web name="News" siteDefinition="BLANKINTERNET#1"
        displayName="News" description="">
        <webs>
          <web name="PressReleases" siteDefinition="BLANKINTERNET#1"
            displayName="Press Releases"  description="" />
          <web name="Announcements" siteDefinition="BLANKINTERNET#1"
            displayName="Announcements" description="" />
        </webs>
      </web>
      <web name="Services" siteDefinition="BLANKINTERNET#1"
        displayName="Services" description="" />
      <web name="Products" siteDefinition="BLANKINTERNET#1"
        displayName="Products" description="" />
      <web name="Search" siteDefinition="SRCHCENTERLITE#1"
        displayName="Search Center" description="" />
    </webs>
  </web>
</portal>
```

An *IISRESET* has to be done to load these new XML files into the worker process for SharePoint to use them. After this, you can test your work. It is necessary to create a new site collection since the publishing portal is marked with the attribute *RootWebOnly* in the webtemp* file. Illustrated by Figure 6-3, the list of available templates now includes your new template: Litware Internet Starter Kit.

Figure 6-3   The new custom site template in the Template Selection list

When continuing, the script will be handed over to the provisioning engine, and you'll have a site like the one portrayed in Figure 6-4.

Figure 6-4   A site for Contoso Pharmaceuticals following the site hierarchy as defined by the XML script

Anonymous Access and Forms-Based Authentication

Public sites are typically configured to allow anonymous access. Visitors navigate to the site or parts of the site without the need to explicitly sign in with an account. In some scenarios, however, there's also the requirement to allow users to create an account, use that account to sign in, and personalize the site experience or perform certain operations, such as dropping items out of a catalog in a shopping basket. These users typically are not part of your domain and have no valid Windows account.

In the previous version, this caused some problems since the whole authentication was focused on working with Windows accounts—local accounts or domain accounts. The current version allows you to store the membership and role information for users in any identity store, ranging from formal data stores such as Microsoft SQL Server to more generic stores such as plain XML files. However, this means that you'll have to come up with your own logic to get users authenticated, rather than relying on the Internet Information Server to do this for you.

In the following pages, I will cover these two topics explaining the configuration and administration tasks as well as some options for customizing and extending the out-of-the-box experience.

Anonymous Access

The configuration of anonymous access is done at two levels. The first level is the Internet Information Server where anonymous access must be allowed for the IIS Web application extended by SharePoint. You can do this without being logged on locally to the Web server using the SharePoint 3.0 Central Administration. In the Application Management page, there is a link under the Application Security group to navigate to the Authentication Providers page. A link for the default zone brings you to the page with the option to allow anonymous access.

> **Warning**   Before proceeding, make sure that you work with the correct IIS Web application. Verify the URL at the top of your admin page to avoid unpleasant consequences in other sites hosted on the Web server.

The second place to make a change is at the level of the publishing portal with anonymous access enabled at the top-level site. Subsites inherit this setting but can overrule it at the individual site level. On the top-level site, the anonymous access is configured by opening the Site Settings page and navigating to the Advanced Permissions page under the Users and Permissions group. Here, use the Settings menu and the Anonymous Access option to open the configuration page, as displayed in Figure 6-5. Typically for a publishing portal, access to the entire site is turned on.

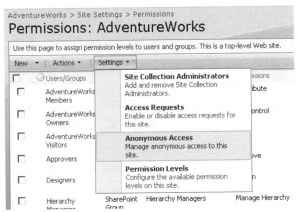

Figure 6-5   Allowing access to the entire top-level site for anonymous users

Users can now anonymously navigate to the site. Figure 6-6 shows the home page, and a Sign In link at the top allows users to sign in with an account. When done, they are authenticated and recognized by SharePoint and can then perform personalization, content authoring, or administration tasks for the site.

Figure 6-6 Anonymous users visiting the AdventureWorks publishing portal

Forms-Based Authentication

Now let's say that you want to build an Internet site where you'd like to allow registered visitors to personalize pages or give them the role of content authors. These visitors do not have an account in the Active Directory because they are not employed by the company and the domain administrator doesn't want them to end up in the Active Directory. Or maybe there are simply too many of these visitors, such as when the site is an e-commerce type of site accessible to the general public.

If you don't store the membership information in the Active Directory, then what are your options? You'll have to store the account information somewhere. The good news is that you can store the accounts in any identity store now. Microsoft SQL Server 2000/2005 databases and any LDAP-enabled identity store are possible candidates supported directly out-of-the-box with Windows SharePoint Services 3.0. Other types of identity stores, such as XML, an Oracle database, or flat files, are also options, but they require additional work. To access these stores, you have to register and configure a custom authentication provider (a topic discussed later).

Forms-based authentication is based on the verification of authentication cookies. Let me explain this a bit more. When a user tries to access the portal, a check is done to see if an authentication cookie is passed along with the HTTP request. If this is not the case, the user is redirected to a login page giving him or her the user interface controls to enter the credentials as needed. The verification of these credentials with the custom identity store is performed within this login. In addition, an authentication cookie for the user is created and there is a redirect back to the page that was originally requested.

The Identity Store and *ConnectionStrings*

The identity store is the place to store the user credentials that can be used during the authentication. If you have done some work with ASP.NET, you've probably read about this and have heard it referred to as membership information. Without doing any additional custom work, Windows SharePoint Services 3.0 supports the use of Active Directory and a Microsoft SQL Server database. First, let's see what the last one can do for you.

The database for the membership information can have any schema, but if you want to do this with minimal effort, a database has to be created that recognizes both ASP.NET 2.0 and Windows SharePoint Services 3.0 . This is the *aspnetdb* database, and you can create it by executing a small utility called *aspnet_regsql.exe*, found in the \windows\Microsoft.NET\ Framework\v2.0.50727 folder. Execute it either at the command line or by double-clicking on it to initiate the ASP.NET SQL Server Setup Wizard as shown in Figure 6-7. The wizard guides you through some short steps to configure and create the *aspnetdb* database. The command-line approach provides more options to configure the creation process, but the outcome will be the same: a Microsoft SQL Server database with a structure ready to store not only membership information but also roles, profile, and personalization information.

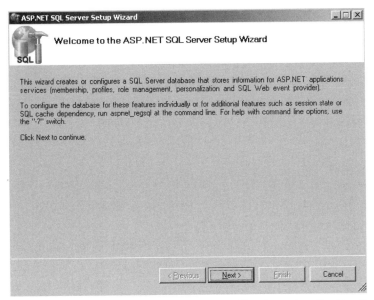

Figure 6-7   The ASP.NET SQL Server Setup Wizard creating the identity store

Populating the database with membership information (users and credentials) can be done in three ways:

- The *aspnetdb* database has a number of stored procedures. Executing the *aspnet_Membership_CreateUser* stored procedure drops new users in the database.

- Another option is the ASP.NET Web Site Administration Tool (part of Microsoft Visual Studio.NET 2005), displayed in Figure 6-8.

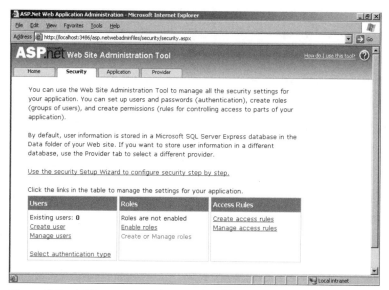

Figure 6-8 Adding users to the membership store using the ASP.NET Web Site Administration Tool

■ A final approach is programmatic and calls the *CreateUser* method of the *Membership* class—a class encapsulated in the *System.Web.dll*. All of the access to, configuration for, and management of the membership store is exposed by classes in the *System.Web.Security* namespace. There is a small application called the *AspMembershipAdminTool* on the companion Web site that illustrates the programming steps to add a couple of users. The code to create a user is as follows:

```
MembershipCreateStatus status;
Membership.CreateUser("Mike Fitzmaurice", "pass@word1",
    "mikef@litwareinc.com", "question","answer", true, out status);
MessageBox.Show(status.ToString());
```

Now, if you run that sample application, you'll possibly encounter some problems because of the default configuration of the proper *ConnectionString* elements in the configuration files. These entries indicate where the *aspnetdb* database is located to the custom application and even to the ASP.NET Web Site Administration Tool. The *ConnectionString* elements are stored in a *config* file (a *web.config* for ASP.NET and an *app.config* for Windows Forms). By default, there is already a *ConnectionString* defined, but you have to check whether it points to the local Microsoft SQL Server Express. If so, there are two options for changing this. One is to open the \WINDOWS\Microsoft.NET\Framework\v2.0.50727\CONFIG\machine.config and look up the *ConnectionString* element. You replace the element with the following:

```
<add name="LocalSqlServer" connectionString="data source=MOSS;Integrated
Security=SSPI;Initial Catalog=aspnetdb" />
```

Changing the *machine.config* has an immediate effect on all of the .NET applications running on the machine since they will now follow this configuration. If you want to be more granular, add a *web.config* or an *app.config* and insert the following:

```
<connectionStrings>
    <remove name="LocalSqlServer" />
    <add name="LocalSqlServer" connectionString="data
     source=MOSS;Integrated Security=SSPI;Initial Catalog=aspnetdb" />
  </connectionStrings>
```

The name of the SQL Server is MOSS in the above XML.

Using a Microsoft SQL Server database is not your only option as the identity store. You can also use an Active Directory or any LDAP store. A practical example of this can be a scenario where the SharePoint site is hosted in the Perimeter Network where you have a domain configured to store the credentials of the visitors in a secure way, not interfering with the accounts that are defined within the internal network.

The connection string below is an example of a possible connection to the *LitwareInc* domain where accounts for external visitors are stored. You have to add this to the *web.config* files of any SharePoint-extended IIS Web application wherever you want to use this type of authentication (including the SharePoint 3.0 Central Administration).

```
<connectionStrings>
 <add name="AD" connectionString=
      "LDAP://moss.litwareinc.com/CN=Users,DC=litwareinc,DC=com"/>
</connectionStrings>
```

ASP.NET Authentication Provider Primer

In this version of SharePoint, we rely on the ASP.NET 2.0 authentication providers to support forms-based authentication. Let's discuss this provider model more in detail to give you an understanding of how it works, what's delivered right out-of-the-box, and, very important, how you can leverage the model to build your own custom providers.

Not working with Windows authentication means that instead of letting IIS do the authentication work, you and SharePoint have to do the work for the SharePoint sites that are enabled for forms-based authentication. There is excellent support in ASP.NET 2.0 to accomplish this in a very clean and organized manner, allowing you to concentrate only on the high-level layer of the problem. All the low-level plumbing is handled in a unified and consistent way through the membership providers in ASP.NET 2.0: enabling the connections to the identity stores, getting access to the membership information, pushing changes back to the membership store, validating users, and much more. Figure 6-9 summarizes all of the options.

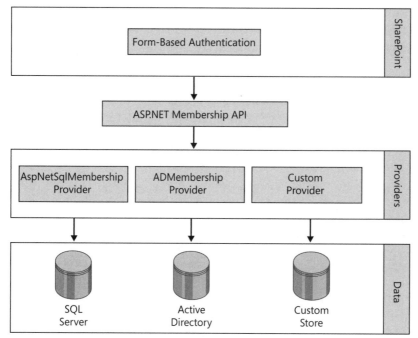

Figure 6-9   The ASP.NET 2.0 authentication providers

Two membership providers are available straight away—no extra coding required:

- The first provider is the *SQLMembershipProvider*, a provider that can connect to membership information stored in a Microsoft SQL Server database (by default *aspnetdb*).

- The other one is the *ActiveDirectoryMembershipProvider*, a provider that connects to an Active Directory and the membership information it stores.

Each of these providers must be registered in the *web.config* of the sites where you want to use them. The *SQLMembershipProvider* registration is available by default in the *machine.config* file.

```
<membership>
  <providers>
    <add name="AspNetSqlMembershipProvider"
    type="System.Web.Security.SqlMembershipProvider, System.Web,
      Version=2.0.0.0, Culture=neutral, PublicKeyToken=b03f5f7f11d50a3a"
    connectionStringName="LocalSqlServer" enablePasswordRetrieval="false"
    enablePasswordReset="true" requiresQuestionAndAnswer="true"
    applicationName="/" requiresUniqueEmail="false"
    passwordFormat="Hashed" maxInvalidPasswordAttempts="5"
    minRequiredPasswordLength="7" minRequiredNonalphanumericCharacters="1"
    passwordAttemptWindow="10" passwordStrengthRegularExpression="" />
  </providers>
</membership>
```

As you see, there are a lot of possible settings for the provider. I better refer to the ASP.NET documentation for a full explanation of each of these because it is outside the scope of this book. If you're happy with them, just leave them as they are in the *machine.config*. If not, override them in your local *web.config*.

It's a different story for the *ActiveDirectoryMembershipProvider*, because there is no default registration in the *machine.config*. So, you have the choice to add the provider details in the *machine.config* or in the local *web.config*. Here are the details:

```
<add name="AspNetActiveDirectoryMembershipProvider"
 type="System.Web.Security.ActiveDirectoryMembershipProvider, System.Web,
 Version=2.0.3600.0, Culture=neutral, PublicKeyToken=b03f5f7f11d50a3a"
 connectionStringName="AD"  connectionUsername="litwareinc\Administrator"
 connectionPassword="pass@word1"/>
```

Overall, the two membership providers will be sufficient for most scenarios. But if not, the ASP.NET provider model is designed to be extensible. You can create, deploy, and register your own custom membership provider by taking the following steps:

- Create and prepare your custom identity store. Examples are a Microsoft Access database, a simple XML file, an Oracle database, or any store that fits the requirements of your solution.

- Create a .NET class library with a class that inherits from the *System.Web.Security .MembershipProvider* base class. This is also the base class for the two membership providers discussed before and summarized in Figure 6-10.

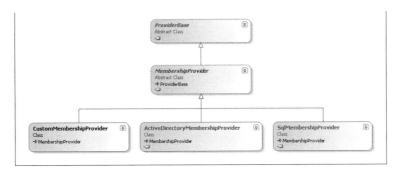

Figure 6-10   The class hierarchy for the membership providers

- Implement the members of the base class: the *MembershipProvider* class. It is fully equipped with dozens of methods that can be overridden and used for coding the communication with your identity store. The ASP.NET 2.0 documentation contains the full details for each of them.

- Build the .NET assembly, possibly signing it. If you are not going for a strong-named assembly, you limit your choice of deploying the .NET assembly.

- Deploy the .NET assembly. You have two options. The first is the bin folder part of the physical folder of your IIS Web application where you want to use the custom membership provider. Note that this is your only option if you decided not to build a strong-named assembly. In the case of a strong-named assembly, you can deploy the .NET assembly in the global assembly cache.

■ Register the custom membership provider in the *web.config* of every IIS Web application where you want to make use of it. In the case of SharePoint, this means the SharePoint 3.0 Central Administration and the IIS Web application that hosts the site you want to configure.

Walkthrough: Creating a Custom Authentication Provider

Let's work out an example of a custom membership provider authenticating the user credentials stored in a small Microsoft Access 2007 database. Note that there is more meat you can add to this membership provider, but I'll leave it up to you to finish it.

To start, create a small Microsoft Access 2007 database with a table called *users*. The table stores the following information in the different columns: *username*, *e-mail*, *password*, *question*, and *answer*. The bulk of the work is done in Microsoft Visual Studio.NET 2005 where you can start by creating a new class library, *LitwareMembershipProviders*. There are a number of references to add because you've started with the bare minimum here. The references to add are *System.Web.dll* and *System.Configuration.dll*.

It's not a bad idea to rename the class to *MicrosoftAccessMembershipProvider* and the namespace to *InsideMOSS.Samples*. Finish the initial work by adding the using statements for namespaces you are about to employ within your code.

```
using System;
using System.Collections.Generic;
using System.Text;
using System.Web.Security;
using System.Configuration;
using System.Collections.Specialized;
using System.Data.OleDb;

namespace InsideMOSS.Samples
{
    public class MicrosoftAccessMembershipProvider
    {}
}
```

To transform your class into a membership provider, the class must inherit from the *MembershipProvider* base class, and all the members of this abstract class have to be implemented (easy to do with the smart tag in Visual Studio.NET). For our walkthrough, it's enough to implement the five methods that are required to support forms-based authentication in a SharePoint environment: *GetUser*, *GetUserNameByEmail*, *FindAllUsers-ByName*, *FindAllUsersByEmail*, and *ValidateUser*. The first four are needed by the *People Picker* control, and the *ValidateUser* method is the one called in the login page to verify the credentials.

Very often, there is a need for administrators to configure the provider with some parameter values while registering the membership provider in the *web.config*. The settings are then mapped to properties exposed in the membership provider class. The base *MembershipProvider* class already contains the most relevant settings you want to support, but to illustrate the process of adding your own custom setting, you'll add one more: *MinRequiredUserNameLength*. With this extra configuration, administrators can enforce that the username consists of a minimum number of characters.

Start by adding a new property to your class using the snippet feature in Microsoft Visual Studio.NET to generate the wrapper for the property. Change the name of the property to *MinRequiredUserNameLength* and *minRequiredUserNameLength* for the member variable. Read-only access is more than enough.

```
private int minRequiredUserNameLength = 5;
public int MinRequiredUserNameLength
{
   get { return minRequiredUserNameLength; }
}
```

There's also another piece of information set by the administrator in the *web.config* that is required internally in your code: the connection string to the Microsoft Access 2007 database. No need to expose this one as a property; a class member variable is sufficient.

```
private string connectionstring = string.Empty;
```

Read the values out of the *web.config* and assign them to the member variables in the *Initialize* method of your class. It is a method that you override from the base *Membership-Provider* class, and it passes you the information from the *web.config* via the *config* parameter (type *NameValueCollection*). It is used to extract the settings from the config file and to pass them to the member variables.

```
public override void Initialize(string name, NameValueCollection config)
{
  if (config["minRequiredUserNameLength"] != null)
    this.minRequiredUserNameLength =
            int.Parse(config["minRequiredUserNameLength"]);
  this.connectionstring = config["connectionString"].ToString();
  base.Initialize(name, config);
}
```

This was only the prep work! Now it's time to concentrate on the five membership methods that code the communication to the Microsoft Access 2007 database. The steps are always basically the same, so you might want to create a helper class to encapsulate all of this logic. We'll keep it fairly simple.

 Note   The completed version of the custom Microsoft Access membership provider is available on the companion Web site.

Let's start with the *ValidateUser* method. The two incoming parameters are the values entered by the user on the login pages: the *user name* and *password*. Use this information to connect to the database, and execute a command to verify whether the combination is valid:

```
public override bool ValidateUser(string username, string password)
{
  bool returnFlag = false;
  try
  {
    OleDbConnection conn = new OleDbConnection(this.connectionstring);
    conn.Open();
    OleDbCommand cmd = new OleDbCommand
        ("SELECT * FROM Users WHERE username=@username AND
         password=@password", conn);
    cmd.Parameters.AddWithValue("@username", username);
    cmd.Parameters.AddWithValue("@password", password);
    OleDbDataReader rd = cmd.ExecuteReader();
    returnFlag = rd.HasRows;
  }
  catch (Exception ex)
  {
    //-- throw exception
  }
  finally
  {
    //-- clean up and close connection
  }
  return returnFlag;
}
```

Next, you have the different methods used by the *People Picker* control. Administrators are sometimes desperate to find users based on certain criteria, and your provider should be able to cope with these requests. In all of them, you'll connect to the database again and execute a query returning either one object of type *MembershipUser* or a collection of it. The *GetUser-NameByEmail* is a bit different and has a *string* return value.

 Note   Please refer to the companion Web site for the complete listing of the code since it is quite lengthy.

There are two options for the deployment of the .NET assembly: as a private assembly or as a shared assembly. For the former approach, copy the assembly to the bin folder associated with the IIS Web application hosting the SharePoint site where you want to use that provider. For the latter, you'll have to sign the .NET assembly and deploy it in the Global Assembly Cache. On your development machine, I would select the first option to ease the testing and debugging of your code, but it is a good idea to have the assembly already signed so that you can register it properly.

The only step left is to register your new membership provider in the *web.config* files of the SharePoint 3.0 Central Administration and the SharePoint site where you want to use it.

If you don't want to repeat these steps for every IIS Web site you extend, register the provider in the *machine.config*. Whatever scenario you're aiming for, the registration XML looks like this (note that the *PublicKeyToken* is different if you used your own key):

```
<membership>
  <providers>
    <add name="MicrosoftAccessMembershipProvider"
     type="Litware.Security.MicrosoftAccessMembershipProvider,
LitwareMembershipProviders, Version=1.0.0.0, Culture=neutral,
PublicKeyToken=165383999e79f2c6"
      connectionString="Provider=Microsoft.ACE.OLEDB.12.0;Data Source=
C:\data\Users.accdb;Persist Security Info=False"
      minRequiredUserNameLength="3"/>
  </providers>
</membership>
```

You'll make use of this custom provider later in the chapter.

Turning On Forms-Based Authentication

Now, let's get back to the topic of forms-based authentication with the steps administrators have to do to turn on forms-based authentication for an IIS Web application. The SharePoint 3.0 Central Administration is the key place for administrators. On the Applications Management page, under the Application Security group, click on the Authentication Providers link. The zone(s) that are currently active are displayed on the next page. Clicking on one of them opens the page where the configuration change from Windows to the Forms option in the Authentication Type section can be made. If done, two additional settings, one for defining the membership provider and one for the role provider (optional), are now visible on the page. You'll add the name of both. The name has to match the way they are registered in the config file. If you decide to authenticate against the *aspnetdb* Microsoft SQL Server database, the name of the membership provider is *aspnetsqlmembershipprovider* as displayed in Figure 6-11. A the bottom of the page, there is an option to enable the smart client integration. I'll explain what that means in a moment.

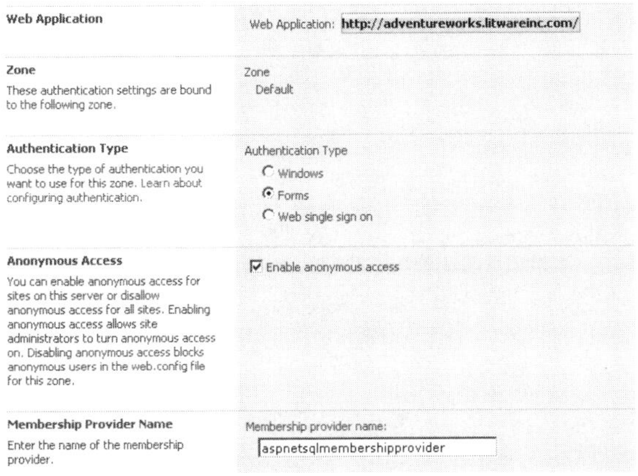

Figure 6-11   Configuring the IIS Web application for forms-based authentication and defining the membership provider to use

But do try out this configuration with the Microsoft Access membership provider discussed before. The only difference is of course the name of the membership provider. It must be set to *microsoftaccessmembershipprovider* (as you have registered it in the *web.config* or the *machine.config*).

No matter what provider you use, applying this new configuration has big consequences for the publishing portal. The authentication type modification is pushed to the *web.config*, and, therefore, users who want to get more than anonymous access will have to pass through a login page, as depicted in Figure 6-12.

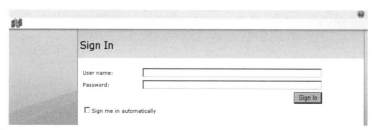

Figure 6-12   The login page displayed to users when forms-based authentication is turned on for a site

Now, what account do you use to sign in? There is a small problem here as we have nobody from our SQL Server data store able to access the site. There is no one listed as a user in the SharePoint site. It's also not possible to invite the SQL users when the site was configured for Windows authentication since the *People Picker* control only accepted valid Windows accounts at that time. If you're starting to sweat now and want to switch back to Windows authentication for the publishing portal, don't worry. The SharePoint product team has supplied a place in the SharePoint 3.0 Central Administration that allows administrators to invite users to a site and give them a role—and all of this without actually being logged on to that site. The administration page in question is the Policy for Web Application page accessible from the Application Management page, shown in Figure 6-13, in the SharePoint 3.0 Central Administration.

Central Administration > Application Management > Policy for Web Application
Policy for Web Application

	Zone	Display Name	User Name	Permissions
	(All zones)	NT AUTHORITY\LOCAL SERVICE	NT AUTHORITY\LOCAL SERVICE	Full Read
	(All zones)	NT AUTHORITY\NETWORK SERVICE	NT AUTHORITY\NETWORK SERVICE	Full Read

Add Users | Delete Selected Users | Edit Permissions of Selected Users   Web Application: **http://adventureworks.litware**

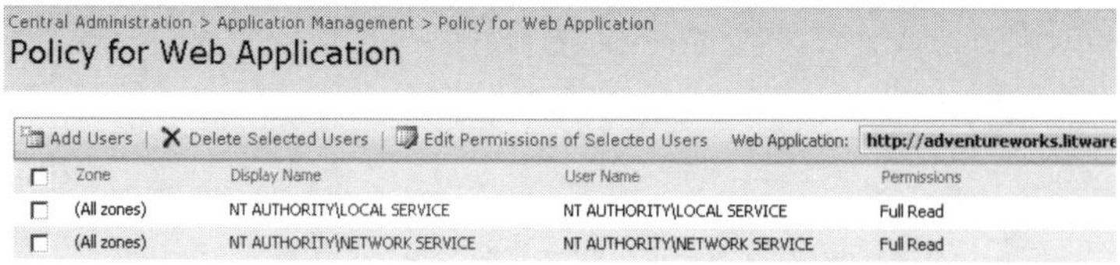

Figure 6-13   The Policy for Web Application page

A number of accounts have already been created. More can be created using the Add Users button in the toolbar. For a publishing portal, the user is added in the default zone. Note that the *People Picker* control knows about the authentication mode and has switched from verifying the entry against the accounts in Active Directory to checking what you have in your own identity store. Figure 6-14 shows how the control can display the different matching names.

Troubleshooting   If this is causing a problem, check whether the *ConnectionString* element has been defined properly in the *web.config* of the SharePoint 3.0 Central Administration or if the change you've made in the *machine.config* points to the correct *aspnetdb* database.

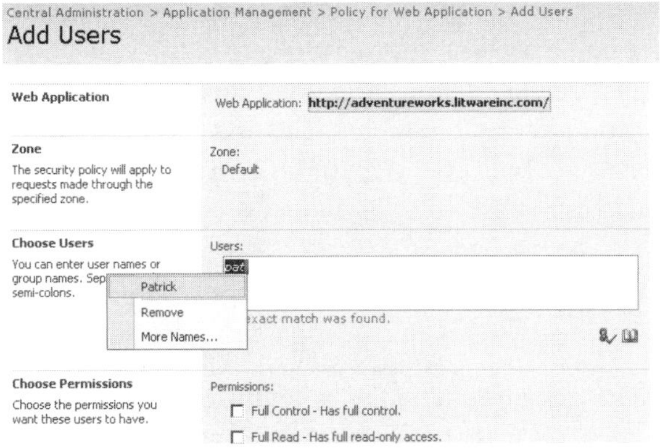

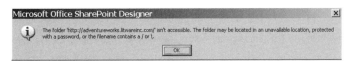

Figure 6-14   Adding one of the SQL Server accounts to the list of users in the AdventureWorks site

With access to the AdventureWorks site, users can sign in and start inviting other people via the People and Groups administration page. This is possible because the AdventureWorks site is configured for forms authentication, and the *People Picker* control is able to connect to the *aspnetdb* and perform a verification against the membership table.

The Smart Clients

The smart clients, such as all of the Microsoft Office 2007 clients including Microsoft SharePoint Designer 2007, will have trouble accessing a site configured for forms-based authentication. Bear in mind that forms-based authentication uses authentication cookies. These cookies are memory cookies by default. This means that when signing in for a site, a cookie is created and kept alive as long as the browser session is open. On the other hand, the smart clients do not have access to this cookie for authentication with the SharePoint site, so they return an error, as displayed in Figure 6-15.

Figure 6-15   The Microsoft Office SharePoint Designer is not able to access a site configured with forms-based authentication when there is no persistent cookie created.

To resolve this problem, two things need to be done. First, in the Policy for Web Application page, you have to enable smart client support. Remember the last setting at the bottom of the page? You'll need to have it turned on. Next, you'll have to force SharePoint to create a persistent cookie instead of a memory cookie. This can easily be done by selecting the Sign

Me In Automatically option available on the login page. After that, you'll be able to access the site with your smart clients such as Microsoft Office SharePoint Designer 2007.

Customizing and Extending Publishing Portals

Consider the out-of-the-box site template for a publishing portal as a decent example of an Internet site. But hopefully, you're going to want to make changes to the look and feel, customize, brand the pages, and perhaps extend the infrastructure with custom page layouts (a.k.a. templates), additional field controls (a.k.a. placeholders), master pages, and extensions to the publishing cycle. The basics have been covered in the chapter on collaboration portals. Here, we'll go a step further.

The *Microsoft.SharePoint.Publishing.dll*

Microsoft.SharePoint.Publishing.dll is the .NET assembly that contains the majority of the code supporting the content management integration in Microsoft Office SharePoint Server 2007. Knowledge of a number of the namespaces is essential before starting to customize or extend publishing portals.

- The *Microsoft.SharePoint.Publishing* namespace contains the classes encapsulating the code-behind for supporting the publishing cycle and related operations. There is support for page layouts, variations, caching, different server controls, Web Parts, and more.

- Next you have the *Microsoft.SharePoint.Publishing.Administration* namespace with the classes used for the content deployment and migration of publishing sites.

- The *Microsoft.SharePoint.Publishing.Fields* is the namespace that makes available the code for all of the additional field types and field controls one can use and drop on the page layouts. Examples are the *HTML* and the *Image* field types. The *fldtypes_publishing.xml* in the \12\Template\XML folder stores the schema information for the publishing field types.

- The *Microsoft.SharePoint.Publishing.Navigation* namespace defines the code-behind for supporting the navigation controls, strongly following the ASP.NET 2.0 provider model. Here, find the *PortalSiteMapProvider* responsible for the retrieval of the site hierarchy data stored in the database.

- The *Microsoft.SharePoint.Publishing.WebControls* contains the code-behind classes for the various ASP.NET server controls and Web Parts. Examples are the HTML editor, authoring console controls, SummaryLink, and TableOfContents Web Parts.

- The *Microsoft.SharePoint.Publishing.WebControls.EditingMenuActions* namespace is interesting. The Page Editing toolbar is a UI component for the content author that exposes the publishing status and operations. All of the code-behind for the controls on the toolbar is provided by classes within this namespace.

- The last one is the *Microsoft.SharePoint.Publishing.WebService* where the most important class is the one working behind the scenes of the *PublishingService.asmx*, a Web Service to communicate remotely with the different steps in the publishing of pages in the portal.

Master Pages in the Publishing Portal

Every one of the pages in the publishing portal is connected to a master page stored in the Master Page Gallery at the level of the site collection. Chapter 2 covered master pages, the different types, how to switch to other master pages, the different controls used on the *default.master*, and how to customize a master page with Microsoft Office SharePoint Designer 2007. All of this is applicable to the publishing portal, but you are typically not going to work with the *default.master* as your master page. Instead, you'll use one of the alternatives available in the Master Page Gallery. Later, there will be a small overview of your different options. If you're not happy with any of these, there is still the option to create your own master page. A walkthrough covers the different steps involved.

The out-of-the-box publishing portal uses the BlueBand master page. If you open that page in Microsoft Office SharePoint Designer 2007, you'll see a lot more controls than the one available in the *default.master*. One group of controls in addition to the ones described in Chapter 2 are referred to as the publishing controls. These controls are prefixed with *PublishingWeb-Controls* and *PublishingNavigation* and deliver the publishing features for the site. The first group, the *PublishingWebControls*, are controls not directly found in the master pages. They are made available in the page layouts that define the diverse field controls that are part of the *Microsoft.SharePoint.Publishing.Fields* namespace. Examples of these are the *RichHtmlField* an the *RichImageField*.

The *PublishingNavigation* prefix is used for the various *PortalSiteMapDataSource* controls that are used by the navigation controls to communicate to the site map providers. Also, in addition to the ASP.NET user controls discussed in Chapter 2, in the *blueband.master*, you'll find three controls dedicated to publishing portals. All of them are stored in the \12\Template\Controltemplates folder:

- The *VariationsLabelMenu.ascx*, a user control displayed to the user when viewing a page that is part of a variation hierarchy. Using this control, the user can quickly jump to the same page in one of the other variations.

> **Important**   At the time of writing, in the ASP.NET user control, the control that actually displays the label is commented out for some reason. You can just uncomment it to start making use of it when switching between different languages in the site (see later).

- The *PublishingConsole.ascx*, an important user control since it allows for control of all the steps during the publishing cycle of a page.

- The *PublishingActionMenu.ascx*, a user control delivering the Site Actions fly-out menu.

Out-of-the-Box Master Pages

A variety of master pages are available out-of-the-box with Windows SharePoint Services 3.0 and Microsoft Office SharePoint Server 2007. We have discussed some of the internals of the *BlueBand.master*, but you can switch one or all of your sites in the publishing portal to any of the master pages that are stored in the Master Page Gallery. The place where you actually do this is the Site Master Page Settings page, displayed in Figure 6-16. Navigate to this page via the Master Page link under the Look and Feel section in the Site Settings page. The page shows the list of available candidates, and you'll be able to select one and apply it to a site, pushing the change to any subsites. At the level of the subsites, it's possible to break the inheritance and associate the site with another master page.

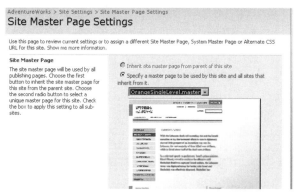

Figure 6-16   Changing to another master page using the Site Master Page Settings page

Let's quickly describe the candidate master pages that are provisioned with the publishing portal.

- The first one is the *default.master*, which was discussed in detail in Chapter 2. If you want, you can make the publishing pages within your publishing portal follow the traditional SharePoint look and feel shown in Figure 6-17. But remember that the *default.master* is somewhat of a chameleon master page, because it uses the *DelegateControl* in many places to adapt itself at runtime to the many types of sites where it is used. Because of this, the *default.master* is not a good candidate to learn from when you build your own master page.

Figure 6-17   A publishing portal following the same look and feel as the SharePoint administration pages

■ Better candidates from which to learn are the three master pages that belong to the same family: the *BlueBand.master*, *BlackBand.master*, and *BlueGlassBand.master*. They display navigation bars on the top and left and are good candidates for the publishing portals. These master pages make a good starting point for your customizations.

■ Two other master pages are also good candidates to start with: the *BlueVertical.master* and *BlackVertical.master*. They present the same look and feel as the three master pages discussed in the previous bullet but do not contain the top navigation bar. Figure 6-18 shows the AdventureWorks site using the *BlueVertical.master*.

Figure 6-18   Applying the *BlueVertical.master* to the publishing portal as the master page

■ Another one you can switch to in the Site Master Page Settings page is the *BlueTabs.master*, also a valid candidate to start with. The difference is that the top navigation bar is tab-based, as illustrated in Figure 6-19.

Figure 6-19   The *BlueTabs.master* applied to the pages

■ The last set of master pages are the *OrangeSingleLevel.master* and the *BlackSingleLevel.master*. Both are variations of the *BlueBand* type of master pages but with different color combinations.

Styling the Publishing Portal

Styling is done with CSS files linked by the master page. Table 6-1 describes the different cascading stylesheets linked by the *BlueBand.master*. The other master pages follow the same approach but use different CSS files.

Table 6-1   CSS Files Linked to the *BlueBand.master* in a Publishing Portal

CSS File	Description
Core.css	Contains the core CSS classes linked to the master page at runtime by the *CssLink* control (located in \12\Template\Layouts\1033\Styles).
PageLayouts.css	Default CSS classes used by the page layouts or templates upon which your publishing pages are based (located in /Style Library/locale/Core Styles).
Band.css	The CSS classes part of the general look and feel definition associated with the *BlueBand.master*. If you switch to another master page for your publishing site, you will get a different CSS file (e.g., the *SingleLevel.css*) retrieved from the same location (located in /Style Library/locale/Core Styles).
Controls.css	Shared by all the master pages, making available the CSS classes defining the style of the various controls used on the publishing pages (located in /Style Library/locale/Core Styles).
Zz1-blue.css	Small CSS file that defines the common look and feel for all of the master pages of the same category. These CSS files are independent of the locale and stored directly under the root of the Style Library (located in /Style Library).

In fact, there are two locations from where your CSS files originate. The first is the \12\ Template\Layouts\1033\Styles where the publishing portal loads the *core.css*. It is possible to override this by specifying an alternate CSS URL in the Site Master Page Settings page. You can upload your own custom *core.css* to the Style Library and notify the *CSSLink* control to activate the uploaded one instead of the default *core.css*. The second location is the database. In the publishing portal, the different CSS files that make it all happen are stored in the Style Gallery. You can review the contents of the Style Gallery in the browser by navigating to the Site Content and Structure page via the Site Actions, as illustrated in Figure 6-20. The Style Library stores two categories of CSS files; one category is dependent on the locale or language, and the other is independent of it.

The CSS files stored in the Style Gallery are linked in the master page with the *CssRegistration* control (a type defined in the *Microsoft.SharePoint.dll*). If you open up the *BlueBand.master* in Microsoft Office SharePoint Designer 2007, at the top you'll find a number of these controls:

```
<SharePoint:CssRegistration name="<% $SPUrl:~SiteCollection/Style
Library/~language/Core Styles/Band.css%>" runat="server"/>

<SharePoint:CssRegistration name="<% $SPUrl:~sitecollection/Style
Library/~language/Core Styles/controls.css %>" runat="server"/>

<SharePoint:CssRegistration name="<% $SPUrl:~SiteCollection/Style
Library/zz1_blue.css%>" runat="server"/>
```

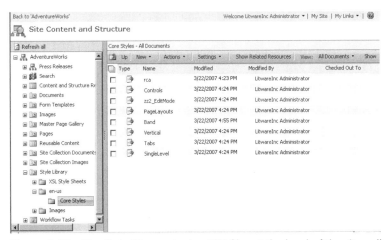

Figure 6-20   The Style Library storing CSS files at the level of the site collection

Microsoft Office SharePoint Designer 2007 is capable of providing very good design when it applies the CSS classes to the various elements within the opened pages in the Designer. From the moment you register one of the CSS files, the Apply Styles pane, shown in Figure 6-21, picks up the CSS file and displays the elements in a WYSIWYG representation so that you immediately have a good understanding of what the CSS class is all about.

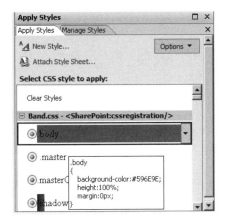

Figure 6-21   The Apply Styles pane in Microsoft Office SharePoint Designer 2007

Walkthrough: Building a Custom Master Page

Your company may require that new master pages be created for the publishing portals. Designers can use various authoring environments and compile the general look and feel along with the common functionality for the pages on the site. One of the candidates could be Microsoft Office SharePoint Designer 2007. Let me take you back to the AdventureWorks publishing portal and walk you through the steps for creating a new master page. It's not my goal to make it super flashy but to simply demonstrate the basic steps to take.

To start, open the AdventureWorks site in Microsoft Office SharePoint Designer 2007. The File New dialog box provides the option to create a new blank master page. Be aware that starting with a blank master page will involve some work and may create problems since SharePoint requires that a certain amount of *ContentPlaceHolder* controls be added to the master page. In addition to these, a *SPWebPartManager* control must be added because your master page will be used for SharePoint pages, and these typically will also contain Web Parts. *RobotsMetaTag* is the last control that's needed. So, begin with the following bare minimum master page:

```
<%@ Master language="C#" %>
<%@ Import Namespace="Microsoft.SharePoint" %>
<%@ Register Tagprefix="SharePoint"
    Namespace="Microsoft.SharePoint.WebControls"
    Assembly="Microsoft.SharePoint, Version=12.0.0.0, Culture=neutral,
PublicKeyToken=71e9bce111e9429c" %>
<%@ Register Tagprefix="WebPartPages"
    Namespace="Microsoft.SharePoint.WebPartPages"
    Assembly="Microsoft.SharePoint, Version=12.0.0.0, Culture=neutral,
PublicKeyToken=71e9bce111e9429c" %>

<html>
  <WebPartPages:SPWebPartManager runat="server" />
  <SharePoint:RobotsMetaTag runat="server" />
  <head runat="server">
    <title>
      <asp:ContentPlaceHolder id="PlaceHolderPageTitle"
       runat="server" />
    </title>
    <asp:ContentPlaceHolder id="PlaceHolderAdditionalPageHead"
     runat="server" />
  </head>

  <body onload="javascript:_spBodyOnLoadWrapper();">
    <form runat="server" onsubmit="return _spFormOnSubmitWrapper();">
      <asp:ContentPlaceHolder id="PlaceHolderMain" runat="server" />
      <asp:Panel visible="false" runat="server">
        <asp:ContentPlaceHolder id="PlaceHolderSearchArea" runat="server"/>
        <asp:ContentPlaceHolder id="PlaceHolderTitleBreadcrumb"
         runat="server"/>
        <asp:ContentPlaceHolder id="PlaceHolderPageTitleInTitleArea"
         runat="server"/>
        <asp:ContentPlaceHolder id="PlaceHolderLeftNavBar" runat="server"/>
        <asp:ContentPlaceHolder ID="PlaceHolderPageImage" runat="server"/>
        <asp:ContentPlaceHolder ID="PlaceHolderBodyLeftBorder"
         runat="server"/>
        <asp:ContentPlaceHolder ID="PlaceHolderNavSpacer" runat="server"/>
        <asp:ContentPlaceHolder ID="PlaceHolderTitleLeftBorder"
         runat="server"/>
        <asp:ContentPlaceHolder ID="PlaceHolderTitleAreaSeparator"
         runat="server"/>
        <asp:ContentPlaceHolder ID="PlaceHolderMiniConsole" runat="server"/>
```

```
        <asp:ContentPlaceHolder id="PlaceHolderCalendarNavigator"
          runat="server" />
        <asp:ContentPlaceHolder id="PlaceHolderLeftActions"
          runat="server"/>
        <asp:ContentPlaceHolder id="PlaceHolderPageDescription"
          runat="server"/>
        <asp:ContentPlaceHolder id="PlaceHolderBodyAreaClass"
          runat="server"/>
        <asp:ContentPlaceHolder id="PlaceHolderTitleAreaClass"
          runat="server"/>
      </asp:Panel>
    </form>
  </body>
</html>
```

After saving the new master page to the Master Page Gallery as *litwareinc.master*, for example, test it out in the publishing portal by navigating to the Site Settings of the top-level site. Under the Look and Feel section, use the Master Page link to switch the site master page to the newly created one. Figure 6-22 displays the result. The page could be more elaborate, but this is just a starter. Here, you only see the content and title of the published page that is rendered inside the *PlaceHolderMain*—the bare minimum.

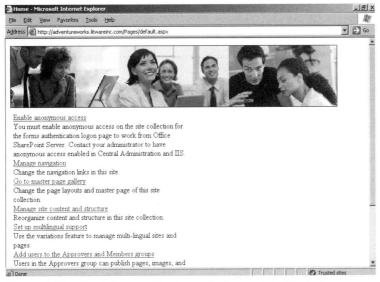

Figure 6-22 The AdventureWorks publishing portal with the bare minimum master page activated

You definitely want to add more functionality to the page, such as the navigation controls, publishing console, welcome control, site actions, and search box. Let's add these one by one using a *TABLE* or *DIV* element to organize the layout of the page and get it ready for the elements that represent all of these additional features. Here is the snippet of HTML with a table added inside the *FORM* element.

```
<table cellpadding="2" cellspacing="2">
  <tr>
    <td width="20%" valign="top">
      <table cellpadding="2" cellspacing="2">
        <tr><td>--logo--</td></tr>
        <tr><td>--welcome--</td></tr>
        <tr><td>--search--</td></tr>
        <tr><td>--site actions--</td></tr>
        <tr><td>--left navigation bar--</td></tr>
      </table>
    </td>
    <td width="80%" valign="top">
      <table cellpadding="2" cellspacing="2">
        <tr><td>--title--</td></tr>
        <tr><td>--breadcrumb--</td></tr>
        <tr><td>--publishing console--</td></tr>
        <tr><td>--content page--</td></tr>
      </table>
    </td>
  </tr>
</table>
```

Start by dropping the *PlaceHolderMain* in the cell that contains the *content page* tag, the important control used by SharePoint to display the content page. Next, the *PlaceHolderTitle-Breadcrumb* goes in the cell with the *breadcrumb* tag, the *PlaceHolderNavSpacer* and *PlaceHolder-LeftNavBar* go in the cell with the *left navigation bar* tag, and finally the *PlaceHolderPageImage* and the *PlaceHolderPageTitleInTitleArea* go in the cell with the *title* tag.

AdventureWorks wants its logo on all of its pages, and because Litware also intends to use the master page for other customers, you'll replace the cell content containing the *logo* tag with an *IMG* element that points to a *logo.jpg* stored in the Site Collection Images Gallery. You can use Microsoft Office SharePoint Designer 2007 or the browser to upload the image in the Site Collection Images Gallery.

```
<img src="<% $SPUrl:~SiteCollection/SiteCollectionImages/logo.jpg %>"
  runat="server">
```

The *SPUrl* makes it very dynamic: execute a piece of server-side code translating the relative URL to the absolute one pointing to the logo image.

The next control you'll add is the *Welcome* control, an ASP.NET user control located in the \12\Template\Controltemplates folder. It is necessary to first add a registration for the control at the top of your master page.

```
<%@ Register TagPrefix="wssuc" TagName="Welcome"
    src="~/_controltemplates/Welcome.ascx" %>
```

After this, you can replace the content of the cell containing the *welcome* tag with the following:

```
<tr>
  <td>
    <wssuc:Welcome id="explitLogout" runat="server"/>
  </td>
</tr>
```

The search box is part of the *Microsoft.SharePoint.Portal.dll*. First, add the register tag with the definition of the prefix to use:

```
<%@ Register Tagprefix="SPSWC"
  Namespace="Microsoft.SharePoint.Portal.WebControls"
  Assembly="Microsoft.SharePoint.Portal, Version=12.0.0.0,
Culture=neutral, PublicKeyToken=71e9bce111e9429c" %>
```

Next, replace the cell that contains the *search* tag with the element by inserting the ASP.NET server control. There are a number of attributes you can assign to a value to customize the appearance and behavior of the search box. In our case, you can do the minimum:

```
<tr>
  <td>
    <asp:ContentPlaceHolder id="PlaceHolderSearchArea" runat="server">
      <SPSWC:SearchBoxEx id="SearchBox" RegisterStyles="false"
        TextBeforeDropDown="" TextBeforeTextBox=
        "<%$Resources:cms,masterpages_searchbox_label%>" TextBoxWidth="100"
        GoImageUrl=
        "<% $SPUrl:~sitecollection/Style Library/Images/Search_Arrow.jpg %>"
        GoImageUrlRTL=
        "<% $SPUrl:~sitecollection/Style Library/Images/Search_Arrow_RTL.jpg
%>"
        UseSiteDefaults="true" DropDownMode = "HideScopeDD"
        SuppressWebPartChrome="true" runat="server" WebPart="true"
        __WebPartId="{3D10784E-D236-4B72-B8F4-B7E473DA276C}"/>
    </asp:ContentPlaceHolder>
  </td>
</tr>
```

A Site Actions menu is required to enable the content authors to work with the pages and the administrators to perform administrative tasks. Once again, this is an ASP.NET user control, and a register tag is required at the top:

```
<%@ Register TagPrefix="PublishingSiteAction" TagName="SiteActionMenu"
    src="~/_controltemplates/PublishingActionMenu.ascx" %>
```

Now, add the control to the master page as the content of the cell with the *site actions* tag.

```
<tr>
  <td><PublishingSiteAction:SiteActionMenu runat="server"/></td>
</tr>
```

The last ASP.NET user control to add is the *publishing console*, also referred to as the *Page Editing toolbar* in the user interface. First, register the control:

```
<%@ Register Tagprefix="PublishingConsole" TagName="Console"
  src="~/_controltemplates/PublishingConsole.ascx" %>
```

Next, replace the content of the cell that has the *publishing console* tag with the definition of the user control.

```
<tr>
  <td><PublishingConsole:Console runat="server"/></td>
</tr>
```

To finish the work on the custom master page, add two navigation controls for the user. The first one enables global navigation for the AdventureWorks site. There is a need to display all of the children of the top-level site. Just add the following new row before the row that displays the breadcrumb:

```
<tr>
  <td>
    <SharePoint:AspMenu ID="GlobalNav" Runat="server"
    DataSourceID="SiteMapDataSource1"
    Orientation="Horizontal" StaticDisplayLevels="1"
    MaximumDynamicDisplayLevels="0"
    StaticSubMenuIndent="0" DynamicHorizontalOffset="0"
    DynamicVerticalOffset="-8"
    StaticEnableDefaultPopOutImage="false" ItemWrap="false"
    SkipLinkText="<%$Resources:cms,masterpages_skiplinktext%>">
    <StaticMenuItemStyle ItemSpacing="10"/>
    <StaticSelectedStyle ItemSpacing="10"/>
    <StaticHoverStyle />
    <DynamicMenuStyle />
    <DynamicMenuItemStyle />
    <DynamicHoverStyle />
    </SharePoint:AspMenu>
    <PublishingNavigation:PortalSiteMapDataSource ID="siteMapDataSource1"
    Runat="server" SiteMapProvider="GlobalNavSiteMapProvider"
    EnableViewState="true" StartFromCurrentNode="true"
    StartingNodeOffset="0" ShowStartingNode="false"
    TreatStartingNodeAsCurrent="true" TrimNonCurrentTypes="Heading"/>
  </td>
</tr>
```

There is no immediate need to create your own custom site map provider. The *PortalSiteMap-Provider* registered as the *GlobalNavSiteMapProvider* is good enough for the *AdventureWorks* site. To connect to this provider, add a *PortalSiteMapDataSource* control to the page and use the *SiteMapProvider* attribute to hook it up with the actual provider registered in the *web.config*. Since this *PortalSiteMapDataSource* control is part of the *Microsoft.SharePoint.Publishing.dll*, you'll have to add another register directive at the top of your page.

```
<%@ Register Tagprefix="PublishingNavigation"
  Namespace="Microsoft.SharePoint.Publishing.Navigation"
  Assembly="Microsoft.SharePoint.Publishing, Version=12.0.0.0,
Culture=neutral, PublicKeyToken=71e9bce111e9429c" %>
```

The *AspMenu* control exposes navigation to the user. Setting the *MaximumDynamicDisplay-Levels* attribute to *0* displays the children of the top-level site.

The second navigation is the left navigation menu. This is again an *AspMenu* control but now configured so that it only displays the subsites and the pages available in the current site. The *AspMenu* control again makes use of a *PortalSiteMapDataSource* control.

```
<asp:ContentPlaceHolder id="PlaceHolderNavSpacer" runat="server" />
<asp:ContentPlaceHolder id="PlaceHolderLeftNavBar" runat="server">
<SharePoint:AspMenu ID="left" Runat="server" DataSourceID="SiteMapDS"
 Orientation="Vertical" StaticDisplayLevels="2"
 MaximumDynamicDisplayLevels="0" StaticSubMenuIndent="10px"
 ItemWrap="true" AccessKey="3" >
 <LevelMenuItemStyles>
   <asp:MenuItemStyle  />
   <asp:MenuItemStyle />
   <asp:MenuItemStyle />
 </LevelMenuItemStyles>
 <DynamicHoverStyle />
 <DynamicMenuStyle />
 <StaticSelectedStyle />
 <DynamicMenuItemStyle />
 <StaticHoverStyle />
</SharePoint:AspMenu>
<PublishingNavigation:PortalSiteMapDataSource ID="SiteMapDS" Runat="server"
 SiteMapProvider="CurrentNavSiteMapProvider" EnableViewState="true"
 StartFromCurrentNode="true" StartingNodeOffset="0"
 showStartingNode="false"
 TrimNonCurrentTypes="Heading"/>
```

Figure 6-23 shows how the home page of the publishing portal looks after modifications to the master page.

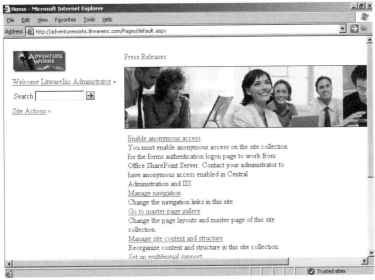

Figure 6-23   The bare minimum master page with the SharePoint administration controls and the different navigation controls

What you see in Figure 6-23 is the result without including CSS elements, but you can see that the various navigation controls are in place, content authors can edit the page, and the publishing console is displayed.

Customizing the Publishing Cycle

Any site that has the publishing features activated works with the page model described previously in the book. In short, pages are stored in the Pages library (you have one per site) and based on page layouts. A page layout is an ASP.NET page stored in the Master Page Gallery associated with a content type, defining what authors can deliver as content and how this content is delivered and inputted. A number of page layouts, listed in Table 6-2, are instantly available for a publishing site or portal.

Table 6-2   Page Layouts in a Publishing Portal

Page Layout	Content Type
Articleleft.aspx	Article Page
Articleright.aspx	Article Page
Articlelinks.aspx	Article Page
Blankwebpartpage.aspx	Welcome Page
Pagefromdoclayout.aspx	Article Page
Redirectpagelayout.aspx	Redirect Page
Variationrootpagelayout.aspx	Redirect Page
Welcomelinks.aspx	Welcome Page
Welcomesplash.aspx	Welcome Page
Welcometoc.aspx	Welcome Page

Page Layouts and Features

Chapter 2 contains a walkthrough that demonstrates the steps for creating a custom page layout in the browser and also discusses the typical flow to follow when authoring content in a publishing site. However, creating custom page layouts purely in the browser is not always the best option—definitely not if there is a need to reuse the page layout in multiple site collections. If your company needs to create many publishing portals and requires that they all have different page layouts for authoring product description pages, you may have a small problem when working with the browser. The level of reusability needed here can only be provided by packaging the page layout (together with the associated content type and the site columns used) into a feature. Administrators can then install the feature at the level of the server farm and activate it when needed. Let me describe in more detail the steps to follow. Figure 6-24 portrays all of the components that will make up the feature.

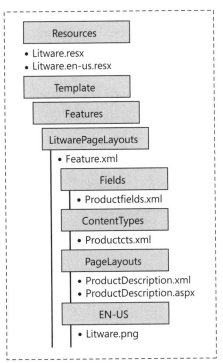

Figure 6-24 The Product Description page layout made available as part of a feature defining custom page layouts created by the Litware company

Skeleton of the Feature   The feature consists minimally of a header file, typically named *feature.xml*. This file must be located in a folder under the Features folder in \12\Template. Every front-end Web server must have the feature made available at that location. As an example, the *feature.xml* for a custom page layout can look like this:

```
<Feature  Id="B13257F3-197A-4331-ABE0-FBDBE412FFA6"
    Title="$Resources:litware,PublishingLayouts_Feature_Title;"
    Description="$Resources: litware,PublishingLayouts_Feature_Description;"
    Version="1.0.0.0" Scope="Site" Hidden="FALSE"
    DefaultResourceFile=" litware "
    xmlns="http://schemas.microsoft.com/sharepoint/">
    <ElementManifests>
     <ElementManifest Location="Fields\productfields.xml"/>
        <ElementManifest Location="ContentTypes\productcts.xml"/>
        <ElementManifest Location="PageLayouts\productdescription.xml"/>
    </ElementManifests>
</Feature>
```

The *Id* has a GUID as a value, and it must be unique within your server farm. Observe that there are no hard-coded strings in the XML file. Resource files, which are XML-based files with an .resx extension and stored in the \12\Resources folder, are used by the feature.

They store the strings as key/value pairs. One resource file contains the defaults, and you can have as many localized copies as you want. In the *feature.xml*, the *title* and the *description* are retrieved from the Litware resource file that matches the locale. The *litware.resx* and the *litware.en-us.resx* must contain the following keys that are used in the *feature.xml* file:

```xml
<?xml version="1.0" encoding="utf-8"?>
<!-- _lcid="1033" _version="12.0.4407.1005" _dal="1" -->
<!-- _LocalBinding -->
<root>
  <Data Name="PublishingLayouts_Feature_Title">
    <Value>Litware Custom Page Layouts</Value>
  </Data>
  <Data Name="PublishingLayouts_Feature_Description">
    <Value>A feature that adds extra page layouts to a publishing
    site.</Value>
  </Data>
</root>
```

The scope of the feature, defined by the *Scope* attribute, is set to the site collection displayed to the administrators in the Site Collection Features page. The display of the feature is the result of setting the *Hidden* attribute to *FALSE*. The final part of the *feature.xml* is the definition of the various manifest files, each containing the details of the different components making up the feature. For the custom page layout, you'll need a manifest for the definition of the site columns, one for the content type and one for the page layout definition itself. All of this can of course be consolidated in one manifest file, but a feature is all about modularity, so let's keep them isolated from each other.

Site Columns The first manifest file is the definition of the six site columns (*code*, *name*, *price*, *category*, *image*, and *description* of the product) that are to become fields of the content type.

```xml
<Elements xmlns="http://schemas.microsoft.com/sharepoint/">
  <Field ID="{0B6F3362-1F9F-4aa7-8FFD-3F375C62A383}"
  Name="ProductCode" SourceID="http://schemas.microsoft.com/sharepoint/v3"
  StaticName="ProductCode" Group="$Resources: litware,Product_Columns"
  DisplayName="$Resources: litware,ProductCode;" Type="Text">
  </Field>
  <Field ID="{DF483F5C-F729-452c-9405-6DD717261479}"
  Name="ProductName" SourceID="http://schemas.microsoft.com/sharepoint/v3"
  StaticName="ProductName" Group="$Resources: litware,Product_Columns"
  DisplayName="$Resources: litware,ProductName;" Type="Text">
  </Field>
  <Field ID="{C9CE3529-1F35-4c13-A452-9D467CBBFCC3}"
  Name="ProductPrice"
  SourceID="http://schemas.microsoft.com/sharepoint/v3"
  StaticName="ProductPrice" Group="$Resources: litware,Product_Columns"
  DisplayName="$Resources: litware,ProductPrice;" Type="Text">
  </Field>
  <Field ID="{D2B58E4A-F3A1-4322-9998-5BE43A7100E4}"
```

```
    Name="ProductCategory"
    SourceID="http://schemas.microsoft.com/sharepoint/v3"
    StaticName="ProductCategory" Group="$Resources: litware,Product_Columns"
    DisplayName="$Resources: litware,ProductCategory;" Type="Text">
    </Field>
    <Field ID="{91D90786-F799-4b4d-8CE4-38AE2DDA7C6F}"
    Name="ProductDescription"
    SourceID="http://schemas.microsoft.com/sharepoint/v3"
    StaticName="ProductDescription"
    Group="$Resources: litware,Product_Columns"
    DisplayName="$Resources: litware,ProductDescription;" Type="HTML">
    </Field>
    <Field ID="{9BFD7528-CF37-4a34-A32D-0383DA27074A}"
    Name="ProductImage"
    SourceID="http://schemas.microsoft.com/sharepoint/v3"
    StaticName="ProductImage"
    Group="$Resources: litware,Product_Columns"
    DisplayName="$Resources: litware,ProductImage;" Type="Image">
    </Field>
  </Elements>
```

There's nothing complicated here. A field is identified by a GUID and a name. The group and display name are retrieved again from the proper resource file. Every field must be associated with a field type. The first four are just *Text* types, but the last two types are the *HTML* and the *Image* field types, which are added to the base Windows SharePoint Services 3.0 field types (see the Fields Feature folder) as part of the Microsoft Office SharePoint Server 2007 installation and the Publishing Features activated for the portal. You can review the definition of the publishing field types in the *fldtypes_publishing.xml* located in the \12\Template\XML folder.

Content Type   The second manifest file is the one that defines the Product Description content type. The identification of a content type is not done with a GUID but with a hexadecimal value that stores all of the information about the type's lineage—that is, the line of parent content types from which your custom content type inherits. The *id* for the Page content type, the one from which to inherit, is *0x010100C568DB52D9D0A14D9B2F DCC96666E9F2007948130EC3DB064584E219954237AF39*. You can just add a new GUID to this to have a unique identifier for your own content type.

```
  <Elements xmlns="http://schemas.microsoft.com/sharepoint/">
    <ContentType  ID="0x010100C568DB52D9D0A14D9B2FDCC96666E9F2007948130EC3D
B064584E219954237AF39004C7B52B5EAFDBE4C85A8730DF1892C35"
    Name="$Resources: litware,ProductDescription_ContentType"
    Group="$Resources: litware,Product_ContentTypes"
    Description="$Resources:
litware,ProductDescription_ContentTypeDescription" Version="0" >
    <FieldRefs>
      <FieldRef ID="{0B6F3362-1F9F-4aa7-8FFD-3F375C62A383}"
      Name="ProductCode" />
      <FieldRef ID="{DF483F5C-F729-452c-9405-6DD717261479}"
      Name="ProductName" />
```

```
        <FieldRef ID="{C9CE3529-1F35-4c13-A452-9D467CBBFCC3}"
          Name="ProductPrice" />
        <FieldRef ID="{D2B58E4A-F3A1-4322-9998-5BE43A7100E4}"
          Name="ProductCategory" />
        <FieldRef ID="{91D90786-F799-4b4d-8CE4-38AE2DDA7C6F}"
          Name="ProductDescription" />
        <FieldRef ID="{9BFD7528-CF37-4a34-A32D-0383DA27074A}"
          Name="ProductImage" />
        </FieldRefs>
        <DocumentTemplate TargetName="/_layouts/CreatePage.aspx" />
      </ContentType>
    </Elements>
```

The manifest additionally contains references to the six site columns defined in the site columns manifest file. The last part is the URL of the page that is displayed when the content author decides to author a page associated with this content type.

Page Layout   The last manifest file stores the definition of the custom page layout:

```
<Elements xmlns="http://schemas.microsoft.com/sharepoint/">
  <Module Name="LitwarePageLayouts" Url="_catalogs/masterpage"
   Path="PageLayouts" RootWebOnly="TRUE">
    <File Url="Product Description.aspx" Type="GhostableInLibrary">
     <Property Name="Title"
     Value="$Resources: litware,PageLayout_ProductDescription_Title;" />
     <Property Name="MasterPageDescription"
     Value="$Resources:litware,PageLayout_ProductDescription_Description;" />
     <Property Name="ContentType"
     Value="$Resources: litware,ProductDescription_ContentType;" />
     <Property Name="PublishingPreviewImage"
      Value="~SiteCollection/_catalogs/masterpage/$Resources:
core,Culture;/Preview Images/Litware.png,~SiteCollection/
_catalogs/masterpage/$Resources:core,Culture;/Preview Images/Litware.png" />
     <Property Name="PublishingAssociatedContentType" Value=";#$Resources:
litware,ProductDescription_ContentType;;#0x010100C568DB52D9D0A14D9B2FDCC9
6666E9F2007948130EC3DB064584E219954237AF39004C7B52B5EAFDBE4C85A8730DF189
2C35;#"/>
        </File>
      </Module>
    <Module Name="PublishingLayoutsPreviewImages" Url="_catalogs/masterpage"
             IncludeFolders="??-??" Path="" RootWebOnly="TRUE">
     <File Url="Litware.png" Name="Preview Images/Litware.png"
      Type="GhostableInLibrary">
     </File>
    </Module>
  </Elements>
```

The first *Module* element indicates to SharePoint the location of the .aspx page. The .aspx page is part of your feature and must be copied along with all of the other parts to the Features folder. During the activation of the feature, it will be dropped in the Master Page and Page

Layouts Gallery. The last action is the result of the value of the *Type* attribute that is set to *GhostableInLibrary*. A number of other attributes are assigned. The *PublishingAssociatedContent-Type* is vital since it connects your *Product Description* page layout with the *Product Description* content type.

The .aspx page is the same as the one that was produced in the previous walkthrough. Simply download a copy of the page to the Features folder using the Send To menu option in the gallery. The only thing to watch out for is that the *FieldName* attributes of the field controls match the names of the fields defined as columns of your content type.

```
<%@ Page Language="C#" Inherits="Microsoft.SharePoint.Publishing.
PublishingLayoutPage,Microsoft.SharePoint.Publishing,Version=12.0.0.0,
Culture=neutral,PublicKeyToken=71e9bce111e9429c"
    meta:progid="SharePoint.WebPartPage.Document" %>
<%@ Register TagPrefix="SharePointWebControls"
  Namespace="Microsoft.SharePoint.WebControls"
  Assembly="Microsoft.SharePoint, Version=12.0.0.0, Culture=neutral,
PublicKeyToken=71e9bce111e9429c" %>
<%@ Register TagPrefix="WebPartPages"
  Namespace="Microsoft.SharePoint.WebPartPages"
  Assembly="Microsoft.SharePoint, Version=12.0.0.0, Culture=neutral,
PublicKeyToken=71e9bce111e9429c" %>
<%@ Register TagPrefix="PublishingWebControls"
  Namespace="Microsoft.SharePoint.Publishing.WebControls"
  Assembly="Microsoft.SharePoint.Publishing, Version=12.0.0.0,
Culture=neutral, PublicKeyToken=71e9bce111e9429c" %>
<%@ Register TagPrefix="PublishingNavigation"
  Namespace="Microsoft.SharePoint.Publishing.Navigation"
  Assembly="Microsoft.SharePoint.Publishing, Version=12.0.0.0,
Culture=neutral, PublicKeyToken=71e9bce111e9429c" %>

<asp:content contentplaceholderid="PlaceHolderPageTitle" runat="server">
 <SharePointWebControls:FieldValue id="PageTitle" FieldName="Title"
  runat="server"/>
</asp:content>
<asp:content contentplaceholderid="PlaceHolderMain" runat="server">

<table style="width: 100%" cellpadding="5" cellspacing="4">
 <tr>
  <td valign="top">
   <div class="headertitle-large" >
    <SharePointWebControls:TextField FieldName="ProductName"
     runat="server" id="TextField1" CssClass="headertitle">
    </SharePointWebControls:TextField>
   </div>
   <hr style="color:gray">
   <div class="bottomLinkBar" >
    <SharePointWebControls:TextField FieldName="ProductCode"
     runat="server" CssClass="breadcrumb">
    </SharePointWebControls:TextField><br><br>
    <u>Model</u>: <SharePointWebControls:TextField
     FieldName="ProductCategory" runat="server" CssClass="breadcrumb">
```

```
        </SharePointWebControls:TextField><br>
        <u>Price</u>: <SharePointWebControls:TextField FieldName="ProductPrice"
        runat="server" CssClass="breadcrumb"></SharePointWebControls:TextField>
      </div>
    </td>
    <td valign="top">
      <PublishingWebControls:RichImageField FieldName="ProductImage"
       runat="server"></PublishingWebControls:RichImageField>
    </td>
  </tr>
  <tr>
    <td colspan="2" valign="top">
      <PublishingWebControls:RichHtmlField FieldName="ProductDescription"
       runat="server" CssClass="level-item" AllowImages="False">
      </PublishingWebControls:RichHtmlField>
    </td>
  </tr>
</table>
</asp:content>
```

Let's go back to the manifest file for the page layout. The second *Module* element indicates the location of the image that will be used as the preview image for the custom page layout. It's the one the content author will see in the Create Page when he or she selects the Product Description page layout. Again, this image is part of the physical files that make up your feature, but, just like the .aspx file, it will be ghosted in the Preview Images folder of the Master Page and Page Layouts Gallery in the publishing portal. There is one special attribute, the *IncludeFolders*, that is handy when you localize this image for a number of languages. The image is stored in the *EN-US* subfolder of the Feature folder. Additional localized versions of the image can be stored each in their own folder. An image for the Flemish content authors for example can be stored in an *NL-BE* subfolder.

> **Note**   The full version of this feature is available on the companion Web site.

Installing and Activating the Feature   Once all of the parts of the feature are copied to the \12\Template\Features folder and the resource files in the \12\Resources folder, the installation can be started. Installing a feature is done with the *STSADM* command line utility. Open a command prompt and then execute the *STSADM* with the option *installfeature* and point to the Feature folder using the filename parameter.

```
stsadm -o installfeature -filename LitwarePageLayouts\feature.xml
```

Activation of the feature is completed either in the browser in the Site Collection Features page or again by using the *STSADM* command line utility. With the last option, you'll use the *activatefeature* option and add the parameter URL to the *filename* parameter to tell SharePoint the URL of the site collection for which you want to have it activated.

```
stsadm -o activatefeature -filename LitwarePageLayouts\feature.xml
    -url http://adventureworks.litwareinc.com
```

The end result is equal to the outcome of the walkthrough in Chapter 2 that describes the steps for creating the custom product description page layout in the browser and Microsoft Office SharePoint Designer 2007.

Custom Field Controls

Going back to the walkthrough that demonstrates how to create a page layout in the browser, field controls were placed on the page layout in Microsoft Office SharePoint Designer 2007. Each of these field controls represents one of the columns defined at the level of the content type associated with the page layout. The type of column identifies the type of field control used to capture the value for the column and the display of this value on the published page.

What if you need to deliver a new type of field control for the content authors that captures and stores content in a customized manner, not directly available with the out-of-the-box field types? Creating custom field controls basically involves creating custom field types and registering these field types in the *web.config* of your IIS Web application so that you can use them in Microsoft Office SharePoint Designer 2007 and on your page layouts. Because the procedures for creating a custom field type are discussed in Ted Patisson's book *Inside Windows SharePoint Services 3.0*, I won't go into all of the details and will simply work out a small example with a *telephone* field control that demonstrates the basic steps. Then, I'll address the additional steps to take for delivering the new field type as a field control in the page layouts.

Walkthrough: Creating a Custom Field Control

Creating a new field type is initiated by creating a .NET assembly containing a number of classes. A reference to the *Microsoft.SharePoint.dll* must be added, and you can immediately sign the project because at deployment time, the .NET assembly has to end up in the Global Assembly Cache (GAC).

> **Note**   The classes to create for the *telephone* field control are only discussed briefly here. The full project is available as a sample on the companion Web site.

The *TelephoneCustomValue* Class   This class stores the definition of the value associated with the custom field. In the case of the *telephone* field, the value is made available as three different parts: the *international code*, the *zone number*, and the *number* itself.

```
using System;
using Microsoft.SharePoint;
namespace Litware.Fields
```

```
{
    public class TelephoneFieldValue : SPFieldMultiColumnValue
    {
        private const int numberOfColumns = 3;
        public TelephoneFieldValue()
            : base(numberOfColumns)
        {}
        public TelephoneFieldValue(string value)
            : base(value)
        {}
        public string InternationalCode
        {
            get { return this[0]; }
            set { this[0] = value; }
        }
        public string Zone
        {
            get { return this[1]; }
            set { this[1] = value; }
        }
        public string TelNumber
        {
            get { return this[2]; }
            set { this[2] = value; }
        }
    }
}
```

The value is stored in one block in the database. Using this class, you'll expose the value in three segments to SharePoint.

The *TelephoneField* Class   The *TelephoneField* class is the actual definition of the field type that contains two parts: the members needed for SharePoint to work with the value of the field, and the control used to render the value in the browser. The rendering of the value is done with a custom ASP.NET server control part of the .NET assembly.

```
using System;
using Microsoft.SharePoint;
using Microsoft.SharePoint.WebControls;
namespace Litware.Fields
{
    class TelephoneField: SPFieldMultiColumn
    {
        public TelephoneField(SPFieldCollection fields, string fieldName)
            : base(fields, fieldName)
        { }
        public TelephoneField(SPFieldCollection fields,
                              string typeName,
                              string displayName)
            : base(fields, typeName, displayName)
        { }
        public override object GetFieldValue(string value)
```

```
        {
            if (string.IsNullOrEmpty(value))
                return null;
            return new TelephoneFieldValue(value);
        }
        public override BaseFieldControl FieldRenderingControl
        {
            get
            {
                BaseFieldControl fldControl = new TelephoneFieldControl();
                fldControl.FieldName = InternalName;
                return fldControl;
            }
        }
    }
}
```

The *TelephoneFieldControl* Class   This class is the ASP.NET server control responsible for the rendering of the user interface elements that capture the value of the field when in edit mode. The actual layout of the user interface elements is delegated to a physical ASCX file that packages the UI elements into a template linked to the server control via the *DefaultTemplate-Name* property of the control.

```
using System;
using Microsoft.SharePoint.WebControls;
using System.Web.UI.WebControls;
namespace Litware.Fields
{
    class TelephoneFieldControl: BaseFieldControl
    {
        protected TextBox textBoxInternationalCode;
        protected TextBox textBoxZone;
        protected TextBox textBoxTelNumber;
        protected override string DefaultTemplateName
        {
            get { return "TelephoneFieldRendering"; }
        }
        protected override void CreateChildControls()
        {
            if (Field == null)
                return;
            base.CreateChildControls();
            if (ControlMode == SPControlMode.Display)
                return;
            textBoxInternationalCode = (TextBox)
                TemplateContainer.FindControl("InternationalCodeBox");
            if (textBoxInternationalCode == null)
                throw new ArgumentException("Corrupted
TelephoneFieldRendering template - missing InternationalCodeBox.");
            textBoxInternationalCode.TabIndex = TabIndex;
            textBoxInternationalCode.CssClass = CssClass;
            textBoxInternationalCode.ToolTip = Field.Title + "
```

```
                     International Code";
           textBoxZone = (TextBox)TemplateContainer.FindControl("ZoneBox");
           if (textBoxZone == null)
               throw new ArgumentException("Corrupted
TelephoneFieldRendering template - missing ZoneBox.");
           textBoxZone.TabIndex = TabIndex;
           textBoxZone.CssClass = CssClass;
           textBoxZone.ToolTip = Field.Title + " Zone Number";
           textBoxTelNumber = (TextBox)
                 TemplateContainer.FindControl("TelNumberBox");
           if (textBoxTelNumber == null)
               throw new ArgumentException("Corrupted
TelephoneFieldRendering template - missing TelNumberBox.");
           textBoxTelNumber.TabIndex = TabIndex;
           textBoxTelNumber.CssClass = CssClass;
           textBoxTelNumber.ToolTip = Field.Title + " Telephone Number";
       }
       public override object Value
       {
           get
           {
               EnsureChildControls();
               TelephoneFieldValue fieldValue = new TelephoneFieldValue();
               fieldValue.InternationalCode =
                   textBoxInternationalCode.Text.Trim();
               fieldValue.Zone = textBoxZone.Text.Trim();
               fieldValue.TelNumber = textBoxTelNumber.Text.Trim();
               return fieldValue;
           }
           set
           {
               EnsureChildControls();
               TelephoneFieldValue fieldValue =
                       (TelephoneFieldValue)value;
               textBoxInternationalCode.Text =
                       fieldValue.InternationalCode;
               textBoxZone.Text = fieldValue.Zone;
               textBoxTelNumber.Text = fieldValue.TelNumber;
           }
       }
   }
 }
}
```

The *ControlTemplates_Telephone.ascx* This is the ASP.NET user control that stores the template and definition of the text box controls used to capture the value for the *telephone* field.

```
<%@ Control Language="C#" Debug="true"  %>
<%@Assembly Name="Microsoft.SharePoint, Version=12.0.0.0,
Culture=neutral, PublicKeyToken=71e9bce111e9429c" %>
<%@Register TagPrefix="SharePoint" Assembly="Microsoft.SharePoint,
Version=12.0.0.0, Culture=neutral, PublicKeyToken=71e9bce111e9429c"
namespace="Microsoft.SharePoint.WebControls"%>
```

```
<SharePoint:RenderingTemplate ID="TelephoneFieldRendering" runat="server">
    <Template>
    <asp:TextBox ID="InternationalCodeBox" MaxLength="5" Size="5"
     runat="server"/>-
    <asp:TextBox ID="ZoneBox" MaxLength="6" Size="6" runat="server"/> 
    <asp:TextBox ID="TelNumberBox" MaxLength="12" Size="12" runat="server"/>
    </Template>
</SharePoint:RenderingTemplate>
```

The *FieldType Manifest* File   The custom field type must be registered as a new field type for SharePoint. To accomplish this, a small XML file with the prefix *fldtypes* is created containing the metadata for the field type along with the definition of the rendering behavior when looking at the value in display mode. That rendering is expressed using the Collaborative Application Markup Language (CAML).

```
<FieldTypes>
    <FieldType>
        <Field Name="TypeName">Telephone</Field>
        <Field Name="ParentType">MultiColumn</Field>
        <Field Name="TypeDisplayName">Telephone</Field>
        <Field Name="TypeShortDescription">Telephone Number</Field>
        <Field Name="UserCreatable">TRUE</Field>
        <Field Name="ShowOnListAuthoringPages">TRUE</Field>
        <Field Name="ShowOnDocumentLibraryAuthoringPages">TRUE</Field>
        <Field Name="ShowOnSurveyAuthoringPages">TRUE</Field>
        <Field Name="ShowOnColumnTemplateAuthoringPages">TRUE</Field>
        <Field Name="FieldTypeClass">Litware.Fields.TelephoneField,
TelephoneCustomField, Version=1.0.0.0, Culture=neutral,
PublicKeyToken=f37bde46697f94a9</Field>
        <PropertySchema>
          <Fields>
            <Field Name="InternationalCode" DisplayName="International Code:"
                MaxLength="5" DisplaySize="5" Type="Text">
            </Field>
            <Field Name="Zone" DisplayName="Zone:" MaxLength="7"
             DisplaySize="7" Type="Text">
            </Field>
            <Field Name="Number" DisplayName="Number:" MaxLength="12"
             DisplaySize="12" Type="Text">
            </Field>
          </Fields>
        </PropertySchema>
        <RenderPattern Name="DisplayPattern">
          <Switch>
            <Expr>
              <Column/>
            </Expr>
            <Case Value="">
            </Case>
            <Default>
              <Column SubColumnNumber="0" HTMLEncode="TRUE"/>
              <HTML><![CDATA[-]]></HTML>
```

```
              <Column SubColumnNumber="1" HTMLEncode="TRUE"/>
              <HTML><![CDATA[ ]]></HTML>
              <Column SubColumnNumber="2" HTMLEncode="TRUE"/>
          </Default>
        </Switch>
      </RenderPattern>
    </FieldType>
  </FieldTypes>
```

Deployment of the Custom Field Type   As mentioned in the beginning of this topic on custom field controls, the .NET assembly encapsulating all of the classes has to be deployed as a strong-named assembly in the Global Assembly Cache (GAC). Two other files must be deployed to a specific folder:

■ The field type manifest file (*fldtypes_telephone.xml*) must be copied to the \12\Template \XML folder. You can find other XML files in this folder prefixed with *fldtypes*. One is the *fldtypes_publishing.xml*, and it contains all of the field types that are enabled when you activate the publishing features for your site collection—the case by default when working with a publishing portal.

■ The ASP.NET user control containing the definition of the user interface elements to be displayed in edit mode must be copied to the \12\Template\Controltemplates folder where the control will be part of the list of user controls used in a variety of places in SharePoint. Remember that in the master page walkthrough, you worked with a number of them such as the *welcome.ascx* and the *publishingconsole.ascx*.

You have to restart SharePoint using an *IISRESET* to activate your new custom field control. After you have done that, you can go to any of your lists or libraries and see in the Create Column page that your new field type will be part of the list of available field types to choose from, as displayed in Figure 6-25.

This now also means that you can extend the content type associated with the page layout for the product description with one additional column, for example the *Product Support Number* column using the *telephone* field as the type.

Using the Field Type as a Field Control   However, in order for the field type to be used as a field control in the page layout, you'll have to do two more steps. The first step is the registration of the field control as a safe control in the *web.config*. An additional *SafeControl* element such as the following can be added (note that the strong name can be different in your case):

```
<SafeControl Assembly="TelephoneCustomField, Version=1.0.0.0,
Culture=neutral, PublicKeyToken=f37bde46697f94a9"
Namespace="Litware.Fields" TypeName="*" Safe="True"
AllowRemoteDesigner="True" />
```

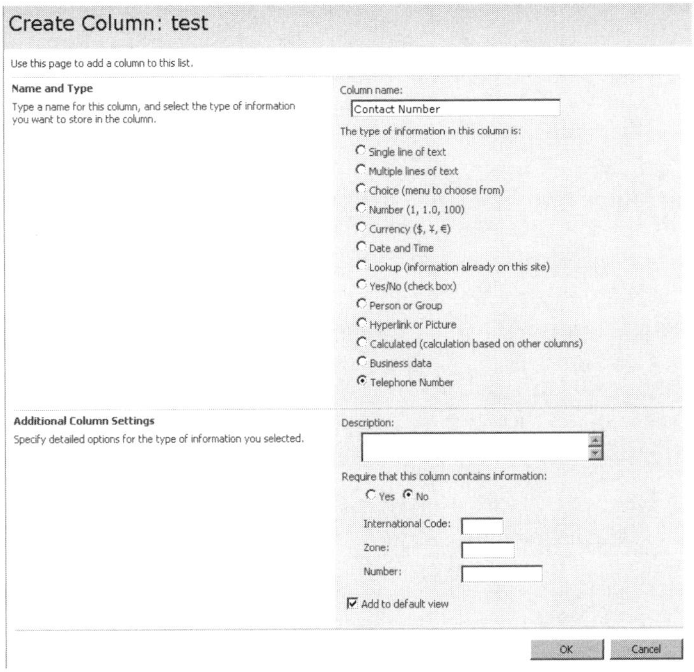

Figure 6-25   The custom telephone field is now part of the list of available field types.

The second step is optional and calls for the creation of a design experience for the control. Microsoft SharePoint Designer 2007 does not really display your *telephone* field control as a control in the designer. If there's a need for a design mode presentation of the *telephone* field control, you will have to add this mode to the server control code part of your project.

Workflow in the Publishing Cycle

By default, an approval workflow is associated at the level of the Pages library in a publishing portal. The Pages library stores the published pages, and each of them is based on one of the page layouts. If needed, this approval workflow can be replaced with one of your own custom workflows. Another approach is to not associate a workflow with the Pages library but instead associate workflows with the content types that drive the page layouts. In the Pages library you will often have pages stored based on different page layouts, and in the real world, each of these types of pages will often follow a different workflow.

Creating Pages Programmatically

Publishing pages can also be programmatically created. The *Microsoft.SharePoint.Publishing.dll* contains the needed types to accomplish this. On the companion Web site, you'll find a small sample application demonstrating a number of the scenarios to work with the publishing types. The application is called PageGenerator, and it is a good idea to just open the project in Visual Studio.NET 2005 and follow along while reading through the following pages that explain the major classes.

The *PublishingSite* Class

The *PublishingSite* class is the first class to explore. The creation of an instance of it requires an instance of the *SPSite*, the type part of the *Microsoft.SharePoint.dll* representing a site collection. Basically, the *PublishingSite* class adds an additional layer to the *SPSite* so that you can access the publishing features for that site collection. Here is the code that is executed when you click the Explore button in the sample application:

```
this.siteCol= new SPSite(textBoxSiteCollectionURL.Text);
this.pubSiteCol = new PublishingSite(this.siteCol);
```

The references are stored in two class-level variables. The *PublishingSite* class allows you to get the page layouts available via two members:

- A property, *PageLayouts*, of type *PageLayoutsCollection* exposes the existing page layouts that are represented as objects of type *PageLayout*.

- There is also a *GetPageLayouts* method that returns a collection of *PageLayout* objects. Filters can be provided as parameters. There is an option to specify that you'd like to see all of the page layouts returned based on a specific content type. In the sample application, I've used this method to populate the combobox listing all of the page layouts. The code follows:

```
PageLayoutCollection pagelayouts = this.pubSiteCol.GetPageLayouts(true);
comboBoxPageLayouts.DisplayMember = "Name";
foreach (PageLayout pagelayout in pagelayouts)
{
  comboBoxPageLayouts.Items.Add(pagelayout);
}
```

In addition to retrieving the collection of page layouts, there is also an option to retrieve the list of content types using the *ContentTypes* property at the level of the *PublishingSite* class.

The *PageLayout* Class

The *PageLayout* class exposes all of the things you can do in the browser with a page layout. There are numerous properties that provide read access to the metadata. This is illustrated in the application when you select a page layout in the dropdown. Some details are retrieved and displayed using the following code:

```
PageLayout pageLayout = (PageLayout)comboBoxPageLayouts.SelectedItem;
this.textBoxPageLayoutDescription.Text =
    pageLayout.Description;
```

```
this.textBoxPageLayoutContentType.Text =
    pageLayout.AssociatedContentType.Name;
this.textBoxPageLayoutCreatedBy.Text =
    pageLayout.CreatedBy.Name;
this.textBoxPageLayoutCreatedOn.Text =
    pageLayout.CreatedDate.ToShortDateString();
```

The *PublishingWeb* Class

You'll probably use this class often if you decide to programmatically work with the publishing pages. You do not create an instance of this class. There is a static *GetPublishingWeb* method that requires an instance of the *SPWeb* and returns the instance of the *PublishingWeb* class. Here is the code illustrating this:

```
PublishingWeb pubweb =
    PublishingWeb.GetPublishingWeb(this.siteCol.RootWeb);
```

Once you have the instance, the real work can begin. One thing you can do is get the collection of publishing pages by calling the *GetPublishingPages* method. This method can be called in a couple of ways. You can just get the list of all of the pages, or you can be more selective. To be more selective, call the method with either a raw CAML query string or one wrapped as part of an instance of the *SPQuery* class. In the treeview control in the sample application, every node that represents a site in your site collection has a *Pages* node. Clicking on it creates subnodes with each representing an instance of the *PublishingPage* class. In the following block of code, a small loop is constructed to create these nodes:

```
PublishingPageCollection pages = pubweb.GetPublishingPages();
foreach (PublishingPage page in pages)
{
  TreeNode node = treeViewItems.SelectedNode.Nodes.Add(page.Url);
}
```

There are also methods, such as the *GetAvailablePageLayouts*, that authors can use to retrieve page layouts. The *SetAvailablePageLayouts* method, on the other hand, can be called to restrict the list exposed to the content authors.

To conclude, a number of properties let you tune the way the navigation controls display the pages. Two examples include the *IncludeInCurrentNavigation* and the *IncludeInGlobalNavigation* flags that can be set to *True* or *False*.

The *PublishingPage* Class

An individual publishing page is represented by a type of the *PublishingPage* class. These objects are actually items in the Pages document library available for every site in the site collection. All of the metadata stored with the item related to the publishing of the page is exposed by a number of properties. The sample application allows you to select a page and then see details such as the page layout on which the page is based, the title, the author, the creation date, and the list of pages that may be linked to it by a setup of variations (discussed more later). Here is the code for retrieving this information:

```
PublishingPage page = (PublishingPage) treeViewItems.SelectedNode.Tag;
textBoxPublishingPageTitle.Text = page.Title;
textBoxPublishingPageCreatedBy.Text = page.CreatedBy.Name;
textBoxPublishingPageCreatedOn.Text = page.CreatedDate.ToShortDateString();
textBoxPublishingPageLayout.Text = page.Layout.Name;
comboBoxPublishingPageVariations.Items.Clear();
if (page.VariationPageUrls.Count > 0)
{
  foreach (string item in page.VariationPageUrls)
  {
    comboBoxPublishingPageVariations.Items.Add(item);
  }
}
```

Creating a *PublishingPage* Object

The steps for creating a publishing page in code are interesting. There are two objects required to get started. A *PublishingWeb* instance is needed because the publishing page you'll create will end up in the *Pages* library of a site. A *PageLayout* instance is also needed because your page is going to be based on a specific page layout. The following lines of code are executed when you click on the button to create a page based on the product description page layout (discussed earlier in the chapter):

```
PublishingPage page =
    web.GetPublishingPages().Add("ProductABC.aspx", pageLayout);
page.Title = "Product ABC";
page.ListItem["ProductCode"] = textBoxProductCode.Text;
page.ListItem["ProductName"] = textBoxProductName.Text;
page.ListItem["ProductPrice"] = textBoxProductPrice.Text;
page.ListItem["ProductDescription"] = textBoxProductDescription.Text;
page.ListItem["ProductCategory"] = textBoxProductCategory.Text;
page.ListItem.Update();
page.CheckIn(string.Empty);
page.Update();
MessageBox.Show("New page created!");
```

A new *PublishingPage* instance can be added to the *PublishingPageCollection* via a call to the *Add* method of the *GetPublishingPages* property, which is available at the level of the *PublishingWeb* instance. Two parameter values are needed: the name of the .aspx page that represents the page and the instance of the *PageLayout* that SharePoint has to use for the creation. The return value, an instance of the *PublishingPage* type, can then be further populated with the required data such as a value for the *Title* property and values for all of the fields accessible with the *ListItem* property. Remember that the *PublishingPage* is an item in the Pages library and follows the content type definition.

There are plenty of other actions you can perform with the types part of the *Microsoft.Share-Point.Publishing.dll*. If you are interested in studying this further, I recommend that you open up the SDK and go through the reference of the classes that make up the many namespaces involved with the publishing features.

Customizing the Page Editing Toolbar

The Page Editing toolbar is a panel of user interface elements that provides page information and methods for interacting with the page. The metadata and actions are used by the content authors to finish their tasks in the publishing cycle. This can range from editing the page, configuring the publication schedule, starting the workflow, publishing the page, updating the variations, and more. Rather than going over the out-of-the-box functionality, I'll instead discuss the steps to take for extending the console or Page Editing toolbar.

The Architecture of the Page Editing Toolbar

The Page Editing toolbar, also called the authoring or publishing console, is embedded in the master page by the *PublishingConsole.ascx* user control, located in the \12\Template\Control-Templates folder. It exposes the page information and related actions using three main areas:

- A Page Status bar displays information about the page, including the version information and status of the page.

- The Page Editing menu enables a user to perform actions such as publish a version, approve a pending version, and check in the page to share a draft.

- And finally, depending on the context and the permissions of the user, Quick Access buttons are displayed for executing actions on the page. Examples include the Approve, Reject, Check in to Share Draft, and Publish buttons.

All of the displayed menu items and Quick Access buttons are defined in XML files located in the \12\Template\Layouts\EditingMenu folder.

The Editing Menu in the Page Editing Toolbar

Figure 6-26 shows the different components of the *EditingMenu.xml* in the \12\Template \Layouts\EditingMenu folder. All of the menu items are displayed in the panel together with the actions that occur when users select a menu item.

Code-behind actions are often encapsulated into .NET assemblies deployed in Global Assembly Cache (GAC). They are referenced in the *EditingMenu.xml* via the *reference* element at the beginning of the file. The classes hooked up with the menu items must inherit from the *ConsoleAction* class located in the *Microsoft.SharePoint.Publishing.WebControls.EditingMenu* namespace (more about this in a moment). Resource files deliver the localization, and the menu items themselves are defined as nested *ConsoleNode* elements. Table 6-3 summarizes the various attributes and their purposes.

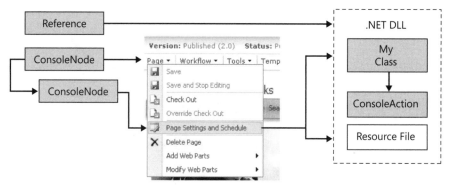

Figure 6-26 The different components that play a role in the construction of the editing menu in the Page Editing toolbar

Table 6-3 *ConsoleNode* **Attributes**

Attribute	Description
Sequence	Attribute used for the top-level menu items that indicates the display order.
NavigateUrl	Attribute used to define what the action is behind the menu item. Nothing is shown for the top-level menu items, but for the menu items under it, it can either point to a URL for a page the user is redirected to or a value can be found that consists of a namespace combined with the name of a class part of the .NET assembly registered with the *reference* element at the top of the XML. An example is *cms:SavePublishingPageAction*.
AccessKey	The keyboard key associated with the menu item.
DisplayText	The text as it is displayed to the user in the browser.
ImageUrl	An image rendered before the display text.
UseResourceFile	*True* or *false* depending on whether you make your strings available in resource files or hard-code them in the XML.
UserRights	Responsible for trimming access to the *ConsoleNode* based on Microsoft Windows SharePoint Services permissions.
PermissionContext	Gets or sets the context in which to evaluate the permissions of the *Console-Node*. For example, certain actions, such as Create Page, must be restricted at the site level. Others, such as Edit Page, must be restricted at the level of the current *SPListItem* object.
HideStates	Context information listing the states when the *ConsoleNode* needs to be hidden. See the SDK for the different options you have here.
ID	The unique identifier of the node.

Customizing the Editing Menu

Custom menu items are not, I repeat *not*, added directly to the *EditingMenu.xml*. The files in the \12\Template\Layouts\EditingMenu folder are untouchable. Figure 6-27 shows the Editing Menus folder in the Master Page Gallery at the level of the site collection.

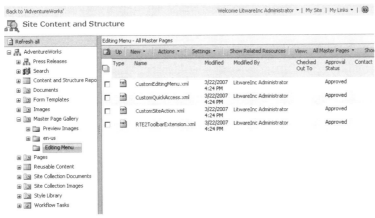

Figure 6-27   The Master Page Gallery contains an empty version of the *CustomEditingMenu.xml* that can be used to add customizations needed in the Page Editing toolbar.

If you open the *CustomEditingMenu.xml* in Microsoft SharePoint Designer 2007, you can add your customizations. An example of a customization can be the addition of a top-level menu item called Templates that lists one or more of the types of pages content authors can create. Take for example the product description page again. Let's say a user clicks on the item and is redirected to a page that is already populated with content retrieved from a database and possibly some additional information guiding the user through the process of creating the page itself. The redirect can be a custom application page deployed in the \12\Template\Layouts folder. Here is the content in the XML that can make this happen:

```
<Console>
  <references>
    <reference TagPrefix="litware" assembly="CustomConsoleActionDemo,
Version=1.0.0.0, Culture=neutral, PublicKeyToken=435ae89fbbd1ddd9"
      namespace="InsideMOSS.Samples" />
  </references>
  <structure >
    <ConsoleNode Sequence="400" NavigateUrl="javascript:" AccessKey="G"
    DisplayText="Templates" ImageUrl="" UseResourceFile="false"
    UserRights="EmptyMask" ID="saTemplates">
      <ConsoleNode Action="litware:CreateProductionDescriptionPage"
      ImageUrl="/_layouts/images/edit.gif"
      DisplayText="Product Description"
      UseResourceFile="false" ID="saProductDescription"/>
    </ConsoleNode>
  </structure>
</Console>
```

The .NET assembly referenced at the top contains one class called *CreateProductionDescription-Page*, which inherits from the abstract *ConsoleAction* class. Here is the code that defines it:

```
using System;
using System.Collections.Generic;
using System.Text;
using Microsoft.SharePoint;
using Microsoft.SharePoint.Publishing.WebControls.EditingMenuActions;
using Microsoft.SharePoint.Publishing.WebControls;
using Microsoft.SharePoint.Utilities;
using System.Web;

namespace InsideMOSS.Samples
{
  public class CreateProductionDescriptionPage: ConsoleAction
  {
    public CreateProductionDescriptionPage()
    {
      this.DisplayText = "Create a new page";
    }
    public override string NavigateUrl
    {
      get
      {
        SPWeb web = SPContext.Current.Web;
        return ("/_layouts/litware/CreateProductDescriptionPage.aspx" +
                "?CancelSource=" + SPHttpUtility.UrlKeyValueEncode(
                HttpContext.Current.Request.Url.OriginalString) +
                "&weburl=" + SPHttpUtility.HtmlEncode(web.ID));
      }
    }
    public override AuthoringStates RequiredStates
    {
      get
      {
        return
        (AuthoringStates.EmptyMask | AuthoringStates.IsPublishingSiteTrue);
      }
    }
    public override Microsoft.SharePoint.SPBasePermissions UserRights
    {
      get
      {
        return
        (SPBasePermissions.EmptyMask | SPBasePermissions.AddListItems);
      }
    }
  }
}
```

The *NavigateUrl* is the most important member to work with in the custom class. In the body, indicate to SharePoint where the user will go when he or she clicks on the menu item. In our example above, the user is redirected to a custom application page, as illustrated in Figure 6-28.

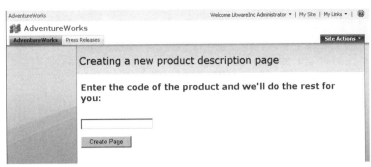

Figure 6-28   The custom application page the user goes to when the custom menu item is selected

The page contains a block of code you should be familiar with if you have read the section in this chapter that discusses the different classes for programmatically creating publishing pages. Here is the code:

```
<%@ Assembly Name="Microsoft.SharePoint, Version=12.0.0.0, Culture=neutral,
    PublicKeyToken=71e9bce111e9429c"%>
<%@ Assembly Name="Microsoft.SharePoint.Publishing, Version=12.0.0.0,
    Culture=neutral, PublicKeyToken=71e9bce111e9429c"%>
<%@ Page Language="C#" MasterPageFile="~/_layouts/application.master"
    Inherits="Microsoft.SharePoint.WebControls.LayoutsPageBase"  %>
<%@ Import Namespace="Microsoft.SharePoint" %>
<%@ Import Namespace="Microsoft.SharePoint.Utilities" %>
<%@ Import Namespace="Microsoft.SharePoint.Publishing" %>

<script runat="server">
  protected void CreatePage(object s, EventArgs e)
  {
    string productcode = textBoxProductCode.Text;
    //-- first retrieve the page layout
    SPSite site = SPContext.Current.Site;
    PublishingSite pubsite = new PublishingSite(site);
    SPContentType ct = pubsite.ContentTypes["Litware Product"];
    PageLayout pagelayout = pubsite.GetPageLayouts(ct,true)[0];
    //-- create a page
    Guid webid = new Guid(SPHttpUtility.HtmlDecode
                    (Request.QueryString["weburl"].ToString()));
    PublishingWeb pubweb = PublishingWeb.GetPublishingWeb
                    (site.AllWebs[webid]);
    PublishingPage page = pubweb.GetPublishingPages().Add
                    ("product_" + productcode + ".aspx", pagelayout);
    //-- set the metadata
    page.Title = "Product " + productcode;
    page.ListItem["ProductCode"] = productcode;
    page.ListItem["ProductName"] = "Small Bike";
    page.ListItem["ProductPrice"] = "$ 100";
    page.ListItem["ProductDescription"] = "description";
    page.ListItem.Update();
    page.Update();
    Response.Redirect(pubweb.Url  + "/" + page.Url);
  }
</script>
```

```
<asp:Content ID="Main" contentplaceholderid="PlaceHolderMain"
 runat="server">
<div>
  <h3>Enter the code of the product and we'll do the rest for you: </h3>
  <br />
  <asp:TextBox ID="textBoxProductCode" runat="server"></asp:TextBox>
  <br /><br />
  <asp:Button ID="buttonCreatePage" OnClick="CreatePage"
   Text="Create Page" runat="server" />
</div>
<asp:Content ID="PageTitleInTitleArea" runat="server"
 contentplaceholderid="PlaceHolderPageTitleInTitleArea" >
  Creating a new product description page
</asp:Content>
```

As you can see, using custom menu items, you have many options for customizing the content authoring functionality depending on the context, the status of the page, and the permissions of the content authors.

The Quick Access Buttons

Another option you have for customizing the Page Editing toolbar is the addition of extra buttons that are displayed again depending on context information. The default list of definitions can be found in the *QuickAccess.xml* file in the \12\Template\Layouts\EditingMenus folder. The elements as well as the steps to customize the experience are the same as with the editing menu.

Supporting Multiple Languages in a Publishing Portal

You may find the need to enable your publishing portals to support multiple languages. In Microsoft Office SharePoint Server 2007, we can do that by using site variations. Site variations make it possible to support not only multilingual but also multidevice or just plain multi-anything Web sites. Generally, site variations are used to modify a source site, and SharePoint duplicates those modifications to any variations of the site.

For example, imagine a multilingual scenario in which a company decides to support three languages for a public site: Flemish, French, and English. Based in Brussels, the company marks the Flemish version of the site as the master or source site. The content managers perform their work within this master site, and all of the work, pages, and potential sites are automatically duplicated in the French and English sites.

Note   Office SharePoint Server 2007 cannot translate pages. Translation of the created content is typically a step in a custom workflow triggered when a content author publishes a page.

Configuring Site Variations

Administrators can configure the site variations at the level of the site collection using a number of administration pages. The walkthrough later on describes all of the steps you need to take. But before that, let's summarize the different artifacts that play a role in the whole site variations story.

- First and most important are variation labels. In the multilingual scenario discussed earlier, Flemish, Dutch, and English are variation labels. One of your variation labels must be the source variation label.

- Office SharePoint Server 2007 allows for a fully scheduled and automatic duplication of work done in the source variation label. Administrators determine schedules to fit their way of working.

- Site variations use the Windows SharePoint Services solutions framework and everything it offers. An internal list named *Relationships* stores all of the metadata involved.

- Resources, such as pictures, can be shared (or referenced) by all variations, or administrators can decide to maintain dedicated resources per variation label.

Walkthrough: Configuring a Site to Support Multiple Languages

By default, site variations are not turned on. Site collection administrators must first configure the site variation settings. To access the site variations settings, open a site, such as the Adventure-Works publishing portal. On the Site Actions menu, choose Site Settings and continue to navigate to the Variations page via the Variation link under the Site Collection Administration group.

Turning Variations On

On this page, displayed in Figure 6-29, you'll need to decide where you want to start varying the site. Your options are to start from the top-level site ("/") or from one of the subsites in the site collection. You can use the Browse button to select a subsite.

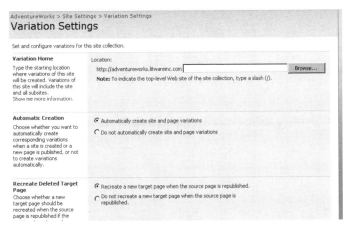

Figure 6-29   Your first administrative step is to configure the variations.

You can take control of the duplication process yourself or let Office SharePoint Server 2007 take care of it. There are also other options:

- Recreate a deleted page in the variations when the source page is republished. This option can enforce consistency between the variations, but in some scenarios you may not want to do so.

- Update Web Parts on target pages. When a content author creates a new source page, you may want to have all of your target pages created, but you may not want to preserve a link to the source page.

- Notify users that need to be aware of the creation of new subsites or pages.

- Reuse a resource, such as a picture, by simply referencing it, or make a local copy of it. The latter choice is useful if the resource needs to be translated.

Creating Variation Labels

Now you are ready to create the variation labels, one for each of the languages you want to support. To create a label for the source variation, navigate via the Site Settings page to the Variation Labels page. On the Variation Labels page, click New Label and then fill in the details.

On the Create Variation Label page, type the name of the label, such as Flemish, and a description. In the Display Name box, type the name that represents the variation in the user interface. In the Locale list, select a locale. The locale allows your site to switch to the language variation based on the culture setting in the browser.

For the final steps, in the Hierarchy Creation section, select the portion of the source variation that you want to duplicate to the other variations and in the Source Hierarchy section. Select Set This Variation To Be The Source Variation (only one source variation per site collection can be defined). Select the site template on which to base the site variation. Figure 6-30 shows all of the above configurations. Click the OK button to create the first variation label.

Next, create all of the other site variation labels that will duplicate the content and infrastructure created in the source variation. Only the title, description, display name, and locale are available to set now. This is because you've already defined the source variation. Remember that you can have only one source variation for your site collection.

As a final step, create the infrastructure by clicking Create Hierarchies in the toolbar of the Variation Labels page. The result will look something like Figure 6-31.

Figure 6-30   The creation of the source variation

Figure 6-31   The variation hierarchy ready to be used

Tuning the Navigation

If you return to the home page of the portal, you can see three subsites—one for each of the variation labels. The Press Releases subsite is not part of the variations infrastructure since that one was already created before you activated the variations. The site variations home pages still need to be approved before they are published, but, as shown in Figure 6-32, you'll see a small control at the top-right corner of the page. In the master page associated with your site, a small ASP.NET user control named *VariationLabelsMenu.ascx* is responsible for this. By using this control, a user can jump to the corresponding page in other variations.

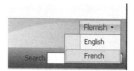

Figure 6-32   The small user control called the VariationsLabel.ascx displaying the options for the user to open the page in one of the other languages

Every possible variation is displayed by the navigation controls. For variations based on language, you probably want to hide all of this. This is because a user is redirected to the appropriate language of the site based on the locale as defined in the language settings of the browser. So, a Flemish visitor with the Flemish locale set in Internet Explorer is redirected to the Flemish variation. If the specified locale is not available as a site variation, the user sees the source variation.

You can hide variations from navigation by clicking Modify Navigation Settings on the Site Settings page at the Site Collection Level.

Authoring Pages

A content author creating a new page in the source variation sees the page duplicated in the other variations. Variation updates can happen automatically, or you can manually activate updates by using the Page Editing toolbar where the Update Variations action is available. The pages created in the variations can be part of a translation process workflow. One example is that an e-mail message notifies a translator to navigate to a new page and translate it.

The Document Conversions Framework

Until now, you have seen two ways of authoring pages for publishing in the portal: the browser and a programmatic approach by using the *Microsoft.SharePoint.Publishing.dll*. There is also an option for allowing content authors to use a smart client such as Microsoft Office Word, Microsoft InfoPath, or any other product for that matter.

Architecture and Configuration Tasks

To start, you'll have to do some configuration tasks in order to prepare the server farm for document conversions. A document converter is made available through an executable installed on the machine within the server farm where the conversions will take place. They are either manually started or are triggered by some kind of event, such as part of a workflow.

In addition to the document converter executables, you have two services that enable the document conversions:

- The Document Conversions Load Balancer manages the availability of document converters.

- The Document Conversions Launcher launches document conversions on an application server.

Each component is run as a service in the SharePoint environment, and the Load Balancer and Launcher must be available in order for conversions to work. When installed in a farm environment, both services should be enabled on application servers in the farm. For example, you may have one server running both a Load Balancer and a Launcher service. Or, you could have one server running a Load Balancer service and one or more servers running a Launcher service.

It would be beyond the scope of this book to detail all of the internals involved with getting the document conversion infrastructure set up in a real-world scenario. I again refer you to *Microsoft Office SharePoint Server 2007 Administrator's Companion* (Microsoft Press) by Bill English for this subject.

Walkthrough: Publishing Pages using Word 2007

Smart client authoring of pages is supported by means of the document conversions framework. Content authors can work in their familiar editor, such as Microsoft Word 2007, create the content as a document, or save the document in a document library where it can be manually or automatically converted to a new publishing page using one of the available page layouts. To conclude this chapter, let's have a quick look at all of this with an example.

> **Important**   Before you follow these steps, make sure that the document conversion services are started and that the document conversion is enabled for the publishing portal you're working with.

Assume that you want users to be able to create press releases on the site using Microsoft Word 2007. First, you'll have to create a place in the publishing portal where they can store their Word documents. Create a document library in the publishing portal called *Press Releases*. Nothing else needs to be done with the document library. Just open up Word and type a press release as displayed in Figure 6-33.

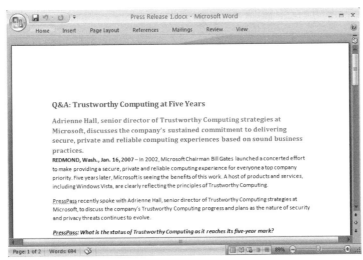

Figure 6-33   A user creating a press release in Word 2007

When you're done, save the document to the newly created document library. To start the scheduling, use the context menu on the document in the document library, as shown in Figure 6-34, to start the conversion of the Word document to a Web page.

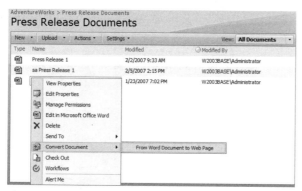

Figure 6-34 Starting the conversion of the Word document in the Web page

Figure 6-35 shows the page displayed where you can enter some important details. The title of the page as well as the name of the .aspx are requested.

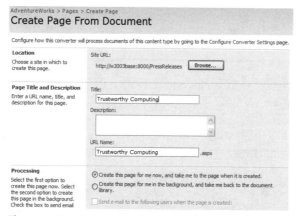

Figure 6-35 Adding the details for the page about to be created

A page layout is used as the basis for the new publishing page. Which one? That depends on the administrator who has the option to configure the converter settings. Clicking on the link at the top of the page displayed in Figure 6-35 takes you to the Configure Settings on Document page. The selection of the page layout is only one of the actions to take here. As shown in Figure 6-36, you can also decide where the content will end up on the page (that is, what field will be used) and whether you'd like to just take over the styles saved along with the document or completely remove them and/or map them to style elements defined in a CSS file.

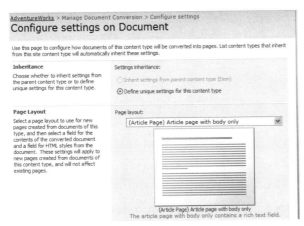

Figure 6-36   Selecting the page layout that will be used for the publishing page

A second section in this page gives you the option to select in which Pages library, or in other words which site, the converted page will be dropped. For our example, select the Press Releases site.

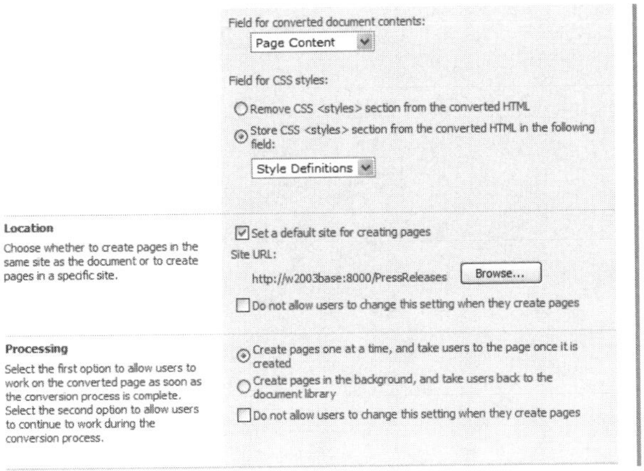

Figure 6-37   Configuring where the new page will be created

After making these final configurations, shown in Figure 6-37, apply them and return back to the previous page to start the conversion process. It will take a moment for the conversion service to do its work, but when complete, the page will look like the one in Figure 6-38. A link is maintained between the page and the source document so that any changes made to the source document will update the publishing page in the portal.

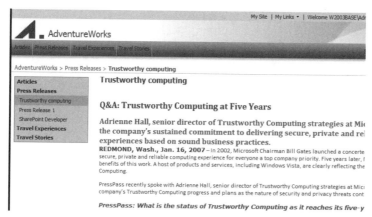

Figure 6-38 The converted page as a new press release on the publishing portal

Summary

Web content management is a vast topic, and a whole book could be written about it. In this chapter, I focused only on some of the important configuration and customization tasks and development options you have when working with a publishing portal. Remember that all of the topics discussed in this chapter are also applicable to the collaboration portal and any site where the publishing features are enabled. A key message to take away is that, in addition to the platform offered by Windows SharePoint Services 3.0, Microsoft Office SharePoint Server 2007 delivers the necessary services and building blocks to produce rich, good-looking, and dynamic public sites that business users can maintain without the help of the IT department or a developer.

Chapter 7
Integrating with Excel Services

- Understand some of the administration and configuration tasks.

- Learn how to prepare and publish an Excel spreadsheet.

- Learn how to create user-defined functions.

- Understand what the Report Center is all about and how to leverage it to create dashboard pages.

- Learn how to communicate with Excel spreadsheets remotely via the Web Service.

Administration and Configuration of Excel Services

A good amount of administration and configuration functionality is involved with Excel Services. We are not going to explain it all in detail since this is a book for developers. However, you should be aware of it since it can impact the way you, the author, extend and deploy your Excel spreadsheets. Configuration of a trusted location is the most important task. When working with Excel Services, the location where the spreadsheets will end up must be trusted, as well as the data connections that are used internally. For example, administrators can only allow connections to be made using data connection files stored in a trusted Data Connection library.

Walkthrough: Configuring a Trusted Location

Let's go through the steps for preparing a document library called Excel Sheets in a Share-Point team site. The document library will be used for storing Microsoft Excel 2007 spreadsheets. As mentioned before, in order to leverage Excel Services, you have to perform some administrative steps.

Start by navigating to the SharePoint 3.0 Central Administration and the administration site of the Shared Services Provider that provides Excel Services for the team site. Under Excel Services Settings, there is a link to navigate to the page where you can define the list of trusted file locations. To add a new entry, use the Add Trusted File Location link in the toolbar.

There are a couple of settings to configure here. First, as shown in Figure 7-1, provide the path to the document library that will store the Excel spreadsheets. It is possible to use the URL of the team site and the Children Trusted option so that all of the document libraries in the team site will be considered as trusted. However, this is not always considered good practice in larger organizations where the publishing of spreadsheets is a process that can only be done under strict control.

Shared Services Administration: SharedServices1 > Excel Services Trusted File Locations > Trusted File Location

Excel Services
Add Trusted File Location

[OK]   [Cancel]

☐ **Location**
A Windows SharePoint Services location, network file share, or Web folder from which a server running Excel Services is permitted to access workbooks.

Address
The full Windows SharePoint Services location, network file share or Web folder address of this trusted location.
`p://moss/SiteDirectory/litware/Sheets`

Location Type
Storage type of this trusted location:
◉ Windows SharePoint Services
○ UNC
○ HTTP

Trust Children
Trust child libraries or directories.
☐ Children trusted

Figure 7-1   Setting the path to a document library as a trusted location for Excel Services

You can stay with the defaults for most of the other settings other than the setting that defines what kind of external data access you'd like to allow for the published spreadsheets. The spreadsheets we will use later all require access to external data sources. So, we need to change the Allow External Data option from None to either Trusted Data Connection Libraries Only or Trusted Data Connection Libraries And Embedded. Your organization may want to enforce the use of data connection files stored in trusted data connection libraries for all of the Excel spreadsheets that will be published. Therefore, let's set the option to only data connection libraries and, in order to avoid unnecessary messages to the user, you can turn off the warning that is normally displayed within the browser when there is an attempt to connect to external data from the Excel spreadsheet. Figure 7-2 portrays the different settings.

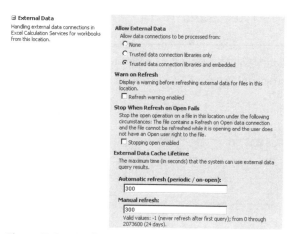

☐ **External Data**
Handling external data connections in Excel Calculation Services for workbooks from this location.

Allow External Data
Allow data connections to be processed from:
○ None
○ Trusted data connection libraries only
◉ Trusted data connection libraries and embedded

Warn on Refresh
Display a warning before refreshing external data for files in this location.
☐ Refresh warning enabled

Stop When Refresh on Open Fails
Stop the open operation on a file in this location under the following circumstances: The file contains a Refresh on Open data connection and the file cannot be refreshed while it is opening and the user does not have an Open user right to the file.
☐ Stopping open enabled

External Data Cache Lifetime
The maximum time (in seconds) that the system can use external data query results.

Automatic refresh (periodic / on-open):
`300`

Manual refresh:
`300`
Valid values: -1 (never refresh after first query); from 0 through 2073600 (24 days).

Figure 7-2   Configuring the connection to external data sources for the trusted file location

To end, you can also check the option to allow user-defined functions as you will need it later. That concludes the work for the trusted file location. Figure 7-3 displays the page with the entry of the trusted document library you'll work with later on.

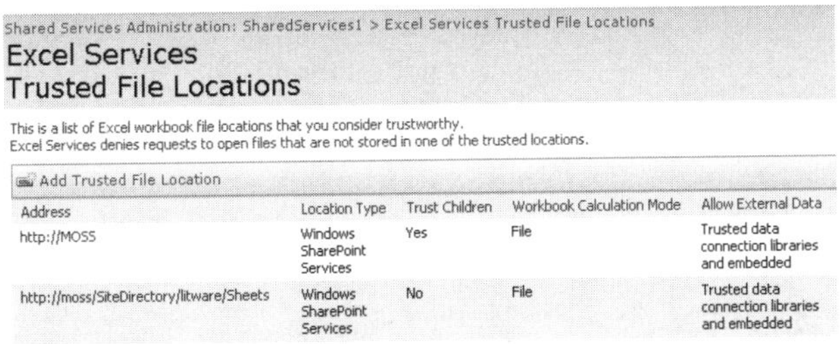

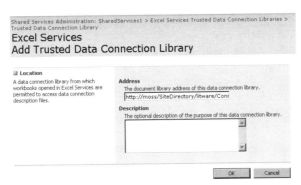

Figure 7-3   The document library added as a new trusted file location for Excel Services

There is one more thing you can do in this walkthrough. Because you specified that external data can only be retrieved by making use of data connections stored in data connection libraries, you'll have to create one and configure it as a trusted place. The data connection library, Excel Connections for example, can be created anywhere, but for simplicity, we'll create it in the same SharePoint site as where we have the trusted document library. The place where you define this data connection library as a trusted library is again at the administration site of your Shared Services Provider. Under the Excel Services Settings section, you'll find the link to navigate to the page where you can create a new entry. No complex configuration here—just provide SharePoint with the path to the data connection library, as displayed in Figure 7-4.

Figure 7-4   Trusting a data connection library that can be used by Excel spreadsheet authors when there is a need to access external data

Excel Spreadsheets on the Server

Excel Services is actually a collection of server-side components running on top of ASP.NET 2.0 and Windows SharePoint Services 3.0 delivering the needed functionality for organizations who want to store, manage, and create their Excel spreadsheets in a centralized manner within the SharePoint server farm. Figure 7-5 depicts the Excel Services architecture and all of the components playing their respective role within the whole story.

To start with, the Excel spreadsheets are published to a normal document library in a SharePoint site and thus end up in one of your content databases. The SharePoint site has to be part of a site collection hosted on an IIS Web Application that is connected to a Shared Services

Provider delivering Excel Services. Don't save the spreadsheet in the document library. Instead, publish the spreadsheet, as you'll see in a moment. Don't forget that Excel Services can only work with trusted document library and that administrators can enforce rules when connecting to external data sources.

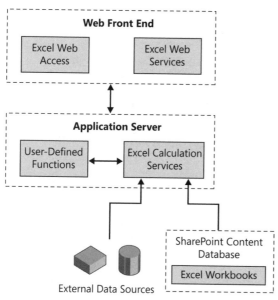

Figure 7-5   Excel Services architecture

Once spreadsheets are published in the document library, users will be able to have the spreadsheets (or parts of it) delivered within the browser. A new Web Part, Excel Web Access, takes care of this. Many spreadsheets are all about executing formulas that process data entered or retrieved within the spreadsheet. Embedded code, such as Visual Basic for Applications, is not allowed, as I'll describe later. There is the option to work with custom code via user-defined functions. Excel Calculation Services is the server-side engine that does the work of loading the workbook, performing the calculations, and maintaining a session for the user with a certain level of interactivity, either directly in the browser or through the different calls done by smart clients with the Web Service. All of these components will be explained in more detail in the following pages.

Preparing an Excel Spreadsheet for Publishing

Not every Excel spreadsheet is a candidate for publishing to Excel Services. There are some important restrictions and limitations you should be aware of:

- The workbooks may not contain embedded code such as Visual Basic for Applications (VBA) procedures that automate certain tasks within Excel. You have support for executing custom code through the use of user-defined functions. That is the only extensibility option supported by this version of Excel Services.

- Excel Services is able to display many, but not all, of the features that have to do with interactivity. Certain advanced visualization for charts will not be possible. The same goes for pivot tables.

- It is very important for you to understand that you do not have access to the Excel object model when running the workbook with Excel Services. For example, dynamic insertion of charts or other Excel objects are not supported.

- The SDK contains a list of other unsupported features you should have a look at before publishing workbooks.

The publishing process itself is very straightforward, and the steps are described in the following walkthrough. The only thing you should have is a trusted document library and connection files in a trusted connection library. As discussed in the beginning of the chapter, you should also be aware of the different configuration and administration settings before publishing.

Walkthrough: Publishing a Spreadsheet

Now that you've read about all of the options for publishing an Excel spreadsheet, let's go through a practical example using the spreadsheet called *ExcelServicesDemo.xlsx*, which can also be found also on the companion Web site. If you open the Excel spreadsheet, you'll find three sheets, one containing a table with data, a second one with a pivot table, and a third one with a simple mortgage calculator. If you have followed the previous walkthrough in this chapter, you're up and running to start the publishing of this spreadsheet to the Excel Sheets document library configured as a trusted library for Excel Services.

The publishing steps are very simple. Select Publish from the File menu and then select the Excel Services option. Point to the document library we've talked about and, before you actually start the publishing process, click on the Excel Services Options button in the Save As dialog box as displayed in Figure 7-6.

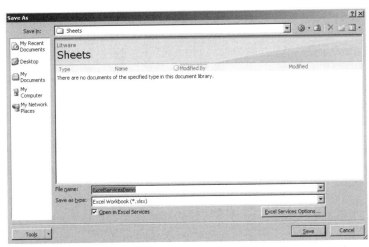

Figure 7-6   Publishing the Excel spreadsheet to the Excel Sheets document library in our SharePoint team site

In the opened dialog box, you have the option to select what you actually want to get published to Excel Services. For this example, proceed to publish the entire workbook. But before doing that, activate the Parameters tab and click the Add button. As shown in Figure 7-7, the Add Parameters dialog box allows you to have all of the named ranges that do not contain any formulas defined as parameters.

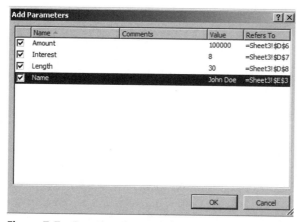

Figure 7-7   Exposing the named ranges in our spreadsheet as parameters to Excel Services

Now you're ready to click the Save button and publish the spreadsheet. A browser session will be opened, and Excel Services will render a thin client representation of the spreadsheet, which gives you access to the three sheets along with the parameters pane. This pane lets you communicate with the named ranges available in the third sheet for the mortgage calculator. Figure 7-8 shows the spreadsheet displayed in the browser.

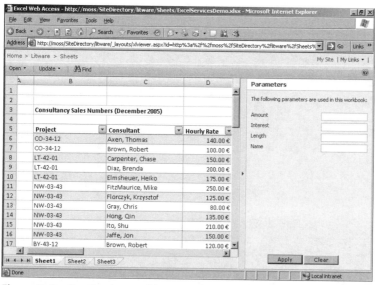

Figure 7-8   Our Excel spreadsheet rendered in the browser

Experiment a bit with the spreadsheet. Notice that there is a certain level of interactivity using the sorting and the filtering options in Sheet1 for the table. The pivot table in Sheet2 allows you to select a consultant, and the data and chart are nicely updated. Moving to Sheet3, you can enter new values for the *amount, interest, length,* and *name* parameters. When you click Apply, all of these new values are transferred to their respective named ranges in the spreadsheet, and a new result is immediately calculated.

This representation of the Excel spreadsheet can be requested any time now by simply going to the Excel Sheets document library and selecting the View in Web Browser option.

User-Defined Functions

As discussed above, no VBA code is allowed by Excel Services! If you need to call custom code, your only (but powerful) option is to use managed .NET assemblies that encapsulate user-defined functions (UDFs). It is possible to use these types of .NET assemblies client-side, but that is not in the scope of this book. We'll concentrate only on the ability to use formulas in cells to call custom functions written in managed code and deployed to Microsoft Office SharePoint Server 2007.

There are a number of reasons why you would opt for creating UDFs:

- Call custom mathematical functions

- Get data from custom data sources into worksheets

- Call Web services from the UDFs

- Wrap calls to existing native code library functions—for example, existing Excel UDFs

This will be discussed in more detail later, but in short, the development and deployment process is done in the following steps:

- Start by creating a .NET assembly that references the *Microsoft.Office.Excel.Server.Udf.dll* containing the user-defined function support.

- The classes are annotated with the *UdfClass* attribute. The methods you want to expose are annotated with the *UdfMethod* attribute. Classes and methods have to be public, and there are certain restrictions regarding the type of incoming and returned parameter values. In short, only the simple types are supported: *Double, Single, Int32, UInt32, Int16, UInt16, Byte, Sbyte, String, Boolean, Object* arrays, *DateTime,* and *Object (Object* is only for return parameters).

- The .NET assembly can be deployed in the global assembly cache, but it is not required. A folder on the server is sufficient to store all UDF assemblies.

- The path to the .NET assembly must be communicated to Excel Services in the administration site of the Shared Services Provider.

- You call the user-defined functions like a normal Excel formula in your workbook. Of course, the calls will only work when the spreadsheet is under the control of Excel Services.

All of this and more is best demonstrated with a walkthrough using the same spreadsheet used in the previous walkthroughs.

Walkthrough: User-Defined Functions

Remember the *ExcelServicesDemo.xlsx* published to the SharePoint environment in the previous walkthrough? It contains a formula for calculating the amount to be paid for the mortgage. Let's assume that there is a need to have more business logic and more complexity in the calculation of this amount. The native formulas made available by the Excel client do not suffice anymore. Since Excel Services does not allow for embedded code in the spreadsheets, you'll have to create a .NET assembly containing a user-defined function encapsulating the code for calculating the amount.

Start by creating a new class library project in Visual Studio.NET 2005 and naming it *Mortgage-UDF*. It is also a good idea to rename the available class to *MortgageCalculate* and the namespace to *InsideMOSS.Samples*. A reference to the *Microsoft.Office.Excel.Server.Udf.dll* must be added to the project. You'll find the entry in the Add Reference dialog box under the name Excel Services UDF Framework. Finish the preparation work by adding a *using* statement to the *Microsoft.Office.Excel.Server.Udf* namespace as follows:

```
using Microsoft.Office.Excel.Server.Udf;
```

The next step is to mark the class with the *UdfClass* attribute and add a method called *Calculate* marked with the *UdfMethod* attribute.

```
[UdfClass]
public class MortgageCalculator
{
  [UdfMethod]
  public double Calculate(double amount, int length, double interest)
  {
  }
}
```

I'm sure you're not especially interested in the topic of formulas related to mortgages, so we'll keep it simple and use the following code in the *Calculate* method:

```
double result = 0;
result = amount * (1 + (length * interest));
return result;
```

Before building the project, use the properties of the project to create a key to sign the assembly.

The resulting .NET *dll* must be made available on all of the front-end Web servers within your server farm. The location or folder is free to choose, but administrators must add an entry for it in the administration site of the Shared Services Provider. Let's use a folder directly at the root, C:\Udfs, and drop the *MortgageUdf.dll* in it. In the Shared Services Provider administration site, click the link for the User-Defined Function Assemblies page and create a new entry here as shown in Figure 7-9.

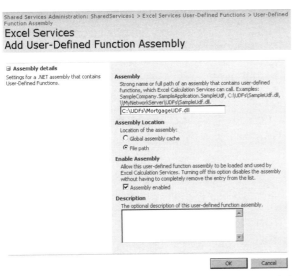

Shared Services Administration: SharedServices1 > Excel Services User-Defined Functions > User-Defined Function Assembly

Figure 7-9 Adding the location of the .NET dll containing the user-defined functions in the Shared Services Provider administration site

Because you are not opting for the Global Assembly Cache, you'll have to change the Assembly Location option to File Path. You may also want to check the list of Trusted File Locations to see whether the entry created for the document library created in the first walk-through allows for user-defined functions.

Time to test your work. Open *ExcelServicesDemo.xlsx* from the document library in Excel and activate the third sheet. In cell D10, you'll find the formula. You will now replace this one with the call to the *Calculate* method in the UDF assembly. As portrayed in Figure 7-10, call the *Calculate* method just like a normal Excel formula giving it the three values it needs as input. Make sure that the three references to the cells are separated from one another using a semicolon. After pressing Enter, you'll see a *#NAME?* value displayed in the cell. Don't worry about this; the user-defined function will do its work only when the Excel spreadsheet is made available to and is under the control of Excel Services.

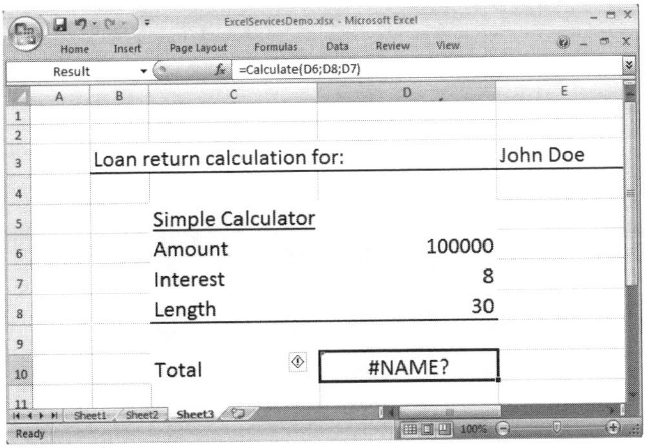

Figure 7-10 Calling the user-defined function in the Excel spreadsheet

Proceed by saving the Excel spreadsheet back to the trusted document library. View the spreadsheet again in the browser and you'll see that the user-defined function is doing its part of the job: calculating the total mortgage amount as shown in Figure 7-11.

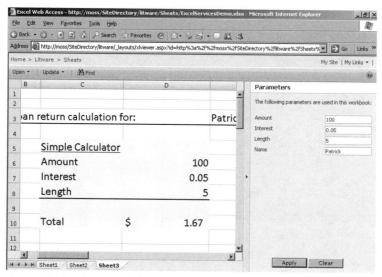

Figure 7-11   The user-defined function calculating the total of the mortgage in a spreadsheet under the control of Excel Services

The Excel Web Access Web Part and Snapshots

The Excel Web Access Web Part is used to deliver either the complete workbook, some sheets from the workbook, or simply different parts from the sheets (such as a chart or a pivot table) in the browser to the SharePoint user. You have already seen it in action with the previous walkthroughs when the spreadsheet was displayed in the browser. However, instead of completely filling up the browser screen, you can also just add it as one of the Web Parts within your SharePoint pages.

The Excel Web Access Web Part is advertised in the Add a Web Part dialog box under the category Business Data Web Parts as displayed in Figure 7-12.

> **Note**   You'll only see the Business Data Web Parts when the Office SharePoint Server Enterprise Site Features are active for your site. This is not the case if you work on a team site that is not part of a site collection of a portal. And of course, as mentioned in Chapter 1, "Introducing the Microsoft Office SharePoint Server 2007," both the Business Data Catalog and Excel Services are part of the enterprise CAL of Microsoft Office SharePoint Server 2007.

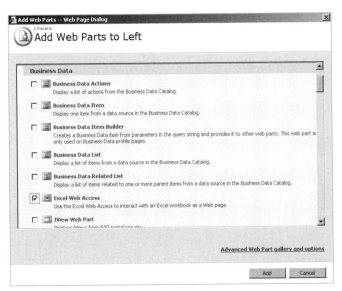

Figure 7-12   Adding the Excel Web Access Web Part to a SharePoint page

The tool pane exposes all of the properties of the Web Part. Use the properties to locate the spreadsheet that must be loaded by Excel Services. Additionally, you can specify the ID of the object you want displayed. Figure 7-13, for example, shows the settings for asking the Web Part to display only the chart.

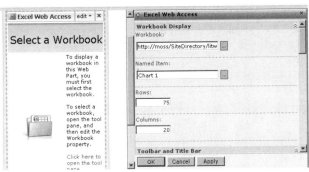

Figure 7-13   Configuring the Excel Web Access to display a snapshot from the workbook

You can decide the level of interaction along with other settings such as the type of toolbar, the choice of menu commands shown, and the navigation options for the user. Figure 7-14 displays the chart from *ExcelServicesDemo.xlsx* with all of the options turned off.

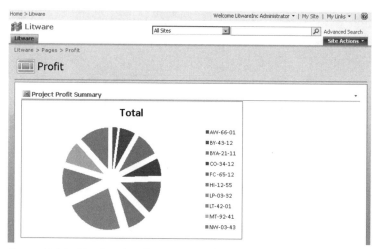

Figure 7-14 The Excel Web Access Web Part showing a chart representing the profits per project

The Report Center

The Report Center is a new type of site delivered with Microsoft Office SharePoint Server 2007 (enterprise CAL) and, by default, is part of the site collection provisioned when opting for a collaboration portal. Just as with the Document and Search Center, the goal of the Report Center is to be a place within the site collection for the delivery of a specific type of content or functionality. In the case of the Report Center, it involves the storage and maintenance of reports, lists that can display key performance indicators (KPIs), and the creation and delivery of dashboards that display business intelligence information often sliced by means of various filter Web Parts.

The Report Library

On the Report Center, you'll find one special list instance already provisioned: the Reports Library. Many more can be created based on the Report Library template. This document library is specially designed to properly version reports and store reports and dashboards of all of the needed metadata. As shown in Figure 7-15, two content types are associated with the Report Library: Report and Dashboard.

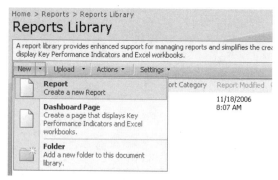

Figure 7-15 The Report Library with the two content types: Report and Dashboard

Versioning is important when storing reports. This is different from versioning a document. You'll have a version of a new document every time you change something with the document. For a report, a new version is created every time you view a report. This is because the underlying data source can receive new or modified data continuously, and your report is a view on that data. Every new view can thus result in a report containing different information. All of this can be easily versioned by the Report Library.

What kind of reports can we store in the Report Library? Out-of-the-box, you can store Excel spreadsheets and manage them in the library. However, don't forget to configure the Report Library as a trusted location if you intend to make the Excel workbooks available via Excel Services, which is probably what you want. Another type of report you can store in the library are reports created with SQL Server Reporting Services. When installing the latest service pack of Microsoft SQL Server 2005, you'll get integration between the SQL Server Reporting Services and Microsoft Office SharePoint Server 2007. The Report Library becomes an additional place where you can deploy your created reports, and there is also a Web Part that is installed and activated giving you the option to visualize and work with the SQL Server Reporting Services reports. A good place for this is a dashboard page.

Dashboards

Dashboards are SharePoint pages that are able to display Web Parts outputting report information (as with Excel spreadsheets or SQL Server Reporting Services reports) combined with an area where you can drop Filter Web Parts that can slice the data shown in the reporting Web Parts. Of course, because it is a normal SharePoint Web Part page following a specific layout, you are permitted to add any other type of Web Part on the dashboard pages. An example of a dashboard page is displayed in Figure 7-16.

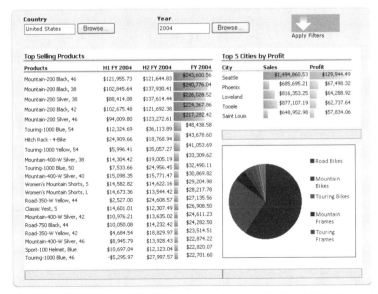

Figure 7-16   An example of a dashboard page with Excel Web Access Web Parts and Filter Web Parts displaying business information

In a moment, you'll go through the steps for creating a similar dashboard.

Filter Web Parts

The concept of a Filter Web Part is simple: capture or retrieve a certain value from the user, a data source, or a context, and pass it to one or more of the Web Parts on the dashboard page. Various Filter Web Parts are immediately available, and there is the option to create additional custom Web Parts. Table 7-1 summarizes which ones you can directly add to a dashboard page:

Table 7-1   List of Filter Web Parts

Web Part	Description
Business Data Catalog Filter	This one filters the contents using a list of values retrieved from an external data source using the Business Data Catalog.
Choice Filter	When adding the filter to the dashboard page, you have the option to populate a choice list manually with options for the user to slice the data.
Current User Filter	This one will not be displayed to the user. This hidden Web Part can retrieve information about the user and pass it to the connected Web Parts. This can simply be the name of the user, the account, or any value of exposed properties from the user profile for that user.
Date Filter	This one allows a user to enter a date and send it to the connected Web Parts.
Page Field Filter	Remember how we discussed the rich page model that underlies the portals? Every page that is part of the Report Center, such as dashboard pages, is stored in the Pages library and is based on page layouts. With this Filter Web Part, you can retrieve values from columns that are associated with the content type driving the page layout.
Query String Filter	Users can be redirected to a dashboard page, and data can be sent along with the redirection in the query string or URL. This Filter Web Part can pick them up and send the values to the connected Web Parts.
SharePoint List Filter	This one can be configured to retrieve a value from a SharePoint list.
SQL Server 2005 Analysis Server Filter	This one can be configured to retrieve filtering values from a cube maintained by SQL Server 2005 Analysis Server.
Text Filter	This one is probably the most simple: a value can be entered and just passed to the connected Web Parts.

As mentioned, you are not restricted to these Web Parts. It is possible to create your own Filter Web Parts.

KPI Lists

The Report Center contains a new list template for storing key performance indicators. Note that this is a lightweight implementation of the concept of KPIs, and if you want richer support, you should have a look at Business Scorecard Manager 2005 and the forthcoming Microsoft PerformancePoint Server. Both run on the latest version of the SharePoint platform.

In short, key performance indicators allow you to communicate goals and trends and track progress within your dashboard pages. They are stored in a custom list that has a number of content types associated with it. These content types basically define how the key performance indicator will get its value. Here are your options:

Indicator Using Data in SharePoint List

This indicator connects to a value stored in the SharePoint list. As shown in Figure 7-17, you have to provide the URL and the view and then define the details of how the value that has to be compared with the indicators (or targets) needs to be calculated. There is the option to just retrieve the number of items, work with a percentage of the items following certain criteria, or make use of a calculation, such as the sum of the values for a specific column in the view.

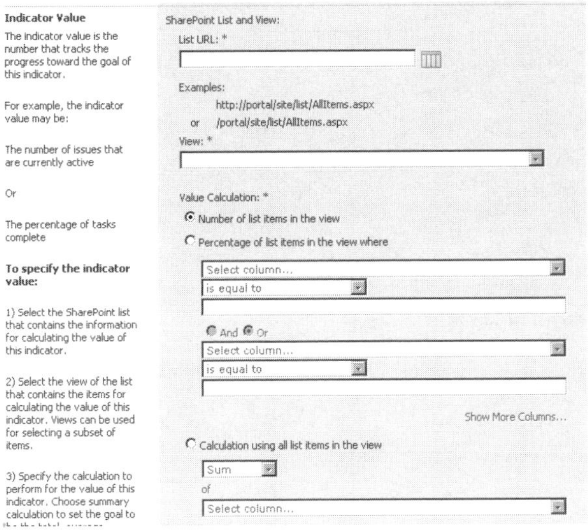

Figure 7-17   The information to be provided when creating a key performance indicator using data in a SharePoint list

Indicator Using Data in an Excel Workbook

A second indicator can be used if the data is stored in an Excel workbook. The indicator as depicted in Figure 7-18 is based on the value from a cell in a workbook.

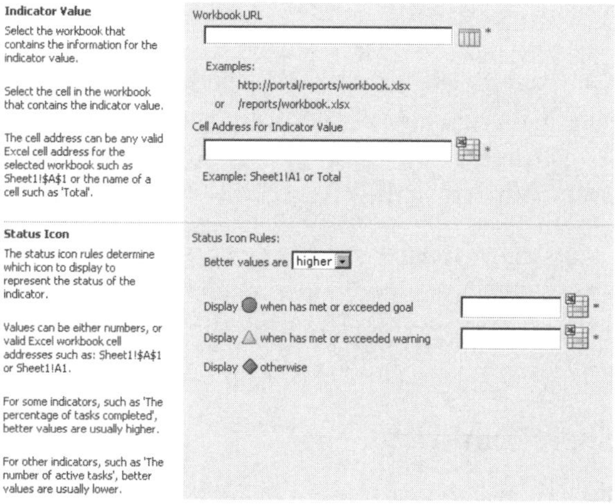

Figure 7-18   The information to be provided when creating a key performance indicator using data in an Excel workbook

Indicator Using Data in a SQL Server 2005 Analysis Server

This indicator is more tuned toward a real-world scenario where a data warehouse is set up and maintained using the SQL Server 2005 Analysis Server. The data warehouse continuously collects data from any resource and exposes it through a cube. With this indicator, you can connect to such a cube by first adding a connection to the Data Connection library that is also part of the Report Center by default. As shown in Figure 7-19, you can select the type of KPIs made available by that cube and then the KPI itself. The details of the selection are immediately displayed.

Figure 7-19   The information to be provided when creating a key performance indicator using data in a SQL Server 2005 Analysis Services cube

Indicator Using Manually Entered Data

This is of course the simplest of all of the possible indicators. You just have to provide a static value when creating an item like this.

Walkthrough: Creating a Dashboard Page

In this walkthrough, you'll get some practical experience with most of the topics we've previously discussed, compiling everything in a nice dashboard page for business users.

Before you begin the walkthrough, make sure that the Reports Library in the Reports Center is known by Excel Services as a trusted location. Refer to the first walkthrough in this chapter for the steps to accomplish this. Additionally, you're also going to make use of the data connection library in the Report Center. This also has to be defined as a trusted location. Again, in the Shared Services Provider administration site, under the Excel Services Settings group, you'll find the link to the list that stores the trusted data connection libraries. Make sure the one in the Report Center is part of this list.

Creating a Data Connection

The first task is to make sure that the Excel spreadsheet you have available on the companion Web site as *Top10ProductsSubCategories.xlsx* is connected to the AdventureWorks data warehouse running under the control of the Microsoft SQL Server 2005 Analysis Services. The SharePoint administrator has configured Excel Services to not allow embedded data connections, so your only choice is to work with the Data Connection library that is already in place in the Report Center.

The data connection file to use is available on the companion Web site as *AdventureWorks.odc*. It has to be uploaded in the data connection library already available in the Report Center. Just navigate to this library and select Upload Document from the toolbar. Browse to the connection file and add it to the library. Don't forget to approve the entry, as shown in Figure 7-20.

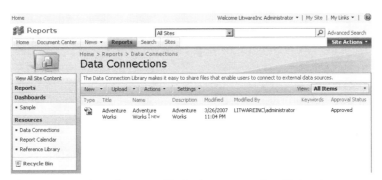

Figure 7-20   The Adventure Works data connection file has been approved and is ready to be used by clients such as Microsoft Excel 2007

Next, open the Excel spreadsheet and you'll see that no data is currently retrieved. Use the Data tab to activate the Data ribbon where you find the different controls to create or use an existing connection. As shown in Figure 7-21, you'll start with the creation of a new data connection by clicking the Connections button and then the Add button.

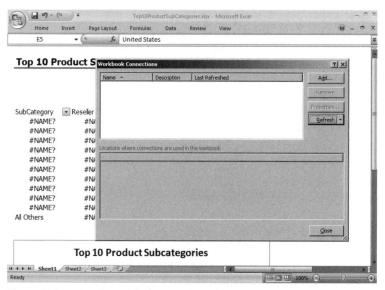

Figure 7-21 Starting with the creation of a new data connection to the AdventureWorks data warehouse

The Add button shows you a dialog box where you can select one of the existing connections already available either locally or on the network (for example, in one of the Data Connection libraries in SharePoint). I assume you don't have any connection yet. Click the Browse for More button at the bottom of the dialog box. The dialog box that allows you to create a new data source is displayed. Now enter the full URL to the data connection file you've previously uploaded in the data connection library in the Report Center. Notice in Figure 7-22 how the spreadsheet is immediately refreshed and all of the data is now nicely retrieved. You can close the dialog box.

Try changing the date to *2003* and the geography to *Australia* and you'll see new data appearing. You're ready to publish this workbook to the Reports Library in the Report Center.

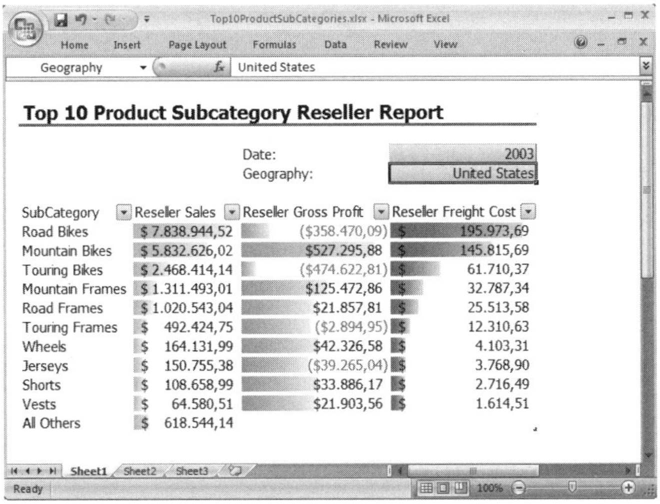

Figure 7-22   The spreadsheet showing the data retrieved from the data warehouse

Publishing the Workbook

Use the File menu and select Publish and then Excel Services to open the dialog box for entering the URL to the Reports Library (*http://moss/Reports/ReportsLibrary*). Before clicking the Save button, have a look at the current status of the Excel Services options by clicking the Excel Services Options button. The goal is to only visualize *Sheet1*. In the Show tab, select Sheets from the dropdown menu and check *Sheet1*. *Sheet2* also contains information that is required to retrieve the data, and it will be published along with the other sheets. However, Excel Services will only show *Sheet1* to the user. The Parameters tab normally shows the two parameters that will be displayed so that there is a level of interactivity with the workbook. After closing this dialog box and clicking the Save button, a dialog box is displayed showing the different document types. Make sure you selected Report here. Excel Services will immediately pick up the spreadsheet and display it in the browser. Figure 7-23 shows what the result should be look like. It is possible to get a warning because you are connecting to external data. If so, just confirm the message and, if desired, deactivate it at the level of the Shared Services Provider for the trusted location.

Again, try to enter different parameters and verify whether you are allowed to refresh the data without any problems. There are other spreadsheets we could add to the dashboard, but for simplicity, let's just stick to one.

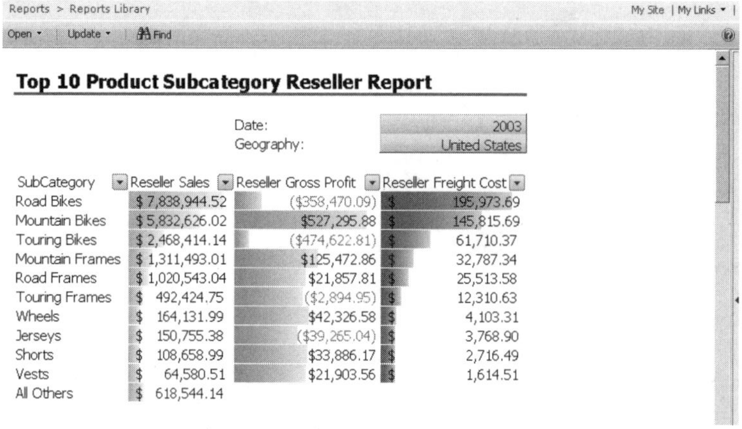

Figure 7-23 The spreadsheet displayed by Excel Services in the browser

Creating the Dashboard

Your next step is to create the dashboard itself. Go to the Reports Library in the Report Center and click the New button to create a new dashboard page. Name the page *Adventure-Works.aspx* and the title *Adventure Works*. In the Dashboard Layout options, select One Column Vertical Layout. That will be more than enough since we will only work with one Web Part in the dashboard. For the rest, keep the defaults, including the one to have a KPI list created automatically. Figure 7-24 shows the settings needed for the new dashboard page.

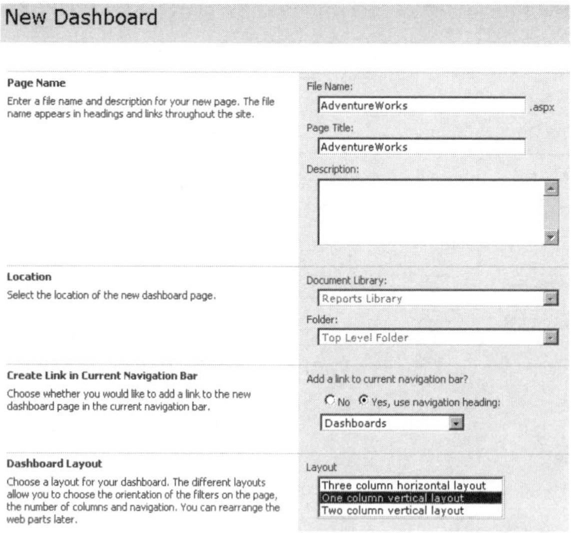

Figure 7-24 The first step to creating a new dashboard page

The page is created, and you'll find two Web Parts already in place. The first one shows the KPI list that was created, and the second one is an Excel Web Access Web Part ready to be configured. Let's start with the last one. Open the tool pane and click the Select A Link button to find the Excel workbook previously published, as shown in Figure 7-25.

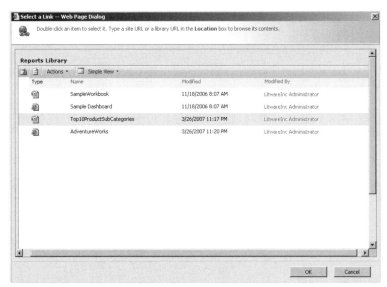

Figure 7-25   Selecting the *Top10ProductSubCategories.xlsx* to be displayed in the Excel Web Access Web Part

The dashboard will display the entire *Sheet1*, as shown in Figure 7-26, so no need to select a value for the *Named Item* field. However, you can set the type of toolbar to *None* and uncheck nearly all of the properties in the tool pane, except the options for *Workbook Interactivity* and *Parameter Modification*, which have to be on in order for the filter Web Parts to work. You may want to set a title for the Web Part and a fixed height value so that you can see the complete sheet in the Web Part body.

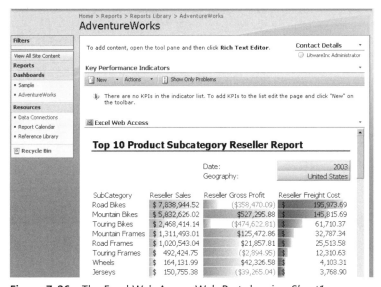

Figure 7-26   The Excel Web Access Web Part showing *Sheet1*

You have also disabled the parameters pane, so there is no direct way of modifying the date or the geography. But, since this is a dashboard page, you can now add some filter Web Parts that can be used to set the values for the two parameters.

Adding Filter Web Parts

Two filter Web Parts will be made available to users visiting the dashboard page. A first one is a simple Text Filter Web Part that can be used to enter the value for the *Date* field. You'll select the Text Filter Web Part instead of the Date Filter Web Part since you only need to have the year. Make sure the page is in edit mode, and in the top left corner of the page, you'll see the Filter Zone. Here, click the Add a Filter button. In the Add Web Parts dialog box, select the Text Filter Web Part. You'll notice a link to the tool pane. Open it and just provide *Date* as the name for the filter. You then have to connect it to the Excel Web Access Web Part to feed it with the inputted date if the user clicks the Apply Filters button in the zone. Use the Edit menu on the Web Part to connect it and send the filter values to the workbook. A popup is shown where you'll have to map the inputted year to the Date parameter exposed in the workbook. Click the Configure button to do this.

Your next filter Web Part is a hidden one or also referred to as a *context filter*. The Current User Filter Web Part will make sure that the user will only see the data for his or her geography. This information is retrieved from the current user's profile. So, if you want to continue with this walkthrough, make sure that you have a property called *Geography* as part of the list of user profile properties and have one or more of the user profiles modified to contain a value for this property. Make sure that everyone can see the property so that you, as the author of the dashboard page, can use it. For example, Brian Cox can have a value for the *Geography* property equal to *United States*, while Mike Fitzmaurice has a value equal to *Australia*.

Edit the dashboard page again, and in the filter zone, add the Current User Filter Web Part. Figure 7-27 shows the configuration in the tool pane. The new *Geography* user profile property should be available in the list. You simply select it to complete the mapping.

Figure 7-27 Configuring the Current User Filter Web Part

Once done, you again have to connect the Current User Filter Web Part to the Web Part that shows the Excel workbook. This time, map the filter value to the *Geography* parameter exposed by the workbook.

You can now just publish the page and try out the dashboard using the two users in combination with an explicitly set value for the year. Figure 7-28 shows the page as shown to Brian.

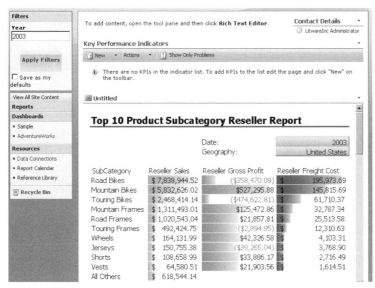

Figure 7-28   The Current User Filter Web Part picks up the value of the *Geography* parameter from Brian's user profile and sends it to the workbook.

Configuring the KPI List

The last part of the dashboard is the KPI list. Many indicators can be added here. We'll just use one to learn about the different steps to take. The indicator will show the visitor of the dashboard whether the company is on target for Internet revenue. It is an indicator that is based on data coming directly from the data warehouse in the SQL Server 2005 Analysis Services.

On the Web Part showing the key performance indicators at the top of the page, use the New button to create a new indicator from SQL Server 2005 Analysis Services. In the New Item page, select the data connection you have used before to pump the data into the workbook. Next, select Financial Perspective\Grow Revenue from the dropdown menu and then select Internet Revenue. All of the information about the targets that have to be achieved is defined in the analysis server, so you don't have to worry about this. Just save the new item under the name *Internet Revenue* and test it out. Figure 7-29 displays the result.

Figure 7-29   A key performance indicator showing whether the company is on target for Internet revenue

The only thing to do now is just publish the dashboard page, and your business users will be able to visit it.

The Excel Services Web Service

As a final topic, let's have a look at what you can do with the Web Service that is part of the Excel Services architecture. It allows you to communicate with the published workbooks in a remote way. You can create a Windows application, a mobile device application, an extension to the Microsoft Office clients, or even a Java-based application running on a non-Windows platform, communicating everything to the workbooks. Excel Services Web Service is physically represented as *excelservice.asmx*, and there are plenty of methods exposed.

The Web Service follows the standard SOAP protocol and is consumed pretty much like any other .NET Web Service. However, it is important that a user session be maintained while calling the different methods that expose the interaction. So, in your client-side code, you'll have to store the session ID and always send it along with the different calls you are making.

Walkthrough: Working with the Excel Services Web Service

The final walkthrough of this chapter will illustrate the steps to take to see the Web Service in action. You'll work again with the workbook that contains the mortgage calculation sheet by sending it some data and letting it recalculate the amount and show the results to the user. To make it simple, you'll have a Windows application with just a couple of user interface controls on it. A starter project for this can be found on the companion Web site as *ExcelCalculation*.

Open the project in Visual Studio.NET 2005. The first thing we'll do is generate the Web Service proxy. Right-click the project in the Solution Explorer and select Add Web Reference. Enter the URL to *excelservice.asmx* or browse for it using the Web Services On The Local Machine link in the Add Web Reference dialog box. Figure 7-30 illustrates an example entry.

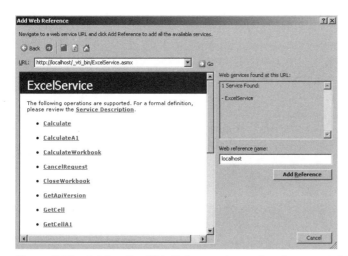

Figure 7-30 Adding the Web Reference to *excelservice.asmx* in Visual Studio.NET 2005

Now open the code editor behind the form you have in the project. There is already an event handler defined for the *Click* event of the button you have on the form. The first block of code to write is the creation of an instance of the Web Service proxy created. Since you're working with a SharePoint Web Service, you'll have to send some credentials with the calls. There are two options: you can use the credentials of the current user or create an instance of *System.Net.NetworkCredential* and provide the constructor with the credential information. In the code below, the account of the current user is sent to the server.

```
WebService.ExcelService ws = new WebService.ExcelService();
ws.Credentials = System.Net.CredentialCache.DefaultCredentials;
```

Your next block of code opens the workbook with a couple of parameters that are passed along with the call. The first parameter is the URL to the Excel workbook. The second and third parameters are used to define the local settings, and the final one is an empty array of type *Status*. This array will be filled up by Excel Services when it encounters non-critical errors and warnings while doing the server-side operations. An array of this type is returned with many of the subsequent calls. The *OpenWorkbook* method returns a string containing the session ID. You'll need to store this one in a variable since you'll have to pass it as a first parameter value with all of the next calls to the Web Service. Here is the code that opens the workbook:

```
WebService.Status[] status = null;
string sessionID =
   ws.OpenWorkbook(textBoxURL.Text, "en-us", "en-us", out status);
```

One by one, the values entered by the user in the Windows application have to be transmitted to the opened workbook. You can do this either with the *SetCell* or the *SetCellA1* method. The former accepts a row/column combination, such as A1. The latter can be used if the workbook makes use of named ranges. That is exactly what you have in the workbook you're targeting with this walkthrough. Here is the code:

```
status = ws.SetCellA1
   (sessionID, "Sheet3", "Name", textBoxCustomerName.Text);
status = ws.SetCellA1
   (sessionID, "Sheet3", "Amount", textBoxAmount.Text);
status = ws.SetCellA1
   (sessionID, "Sheet3", "Interest", textBoxInterestRate.Text);
status = ws.SetCellA1
   (sessionID, "Sheet3", "Length", textBoxLength.Text);
```

When all of the values are transferred to the workbook, you'll make a call to recalculate the workbook via the *CalculateWorkbook* method.

```
status = ws.CalculateWorkbook
   (sessionID, WebService.CalculateType.Recalculate);
```

When all of this has been done, you simply retrieve the value that results from the calculation of the corresponding cell in the workbook. You can again use two methods to do this: *GetCell* and *GetCellA1*. They follow pretty much the same signature as with the *SetCell* and *SetCellA1* methods except that you get the result back as an object and you have to pass the array of type *Status* as an *out* parameter. Here is how you retrieve the value out of the named range called *Results* in the workbook:

```
object result = ws.GetCellA1
  (sessionID, "Sheet3", "Result", false, out status);
```

The final piece of code is the display of the result and the closing of the workbook:

```
if (result != null)
    MessageBox.Show("The result is " + result.ToString());
status = ws.CloseWorkbook(sessionID);
```

Figure 7-31 shows the result in the Windows application when feeding it with data.

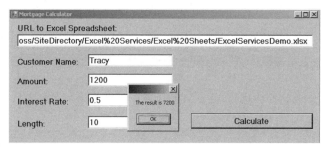

Figure 7-31   A smart client sending data for calculating a mortgage amount to an Excel spreadsheet

Summary

When I speak to sales people about typical business scenarios for using Excel Services, I always use the example of an insurance company facing the following challenges:

- A company employs 50 insurance agents all visiting customers throughout the country. Every insurance agent uses a couple of Excel spreadsheets authored by experts within the company. The spreadsheets are individually stored on each of their laptops, and it's always a struggle when updates to the spreadsheets have to be pushed to every laptop. A lot of time and energy is wasted with the maintenance of all of the distributed spreadsheets.

- It already happened a couple of times last year: an insurance agent leaves the company and makes a copy of the intellectual property (that is, the spreadsheets), and although we have some protection built in to the workbooks, we cannot 100% guarantee that no one is able to steal the complex formulas that drive the calculation.

- The insurance company has a Web site that is growing in popularity. Many of the customers would like to see tools on the site, such as the calculation of their mortgage done via the Web site rather than have a home visit from the insurance agent. However, after a study last year, the company is against custom development of an application that would translate all of the business logic embedded within the spreadsheets to an ASP.NET application.

- The insurance agents have also received mobile devices instead of laptops but are then unable to satisfy customers with the results needed for a calculation that is normally done within the spreadsheets. They would like to just see a central system where they can send the parameter values and get the results back.

If you have read the complete chapter and worked through the walkthroughs, you have an idea of how Excel Services delivered with the Enterprise version of Microsoft Office Share-Point Server 2007 can help the insurance company. Excel Services solves the problems of the distribution of the spreadsheets. You can make the workbooks (or parts of it) available from central locations, and this means better upgrading and maintenance of the workbooks. You do not need to rewrite the business logic in ASP.NET. The insurance experts can simply continue to add their expertise inside the workbooks and, by simply publishing them, make that expertise immediately available for consumption both in the browser as well as via Web Services by any type of client application. In short, this first version of Excel Services definitely answers a wide set of real-world business challenges for anybody who works extensively with Excel spreadsheets. There are limitations to consider, but the course definitely has a lot of promises.

Chapter 8
Policies and the Records Repository

- Understand the many new concepts and terms related to information management policies.

- Learn how to leverage the Microsoft Office SharePoint Server 2007 policy framework to build and deploy custom policies.

- Understand the new Records Center site and experience the out-of-the-box functionality directly available.

- Learn how to customize and extend the Records Center so that it fits the needs of your organization.

- Create custom document routers for the record managers.

The Microsoft Office SharePoint Server 2007 Policy Framework

Enforcing content rules is what policies are all about. Your company may require you to be compliant with all kinds of government or industry-specific regulations for the content that you store and make available within your infrastructure, and that infrastructure can of course be a SharePoint environment. Examples are Sarbanes-Oxley in the financial and accountancy world, HIPAA in the healthcare sector, ISO in the manufacturing sector, and DOD 5012.2 regulations for the government sector. But rules are not limited to these types of official regulations. The company itself can have its own set of procedures and guidelines in place that need to be enforced on all of the content and documents that are made available electronically.

Information workers often consider enforced rules to be annoying, and they often don't want to be hindered by restrictive rules while doing their work. This is why you need an infrastructure that enforces all of these policies without any intervention from information workers. Whatever workers do with the content or documents, policies should be applied that users won't notice and that prevent them from finding workarounds.

Microsoft Office SharePoint Server 2007 adds a rich information management policy framework on top of the Windows SharePoint Services 3.0 platform with a number of directly usable policies, plus plenty of options for developers to create custom policies and provide the means for administrators to deploy and make these policies active at different levels within the SharePoint server farm.

Policies are the focus of the first part of this chapter. I'll start with an explanation of the various terms and concepts involved, continue with a quick look at the various out-of-the-box information management policies, and conclude with the steps to take when you decide to create and deploy your own custom policies. A walkthrough at the end will put all of this into practice.

Information Management Policy Terminology

There are a number of concepts and new terms to know about when working with the policies in a Microsoft Office SharePoint Server 2007 server farm. All of the terms are not directly related with any type of official compliance policy or guideline; they are just part of a new vocabulary that is important to understand before we proceed with the rest of the chapter. Figure 8-1 depicts the interaction between all of these concepts.

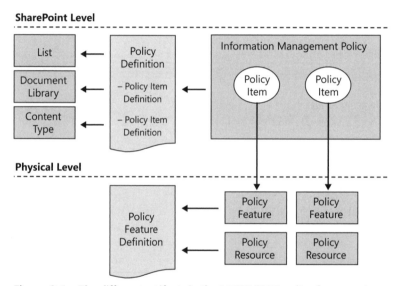

Figure 8-1   The different artifacts in the MOSS 2007 policy framework

Information Management Policy

An *information management policy*, going forward simply referred to as *policy*, is defined by a collection of one or more rules assembled together for the purpose of enforcing rules on content that is stored in SharePoint containers as well as content that is downloaded to clients. One example is an administrator who enforces a label and retention period to all content stored within a document library by associating a policy at the level of the library.

Associating a policy directly to a container or the definition of what goes into that container (in other words, a content type) is not your only option. Site collection administrators may also create and configure policies at the level of the site collection, thus having one central place for configuration and maintenance. Once defined at the level of the site collection, policies are available to anybody who has the required permission to use them at the lower levels within that site collection: the list, library, or content type. I'll detail the configuration options in more detail later in this chapter.

Each policy that can be activated consists of one or more policy items that are physically represented by a .NET assembly, and often, they are associated with ASP.NET user controls that expose the various configuration options in the browser.

A Policy Feature

The individual instruction sets that collectively make up a policy are code-wise represented as policy features. A policy feature should not be confused with the concept of the *feature*, which is part of the Windows SharePoint Services 3.0 framework and is used for installing and activating the many *things* we can do within a SharePoint site. A *policy feature* is delivered through a .NET assembly with the execution logic encapsulated in a class that implements a specific interface. The out-of-the-box policy features, for example, are all compiled within *Microsoft.Office.Policy.dll*.

A Policy Item

We use the term *policy item* to refer to the individual instruction set in the policy at the SharePoint level. Administrators can collect the label and a retention policy item together in a policy that is then applied to a document library. All of the details of a policy item are defined within an XML file, also referred to as the *policy item definition*.

A Policy Definition

So, when an administrator activates a policy on a container, all of the details of that policy are represented in an XML file, called the *policy definition file*. The following is an example of such a policy definition file:

```
<p:Policy xmlns:p="office.server.policy" local="false"
   id="bb4f19fd-a429-4732-8de8-75f9c92a8740">
  <p:Name>Policy 1</p:Name>
  <p:Description />
  <p:Statement />
  <p:PolicyItems>
    <p:PolicyItem featureId=
        "Microsoft.Office.RecordsManagement.PolicyFeatures.Expiration">
      <p:Name>Expiration</p:Name>
      <p:Description>Automatic scheduling of content for processing,
                    and expiry of content that has reached its due
                    date.</p:Description>
      <p:CustomData>
        <data>
          <formula id="Microsoft.Office.RecordsManagement.
              PolicyFeatures.Expiration.Formula.BuiltIn">
            <number>1</number>
            <property>Modified</property>
            <period>years</period>
          </formula>
          <action type="action"
```

```
                    id="Microsoft.Office.RecordsManagement.PolicyFeatures.
                       Expiration.Action.MoveToRecycleBin" />
            </data>
          </p:CustomData>
       </p:PolicyItem>
     </p:PolicyItems>
   </p:Policy>
```

This is actually the XML file that is the result of an export operation of a policy configured at the level of the SharePoint 3.0 Central Administration. The Microsoft Office SharePoint Server 2007 software developer kit (SDK) has a detailed description of the policy schema and the different elements that can be used here.

Policy Item Definition

Within the policy definition file, you'll see an XML block per *policy item* included with the policy. For example, you can identify the expiration or retention policy item defined by the *PolicyItem* element. Notice that the *PolicyItem* element contains the *featureId* attribute pointing to the policy feature, that is the .NET class, representing the policy item. Again I refer to the SDK for a full explanation of all the elements involved since there is no need for you to actually create this XML yourself.

Policy Feature Definition

As I'll discuss later, developers can create additional custom policy items. It involves some coding, and at the end, when you want your policy to be known by SharePoint, you'll have to create a *policy feature definition* file, which is an XML-based file that describes what the policy feature is all about, its metadata, and any information about the different controls that Sharepoint has to display to the administrators when configuration is required. This interface with the administrators is done by means of ASP.NET user controls, which are displayed and used at the global level in the SharePoint 3.0 Central Administration where the administrators can configure defaults for the policy features. The controls can also be displayed at the local level, such as the Edit Policy page that's rendered when a policy is created for a document library, where administrators can override the default settings and configure the policy feature for a specific scenario.

Policy Resource

Policy resources are the ASP.NET user controls that accompany the policy feature and take care of the configuration by the administrators in the browser. Two policy resources are possible, one at the global level and one at the local level. Both are optional. As we will see later, the ASP.NET user control is not the only part that makes up a policy resource. There is also a policy resource class involved, typically encapsulated along with the policy feature class in the same .NET assembly. Consider the policy resource class as the code-behind for the ASP.NET user control, but there are specifics I'll talk about in the walkthrough later in this chapter.

Policy Resource Definition List

A last term to know about is the policy resource definition list. Each policy feature has its own *policy resource definition list*, which lists the policy resources available to it. We're talking again about a section in the policy feature definition file following a specific schema that contains the URLs of the Web controls.

OOB Information Management Policies

A lot is involved with information management policies, and the good news is that you have excellent support via the Microsoft Office SharePoint Server 2007 object model to start building your own custom information management policy features. But before we dive into that topic, let's first discuss the four information management policy features delivered out-of-the-box with Microsoft Office SharePoint Server 2007. We'll take a quick look at each of them before we immerse ourselves in the development process for a custom policy feature.

Labels

The *label policy* allows an administrator to define a label that will be inserted in the document. The label can be a static label or it can be built up in a more dynamic way by using values that are part of the metadata of the item. An example can be the author, the creation date of the document, or a custom piece of metadata such as the Department in Figure 8-2.

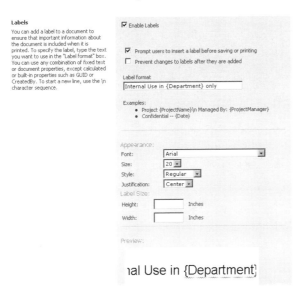

Figure 8-2 Configuring a label policy with the goal of inserting a text dynamically made up with the department—part of the custom metadata for a document in the library

After associating the policy with one of your document libraries, you end up with documents with headers such as the one depicted in Figure 8-3.

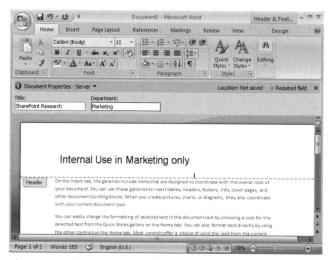

Figure 8-3   A document with a label as defined by the policy configured in Figure 8-1

Auditing

Another information management policy that you can directly associate with a document library or list is the auditing policy, shown in Figure 8-4. The *auditing policy* enforces auditing for a number of events that are triggered for the document subject to the policy.

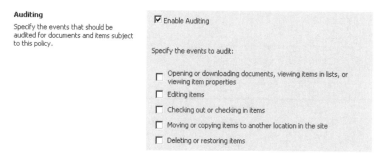

Figure 8-4   The different events that can be audited for the auditing policy

Expiration

The *expiration policy* allows for the definition of a retention period for the item that is subject to the policy. The period can be set in a number of ways, either by adding an interval to the current date (for example, keeping the document alive for the next three months) or in a programmatic way (for example, as one of the steps within a workflow). Additionally, you can specify what has to happen when the item expires. Figure 8-5 displays the options, including deleting the item or starting one of the available workflows.

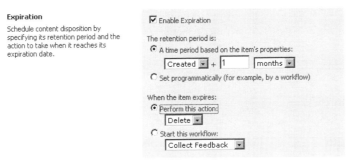

Figure 8-5   The configuration options for an expiration policy

Barcodes

A final policy you can use is the *barcode policy*, which can generate a barcode for an item in a list or document library. We'll have a closer look at this one in the following walkthrough.

Walkthrough: Working with Policies

We've discussed what information management policies are all about, what players are in the story, and the policy items that are available out-of-the-box. Now, let's take a look at the different steps to follow to associate a policy containing the barcode policy item to a list.

Before starting, following Figure 8-6 as an example, you have to create a new list in a SharePoint team site storing product information with custom columns such as the code, price, model, and description.

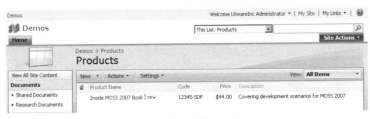

Figure 8-6   The list storing product information

Now assume your company has required that every product stored in the list has to have a barcode associated with it. And all of this with no manual intervention of users. The good news is that the barcode information management policy is designed to accomplish exactly this. So let's play the role of the administrator of the product list and configure the policy. Every list and document library has an option on the Settings page to create or manage the information management policy settings as shown in Figure 8-7.

Given that this policy will target only this one list, you can opt for the Define A Policy option instead of using one of the site collection policies. Managing information management policies defined at the site collection level can be done by going to the Site Settings page of the top-level site within your site collection where you'll find the Site Collection Policies link under the group Site Collection Administration. Here you can pretty much do the same steps as for the rest of the walkthrough except to not associate the policy with a specific container.

Figure 8-7   The Information Management Policy Settings page

In the Edit Policy page, you can finish the process for defining the barcode policy for the products list. Add a description for the administrators managing the policy as well as a statement that will be displayed to the users working with the items subject to the policy. Office 2007 clients are able to show the latter policy statement to the user using the message bar.

On the next page, you'll find all of the policy items that are installed and ready to be used. Later in the chapter, we'll discuss how to create your own custom policy item and have an additional entry added for it on the page. For now, go to the bottom of the page, and as presented in Figure 8-8, the only thing to do is just check the barcode policy. There's no need to prompt a user for it.

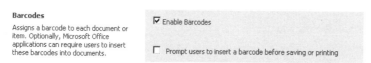

Figure 8-8   Configuring the new policy for the products list

Now, you're ready to test the new policy. In the products list, create a new product item or edit an existing item. Without doing anything yourself, the policy will insert a barcode that now becomes part of the metadata of the item, as shown in Figure 8-9.

Figure 8-9   The barcode policy in action for an item of the products list

Building Custom Policy Features

Although the out-of-the-box information management policy items we've discussed will be helpful in some scenarios, the real world often requires different types of policy items with custom-tailored policy features. Microsoft Office SharePoint Server 2007 comes with a complete Application Programming Interface (API) that supports developers with creating custom information management policy features. Let's have a look first at the different building blocks that make up custom policy features and the deployment steps involved. After that, you can put it into practice with a walkthrough.

Policy Class

The first building block of a custom policy feature is a .NET assembly containing at least one class implementing the *IPolicyFeature* interface defined in the *Microsoft.Office.Server.Records-Management.InformationPolicies* namespace and physically delivered with *Microsoft.Office .Policy.dll*. The interface defines a collection of methods called by SharePoint when the policy feature becomes active as part of a policy. Table 8-1 describes the various methods and their purposes.

Table 8-1   Methods of the *IPolicyFeature* Interface

Method	Description
OnCustomDataChange	Policy items can expose controls that allow administrators to make changes to the custom settings. When this is done, you can process these changes. The *OnCustomDataChange* method is the place to be for that.
OnGlobalCustomDataChange	This serves the same goal as the previous method but instead for the farm-level or global configuration settings.
ProcessListItem	This method is useful in a scenario where you have content already in the document library or list, and administrators decide to make changes to the policy feature settings. The *ProcessListItem* allows you to one by one apply these changes to any of the existing items in the container.
ProcessListItemOnRemove	This method lets you specify item level un-registration that needs to be performed when the policy feature is removed from a policy.
Register	This method is called when administrators assign a new policy feature to the list or document library giving you the place to typically register event handlers or extend the schema of the list or document library with additional fields that are needed for the policy feature.
UnRegister	This is the method that is called when you remove the policy feature for the list or document library. Here you can clean up what you have done at the level of the list or document library.

The *Register* method is definitely the most important method in the *IPolicyFeature* interface. This method is called when the policy feature gets associated with a list or a document library and an appropriate place to add the code to write your initialization code, the programmatic registration of event handlers that will do the actual work on the item or document subject to the policy feature, and the possible changes that may be required for the schema of the list or document library in order for the policy feature to properly function. For the last method, reflect back to the barcode policy item you worked with in the previous walkthrough. When applied, extra columns were added to the list.

```
public void Register(SPContentType ct)
{
    //-- Initialization Code
    //-- Registering Event Handlers
    //-- Making modifications to the schema of the list or document library
}
```

The *Register* method has a signature containing one incoming argument of type *SPContentType*. This parameter is important since it gives you access to the content type of the item, the actual list or document library, the site, and any other SharePoint objects you may need for the implementation of the policy feature.

Event Handlers

Policy items in the information management policy typically act on items or documents when a certain event happens at that level. For example, the barcode policy item generates a barcode when a new item is created or when an existing item doesn't yet have a barcode.

Consequently, SharePoint event handlers are the second type of .NET assembly that you'll have to create during the development of a custom information management policy feature. There is nothing special with these event handlers. They are .NET classes that inherit from the *Microsoft.SharePoint.SPItemEventReceiver* class and subsequently implement one or more base methods that correspond to the events that need to be handled. For example, the following code shows the skeleton of a class that handles the *ItemAdded* and the *ItemUpdated* events.

```
using System;
using System.Collections.Generic;
using System.Text;
using System.Diagnostics;
using Microsoft.SharePoint;

namespace InsideMOSS.Samples
{
    public class PolicyEventHandler: SPItemEventReceiver
    {
        public override void ItemAdded(SPItemEventProperties properties)
        {
            base.ItemAdded(properties);
        }
```

```
        public override void ItemUpdated(SPItemEventProperties properties)
        {
            base.ItemUpdated(properties);
        }
    }
}
```

Both are asynchronous events that are fired after SharePoint has performed the action in the database. There is also the option to handle synchronous before events, for example, the *ItemAdding* and the *ItemUpdating* events. I recommend that you refer to *Inside Windows SharePoint Service 3.0* (Microsoft Press), by Ted Pattison, for more information on event handlers.

Registration of the Event Handlers

Registration of the event handlers is done in the *Policy* class within the *Register* method. Examine the following block of code:

```
public void Register(SPContentType ct)
{
  SPEventReceiverDefinition evdef = ct.ParentList.EventReceivers.Add();
  evdef.Assembly = "full strong name of .NET assembly";
  evdef.Class = "fully qualified name of the class";
  evdef.Data = "some data passed to the event handler";
  evdef.Name = "Item added event handler";
  evdef.Type = SPEventReceiverType.ItemAdded;
  evdef.SequenceNumber = 1001;
  evdef.Update();
}
```

Event handlers are registered at the level of the list or document library, and therefore, you have to get a reference to the *SPList* object. This can be done by using the *ParentList* property of the incoming *SPContentType* argument. Next, add a new *SPEventReceiverDefinition* object to the *EventReceivers* collection of the *SPList*. The event handling code is ready for action after assigning the needed information, such as the class that encapsulates all of the event handling code, the name, type, and the sequence number of the event handler, and the information regarding the .NET assembly.

Configuration Controls

When a user selects a policy item on the Edit Policy page, there is the option to provide him or her with controls to configure the policy item. For example, the four out-of-the-box policy items all have some kind of configuration settings associated with them. Figure 8-10 shows the configuration options for an expiration policy item.

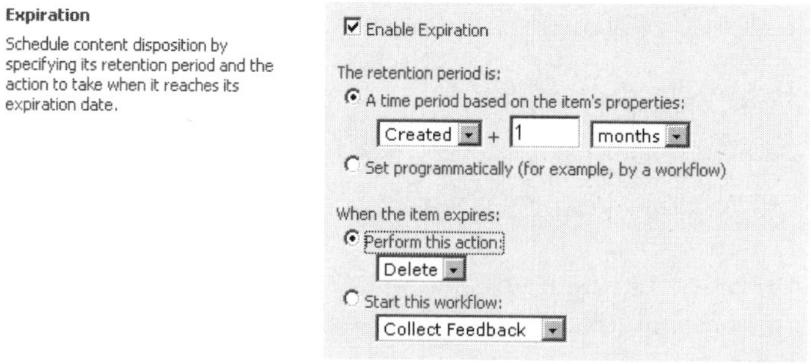

Figure 8-10 The configuration settings for an expiration policy item

This is not the only option you have for allowing users to specify configuration settings. It is also possible to allow users with access to SharePoint 3.0 Central Administration options to set global configuration values, which consequently become the default values for the policy items at the local level (but they can be overridden if needed). The place to go for this type of configuration is the Operations page in SharePoint 3.0 Central Administration. Under the Security Configuration group is the Information Management Policy Configuration link that brings you to a page where each of the installed policy items is listed, as shown in Figure 8-11.

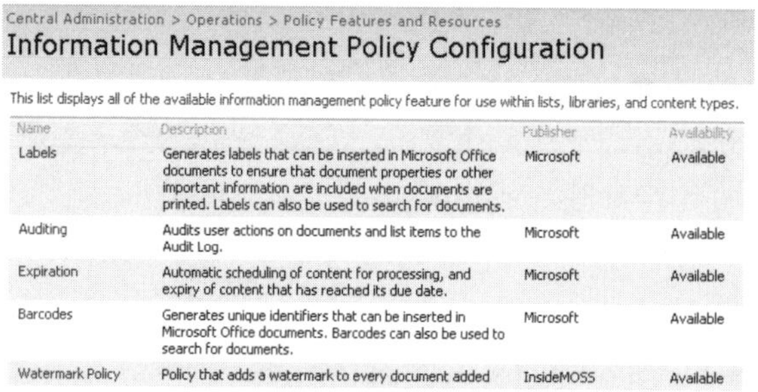
Central Administration > Operations > Policy Features and Resources

Information Management Policy Configuration

This list displays all of the available information management policy feature for use within lists, libraries, and content types.

Name	Description	Publisher	Availability
Labels	Generates labels that can be inserted in Microsoft Office documents to ensure that document properties or other important information are included when documents are printed. Labels can also be used to search for documents.	Microsoft	Available
Auditing	Audits user actions on documents and list items to the Audit Log.	Microsoft	Available
Expiration	Automatic scheduling of content for processing, and expiry of content that has reached its due date.	Microsoft	Available
Barcodes	Generates unique identifiers that can be inserted in Microsoft Office documents. Barcodes can also be used to search for documents.	Microsoft	Available
Watermark Policy	Policy that adds a watermark to every document added	InsideMOSS	Available

Figure 8-11 The list of registered policy items at the level of the server farm

If the policy item has a global configuration control associated with it, you'll be able to navigate to the page displaying it and change the settings to the values. Figure 8-12 displays the options administrators have to change the barcode generation settings.

Creating a control at the local or global level is basically done in the same way. You'll start by creating a class that inherits from the *CustomSettingsControl* class defined in the *Microsoft.Office.RecordsManagement.InformationPolicy* namespace. This is actually the code-behind class of the ASP.NET user control, the .ascx file, that you'll have to create. The .ascx file contains the user interface layout for the configuration settings. In the walkthrough later on, I'll go through the various steps to take to actually realize this.

Once the ASP.NET user control is up and running, you'll have to tell SharePoint about it. The policy feature definition file is the place to do this. In this XML file, you can use the *ConfigPage* and the *GlobalConfigPage* to point to the ASP.NET user controls used for either the local or global configuration settings.

Figure 8-12   The global configuration of the barcode policy item

Deployment Steps

Deploying a custom policy item is realized by dropping the different .NET assemblies in the Global Assembly Cache (GAC) and then programmatically registering the new policy item within the server farm. This registration is done by a simple call to the *PolicyFeatureCollection* defined within the *Microsoft.Office.RecordsManagement.InformationPolicy* namespace. The policy feature definition file is the argument to provide.

```
PolicyFeatureCollection.Add(manifestXML);
```

The local configuration controls have to be copied to the \12\Template\Layouts folder where they will be picked up by SharePoint when they need to be displayed. The global configuration controls go into the \12\Template\Admin folder.

Walkthrough: Creating and Deploying a Custom Policy Item

It's time to walk through an example demonstrating how to create a custom policy and make it available within your SharePoint server farm. The sample demonstrates a policy that administrators can activate for a document library if there is the need to enforce a watermark in every new Microsoft Word 2007 document. So, in addition to demonstrating the steps for creating a custom policy item, the example is also a nice example of how to use the *System.IO.Packaging* API and communicate from within your SharePoint code with a Word 2007 document stored in the new Office Open XML File Format. The event handler in question is a normal SharePoint event handler exposed as a .NET class that inherits from the *Microsoft.SharePoint.SPItemEventReceiver* class. The entire project is available on the companion Web site. The event handler overrides the *ItemAdded* base method and calls code from a helper class that does all of the interaction with the Microsoft Word 2007 document. This is not the topic of this chapter, so I won't go into detail for that code but will instead focus on the building of the custom policy item. However, I do encourage you to have a look at the helper class part of the event handler project and the techniques used to insert the watermark in the Microsoft Word 2007 document.

We'll break up the walkthrough in two parts. As a starter, you'll go through all of the essential steps for creating and deploying a custom policy item. In the second part, I'll show you how to build an ASP.NET user control and register it as part of the policy feature. This way, you'll enable administrators to set the text for the watermark to be inserted in the document while configuring the policy.

The Simple Watermark Policy   We'll get started by opening up Microsoft Visual Studio.NET 2005 and creating a new class library named *InsideMOSSPolicies*. There are two assemblies to reference: *Microsoft.Office.Policy.dll* and *Microsoft.SharePoint.dll*. You'll probably want to rename the class delivered as part of the class library project to something like *PolicyWatermark*, and while you're doing that, go ahead and change the namespace to *InsideMOSS.Samples* and add the following *using* statements for the namespaces you'll use in addition to the ones already defined:

```
using Microsoft.Office.RecordsManagement.InformationPolicy;
using Microsoft.SharePoint;
```

Next, to have SharePoint recognize the class as a policy class, it has to implement the *IPolicy-Feature* interface, defining six methods I explained earlier in the chapter. You only have to worry about the *Register* method for the watermark policy we are creating here, but make sure that no exceptions are thrown when SharePoint starts calling each of the other methods implemented with the interface. To be clear, here is the policy item class ready to be connected to the event handler discussed in the beginning of the walkthrough:

```
public class PolicyWatermark: IPolicyFeature
{
    #region IPolicyFeature Members
    public void OnCustomDataChange(PolicyItem policyItem, SPContentType ct)
    {}
    public void OnGlobalCustomDataChange(PolicyFeature feature)
    {}

    public bool ProcessListItem
      (SPSite site, PolicyItem policyItem, SPListItem listItem)
    {
        return true;
    }
    public bool ProcessListItemOnRemove(SPSite site, SPListItem listItem)
    {
        return true;
    }
    public void Register(SPContentType ct)
    { }
    public void UnRegister(SPContentType ct)
    { }
    #endregion
}
```

On the companion Web site, you'll find the *WatermarkAdditionHandler* project containing the event handler class that takes care of the code for the insertion of the watermark in the Microsoft Word 2007 documents added to the document library. The registration of the event handlers is something you'll have to do in the body of the *Register* method of your policy class. An instance of the *SPEventReceiverDefinition* is created by calling the *Add* method for the collection that stores all of the event handler registrations for the list or document library. This collection is exposed with the *EventReceivers* property of the *SPList* object. Referring to our example in the document library, the way to get to the *SPList* is by using the *ParentList* property of the incoming *SPContentType* type of parameter for the *Register* method. Here is the code to create the object of type *SPEventReceiverDefinition* and then set each of the necessary properties along with the passing of a hard-coded watermark text before performing an update operation:

```
public void Register(SPContentType ct)
{
  try
  {
    SPEventReceiverDefinition evdef = ct.ParentList.EventReceivers.Add();
    evdef.Assembly = "WaterMarkAdditionHandler, Version=1.0.0.0, " +
                        "Culture=neutral, PublicKeyToken=a9ad4fa2c3c498c6";
    evdef.Class = "InsideMOSS.Samples.WaterMark";
    evdef.Data = "My Watermark";
    evdef.Name = "Document Watermark Addition";
    evdef.Type = SPEventReceiverType.ItemAdded;
    evdef.SequenceNumber = 1001;
    evdef.Update();
  }
  catch (Exception ex)
  {
    throw new Exception("Unable to register event handler.", ex);
  }
}
```

You should also clean up when the policy gets unregistered by removing the event handler from the *SPEventReceiverDefinitionCollection* of the list or library you're dealing with. The following code, part of the *Unregister* method, illustrates a possible approach:

```
public void UnRegister(SPContentType ct)
{
  if (ct != null)
  {
    foreach(SPEventReceiverDefinition evdef in ct.ParentList.EventReceivers)
    {
      if (evdef.Name == "Document Watermark Addition")
        evdef.Delete();
    }
  }
}
```

When all of this is done, you have completed the coding part of this first version of the watermark policy item. Save all of your code and then, before you build the .NET assembly, just go to the properties of the project and make sure you have the .NET assembly signed and that it is set to receive a strong name after the build. This is necessary because these custom policy assemblies must be deployed in the Global Assembly Cache as well as the .NET assemblies containing the event handlers that do the work for the policy.

If the build is succesfull, you're ready for a final piece of the project. It is time to create the XML file that defines what the policy feature is all about. Here is the content of the policy feature definition, but make sure you replace the *PublicKeyToken* value with the one created for your assembly:

```
<PolicyFeature id="InsideMOSS.Samples.PolicyWatermark"
    xmlns="urn:schemas-microsoft-com:office:server:policy">
 <Name>Watermark Policy</Name>
 <Description>Policy that adds a watermark to every document
  added</Description>
 <Publisher>InsideMOSS</Publisher>
 <AssemblyName>InsideMOSSPolicies, Version=1.0.0.0, Culture=neutral,
  PublicKeyToken=7df9ac27d313b844</AssemblyName>
 <ClassName>InsideMOSS.Samples.PolicyWatermark</ClassName>
</PolicyFeature>
```

The XML starts with a root element called *PolicyFeature*. The *Id* attribute is not strictly necessary for the first version of the custom policy, but you'll need it in the second part. Next, you have three child elements that provide some identification information to SharePoint: a *Name*, *Description*, and a *Publisher* element. The *AssemblyName* and *ClassName* finish it off. The first receives the strong name of the .NET assembly containing your custom policy code, and the second gets the fully qualified name of the class that has to be instantiated.

For this walkthrough, we'll stick with a manual deployment and activation of the policy. It is also possible to package your work into a solution and install the solution with STSADM. We have done this a couple of times in the book, and I refer to those specific chapters for more details.

The two .NET assemblies, one containing the policy class and one containing the event handlers, need to end up in the Global Assembly Cache. Next, to tell SharePoint about your new policy feature, you have to add the new policy feature definition to the *PolicyFeature-Collection* that is defined within the *Microsoft.Office.RecordsManagement.InformationPolicy*. The argument to provide is the path to the XML file containing the policy feature definition. Here is the one line of code that accomplishes this:

```
PolicyFeatureCollection.Add(manifestXML);
```

On the companion Web site, you'll find a Windows application called *MOSS Policy Explorer* that you can use to quickly perform this. When you run it, it loads all of the policies that are active and ready to use. Figure 8-13 shows the four out-of-the-box policy features with their details.

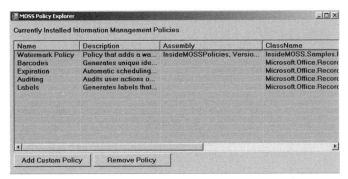

Figure 8-13   The *MOSS Policy Explorer* application you can use to register new custom policy features

Click the *Add Custom Policy* button and load the policy feature definition file. Within seconds, the watermark policy is added and ready to be used in a SharePoint site.

Now let's have a look at the result of our efforts. Open a SharePoint site and create a new document library. Make sure you use the Microsoft Word 2007 document template since the code for inserting the watermark only works with documents that are stored in the Office Open XML File format. When done, open the Document Library Settings page and navigate via the Information Management Policy Settings link to the page where a new policy can be defined. You can opt for the definition of a local policy. As you proceed, you'll see that the page displays a fifth possible policy item to include in the information management policy, the watermark policy item as shown in Figure 8-14.

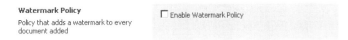

Figure 8-14   The watermark policy is available as one of the information management policies.

There is nothing really difficult to do here. Just select the Enable Watermark Policy check box and apply it to the document library. A new document added to the document library will now have a watermark. Figure 8-15 shows the end result of your work.

This concludes the first version of the watermark policy item. Now let's go a step further. Instead of having a hard-coded string for the watermark, we'll make it more dynamic by allowing administrators to configure the text of the watermark in the Edit Policy page.

Note   The sample created in the walkthrough can also be reworked so that the both the policy class as well as the event handler are included in the same assembly. This will simplify the development and the maintenance of the custom policy. For the sake of clarity however, I decided to split the two here in the book.

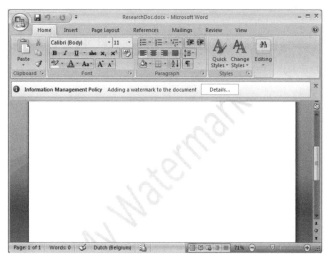

Figure 8-15   The policy enforces the insertion of a watermark for every new document.

Adding Configuration Options for the Watermark Policy   There are two options to provide administrators with a place for configuring the text of the watermark. You can prepare an ASP.NET user control that is delivered at the level of the SharePoint 3.0 Central Administration site for a global type of configuration, or you can work with an ASP.NET user control that is displayed at the level of the site collection within the Edit Policy page. For this walkthrough, we'll opt for the latter approach, but if you're interested, you can work out a global configuration scenario with pretty much the same steps.

Begin by adding a new *Web User Control* item named *WatermarkSettings.ascx* to the *InsideMOSSPolicies* project. There are a couple of directives to add to the user control. First there is an *Assembly* directive containing the full strong name of the *InsideMOSSPolicies* assembly. Next, you have the *Control* directive pointing to the code-behind class called *InsideMOSS.Samples* *.WaterMarkSettingsControl* that you'll create in a moment. In order for the code in your policy class to be able to communicate with the user control where the user interface layout is defined, you'll need to wrap up the code-behind for the user control in a class that inherits from the *CustomSettingsControl* class defined in the *Microsoft.Office.RecordsManagement* *.InformationPolicy* namespace. This base class has all of the required methods to set up an interaction with the policy feature (see later) and is itself based on the *UserControl* class of the *System.Web.UI* namespace. Here are the two directives you need in your ASP.NET user control:

```
<%@ Assembly Name="InsideMOSSPolicies, Version=1.0.0.0, Culture=neutral,
    PublicKeyToken=7df9ac27d313b844"%>
<%@ Control Language="C#"
    Inherits="InsideMOSS.Samples.WaterMarkSettingsControl"%>
```

For the rest, the layout is going to be pretty simple. You only have to add a *TextBox* prefixed with text explaining its purpose:

```
<div>Enter the text of the watermark here:<br />
<asp:TextBox ID="WaterMarkTextBox" runat="server"
 Width="272px"></asp:TextBox>
</div>
```

As mentioned, the code-behind for this user control goes into a class inheriting from the *CustomControlSettings* class. Add a new class to the *InsideMOSSPolicies* project named *Water-MarkSettingsControl*. Then add the using statements for the *System.Web.UI.WebControls* and the *Microsoft.Office.RecordsManagement.InformationPolicy* namespaces, and let your class inherit from the *CustomControlSettings* class. If not done already, also add a reference to the *System.Web.dll* in your project. Here is the starter for that class:

```
using System;
using System.Collections.Generic;
using System.Text;
using System.Web;
using System.Web.UI.WebControls;
using Microsoft.Office.RecordsManagement.InformationPolicy;

namespace InsideMOSS.Samples
{
    public class WaterMarkSettingsControl: CustomSettingsControl
    {
    }
}
```

There are some methods and properties of the base class that have to be implemented in your class. You can use the smart tag when placing your cursor in the *CustomSettingsControl* text in the editor to generate the skeletons of these members to override. There are three properties and two methods. You'll only use one of the properties, *CustomData*, for this walk-through, but you'll have to make sure that SharePoint does not get exceptions when calling all of the non-used members. So, after a clean-up, the inside of your class looks like this:

```
public override Microsoft.SharePoint.SPContentType ContentType
{
    get { return this.ContentType; }
    set { this.ContentType = value;}
}

public override string CustomData
{
    get { return string.Empty; }
    set { this.CustomData = value; }
}

public override Microsoft.SharePoint.SPList List
```

```
{
    get { return this.List; }
    set { this.List = value; }
}

public override bool LoadPostData(string postDataKey,
    System.Collections.Specialized.NameValueCollection values)
{
    return true;
}

public override void RaisePostDataChangedEvent()
{ }
```

The class is intended to be the code-behind class for the ASP.NET user control created previously. Therefore, one thing to do at the start of the execution of the logic within this class is the hook-up with the *TextBox* control that is available in the user control. A class-level variable and a call to the *FindControl* method in the *OnLoad* event handler for the class will do the trick. Here is the code you have to add:

```
private TextBox WaterMarkTextBox = null;

protected override void OnLoad(EventArgs e)
{
    this.WaterMarkTextBox = (TextBox)this.FindControl("WaterMarkTextBox");
    base.OnLoad(e);
}
```

The final part for the code in this class is to configure the steps to do a little bit more in the *CustomData* property than just return and set an empty string. The *CustomData* property is very important since it is the one called by SharePoint to save and deliver again the custom setting for the watermark text. This is now a simple call to the *Text* property of the *TextBox* you've just found in the *OnLoad* event handler:

```
public override string CustomData
{
    get
    {
        return this.WaterMarkTextBox.Text;
    }
    set
    {
        if (this.WaterMarkTextBox != null)
            this.WaterMarkTextBox.Text = value;
    }
}
```

Now return to the *PolicyWatermark* class. There is just one custom static field you have to add called the *PolicyID*. The custom watermark text, when modified using the user control, will be stored in the policy item definition, the XML block we've discussed earlier in the chapter. So instead of giving the watermark directly as data to the event handler during the registration of the event handler, you'll let the event handler pick up the data from the

XML that is part of the policy item definition. We have to do this because passing the data to the event handler in the Register method can only happen once. Changing the watermark text can be done very frequently, but this modification by the administration does not call the *Register* method anymore. The policy is already registered. Here is the static field you have to add to the *PolicyWatermark* class:

```
public static string PolicyID = "InsideMOSS.Samples.PolicyWatermark";
```

The first version of our solution here did not allow any custom modification to the watermark text. Now you have a version up and running, but SharePoint does not yet know about your ASP.NET user control. Therefore, open the *manifest.xml* that is part of the *InsideMOSSPolicies* project and add the XML elements *ConfigPage* and *DefaultCustomData* before the element defining the strong name of the assembly. It must be added before the *Assembly* element since the schema defines a fixed order. The *ConfigPage* element just points to your ASP.NET user control, and with the *DefaultCustomData* and the *customData* child element, you can set a default value for the watermark text. If you are trying out a custom configuration at the level of the SharePoint 3.0 Central Administration, you'll have to add the *ConfigGlobalPage* element. Here is the snippet to add to the XML file:

```
<ConfigPage>WaterMarkSettings.ascx</ConfigPage>
<DefaultCustomData>
    <customData>Default Watermark</customData>
</DefaultCustomData>
```

Well, you're almost finished now. All the work has been done in the custom policy item project, but there is one change you have to do to the project containing the event handler. This change is going to make the event handler dependant on the custom policy feature. After opening up the *WaterMarkAdditionHandler* project from the companion Web site, a reference is immediately added to the *InsideMOSSPolicies* project. And while you're in the *Add References* dialog box, also add the reference to the *Microsoft.Office.Policy.dll*. Open the *WaterMark.cs* file and add two *using* statements, which will be helpful:

```
using Microsoft.Office.RecordsManagement.InformationPolicy;
using InsideMOSS.Samples;
```

In the *WaterMark* class, you'll see the code for the *ItemAdded* event handler. Remember that in the initial scenario you passed the text of the watermark to the event handler during registration. Now, you have a more dynamic approach and the text is stored in the policy item definition. So, you need to get access to that definition. The approach to take is to use the static method called *GetPolicy* of the *Policy* class and call it with the *ContentType* of the document or list item that triggered the event. Remember that a policy is a collection of policy items, and therefore you have to pick up the one for the watermark. The *PolicyID* field created before now becomes very handy. Here is the code you add at the beginning of the *ItemAdded* event handler:

```
Policy policy = Policy.GetPolicy(properties.ListItem.ContentType);
PolicyItem policyItem = policy.Items[PolicyWatermark.PolicyID];
```

Delete the line where the *AddWaterMark* method of the *Helper* class is called and replace it with the following call:

```
Helper.AddWaterMark(tempfile, policyItem.CustomData);
```

You just grab the value of the *CustomData* property that will give you what you need for the rest of the process.

When you're done with all of this, you're ready to deploy and activate the policy feature in your server farm. Remove and re-add the new policy feature. Just proceed by following the same steps described for the simple version of your policy feature. Since you have made changes to the event handler code, you have to deploy that .NET assembly again to the Global Assembly Cache along with the .NET assembly of your policy feature. An *IISReset* will be necessary before you test it out. The .ascx file that you have created for the configuration settings has to be copied to the \12\Template\Layouts folder.

Now, administrators who navigate to the Edit Policy page will be able to check the watermark policy item and fill out the text of the watermark in the textbox, as displayed in Figure 8-16.

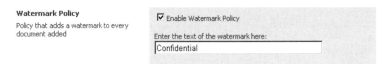

Figure 8-16   The configuration control allowing the administrator to set the text of the watermark to be inserted in the Microsoft Word 2007 document

The Records Center

The Records Center is a new type of site you can create using Microsoft Office SharePoint Server 2007 with the goal of creating a highly controlled and safe place within your server farm where records can be stored and managed by record managers. This is often a requirement in organizations that have to comply with many different guidelines and regulations, both official and non-official. Records in the active collaboration workspaces that are not needed anymore, such as the team sites or the collaboration portals, can be moved to the Records Center where they can be stored and highly regulated in their specific libraries for many years under strict conditions.

Creating a Records Center

Creating a Records Center is done in pretty much the same way as when provisioning any other type of site in SharePoint. Typically, these types of sites are provisioned on a dedicated Web server—machines that are kept under strict surveillance and locked away. The job of the Record Center is to store records that may play a crucial role in the future such as when the company faces a lawsuit and lawyers need to be able to track everything related to the case, including the records that were created and used in the collaboration spaces. The following steps create a new Records Center:

1. Using SharePoint 3.0 Central Administration, extend an IIS Web site and provide it with the required information such as the description, the port number, optional host header, and the physical folder associated with the IIS Web site. Configure the authentication, Kerberos and NTLM, and definitely keep the anonymous setting turned off for these types of sites. The Records Center should be a very secure environment accessible to only a few people: the records managers, laywers, and so on. As a final step in the data, provide the information for the application pool and the details of the content database to be created.

2. Once the IIS Web site is extended, it becomes an IIS Web application ready to host your Records Center as the top-level site in a new site collection, a site provisioned based on the *Records Center* template as shown in Figure 8-17.

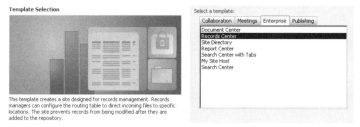

Figure 8-17   Selecting the Records Center template

3. When all of this is finished, you'll be able to navigate to the home page of the Records Center and discover the different lists and document libraries that are already instantiated in the site upon creation. Figure 8-18 shows the out-of-the-box experience with a new Records Center.

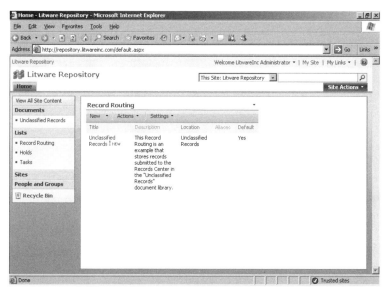

Figure 8-18   The Records Center as it is delivered out-of-the-box with Microsoft Office SharePoint Server 2007

For your information, the Records Center is not provisioned like the Publishing Portal where a provisioning assembly basically gets an XML-based script of what the site hierarchy is going to be about. The Records Center is provisioned very much like a normal team site. In the \12\Template\SiteTemplates\SPSReportCenter folder, you can find the site definition for the Records Center.

Table 8-2 describes the different artifacts that are provisioned upon creation of the Records Center.

Table 8-2   What Do You Get Out of the Box with the Records Center?

Feature	Description
Record Routing List	This is a list storing the record routing types. A *record routing type*, sometimes also referred to as a *file plan*, can process incoming records and route them to their final destination, a document library within the Records Center, for example. The list by default contains one record routing type, the *Unclassified Records*, that routes any incoming record for which there is no specific custom routing type defined to the Unclassified Records document library.
Unclassified Records	This document library stores not only the document, but also the metadata of the incoming record in the form of an XML file and the audit history. The Unclassified Records document library is the place where records will end up that are not processed by a custom record routing type (see later).
Records Pending Submission	This document library can act as a temporary place for documents and their metadata and auditing history that are submitted to the Records Center but are missing one or more of the required metadata fields. They will remain here until the submitters complete all of the needed metadata.
Missing Properties	Every submitted document that has a missing value for a required metadata element results in an entry in this document library. Submitters completing the data will actually be redirected to the Edit Item page showing the properties of the submitted document with the option for the submitters to complete the data.
Hold Reports	This is another document library that stores all of the documents that are on hold by lawyers, for example, that do not want any further actions to occur on the documents.
Holds	Use this list to track external actions such as litigations, investigations, or audits that require you to suspend record disposition. Placing an item on one or more holds will suspend the item's disposition until the item is no longer managed by any holds.
Submitted E-mail Records	This list is used by the Records Center to temporarily store received e-mail records. As we will discuss in a moment, records can be sent in many ways to the Record Center.

The Send To Feature

A Records Center is a place where we can send records to or from anywhere within the server farm. We'll detail the different options for sending records to the Record Center in a moment, but first we'll discuss the interaction between the document libraries in a SharePoint site and the Records Center.

Windows SharePoint Services 3.0 makes the document libraries available with the Send To option. This *Send To* option is a menu item you can access from the ECB (enhanced combobox) associated with every item in the document library. By default, the Send To feature comes with a number of pre-defined locations where you can send a document, as displayed in Figure 8-19.

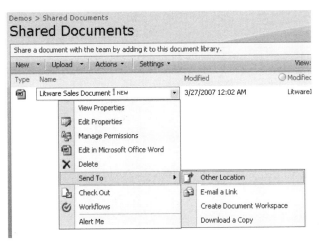

Figure 8-19   Making copies of the document in a Windows SharePoint Services 3.0 document library with the Send To option

Because Send To is a Windows SharePoint Services 3.0 feature, it will not be discussed in detail in this book. However, it can be extended with an option to send a document to one of the Records Centers that is available in the server farm. To accomplish this, you only have to perform one small administrative task in SharePoint 3.0 Central Administration. If you navigate to the Applications Management page, there is a link under the External Service Connections group to configure the Records Center. This brings you to a page, shown in Figure 8-20, where you can connect to a Records Center. You only need to provide the URL to the *officialfile.asmx* Web service (more on this Web service later) and enter a display name.

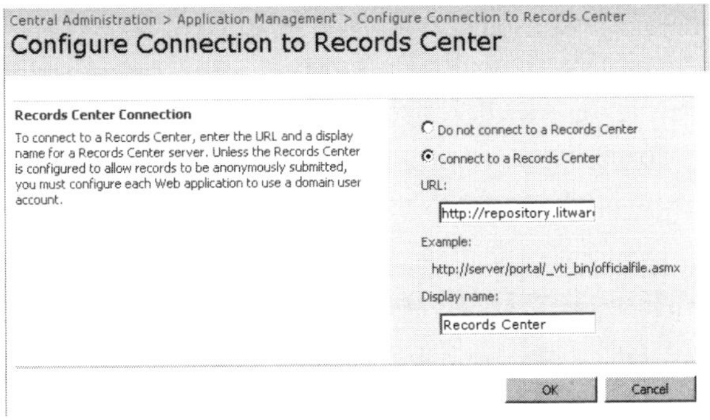

Central Administration > Application Management > Configure Connection to Records Center
Configure Connection to Records Center

Records Center Connection

To connect to a Records Center, enter the URL and a display name for a Records Center server. Unless the Records Center is configured to allow records to be anonymously submitted, you must configure each Web application to use a domain user account.

○ Do not connect to a Records Center
◉ Connect to a Records Center

URL:
http://repository.litware

Example:
http://server/portal/_vti_bin/officialfile.asmx

Display name:
Records Center

OK   Cancel

Figure 8-20   Configuration of an extra Send To option to the Records Center in SharePoint 3.0 Central Administration

If you press OK, every document library's Send To option in the server farm will have an extra option with the name as entered in the configuration page. As shown in Figure 8-21, selecting the option will result in your document being sent to the Records Center where, if you have not configured anything other than what you get out-of-the-box with the template, your document will be routed to the Unclassified Records document library as depicted in Figure 8-22.

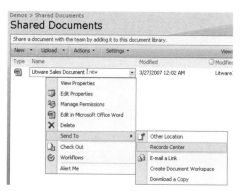

Figure 8-21 Sending the document to the Records Center using the Send To menu in a document library

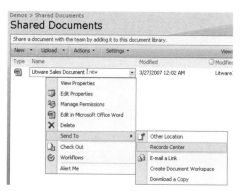

Figure 8-22 The document routed to the Unclassified Records document library in the Records Center

Options for Communicating with the Records Center

The Send To feature is not the only option for submitting records to the Records Center. The Records Center is open and accessible thanks to Simple Mail Transfer Protocol (SMTP) (for sending e-mails) and the *OfficialFile* Web service. Actually, this Web service is also used under the hood by the Send To feature, but as I'll show you in the walkthrough, you can build any type of application on any platform and communicate with the Records Center using the Web service. Figure 8-23 depicts the different options.

Incoming records are processed by record routing types, sometimes with the help of a custom repository router, and end up in a document library along with the metadata and auditing history.

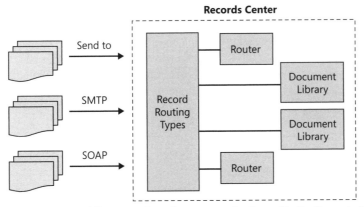

Figure 8-23   Different options for communicating with the Records Repository

Configuring the Records Center

Go back to the document we sent to the Records Center with the Send To feature. It ended up in Unclassified Records. This is the default document library for storing incoming records that are assigned to the *Unclassified Records* record routing type. A *record routing type* is defined as an entry in a specific list called the Record Routing list. The home page of the Records Center, shown in Figure 8-17, shows the content of that list and only one entry is there by default: Unclassified Records. The walkthrough later in the chapter will show how to create additional Record Routing entries. Basically, you start by creating a new item in the Record Routing list and assign each of the fields a value. Table 8-3 summarizes the fields and their purpose.

Table 8-3   Fields for a Record Routing Type

Field	Description
Title	The name of the record routing type.
Description	The description of the record routing type.
Location	The name of the document library where the routed record will eventually be stored.
Aliases	The value of the *Title* field of the record routing type is going to be the main criteria for routing the document. For example, a document that is based on a content type that listens to the *Report* name will immediately be handled by the record routing type called *Report*. Aliases can help provide multiple potential names to which to match the incoming record. You have to separate them with a slash ('/').
Default	Makes this record routing type the default instead of the *Unclassified Records* record routing type.

Walkthrough: Configuring the Records Center

Let's work through a practical scenario demonstrating how you can configure the Records Center and route documents to it. We'll assume that we're working in a hospital where personnel work with patient records stored in specific SharePoint team sites while a patient is in the hospital. After the patient leaves, the records are no longer needed in the collaboration spaces and can be transferred to the Records Center.

It is important that administrators of the collaboration workspaces sync up with records managers. For SharePoint administrators, it is important to create content types that define the patient record. Records managers need to know about these content types since the file plans or record routing types should be tuned to match them.

So, let's start defining a content type called Patient Record by associating three columns with it: Patient Name, Treatment, and Doctor. In the real world, there would be many more fields to create, but for simplicity let's stick to those three. The content type can be created at the level of one of your site collections by going to the Content Types Gallery and using the Create option on the toolbar. In the New Content Type page, displayed in Figure 8-24, proceed by first entering the name of the content type—remember this is very important for the other side, the Records Center. Next, select the Document Content Types group and base the Patient Record content type on the Document content type.

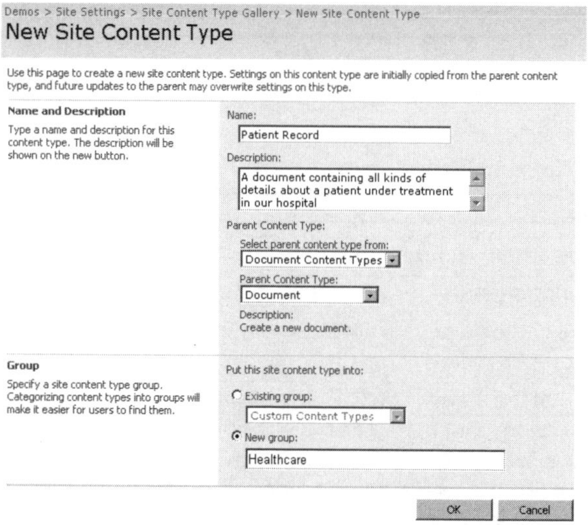

Figure 8-24   The Patient Record content type

Continue and finish the creation of the content type by adding the three columns—Patient Name, Treatment, and Doctor—typed all in a single line of text.

Next, create a document library named Patient Records and associate the Patient Record content type with this document library. Create some sample documents to play with and then go to the Records Center where you'll play the role of the records manager.

To start, define a new record routing type that will move incoming records that are based on the Patient Record content type into the new Patient Records document library. Create this document library by following the steps you normally take when you create a document library within a SharePoint site. Open the Record Routing list where you create a new item. The new record routing type is called *Patient Record* and, in addition to a small description, you have to enter the name of the Patient Records document library. Figure 8-25 displays the new record routing type.

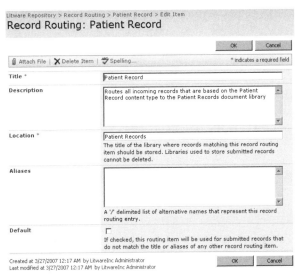

Figure 8-25   The definition of a new record routing type in the Record Routing list routing incoming patient records to the Patient Records document library

You're finished for now! You can test it out by going back to your SharePoint team site and using the Send To option to send one of your sample documents based on the *Patient Record* content type to the Records Center. Check out the Patient Records document library in the Records Center and you'll find a new folder named as the current date and time. Figure 8-26 displays the document you've sent to the Records Center along with a folder named Properties that contains the metadata of the document in question converted into an XML file.

Figure 8-26   The document and the metadata converted into an XML file routed to and stored in the Patient Records document library in the Records Center

The lesson learned here is that the content type defines where the document ends up in the Records Center. But suppose that different administrators use conflicting names for the content types defining the information stored for a patient. Maybe one administrator uses

Patient Document and another uses Patient Sheet. In the Records Center, however, we want those types of documents to both end up in the Patient Records document library in order to avoid the records manager having to create multiple record routing types. That is where the *Aliases* field of the record routing type enters the picture.

To test this out, you need to create two more content types in your site collection, and then you can go back to the Records Center and edit the Patient Record item in the Records Routing list. You now simply have to add *Patient Sheet/Patient Document* as the value of the *Aliases* field, save your work, and from now on, documents based on any of the three content types will be routed to the same Patient Records document library.

Every incoming record's metadata is immediately converted to an XML file that is stored along with the record in the Patient Records document library. If you create three extra columns for this document library in the Records Center matching up with the three columns you created for the Patient Record content type, you'll notice that when sending a document to the repository, all of the metadata is actually promoted to become values of these columns. Figure 8-27 illustrates this.

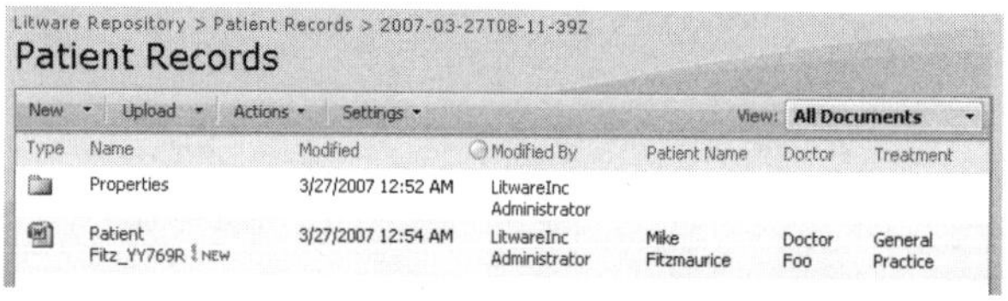

Figure 8-27 Metadata of the incoming record is automatically promoted in the document library in the Records Center.

But what if some of the required metadata is missing? Try it out by going back to the Patient Records document library in the Records Center and changing the Patient Name column to a required column. Now, send a new document to the Records Center without providing a name for the patient. You will not get a confirmation for the Send To operation. In fact, you are redirected to a page, shown in Figure 8-28, that is part of the Records Center itself where you are asked to provide the values for the missing metadata.

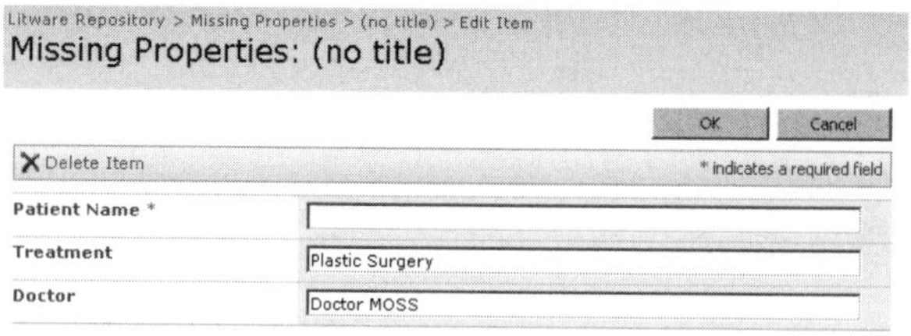

Figure 8-28 The incoming record does not have the required metadata. This page is provisioned to the user asking for the values for the missing properties.

If you take a further look, you'll notice that the document is now temporarily stored in the Missing Properties document library, also part of the Records Center site. Go to the View All Site Content page to see the link to this document library. There, you'll see the document, as displayed in Figure 8-29.

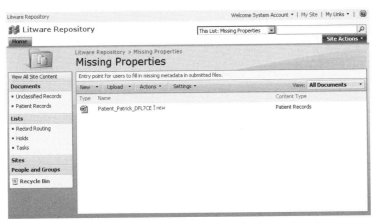

Figure 8-29 The document missing the required metadata is temporarily stored in the Missing Properties document library of the Records Center.

When you enter the name of the patient and then proceed, you'll get a confirmation page and a redirect back to the SharePoint site from where you've sent the document. The document is also removed from of the Missing Properties document library.

We also discussed other options for communicating with the Records Center. Let's work out an example where a Windows client allows a user to pick up a document and send it to the Records Center. In the application, you'll communicate with the Records Center by consuming the *OfficialFile* Web service. We'll ignore any aesthetics for the user interface and just have a form with a button on it. The first thing to do in your new Windows application is to add a Web reference and enter the URL to the *OfficialFile.asmx* that is linked to your Records Center. Figure 8-30 shows the Add Web Reference dialog box where you ask Visual Studio.NET 2005 to generate a proxy using the URL to the *officialfile.asmx*.

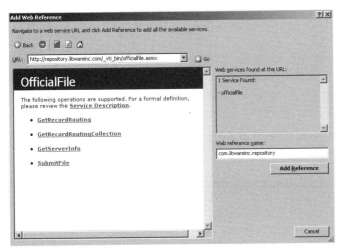

Figure 8-30 Generating the Web service proxy for the *OfficialFile* Web service

There are a couple of namespaces to add before you start with the handling of the *Click* event for the button on the form. Here is the list of *using* statements to add assuming you have *InsideMoss.Samples* as the namespace of your class and *com.litwareinc.repository* as the additional namespace of the proxy:

```
using System.IO;
using System.Net;
using InsideMoss.Samples.com.litwareinc.repository;
```

In the *Click* event handler, you'll first write the code to have the user select one of the files on his or her file system. The following is interaction code with an *OpenFileDialog* instance:

```
using (OpenFileDialog fd = new OpenFileDialog())
{
    if (fd.ShowDialog() == DialogResult.OK)
    {
        Stream s = fd.OpenFile();
        byte[] buffer = new byte[s.Length];
        s.Read(buffer,0,(int)s.Length);
        s.Close();
        string[] tmp = fd.FileName.Split('\\');
        string fileName = tmp[tmp.GetUpperBound(0)];
    }
}
```

Now for the best part. First, create a new instance of the Web Service proxy and pass the credentials, either explicit credentials or the credentials of the currently logged-on user. Here is the code for it:

```
RecordsRepository ws = new RecordsRepository();
ws.Credentials = CredentialCache.DefaultCredentials;
```

You'll have the opportunity to pass metadata for the document to the Web Service. This metadata will be converted to an XML file that will be stored in the Properties folder exactly as was done when sending the document to the Records Center via the Send To option from a Windows SharePoint Services 3.0 document library. For each of the metadata elements you want to pass, you have to create a *RecordsRepositoryProperty* object and collect them all in an array. The following code shows how you prepare an array with the three metadata elements defined at the level of the Patient Records document library in the Records Center:

```
RecordsRepositoryProperty prop1 = new RecordsRepositoryProperty();
prop1.Name = "Patient Name";
prop1.Type = "Text";
prop1.Value = "Brian Cox";
RecordsRepositoryProperty prop2 = new RecordsRepositoryProperty();
prop2.Name = "Treatment";
prop2.Type = "Text";
prop2.Value = "General Practice";
RecordsRepositoryProperty prop3 = new RecordsRepositoryProperty();
```

```
prop3.Name = "Doctor";
prop3.Type = "Text";
prop3.Value = "Doctor Zoe";
RecordsRepositoryProperty[] props = new RecordsRepositoryProperty[3];
props[0] = prop1;
props[1] = prop2;
props[2] = prop3;
```

The next line is the actual call to the *SubmitFile* Web method of the *OfficialFile* Web service. The first parameter is the document itself. Next, you have the metadata and then the very important string identifying the record routing type you want. The last parameters are the name of the user and the name of the document as it will be stored in the document library.

```
string retValue = ws.SubmitFile(buffer, props, "Patient Record",
                  fd.FileName, @"litwareinc\administrator");
```

The Web method call sends back the following XML string:

```
<ResultCode>Success</ResultCode>
<AdditionalInformation>http://repository.litwareinc.com/Patient
 Records/2006-11-30T06-09-07Z/Patient_Bria.docx</AdditionalInformation>
```

The metadata supplied here is remotely wrapped in one or more objects of the *Records-RepositoryProperty* object and sends them as part of the HTTP request. What happens if there are missing pieces for this metadata? Assume, for example, that you did not supply the value for the *Patient Name* property. If this is the case, the *OfficialFile* Web service returns an XML string containing the *MissingInformation* as the *ResultCode* and the URL of the page where you can redirect the user. This is the page where he or she can supply the missing values.

```
<ResultCode>MoreInformation</ResultCode>
<ResultUrl>http://repository.litwareinc.com/Missing
   Properties/Forms/EditForm.aspx?ID=5&amp;
   Source=http%3a%2f%2frepository.litwareinc.com%2
   f_layouts%2fofficialfilesuccess.aspx%3
   fItemId%3d8ac4929b-a3b6-4b59-b48c-5097aade707e
</ResultUrl>
```

This concludes the work for this walkthrough.

Custom Records Repository Routers

The last topic I'll discuss is how to customize and extend the way records that are submitted to the Records Center are processed. This custom processing can be accomplished by creating custom records repository routers, which are .NET assemblies that implement the *IRouter* interface.

You may want to create a custom records repository router when the default processing of incoming records is not sufficient. Here are a number of scenarios:

- Modifying the contents of the submitted document. An example can be a label, header, or watermark added to the document before it arrives in the Records Center.

- Modifying the destination and routing the incoming document elsewhere based on some custom business logic.

- Editing the submitted document metadata, such as completing extra metadata that the records manager needs.

- Communicating detailed information about processing results. The custom router can write any detailed processing information necessary to the *resultData* parameter. If the router fails, or if the router informs the records repository to cancel its own processing of the submitted document, the record repository returns this information to the calling application.

IRouter Interface

The *IRouter* interface is very simple. It defines one method, *OnSubmitFile*, with the following incoming parameters summarized in Table 8-4.

Table 8-4   *OnSubmitFile* Method Signature

Parameter	Description
recordSeries	The record series type specified for the document by the document submitter. This matches up with the record routing type that processes the incoming record.
sourceUrl	The URL from where the document is submitted.
userLoginName	The login name of the user submitting the document.
fileToSubmit	The document submitted, passed by reference so that within your custom router you can make changes to the document contents, such as adding additional labels.
properties	All of the metadata that comes along with the submitted document. As I've discussed previously, all of this metadata is converted at the end in an XML file stored along with the document in its final destination at the document library. This parameter is also defined by reference so that it is possible to make changes to the metadata.
destination	The final destination of the submitted document, passed by reference so that, for example, a custom router can redirect the document based on specific business logic to another destination as the one defined in the Records Center by the records manager.
resultData	Any additional information from the router regarding its processing of the document.

After the custom router finishes the custom processing of the submitted document, it has to tell the record routing type to which it's associated the next steps it needs to take. This is done by returning a *RouterResult* enumeration value with the following possible options summarized in Table 8-5.

Table 8-5 *RouterResult* **Enumeration Values**

Value	Description
SuccessContinueProcessing	The router has finished its job and returns a flag to the record routing type indicating that it can now continue with processing the document.
SuccessCancelFurtherProcessing	The router has successfully completed its processing, but the record repository discontinues its processing of the document. The record repository returns the contents of the *resultData* parameter as well as a success value to the calling application. This is useful when the router takes over storing the submitted document in its final destination from the record routing type definition.
RejectFile	The router did not complete its processing successfully. The record repository returns an error to the calling application, as well as the contents of the *resultData* parameter.

Deployment of Custom Routers

Figure 8-31 displays the different players involved in the deployment and activation of a custom records repository router.

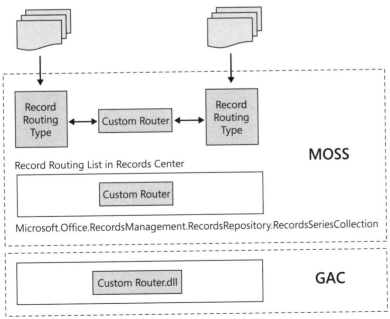

Figure 8-31 Deployment of custom record repository routers

The custom router class implementing the *IRouter* interface has to be compiled within the .NET assembly and deployed in the Global Assembly Cache. Once it is there, SharePoint is told of the existence of the custom router after the router is programmatically added to the record repository's record series collection, a collection of *RecordSeries* instances defined in the *Microsoft.Office.RecordsManagement.RecordsRepository* namespace. A *RecordSeries* object actually stores the definition of a record routing type created and made available through the Record Routing list in the Records Center. Table 8-6 describes the different properties and methods exposed by the *RecordSeries* class.

Table 8-6 *RecordSeries* Properties

Property	Description
ContentType	A property not immediately accessible by the records manager in the browser. It stores the content type that is active for the document library where the incoming records processed by this record routing type will be dropped. For the *Patient Record* routing type created in the walkthrough, the value for this property is *Document*.
Default	Boolean indicating whether this is the default record routing type. Out-of-the-box, the default type is the *Unclassified Records* record routing type that is available in the Record Routing list. Record managers can point to a custom created one as the default. The default record routing type will handle all of the incoming records for which we do not have a dedicated record routing type.
Description	The description of the record routing type.
Location	The name of the document library where the incoming records that are processed by the record routing type will be stored.
Mappings	The aliases defined for the record routing type. Incoming records based on a content type matching one of these mappings will also be handled by the record routing type in question.
Name	The name of the record routing type.
RequestedRecordRouting	Automatically takes over the value of the name property. Any incoming record based on a content type with the same name will be processed by the record routing type.
Router	A possible custom records repository router instance that is associated with the record routing type.

The companion Web site contains a Windows application called Router Explorer that you can use to browse what is available as record routing types in the Records Center, retrieve the values of the above properties, and perform operations such as adding or removing a custom records repository router.

When you decide to add a custom records repository router, you can use the *AddRouter* method available at the level of the *RecordSeriesCollection* object with a signature described in Table 8-7.

Table 8-7 *AddRouter* **Method Signature**

Parameter	Description
strName	The name of the custom router as it will be identified in the collection.
strAssembly	The strong name of the .NET assembly that has been deployed in the GAC containing the custom router code.
strCass	The fully qualified name of the class implementing the *IRouter* interface.

The *RecordSeriesCollection* also has a *RemoveRouter* method you can call with the name of a router instance. If found, the custom router instance will be de-attached from the record routing type.

Once the custom repository router has been added to the *RecordSeriesCollection*, record managers can attach it to a record routing type using the *Router* field in the Record Routing list. A record routing type can only have one custom router attached to it. However, a custom router can work for more than one record routing type. After you specify a custom router for a given record routing type, the records repository invokes the router whenever a file of that record routing type is submitted through any mechanism, including the user interface, object model, or SMTP.

Walkthrough: Creating Custom Routers

Let's go through a final walkthrough to illustrate how you can plug in your own custom repository router to extend the records routing type from the previous walkthrough. The goal is to perform some additional logging of the incoming metadata to a custom list before the record routing type continues with the processing of the patient record.

To start with, you need a new custom list in the Records Center that contains columns for each of the three metadata elements defined previously for a patient record: *Patient Name*, *Treatment*, and *Doctor*. Next, open Microsoft Visual Studio.NET 2005 and create a new .NET class library named *CustomPatientRouter*. You have to add a reference to both *Microsoft.Share-Point.dll* and *Microsoft.Office.Policy.dll*. Here are the using statements you can add in addition to the ones already defined:

```
using Records = Microsoft.Office.RecordsManagement.RecordsRepository;
using Microsoft.SharePoint;
```

The alias for the first namespace is added to avoid confusion between the *RecordsRepositoryProperty* type in the *Microsoft.Office.RecordsManagement.RecordsRepository* and the one in the *Microsoft.SharePoint* namespace.

The class, named *PatientMetadataLog*, implements the *IRouter* interface. The only method to implement is *OnSubmitFile*:

```
namespace InsideMOSS.Samples
{
    public class PatientMetadataLog: Records.IRouter
    {
```

```
#region IRouter Members
public Records.RouterResult
    OnSubmitFile(string recordSeries, string sourceUrl,
            string userName,
            ref byte[] fileToSubmit,
            ref Records.RecordsRepositoryProperty[] properties,
            ref SPList destination, ref string resultDetails)
{
    throw new Exception
        ("The method or operation is not implemented.");
}
#endregion
    }
}
```

A lot of information comes in as parameters. The last four—*fileToSubmit, properties, destination,* and *resultDetails*—are defined by *ref*, which allows for changes that are picked up by the default record routing type code to be executed after your custom router has done its logging operation. An example can be your router looking at the metadata and making changes to the destination document library where the document will eventually end up.

We'll keep it simple by consulting the metadata exposed by the array containing *Records-RepositoryProperty* instances. Here is the code to insert in place of the line throwing the exception:

```
SPWeb web = destination.ParentWeb;
SPList list = web.Lists["Patient Record Log"];
SPListItem item = list.Items.Add();

for (int i = 0; i < properties.Length - 1; i++)
{
    Records.RecordsRepositoryProperty prop =
        (Records.RecordsRepositoryProperty)properties[i];
    switch (prop.Name)
    {
        case "Patient Name":
            item["Patient Name"] = prop.Value;
            break;
        case "Treatment":
            item["Treatment"] = prop.Value;
            break;
        case "Doctor":
            item["Doctor"] = prop.Value;
            break;
        default:
            break;
    }
}
item.Update();
```

When you're done with your custom code in the router, you have to return what should be done next to the record routing type. The *RouterResult* enum has three options from which to select: tell the record routing type that it should continue processing the patient record, return a failure to the SharePoint site initiating the transfer of the record to the Records Center, or return a message to the record routing type saying that everything is fine and that what had to be done in the custom code has been completed.

```
return Records.RouterResult.SuccessContinueProcessing;
```

That's all of the code for the custom router assembly. Now, let's take a look at the steps for making this custom router available to the records managers.

First of all, the custom router .NET assembly has to be deployed in the Global Assembly Cache. Therefore, sign the project before you build it and then deploy the assembly in the Global Assembly Cache using the command prompt and the *gacutil.exe* tool with the option /i.

```
Gacutil /i CustomPatientRouter.dll
```

The custom router is registered with a couple of calls to the object model. The companion Web site contains a Windows application called Router Explorer that demonstrates the registration process and a couple of other operations you can do with the classes involved. Here is the core code for the addition of the custom router:

```
SPSite site = new SPSite("http://repository.litwareinc.com");
SPWeb web = site.RootWeb;
RecordSeriesCollection rsColl = new RecordSeriesCollection(web);
rsColl.AddRouter("Patient Metadata Logging",
  "CustomPatientRouter, Version=1.0.0.0,
  Culture=neutral, PublicKeyToken=2336f55d85d3d348",
  "InsideMOSS.Samples.PatientMetadataLog");
MessageBox.Show("Router added!");
```

The new Router object is added to the *Microsoft.Office.RecordsManagement.RecordsRepository .RecordSeriesCollection* by calling the *AddRouter* method with the instance of the *SPWeb* class that represents the Records Center site. The parameters to provide are the router name, the strong-name for the .NET assembly, and the fully qualified name of the class implementing the *IRouter* interface.

The records manager has to do the next step in the Records Center. The custom router must be associated with the *Patient Record* record routing type created in the previous walkthrough. To do this, navigate to the Record Routing list and edit the *Patient Record* item. There is now an extra column that you can set: the *Router* field. It shows a dropdown, as displayed at the bottom of Figure 8-32, where you'll find the custom router you've built and deployed in the previous steps.

Now, whenever you send a patient record to the Records Center, it will be mapped as before to the record routing type, but it will first execute the code of the custom router and, depending on the outcome, further process the incoming record. If all went well, you'll have the metadata in the *Patient Record Log* list for each of the incoming records.

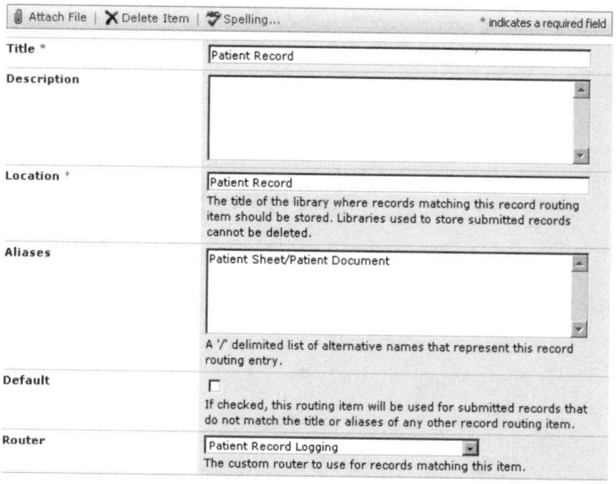

Figure 8-32 Associating the custom router with the record routing type

Summary

This final chapter discussed two major frameworks that are delivered with Microsoft Office SharePoint Server 2007: the policy framework and the document routing framework. Both frameworks are very important in the overall enterprise content management story and, as described, policy administrators can immediately use out-of-the-box functionality and a new type of SharePoint site called the Records Center with all of the necessary infrastructure in place for receiving, routing, managing, and holding the important records within the organization. A key message to take away from this chapter is that the underlying frameworks are very powerful and provide the necessary artifacts and APIs to build rich enterprise management solutions for information workers, both within and outside the company.

Index

What do you think of this book?

We want to hear from you!

Do you have a few minutes to participate in a brief online survey?

Microsoft is interested in hearing your feedback so we can continually improve our books and learning resources for you.

To participate in our survey, please visit:

www.microsoft.com/learning/booksurvey/

...and enter this book's ISBN-10 number (appears above barcode on back cover*).
As a thank-you to survey participants in the United States and Canada, each month we'll randomly select five respondents to win one of five $100 gift certificates from a leading online merchant. At the conclusion of the survey, you can enter the drawing by providing your e-mail address, which will be used for prize notification only.

Thanks in advance for your input. Your opinion counts!

* Where to find the ISBN-10 on back cover

ISBN-13: 000-0-0000-00000-0
ISBN-10: 0-0000-00000

00000

0 000000 000000

Example only. Each book has unique ISBN.

Microsoft
Press

No purchase necessary. Void where prohibited. Open only to residents of the 50 United States (includes District of Columbia) and Canada (void in Quebec). For official rules and entry dates see:

www.microsoft.com/learning/booksurvey/